★★★★ A TASTE OF ★★★★
AMERICA

★★★★ A TASTE OF ★★★★
AMERICA

More than 400 delicious regional recipes shown
step by step in over 1750 stunning photographs
that guide you clearly through each recipe

Carole Clements, Laura Washburn & Patricia Lousada

HERMES
HOUSE

This edition is published by Hermes House

Hermes House is an imprint of Anness Publishing Ltd
Hermes House, 88–89 Blackfriars Road, London SE1 8HA
tel. 020 7401 2077; fax 020 7633 9499

www.hermeshouse.com; www.annesspublishing.com

If you like the images in this book and would like to investigate using them for publishing, promotions
or advertising, please visit our website www.practicalpictures.com for more information.

A CIP catalogue record for this book is available from the British Library

Publisher: Joanna Lorenz
Editor: Sophy Friend
Indexer: Pat Coward
Designer: Sheila Volpe
Photography: Amanda Heywood
Food for Photography: Elizabeth Wolf-Cohen, Carla Capalbo
Steps by Marilyn Forbes, Cara Hobday, Teresa Goldfinch, Nicola Fowler

Previously published as *The Ultimate American Cookbook*

1 3 5 7 9 10 8 6 4 2

NOTES

Bracketed terms are intended for American readers.

For all recipes, quantities are given in both metric and imperial measures and, where appropriate, in standard
cups and spoons. Follow one set of measures, but not a mixture, because they are not interchangeable.
Standard spoon and cup measures are level. 1 tsp = 5ml, 1 tbsp = 15ml, 1 cup = 250ml/8fl oz.

Australian standard tablespoons are 20ml. Australian readers should use 3 tsp in place of 1 tbsp
for measuring small quantities of gelatine, flour, salt, etc.

American pints are 16fl oz/2 cups. American readers should use 20fl oz/2.5 cups in place of
1 pint when measuring liquids.

Electric oven temperatures in this book are for conventional ovens. When using a fan oven, the temperature
will probably need to be reduced by about 10–20°C/20–40°F. Since ovens vary, you should check with your
manufacturer's instruction book for guidance.

Medium (US large) eggs are used unless otherwise stated.

CONTENTS

THE BEST OF AMERICA

American families – with their diverse culinary traditions – have always been on the move. Hardy immigrants crossed oceans, and pioneers followed a trail or a river to the West. Today they chase down jobs far from where they grew up and retire to where the sun shines. As people criss-cross the country, they adapt their favourite recipes to the local produce and, in mixed communities, adopt entirely new foods and flavours. What has evolved is the richest and most varied cuisine imaginable. Even now, new dishes are continually entering the changing repertoire.

This unique volume explores this gastronomic heritage. We take you through America's regional cooking, passing on historical tastes with vintage recipes as well as offering new dishes made with local ingredients. All the recipes are presented in a simple step-by-step format with pictures to guide you every inch of the way.

We have taken the compass points as general divisions and look at each region in terms of its most important and characteristic ingredients and its unique traditions, offering a varied and representative selection of the food from each area.

Cooking from New England and the Mid-Atlantic seaboard evokes some of America's oldest food traditions, from the first Thanksgiving to Thomas Jefferson's waffle iron. With such a long coastline, seafood has always played a key role, and cold winters promoted the hearty fare we associate with this region. For many people, the South conjures up Spanish moss, French quarter architecture, and plantations. In fact, the Spanish, French, and African-American influences are the most important ones in terms of local food, and Cajun, Creole, and soul food mingle with customs of gracious dining carried over from earlier times.

Moving westward, the Midwest has always been the breadbasket of the country and, although much fertile farmland has been urbanized today, raising crops and animals for the table is still important. The Southwest draws on heirloom traditions, gleaned from Native Americans and Spanish settlers of the areas. Since the state of California occupies much of the West coast and has had such an influence on culinary trends, we have treated it on its own. With well stocked coastal waters and orchards laden with apples, the Pacific Northwest and the Mountain States conclude the culinary tour.

Today cooking at home has changed from an everyday event starting from scratch to more of a hobby. But whether you're preparing for a festive meal to share with friends or simply putting together a quick dinner, this wonderful cookbook has recipes to suit.

NEW ENGLAND & THE MID-ATLANTIC STATES

THE FIRST SETTLERS FOUND REFUGE IN THIS PART OF THE COUNTRY AND WORKED THE FERTILE LAND, CREATING A RICH CULINARY HERITAGE. SINCE COLONIAL DAYS, THE TRADITION OF GOOD EATING THAT DEVELOPED HERE SPREAD TO OTHER AREAS. WITH SO MUCH COASTLINE, SEAFOOD HAS ALWAYS BEEN A KEY INGREDIENT IN THE COOKING OF THIS REGION.

New England Clam Chowder

SERVES 8

48 clams, such as cherrystone or
    littleneck, scrubbed

1.3 litres/2¼ pints/6 cups water

40g/1½oz/¼ cup finely diced salt pork

3 onions, finely chopped

1 bay leaf

5 potatoes, diced

salt and pepper

475ml/16fl oz/2 cups milk, warmed

250ml/8fl oz/1 cup single (light) cream

chopped fresh parsley, to garnish

1 Rinse the clams well in cold water.
Drain. Place them in a deep pan with
the water and bring to the boil. Cover
and steam until the shells open, about
10 minutes. Remove the pan from
the heat.

2 When the clams have cooled
slightly, remove them from their
shells. Discard any clams that have
not opened. Chop the clams coarsely.
Strain the cooking liquid through a
strainer lined with muslin (cheesecloth), and reserve it.

3 In a large heavy pan, fry the salt
pork until it renders its fat and begins
to brown. Add the onions and cook
over a low heat until softened,
8–10 minutes.

4 ▲ Add the bay leaf, potatoes and
clam cooking liquid. Stir. Bring to the
boil and cook for 5–10 minutes.

5 ▲ Stir in the chopped clams.
Continue to cook until the potatoes
are tender, stirring occasionally.
Season with salt and pepper.

Reduce the heat to low and stir in
t   rmed milk and cream. Simmer
     ·ly for 5 minutes more. Discard
     y leaf, and taste and adjust the
     ing before serving, sprinkled
wi.ı parsley.

~ COOK'S TIP ~

If clams have been dug, purging
helps to rid them of sand and
stomach contents. Put them in a
bowl of cold water, sprinkle with
50g/2oz/½ cup cornmeal and some salt.
Stir lightly and leave to stand in a
cool place for 3–4 hours.

Chilled Asparagus Soup

Serves 6

900g/2lb fresh asparagus

60ml/4 tbsp butter or olive oil

175g/6oz/1½ cups sliced leeks or spring
   onions (scallions)

45ml/3 tbsp plain (all-purpose) flour

1.5 litres/2½ pints/6¼ cups chicken stock

salt and pepper

½ cup single (light) cream

15ml/1 tbsp finely chopped fresh
   tarragon or chervil

1 ▲ Cut the top 6cm/2½in off the
asparagus spears. Blanch these tips in
boiling water until just tender, about
5–6 minutes. Drain. Cut each tip into
two or three pieces, and set aside.

2 Trim the ends of the stalks,
removing any brown or woody parts.
Chop the stalks into 1cm/½in pieces.

3 ▲ Heat the butter or oil in a heavy
pan. Add the leeks or spring onions
and cook over a low heat until softened,
5–8 minutes. Stir in the chopped
asparagus stalks, cover and cook for
6–8 minutes more.

4 Add the flour and stir well to blend.
Cook for 3–4 minutes, uncovered, stirring occasionally.

5 ▼ Add the chicken stock. Bring to
the boil, stirring frequently, then
reduce the heat and simmer for 30
minutes. Season with salt and pepper.

6 ▲ Purée the soup in a food processor
or blender. If necessary, strain it to
remove any coarse fibres. Stir in the
asparagus tips, most of the cream and
the herbs. Chill well. Stir thoroughly
before serving, and check the seasoning. Garnish with swirled cream to
make an attractive pattern, then serve.

Chesapeake Melon and Crab Meat Salad

SERVES 6

450g/1lb fresh crab meat

115g/4oz/½ cup mayonnaise

50ml/2fl oz/¼ cup sour cream or natural (plain) yogurt

30ml/2 tbsp olive oil

30ml/2 tbsp fresh lemon or lime juice

20g/¾oz/¼ cup finely chopped spring onions (scallions)

30ml/2 tbsp finely chopped fresh coriander (cilantro)

1.5ml/¼ tsp cayenne pepper

salt and pepper

1½ canteloupe or small honeydew melons

3 heads of Belgian endive

fresh coriander sprigs, to garnish

1 ▲ Pick over the crab meat very carefully, removing any bits of shell or cartilage. Leave the pieces of crab meat as large as possible.

2 ▲ In a medium bowl, combine all the other ingredients except the melon and endive. Mix well. Fold the crab meat into this dressing.

3 ▲ Halve the melons and remove the seeds. Cut into thin slices and remove the rind.

4 ▲ Arrange the salad on individual serving plates, making a decorative design with the melon slices and whole endive leaves. Place a mound of dressed crab meat on each plate. Garnish each salad with fresh coriander sprigs.

Long Island Scallop and Mussel Kebabs

SERVES 4

65g/2½oz/5 tbsp butter, at room temperature
30ml/2 tbsp finely chopped fresh fennel fronds or parsley
15ml/1 tbsp fresh lemon juice
salt and pepper
32 bay or small scallops
24 large mussels in shell
8 bacon rashers (strips)
50g/2oz/1 cup fresh breadcrumbs
50ml/2fl oz/¼ cup olive oil
hot toast, to serve

1 ▲ Make the flavoured butter by combining the butter with the chopped herbs, lemon juice and salt and pepper to taste. Mix well. Set aside.

2 ▲ In a small pan, cook the scallops in their own liquor until they begin to shrink. (If there is no scallop liquor – retained from the shells after shelling – use a little fish stock or white wine.) Drain and pat dry with kitchen paper.

3 Scrub the mussels well, and rinse under cold running water. Place in a large pan with about 2.5cm/1in of water in the bottom. Cover and steam the mussels over a medium heat until they open. Remove them from their shells, and pat dry on kitchen paper. Discard any mussels that have not opened.

4 ▼ Take eight 15cm/6in wooden or metal skewers. Thread on each one, alternately, four scallops, three mussels and a rasher of bacon, weaving the bacon between the scallops and mussels.

5 Preheat the grill (broiler).

6 ▲ Spread the breadcrumbs on a plate. Brush the seafood with olive oil and roll in the crumbs to coat all over.

7 Place the skewers on the grill (broiling) rack. Grill (broil) until crisp and lightly browned, 4–5 minutes on each side. Serve at once with hot toast and the flavoured butter.

Oyster Stew

SERVES 6

475ml/16fl oz/2 cups milk

475ml/16fl oz/2 cups single (light) cream

1.2 litres/2 pints shelled oysters, drained, with their liquor reserved

pinch of paprika

salt and pepper

25g/1oz/2 tbsp butter

15ml/1 tbsp finely chopped fresh parsley

1 Combine the milk, cream and oyster liquor in a heavy pan.

2 ▼ Heat the mixture over a medium heat until small bubbles appear around the edge of the pan. Do not allow it to boil. Reduce the heat to low and add the oysters.

3 Cook, stirring occasionally, until the oysters plump up and their edges begin to curl. Add the paprika, and salt and pepper to taste.

4 Meanwhile, warm six soup plates or bowls. Cut the butter into six pieces and put one piece in each bowl.

5 Ladle in the oyster stew and sprinkle with the chopped parsley. Serve at once.

Oysters Rockefeller

SERVES 6

450g/1lb fresh spinach leaves

40g/1½oz/½ cup chopped spring onions (scallions)

50g/2oz/½ cup chopped celery

25g/1oz/½ cup chopped fresh parsley

1 garlic clove

2 anchovy fillets

50g/2oz/¼ cup butter or margarine

30g/1¼oz/½ cup dried breadcrumbs

5ml/1 tsp Worcestershire sauce

30ml/2 tbsp anise-flavoured liqueur (Pernod or Ricard)

2.5ml/½ tsp salt

hot pepper sauce

36 oysters in the shell

fine strips of lemon rind, to garnish

~ COOK'S TIP ~

To open an oyster, push the point of an oyster knife about 1cm/½in into the "hinge". Push down firmly. The lid should pop open.

1 ▲ Wash the spinach well. Drain, and place in a heavy pan. Cover and cook over a low heat until just wilted. Remove from the heat. When the spinach is cool enough to handle, squeeze it to remove the excess water.

2 ▲ Put the spinach, spring onions, celery, parsley, garlic and anchovy fillets in a food processor and process until finely chopped.

3 Heat the butter or margarine in a frying pan. Add the spinach mixture, breadcrumbs, Worcestershire sauce, liqueur, salt and hot sauce to taste. Cook for 1–2 minutes. Cool, then chill.

4 Preheat the oven to 230°C/450°F/ Gas 8. Line a baking sheet with crumpled foil.

5 ▲ Open the oysters and remove the top shells. Arrange them, side by side, on the foil (it will keep them upright). Spoon the spinach mixture over the oysters, smoothing the tops with the back of the spoon.

6 Bake until piping hot, about 20 minutes. Serve at once, garnished with the lemon rind.

Oyster Stew (top), Oysters Rockefeller

Cape Cod Fried Clams

SERVES 4

36 clams, such as cherrystone, scrubbed

250ml/8fl oz/1 cup buttermilk

pinch of celery salt

1.5ml/¼ tsp cayenne pepper

oil for deep-frying

65g/2½oz/1 cup dried breadcrumbs

2 eggs, beaten with 30ml/2 tbsp water

lemon wedges and tartare sauce or
tomato ketchup, to serve

1 Rinse the clams well. Put them in a large pan with 475ml/16fl oz/2 cups water and bring to the boil. Cover and steam until the shells open.

2 ▼ Remove the clams from their shells, and cut away the black skins from the necks. Discard any clams that have not opened. Strain the cooking liquid and reserve.

3 ▲ Place the buttermilk in a large bowl and stir in the celery salt and cayenne. Add the clams and 120ml/4fl oz/½ cup of their cooking liquid. Mix well. Leave to stand for 1 hour.

4 Heat the oil in a deep-fryer or large pan to 190°C/375°F. (To test the temperature without a thermometer, drop in a cube of bread; it should be golden brown in 40 seconds.)

5 ▲ Drain the clams and roll them in the breadcrumbs to coat all over. Dip them in the beaten egg and then in the breadcrumbs again.

6 Fry the clams in the hot oil, a few at a time, stirring, until they are crisp and brown, about 2 minutes per batch. Remove with a slotted spoon and drain on kitchen paper.

7 Serve the fried clams hot, accompanied by lemon wedges and tartare sauce or ketchup.

Eggs Benedict

SERVES 4

5ml/1 tsp vinegar

4 eggs

2 English muffins or 4 slices of bread

butter, for spreading

2 slices of cooked ham, 5mm/¼in thick,
  each cut in half crossways

fresh chives, to garnish

FOR THE SAUCE

3 egg yolks

30ml/2 tbsp fresh lemon juice

1.5ml/¼ tsp salt

115g/4oz/½ cup butter

30ml/2 tbsp single (light) cream

pepper

4 ▼ Bring a shallow pan of water to
the boil. Stir in the vinegar. Break
each egg into a cup, then slide it carefully into the water. Delicately turn the
white around the yolk with a slotted
spoon. Cook until the egg is set to
your taste, 3–4 minutes. Remove to
kitchen paper to drain. Very gently cut
any ragged edges off the eggs with a
small knife or scissors.

5 ▲ While the eggs are poaching,
split and toast the muffins or toast the
bread slices. Butter while still warm.

6 Place a piece of ham, which you
may brown in butter if you wish, on
each muffin half or slice of toast. Trim
the ham to fit neatly. Place an egg on
each ham-topped muffin. Spoon the
warm sauce over the eggs, garnish
with chives and serve.

1 ▲ For the sauce, put the egg yolks,
lemon juice and salt in the container
of a food processor or blender. Blend
for 15 seconds.

2 Melt the butter in a sm~
it bubbles (do not let it brown). W~
the motor running, pour the hot butter
into the food processor or blender
through the feed tube in a slow, steady
stream. Turn off the machine as soon
as all the butter has been added.

3 Scrape the sauce into the top of a
double boiler over just simmering
water, or a heatproof bowl set over hot
water. Stir until thickened, about
2–3 minutes. (If the sauce curdles,
whisk in 15ml/1 tbsp boiling water.)
Stir in the cream and season with
pepper. Keep warm over the hot water.

Maryland Crab Cakes with Tartare Sauce

SERVES 4

675g/1½lb fresh crab meat

1 egg, beaten

30ml/2 tbsp mayonnaise

15ml/1 tbsp Worcestershire sauce

15ml/1 tbsp sherry

30ml/2 tbsp finely chopped fresh parsley

15ml/1 tbsp finely chopped fresh chives

salt and pepper

45ml/3 tbsp olive oil

FOR THE SAUCE

1 egg yolk

15ml/1 tbsp white wine vinegar

30ml/2 tbsp Dijon-style mustard

250ml/8fl oz/1 cup vegetable oil

30ml/2 tbsp fresh lemon juice

20g/¾oz/¼ cup finely chopped spring
   onions (scallions)

30ml/2 tbsp chopped drained capers

few finely chopped sour dill pickles

60ml/4 tbsp finely chopped fresh parsley

1 ▲ Pick over the crab meat, removing any shell or cartilage. Keep the pieces of crab as large as possible.

~ COOK'S TIP ~

For easier handling and to make the crab meat go further, add 50g/2oz/1 cup fresh breadcrumbs and one more egg to the crab mixture. Divide the mixture into 12 cakes to serve six.

2 ▲ In a mixing bowl, combine the beaten egg with the mayonnaise, Worcestershire sauce, sherry and herbs. Season with salt and pepper. Gently fold in the crab meat.

3 ▲ Divide the mixture into eight portions and gently form each one into an oval cake. Place on a baking sheet between layers of baking parchment and chill for at least 1 hour.

4 ▲ Meanwhile, make the sauce. In a medium bowl, beat the egg yolk with a wire whisk until smooth. Add the vinegar, mustard and salt and pepper to taste, and whisk for about 10 seconds to blend. Whisk in the oil in a slow, steady stream.

5 ▲ Add the lemon juice, spring onions, capers, pickles and parsley and mix well. Check the seasoning. Cover and chill.

6 Preheat the grill (broiler).

7 ▲ Brush the crab cakes with the olive oil. Place on an oiled baking sheet, in one layer.

8 ▲ Grill (broil) 15cm/6in from the heat until golden brown, about 5 minutes on each side. Serve the crab cakes hot with the tartare sauce.

Baked Fish

SERVES 6

1.2kg/2½lb cod, haddock or bluefish
  fillets, skinned

45ml/3 tbsp olive oil

5ml/1 tsp drained capers

2 garlic cloves

2 ripe tomatoes, peeled, seeded
  and finely diced

30ml/2 tbsp finely chopped fresh basil, or
  10ml/1 tsp dried basil

salt and pepper

250ml/8fl oz/1 cup dry white wine

1 Preheat the oven to 200°C/400°F/
Gas 6.

2 ▲ Arrange the fillets in one layer
in a shallow oiled baking dish. Brush
the fish with olive oil.

3 Chop the capers with the garlic.
Mix with the tomatoes and basil.
Season with salt and pepper.

4 ▼ Spoon the tomato mixture over
the fish. Pour in the wine. Bake until
the fish is cooked, 15–20 minutes.
Test to see if the fish is done with the
point of a knife; the fish should be just
opaque in the centre. Serve hot.

Old Westbury Flounder with Crab

SERVES 6

50g/2oz/¼ cup butter or margarine

25g/1oz/¼ cup plain (all-purpose) flour

250ml/8fl oz/1 cup fish stock, or 175ml/
  6fl oz/¾ cup fish stock mixed with
  50ml/2fl oz/¼ cup dry white wine

250ml/8fl oz/1 cup milk

1 bay leaf

salt and pepper

12 flounder fillets, about 1.2kg/2½lb

250g/9oz/1½ cups fresh crab meat, flaked

40g/1½oz/½ cup freshly grated Parmesan

1 Preheat the oven to 220°C/425°F/
Gas 7.

~ VARIATIONS ~

Other flat white fish, such as sole,
can be substituted for the flounder.
Raw peeled and deveined prawns
(shrimp), chopped if large, can be
used instead of crab meat.

2 ▲ In a medium heavy pan, melt the
butter or margarine over a medium
heat. Stir in the flour and cook for
2–3 minutes.

3 ▲ Pour in the fish stock (or mixed
fish stock and wine) and the milk.
Whisk until smooth.

4 Add the bay leaf. Raise the heat to
medium-high and bring to the boil.
Cook for 3–4 minutes more. Remove
the sauce from the heat, and add salt
to taste. Keep hot.

5 ▲ Butter a large baking dish. Twist
each fillet to form a "cone" shape and
arrange in the dish. Sprinkle the crab
meat over the fish. Pour the hot sauce
evenly over the top and sprinkle with
the cheese.

6 Bake until the top is golden brown
and the fish is cooked, 10–12 minutes.
Test to see if the fish is done with the
point of a knife: the fish should be just
opaque in the centre. Serve hot.

Baked Fish (top), Old Westbury Flounder with Crab

Scallops Thermidor

SERVES 6

900g/2lb scallops

50g/2oz/½ cup plain (all-purpose) flour

115g/4oz/½ cup butter or margarine

65g/2½oz/1 cup quartered
   small mushrooms

25g/1oz/½ cup fresh breadcrumbs

30ml/2 tbsp finely chopped fresh parsley

30ml/2 tbsp finely chopped fresh chives

120ml/4fl oz/½ cup sherry

50ml/2fl oz/¼ cup cognac

5ml/1 tsp Worcestershire sauce

2.5ml/½ tsp salt

1.5ml/¼ tsp black pepper

350ml/12fl oz/1½ cups whipping cream

2 egg yolks

chives, to garnish (optional)

1 Preheat oven to 200°C/400°F/Gas 6.

2 ▲ Roll the scallops in the flour, shaking off the excess. Heat half the butter or margarine in a medium frying pan. Add the scallops and sauté until they are barely golden all over, about 3 minutes. Remove from the pan and set aside.

3 ▲ Melt two more tablespoons of butter or margarine in the pan. Add the mushrooms and breadcrumbs and sauté for 3–4 minutes, stirring. Add the parsley, chives, sherry, cognac, Worcestershire sauce and salt and pepper. Cook for 3–4 minutes more, stirring well.

4 ▲ Add the cream, and cook for another 3–4 minutes, stirring occasionally. Remove from the heat and mix in the egg yolks. Fold in the sautéed scallops.

5 Divide the mixture among six greased individual gratin or other baking dishes. Or, if you prefer, put it all in one large shallow baking dish. Dot with the remaining 30ml/2 tbsp butter or margarine.

6 Bake until bubbling and lightly browned, about 10 minutes. Serve at once in the dishes. Garnish with chives, if you wish.

Spaghetti with Clams

SERVES 4

24 hard-shell clams, such as
    littlenecks, scrubbed

250ml/8fl oz/1 cup water

120ml/4fl oz/½ cup dry white wine

salt and pepper

450g/1lb spaghetti, preferably Italian

75ml/5 tbsp olive oil

2 garlic cloves, finely chopped

45ml/3 tbsp finely chopped fresh parsley

1 ▲ Rinse the clams well in cold water and drain. Place in a large pan with the water and wine and bring to the boil. Cover and steam until the shells open, about 6–8 minutes.

2 Discard any clams that have not opened. Remove the clams from their shells. If large, chop them roughly.

3 ▲ Strain the cooking liquid through a strainer lined with muslin (cheesecloth). Place in a small pan and boil rapidly until it has reduced by about half. Set aside.

4 Bring a large pan of water to the boil. Add 5ml/1 tsp salt. When the water is boiling rapidly, add the spaghetti and stir well as it softens. Cook until the spaghetti is almost done, and still firm to the bite (check the packet instructions for cooking times).

5 ▼ Meanwhile, heat the olive oil in a large frying pan. Add the garlic and cook for 2–3 minutes, but do not let it brown. Add the reduced clam liquid and the parsley. Let it cook over a low heat until the spaghetti is ready.

6 ▲ Drain the spaghetti. Add it to the frying pan, raise the heat to medium and add the clams. Cook for 3–4 minutes, stirring constantly to cover the spaghetti with the sauce and to heat the clams.

7 Season with salt and pepper and serve. No cheese is needed with this clam sauce.

Maine Grilled Lobster Dinner

SERVES 4

4 live lobsters, about 675g/1½lb each

45ml/3 tbsp finely chopped mixed fresh herbs, such as parsley, chives and tarragon

225g/8oz/1 cup butter, melted and kept warm

8 tender corn on the cob, cleaned

salt and pepper

lemon halves, to garnish

1 Preheat the grill (broiler).

2 Kill each lobster quickly by inserting the tip of a large chef's knife between the eyes.

3 ▲ Turn the lobster over on to its back and cut it in half, from the head straight down to the tail. Remove and discard the hard sac near the head, and the intestinal vein that runs through the middle of the underside of the tail. All the rest of the lobster meat is edible. Preheat the grill (broiler).

4 ▲ Combine the finely chopped herbs with the melted butter.

5 ▲ Place the lobster halves, shell side up, in a foil-lined grill (broiling) pan or a large roasting pan. (You may have to do this in two batches.) Grill (broil) for about 8 minutes. Turn the lobster halves over, brush generously with the herb butter, and grill for 7–8 minutes more.

6 ▲ While the lobsters are cooking, drop the corn cobs into a large pan of rapidly boiling water and cook until just tender, 4–7 minutes. Drain.

7 Serve the lobsters and corn hot, with salt, freshly ground black pepper, lemon halves and individual bowls of herb butter. Provide crackers for the claws, extra plates for cobs and shells, finger bowls and lots of napkins.

Prawn Soufflé

SERVES 4–6

15ml/1 tbsp dried breadcrumbs

25g/1oz/2 tbsp butter or margarine

90g/3½oz/⅔ cup coarsely chopped
cooked prawns (shrimp)

15ml/1 tbsp finely chopped fresh
tarragon or parsley

1.5ml/¼ tsp pepper

45ml/3 tbsp sherry or dry white wine

FOR THE SOUFFLÉ MIXTURE

40g/1½oz/3 tbsp butter or margarine

37 ml/2½ tbsp plain (all-purpose) flour

250ml/8fl oz/1 cup milk, heated

4ml/¾ tsp salt

4 eggs, separated, plus 1 white

1 ▲ Butter a 1.5–2 litre/2½–3½ pint
soufflé dish. Sprinkle with the breadcrumbs, tilting the dish to coat the
bottom and sides evenly.

2 Preheat the oven to 200°C/400°F/
Gas 6.

~ VARIATIONS ~

For Lobster Soufflé, substitute
1 large lobster tail for the cooked
prawns (shrimp). Chop it finely and
add to the pan with the herbs and
wine in place of the prawns. For
Crab Soufflé, use 175g/6oz/1 cup fresh
crab meat, picked over carefully to
remove any bits of shell and cartilage,
in place of the prawns.

3 ▲ Melt the butter or margarine in
a small pan. Add the chopped prawns
and cook for 2–3 minutes over a low
heat. Stir in the herbs, pepper and
wine and cook for 1–2 minutes more.
Raise the heat and boil rapidly to
evaporate the liquid. Remove from
the heat and set aside.

4 For the soufflé mixture, melt the
butter or margarine in a medium heavy
pan. Add the flour, blending it well
with a wire whisk. Cook over a low
heat for 2–3 minutes. Pour in the hot
milk and whisk vigorously until
smooth. Simmer for 2 minutes, still
whisking. Stir in the salt.

5 ▼ Remove from the heat and
immediately beat in the egg yolks, one
at a time. Stir in the prawn mixture.

6 In a large bowl, whisk the egg
whites until they form stiff peaks. Stir
about one-quarter of the egg whites
into the prawn mixture. Gently fold in
the rest of the egg whites.

7 Turn the mixture into the prepared
dish. Place in the oven and reduce the
heat to 190°C/375°F/Gas 5. Bake until
the soufflé is puffed up and lightly
browned on top, 30–40 minutes.
Serve at once.

Chicken Brunswick Stew

SERVES 6

1.8kg/4lb chicken, cut into
 serving pieces

paprika, for dusting

30ml/2 tbsp olive oil

25g/1oz/2 tbsp butter

4 onions, chopped

225g/8oz/1 cup chopped green or yellow
 (bell) pepper

450g/1lb/2 cups chopped peeled fresh or
 canned plum tomatoes

250ml/8fl oz/1 cup white wine

475ml/16fl oz/2 cups chicken stock
 or water

15g/½oz/¼ cup chopped fresh parsley

2.5ml/½ tsp hot pepper sauce

15ml/1 tbsp Worcestershire sauce

2 cups corn kernels, fresh, frozen
 or canned

150g/5oz/1 cup butter (lima) beans

45ml/3 tbsp plain (all-purpose) flour

salt and pepper

savoury scones, rice or potatoes, to serve
 (optional)

1 ▲ Rinse the chicken pieces under
cool water and pat dry with kitchen
paper. Dust each piece lightly with salt
and paprika.

2 In a large heavy pan, heat the olive
oil with the butter over a medium-high
heat. Heat until the mixture is sizzling
and just starting to change colour.

3 ▲ Add the chicken pieces and fry
until golden brown on all sides.
Remove the chicken pieces with tongs
and set aside.

4 ▲ Reduce the heat to low and add
the onions and pepper to the pan.
Cook until softened, 8–10 minutes.

5 Raise the heat. Add the tomatoes
and their juice, the wine, stock or
water, parsley and hot pepper and
Worcestershire sauces. Stir and bring
to the boil.

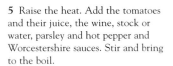

6 ▲ Return the chicken to the
pan, pushing it down into the sauce.
Cover, reduce the heat and simmer for
30 minutes, stirring occasionally.

7 ▲ Add the corn and butter beans
and mix well. Partly cover and cook
for 30 minutes more.

8 ▲ Tilt the pan, and skim off as
much of the surface fat as possible.
In a small bowl, mix the flour with a
little water to make a paste.

9 ▲ Gradually stir in about 175ml/
6fl oz/¾ cup of the hot sauce from the
pan. Stir the flour mixture into the
stew, and mix well to distribute it
evenly. Cook for 5–8 minutes more,
stirring occasionally.

10 Check the seasoning. Serve the
stew in shallow soup plates, with
scones, rice or potatoes, if you like.

Yankee Pot Roast

SERVES 8

1.8kg/4lb chuck steak, rump (round) steak or brisket

3 garlic cloves, cut in half or in thirds

225g/8oz piece of salt pork

4 onions, chopped

115g/4oz/1 cup chopped celery

4–6 carrots, chopped

150g/5oz/1 cup diced turnips

475ml/16fl oz/2 cups beef or chicken stock

475ml/16fl oz/2 cups dry red or white wine

1 bay leaf

5ml/1 tsp fresh thyme leaves, or 2.5ml/½ tsp dried thyme

8 small potatoes

2.5ml/½ tsp salt

2.5ml/½ tsp pepper

50g/2oz/¼ cup butter or margarine, at room temperature

25g/1oz/¼ cup plain (all-purpose) flour

watercress, to garnish

1 Preheat the oven to 160°C/325°F/Gas 3.

2 ▲ With the tip of a sharp knife, make deep incisions in the meat, on all sides, and insert the garlic pieces.

3 In a large, lidded flameproof casserole, cook the salt pork over a low heat until it renders its fat and begins to brown.

4 ▲ Remove the salt pork with a slotted spoon and discard. Raise the heat to medium-high and add the steak or brisket. Brown it on all sides. Remove and set aside.

5 ▲ Add the onions, celery and carrots to the casserole and cook over a low heat until softened, 8–10 minutes. Stir in the turnips. Add the stock, wine and herbs and mix well. Return the steak. Cover and place in the oven. Cook for 2 hours.

6 ▲ Add the potatoes, pushing them down under the other vegetables. Season with salt and pepper. Cover again and cook until the potatoes are tender, about 45 minutes.

7 ▲ In a small bowl, combine the butter or margarine with the flour and mash together to make a paste.

8 Transfer the meat to a warmed serving dish. Remove the potatoes and other vegetables from the casserole with a slotted spoon and arrange around the roast. Keep hot.

9 ▲ Discard the bay leaf. Tilt the casserole and skim off the excess fat from the surface of the cooking liquid. Bring to the boil on top of the stove. Add half the butter and flour paste and whisk to blend. Cook until the gravy is thickened, 3–4 minutes. Add more of the paste if the gravy is not sufficiently thick. Strain into a gravy boat. Serve with the sliced meat and vegetables, garnished with watercress.

> ~ **VARIATION** ~
>
> Add 175g/6oz/1½ cups frozen peas to the casserole about 5 minutes before the potatoes are done.

Philadelphia Scrapple

SERVES 10

1.3kg/3lb pork neck bones or
  pigs' knuckles

3.5 litres/6 pints water

5ml/1 tsp salt

1 bay leaf

2 fresh sage leaves

5ml/1 tsp pepper

300g/11oz/2¾ cups yellow cornmeal

maple syrup, fried eggs and grilled
  (broiled) tomatoes, to serve (optional)

1 Put the bones or knuckles, water,
salt and herbs in a large pan. Bring to
the boil and simmer for 2 hours.

2 ▲ Remove the meat from the
bones and chop it finely or mince it.
Set aside. Strain the broth and skim
off any fat from the surface. Discard
the bones.

3 Put 2.4 litres/4 pints of the broth in
a large heavy pan. Add the chopped or
minced meat and the pepper. Bring to
the boil.

4 ▲ There should be about 1.2 litres/
2 pints of broth left. Stir the cornmeal
into this. Add to the boiling mixture
in the pan and cook until thickened,
about 10 minutes, stirring constantly.

5 Reduce the heat to very low, cover
the pan and continue cooking for
about 25 minutes, stirring often. Check
the seasoning.

6 ▲ Turn the mixture into two loaf
tins and smooth the surface. Leave to
cool, then chill overnight.

7 To serve, cut the loaves into 1cm/
½in slices. Sprinkle with flour and
brown on both sides in butter or other
fat over a medium heat. Serve with
warmed maple syrup, fried eggs and
grilled tomato halves, if you wish.

Red Flannel Hash with Corned Beef

SERVES 4

6 bacon rashers (strips)

175g/6oz/¾ cup finely chopped onion

5 potatoes, boiled and diced

250g/9oz/1½ cups chopped corned beef

350g/12oz/1½ cups diced cooked
  beetroot (beet) (not in vinegar)

50ml/2fl oz/¼ cup single (light) or
  pouring (half-and-half) cream

15g/½oz/¼ cup finely chopped
  fresh parsley, plus sprig to garnish

salt and pepper

3 ▼ Heat 60ml/4 tbsp of the reserved bacon fat, or other fat, in the frying pan. Add the hash mixture, spreading it out evenly with a spatula. Cook over a low heat until the bottom is brown, about 15 minutes. Flip the hash out on to a plate.

4 ▲ Gently slide the hash back into the frying pan and cook on the other side until lightly browned. Serve at once, garnished with the parsley sprig.

1 ▲ Cook the bacon in a large heavy or nonstick frying pan until golden and beginning to crisp. Remove with a slotted spatula and drain on kitchen paper. Pour off all but 30ml/2 tbsp of the bacon fat in the pan, reserving the rest for later.

2 ▲ Cut the bacon into 1cm/½in pieces and place in a mixing bowl. Cook the onion in the bacon fat over a low heat until softened, 8–10 minutes. Remove it from the pan and add to the bacon. Mix in the potatoes, corned beef, beetroot, cream and the finely chopped parsley. Season with salt and pepper and mix well.

Boston Baked Beans

SERVES 8

500g/1¼lb/3 cups dried haricot (navy) or Great Northern beans

1 bay leaf

4 cloves

2 onions, peeled

185g/6½oz/½ cup treacle (molasses)

150g/5oz/¾ cup soft dark brown sugar

15ml/1 tbsp Dijon-style mustard

5ml/1 tsp salt

5ml/1 tsp pepper

250ml/8fl oz/1 cup boiling water

225g/8oz piece of salt pork

1 Rinse the beans under cold running water. Drain and place in a large bowl. Cover with cold water and leave to soak overnight. Drain and rinse again.

2 Put the beans in a large pan with the bay leaf and cover with fresh cold water. Bring to the boil and simmer until tender, 1½–2 hours. Drain.

3 Preheat the oven to 140°C/275°F/ Gas 1.

4 ▲ Put the beans in a large casserole. Stick two cloves in each of the onions and add them to the pan.

5 In a mixing bowl, combine the treacle, dark brown sugar, mustard, salt and pepper. Add the boiling water and stir to blend.

6 Pour this mixture over the beans. Add more water if necessary so the beans are almost covered with liquid.

7 ▲ Blanch the piece of salt pork in boiling water for 3 minutes. Drain. Score the rind in deep 1cm/½in cuts. Add the salt pork to the casserole and push down just below the surface of the beans, skin-side up.

8 Cover the casserole and bake in the centre of the oven for 4½–5 hours. Uncover for the last half hour, so the pork rind becomes brown and crisp. Slice or shred the pork and serve hot.

Harvard Beetroot

SERVES 6

5 cooked beetroot (beets), about 675g/1½lb

75g/3oz/6 tbsp granulated sugar

15ml/1 tbsp cornflour (cornstarch)

2.5ml/½ tsp salt

50ml/2fl oz/¼ cup cider or white wine vinegar

120ml/4fl oz/½ cup beetroot cooking liquid or water

25g/1oz/2 tbsp butter or margarine

1 Peel the beetroot and cut into medium-thick slices. Set aside.

2 ▲ In the top of a double boiler, combine all the other ingredients except the butter or margarine. Stir until smooth. Cook over hot water, stirring constantly, until the mixture is smooth and clear.

3 ▼ Add the beetroot and butter or margarine. Continue to cook over the hot water, stirring occasionally, until the beetroot slices are heated through, about 10 minutes. Serve hot.

Boston Baked Beans (top), Harvard Beetroot

Coleslaw

SERVES 8

225g/8oz/1 cup mayonnaise

120ml/4fl oz/½ cup white wine vinegar

15ml/1 tbsp Dijon-style mustard

10ml/2 tsp caster (superfine) sugar

15ml/1 tbsp caraway seeds

salt and pepper

900g/2lb/8 cups grated green cabbage,
   or a mixture of green and red cabbage

150g/5oz/1 cup grated carrots

2 yellow or red onions, finely sliced

1 Combine the mayonnaise, vinegar, mustard, sugar and caraway seeds. Season with salt and pepper.

2 ▼ Put the cabbage, carrots and onions in a large bowl.

3 ▲ Add the dressing to the vegetables and mix well. Taste for seasoning. Cover and chill for 1–2 hours. The cabbage will become more tender the longer it marinates.

Pennsylvania Dutch Fried Tomatoes

SERVES 4

2–3 large green or very firm red tomatoes

40g/1½oz/⅓ cup plain (all-purpose) flour

50g/2oz/¼ cup butter or bacon fat

granulated sugar, if needed

4 slices hot buttered toast

175ml/6fl oz/¾ cup pouring
   (half-and-half) cream

salt and pepper

1 ▼ Slice the tomatoes into 1cm/½in rounds. Coat lightly with flour.

2 ▲ Heat the butter or bacon fat in a frying pan. When it is hot, add the tomato slices and cook until browned. Turn them once, and season generously with salt and pepper.

3 If the tomatoes are green, sprinkle each slice with a little sugar. Cook until the other side is brown, about 3–4 minutes more.

4 Divide the tomatoes among the slices of toast and keep hot.

5 ▲ Pour the cream into the hot frying pan and bring to the boil. Simmer for 1–2 minutes, stirring to mix in the brown bits and cooking juices. Spoon the gravy over the tomatoes, and serve at once.

~ **VARIATION** ~

For Fried Tomatoes with Ham, top the toast with ham slices before covering with the tomatoes.

Coleslaw (top), Pennsylvania Dutch Fried Tomatoes

Boston Brown Bread

MAKES 2 SMALL LOAVES

15ml/1 tbsp butter or margarine, softened

115g/4oz/1 cup yellow cornmeal

115g/4oz/1 cup wholemeal
    (whole-wheat) flour

115g/4oz/1 cup rye flour

5ml/1 tsp bicarbonate of soda
    (baking soda)

5ml/1 tsp salt

475ml/16fl oz/2 cups buttermilk

275g/10oz/¾ cup treacle

175g/6oz/1 cup chopped raisins

butter or cream cheese, to serve

1 ▲ Grease two 450g/1lb food cans, or two 1.2 litre/2 pint pudding dishes, with the soft butter or margarine.

2 ▲ Sift all the dry ingredients together into a large bowl. Tip in any bran from the wholemeal flour. Stir well to blend.

3 In a separate bowl, combine the buttermilk, treacle and raisins. Add to the dry ingredients and mix well.

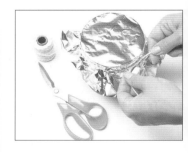

4 ▲ Pour the mixture into the prepared cans, filling them about two-thirds full. Cover the tops with buttered foil, and tie or tape it down so that the rising bread cannot push the foil lid off.

5 Set the cans on a rack in a large pan with a tight-fitting lid. Pour in enough warm water to come halfway up the sides of the cans. Cover the pan, bring to the boil and steam for 2½ hours. Check occasionally that the water has not boiled away, and add more if necessary to keep the level up.

6 Turn the bread out on to a warmed serving dish. Slice and serve with butter or cream cheese for spreading.

Sweet Potato Scones

MAKES ABOUT 24

150g/5oz/1¼ cups plain (all-purpose) flour

20ml/4 tsp baking powder

5ml/1 tsp salt

15ml/1 tbsp brown sugar

65g/2½oz/¾ cup mashed cooked
    sweet potatoes

150ml/¼ pint/⅔ cup milk

60ml/4 tbsp melted butter or margarine

1 Preheat the oven to 230°C/450°F/
Gas 8.

2 ▲ Sift the flour, baking powder
and salt into a bowl. Add the sugar
and stir to mix.

3 ▲ In a separate bowl, combine the
sweet potato mash with the milk and
melted butter or margarine. Mix well
until evenly blended.

4 ▼ Stir the dry ingredients into the
sweet potato mixture to make a
dough. Turn out on to a lightly floured
surface and knead lightly just to mix,
1–2 minutes.

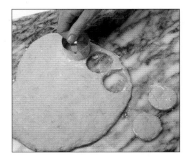

5 ▲ Roll or pat out the scone mixure
to 1cm/½in thickness. Cut out rounds
with a 4cm/1½in pastry (cookie) cutter.

6 Arrange the rounds on a greased
baking sheet. Bake until puffed and
lightly golden, about 15 minutes.
Serve the scones warm.

Boston Cream Pie

SERVES 8

225g/8oz/2 cups self-raising (self-rising) flour

15ml/1 tbsp baking powder

2.5ml/½ tsp salt

115g/4oz/½ cup butter, softened

200g/7oz/1 cup granulated sugar

2 eggs

5ml/1 tsp vanilla extract

175ml/6fl oz/¾ cup milk

FOR THE FILLING

250ml/8fl oz/1 cup milk

3 egg yolks

90g/3½oz/½ cup granulated sugar

25g/1oz/¼ cup plain (all-purpose) flour

15g/½oz/1 tbsp butter

15ml/1 tbsp brandy or 5ml/1 tsp vanilla extract

FOR THE CHOCOLATE GLAZE

25g/1oz cooking (unsweetened) chocolate

25g/1oz/2 tbsp butter or margarine

90g/3½oz/½ cup icing (confectioners') sugar, plus extra for dusting

2.5ml/½ tsp vanilla extract

about 15ml/1 tbsp hot water

1 Preheat the oven to 190°C/375°F/ Gas 5.

2 Grease two 20cm/8in shallow round cake tins (pans), and line the bottoms with greased baking parchment.

3 Sift the flour with the baking powder and salt.

4 Beat the butter and granulated sugar together until light and fluffy. Add the eggs one at a time, beating well after each addition. Stir in the vanilla. Add the milk and dry ingredients alternately, mixing only enough to blend thoroughly. Do not over-beat the mixture.

5 Divide the mixture between the prepared tins and spread it out evenly. Bake until a skewer inserted in the centre comes out clean, about 25 minutes.

6 Meanwhile, make the filling. Heat the milk in a small pan to boiling point. Remove from the heat.

7 ▲ In a heatproof mixing bowl, beat the egg yolks until smooth. Gradually add the granulated sugar and continue beating until pale yellow. Beat in the flour.

8 ▲ Pour the hot milk into the egg yolk mixture in a steady stream, beating constantly. When all the milk has been added, place the bowl over a pan of boiling water, or pour the mixture into the top of a double boiler. Heat, stirring constantly, until thickened. Cook for 2 minutes more, then remove from the heat. Stir in the butter and brandy or vanilla. Leave to cool.

9 ▲ When the cake layers have cooled, use a large sharp knife to slice off the domed top to make a flat surface. Place one layer on a serving plate and spread the filling on in a thick layer. Set the other layer on top, cut side down. Smooth the edge of the filling layer so it is flush with the sides of the cake layers.

10 ▲ For the glaze, melt the chocolate with the butter or margarine in the top of a double boiler, or in a bowl over hot water. When smooth, remove from the heat and beat in the sugar to make a thick paste. Add the vanilla. Beat in a little of the hot water. If the glaze does not have a spreadable consistency, add more water, 5ml/1 tsp at a time.

11 Spread the glaze evenly over the top of the cake, using a metal spatula. Dust the top with icing sugar. Because of the custard filling, any leftover cake must be chilled.

Shaker Summer Pudding

SERVES 6–8

1 loaf of white farmhouse-type bread,
   1–2 days old, sliced

675g/1½lb fresh redcurrants

50g/2oz/¼ cup plus 30ml/2 tbsp
   granulated sugar

50ml/2fl oz/¼ cup water

675g/1½lb berries: raspberries,
   blueberries and blackberries

juice of ½ lemon

whipped cream, to serve (optional)

1 ▲ Trim the crusts from the bread slices. Cut a round of bread to fit in the bottom of a 1.5 litre/2½ pint/6 cup domed pudding basin. Line the sides of the basin with bread slices, cutting them to fit and overlapping them slightly. Reserve enough bread slices to cover the top of the basin.

2 Combine the redcurrants with the 50g/2oz/¼ cup of sugar and the water in a non-metallic pan. Heat gently, crushing the berries lightly to help the juices flow. When the sugar has dissolved, remove from the heat.

3 Tip the currant mixture into a food processor or blender and process until quite smooth. Press through a fine-mesh nylon strainer set over a bowl. Discard the fruit pulp left in the strainer.

4 Put the berries in a bowl with the remaining sugar and the lemon juice. Stir well.

5 One at a time, remove the cut bread pieces from the basin and dip in the redcurrant purée. Replace to line the basin evenly.

6 ▲ Spoon the berries into the lined basin, pressing them down evenly. Top with the reserved cut bread slices, which have been dipped in the redcurrant purée.

7 Cover the basin with clear film (plastic wrap). Set a small plate, just big enough to fit inside the rim of the basin, on top of the pudding. Weigh it down with cans of food. Chill for 8–24 hours.

8 To turn the pudding out, remove the weights, plate and clear film. Run a knife between the basin and the pudding to loosen it. Turn out on to a serving plate. Serve in wedges, with whipped cream if you wish.

Apple Brown Betty

SERVES 6

50g/2oz/1 cup fresh breadcrumbs

150g/5oz/¾ cup soft light brown sugar

2.5ml/½ tsp ground cinnamon

1.5ml/¼ tsp ground cloves

1.5ml/¼ tsp grated nutmeg

50g/2oz/¼ cup butter

900g/2lb tart-sweet apples

juice of 1 lemon

40g/1½oz/⅓ cup finely chopped walnuts

1 Preheat the grill (broiler).

2 ▲ Spread the breadcrumbs on a baking sheet and toast under the grill until golden, stirring so they colour evenly. Set aside.

3 Preheat the oven to 190°C/375°F/Gas 5. Grease a 2.5 litre/4 pint baking dish.

4 ▲ Mix the sugar with the spices. Cut the butter into pea-size pieces; set aside.

5 ▲ Peel, core and slice the apples. Toss immediately with the lemon juice to prevent the apple slices from turning brown.

6 Sprinkle about 37ml/2½ tbsp breadcrumbs over the bottom of the prepared dish. Cover with one-third of the apples and sprinkle with one-third of the sugar-spice mixture. Add another layer of breadcrumbs and dot with one-third of the butter. Repeat the layers two more times, ending with a layer of breadcrumbs. Sprinkle with the nuts, and dot with the remaining butter.

7 Bake until the apples are tender and the top is golden brown, 35–40 minutes. Serve warm. It is good with cream or ice cream.

Maryland Peach and Blueberry Pie

SERVES 8

225g/8oz/2 cups plain (all-purpose) flour

2.5ml/½ tsp salt

5ml/1 tsp granulated sugar

150g/5oz/10 tbsp cold butter
    or margarine, diced

1 egg yolk

30–45ml/2–3 tbsp iced water

30ml/2 tbsp milk, for glazing

FOR THE FILLING

6 peaches, peeled, stoned and sliced

225g/8oz/2 cups fresh blueberries

150g/5oz/¾ cup granulated sugar

30ml/2 tbsp fresh lemon juice

40g/1½oz/⅓ cup plain (all-purpose) flour

pinch of grated nutmeg

25g/1oz/2 tbsp butter or margarine, cut
    into pea-size pieces

1 For the pastry, sift the flour, salt and sugar into a bowl. Using your fingertips, rub the butter or margarine into the dry ingredients as quickly as possible until the mixture is crumbly and resembles breadcrumbs.

2 Mix the egg yolk with 30ml/2 tbsp of the iced water and sprinkle over the flour mixture. Combine with a fork until the pastry holds together. If the pastry is too crumbly, add a little more water, 5ml/1 tsp at a time. Gather the pastry into a ball and flatten into a disk. Wrap in clear film (plastic wrap) and chill for at least 20 minutes.

3 Roll out two-thirds of the pastry between two sheets of baking parchment to a thickness of about 3mm/⅛in. Use to line a 23cm/9in tart tin (pan). Trim all around, leaving a 1cm/½in overhang. Fold the overhang under to form the edge. Using a fork, press the edge to the rim of the tin.

4 ▲ Gather the trimmings and remaining pastry into a ball, and roll out to a thickness of about 6mm/¼in. Using a pastry wheel or sharp knife, cut strips 1cm/½in wide. Chill the pastry case and the strips for 20 minutes.

5 Preheat the oven to 200°C/400°F/Gas 6.

6 ▲ Line the pastry case with baking parchment and fill with dried beans. Bake until the pastry case is just set, 7–10 minutes. Remove from the oven and carefully lift out the paper with the beans. Prick the bottom of the pastry case all over with a fork, then return to the oven and bake for 5 minutes more. Let the pastry case cool slightly before filling. Leave the oven on.

7 ▲ In a mixing bowl, combine the peach slices with the blueberries, sugar, lemon juice, flour and nutmeg. Spoon the fruit mixture evenly into the pastry case. Dot with the pieces of butter or margarine.

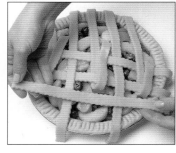

8 ▲ Weave a lattice top with the chilled pastry strips, pressing the ends to the baked pastry-case edge. Brush the strips with the milk.

9 Bake the pie for 15 minutes. Reduce the heat to 180°C/350°F/Gas 4, and continue baking until the filling is tender and bubbling and the pastry lattice is golden, about 30 minutes more. If the pastry gets too brown, cover loosely with a piece of foil. Serve the pie warm or at room temperature.

Brethren's Cider Pie

SERVES 6

175g/6oz/1½ cups plain
   (all-purpose) flour

1.5ml/¼ tsp salt

5ml/1 tsp caster (superfine) sugar

115g/4oz/½ cup cold butter or
   margarine, diced

30–45ml/3–4 tbsp iced water

FOR THE FILLING

550ml/18fl oz/2½ cups cider

15ml/1 tbsp butter

250ml/8fl oz/1 cup maple syrup

50ml/2fl oz/¼ cup water

1.5ml/¼ tsp salt

2 eggs, at room temperature, separated

5ml/1 tsp grated nutmeg

1 ▲ For the pastry, sift the flour, salt and sugar into a bowl. With a pastry blender, cut in the butter until the mixture resembles breadcrumbs, or rub in with your fingertips.

2 Sprinkle 45ml/3 tbsp of the iced water over the flour mixture. Combine with a fork until the pastry holds together. If the pastry is too crumbly, add a little more water, 5ml/1 tsp at a time. Gather the pastry into a ball and flatten into a disk. Wrap in baking parchment and chill for 20 minutes.

3 ▲ Meanwhile, place the cider in a heavy pan. Boil until only 175ml/6fl oz/ ¾ cup remains. Leave to cool.

4 ▲ Roll out the pastry between two sheets of baking parchment to a thickness of about 3mm/⅛in. Use to line a 23cm/9in pie tin (pan).

5 ▲ Trim all around, leaving a 1cm/ ½in overhang. Fold the overhang under to form the edge. Using a fork, press the edge to the rim of the pan and press up from under with your fingers at intervals for a ruffle effect. Chill for 20 minutes.

6 Preheat the oven to 180°C/350°F/ Gas 4.

7 ▲ For the filling, add the butter, maple syrup, water and salt to the cider, bring to the boil and simmer gently for 5–6 minutes. Remove the pan from the heat and let the mixture cool slightly, then whisk in the beaten egg yolks.

8 ▲ In a large bowl, whisk the egg whites until they form stiff peaks. Add the cider mixture and fold gently together until evenly blended.

9 ▲ Pour into the prepared pastry case. Dust with the grated nutmeg.

10 Bake until the pastry is golden brown and the filling is well set, 30–35 minutes. Serve warm.

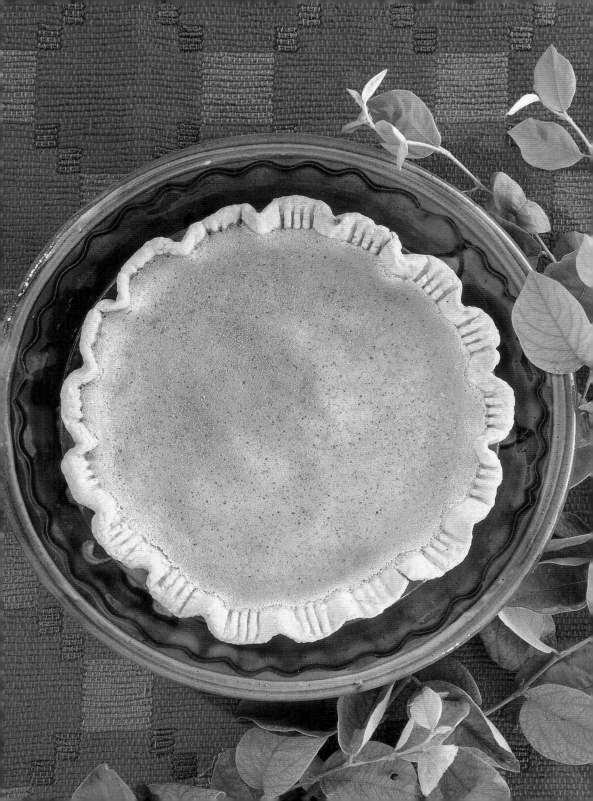

Vermont Baked Maple Custard

SERVES 6

3 eggs

185g/6½oz/½ cup maple syrup

550ml/18fl oz/2½ cups milk

pinch of salt

pinch of grated nutmeg

~ COOK'S TIP ~

Baking delicate mixtures such as
custards in a bain marie helps
protect them from uneven heating,
which could make them rubbery.

1 ▼ Preheat the oven to 180°C/
350°F/Gas 4. Combine all the
ingredients in a bowl and mix
together well.

2 ▲ Set individual ramekins in a
roasting pan half filled with hot water.
Pour the custard mixture into the
ramekins. Bake until the custards are
set, 45–60 minutes. Test by inserting
the blade of a knife in the centre; it
should come out clean. Serve warm
or chilled.

Cranberry Ice

MAKES ABOUT 1.75 LITRES/3 PINTS/7½ CUPS

2.5 litres/4 pints cranberries

475ml/16fl oz/2 cups water

350g/12oz/1¾ cups granulated sugar

1.5ml/¼ tsp grated orange rind

30ml/2 tbsp fresh orange juice

1 Check the manufacturer's
instructions for your ice cream maker,
if using one, to find out its capacity.
If necessary, halve the recipe.

2 ▲ Pick over and wash the
cranberries. Discard any that are
blemished or soft.

3 ▼ Place the cranberries in a non-
metallic pan with the water and bring
to the boil. Reduce the heat and
simmer until the cranberries are soft,
about 15 minutes.

4 Push the cranberry mixture through
a fine-mesh nylon strainer set over a
bowl. Return the purée to the pan,
add the sugar and stir to dissolve. Boil
for 5 minutes. Stir in the orange rind
and juice. Remove from the heat and
let the cranberry mixture cool down to
room temperature.

5 To freeze in an ice cream maker,
pour the cranberry mixture into the
machine and freeze following the
manufacturer's instructions.

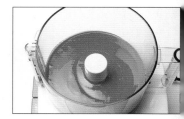

6 ▲ If you do not have an ice cream
maker, pour the mixture into a metal
or plastic freezer container and freeze
until softly set, about 3 hours. Remove
the frozen cranberry mixture from the
container and chop roughly into 7.5cm/
3in pieces. Place in a food processor and
process until smooth. Return the mixture to the freezer container and freeze
again until firm. Repeat this freezing
and chopping process two or three
times, then leave to freeze until firm.

Vermont Baked Maple Custard (top), Cranberry Ice

THE SOUTH

RICH AND DIVERSE CULINARY
INFLUENCES – FRENCH, SPANISH,
NATIVE AMERICAN AND AFRICAN –
HAVE BROUGHT ABOUT SEVERAL
DISTINCT CUISINES, CAJUN BEING
PERHAPS THE MOST WELL KNOWN.
ALL HAVE CAPITALIZED ON THE
BOUNTY OF FIELD AND FOREST,
THE PROXIMITY OF WATER
THROUGHOUT MUCH OF THE
REGION AND A WARM CLIMATE.

Miami Chilled Avocado Soup

2 large or 3 medium ripe avocados

15ml/1 tbsp fresh lemon juice

75g/3oz/¾ cup coarsely chopped peeled cucumber

30ml/2 tbsp dry sherry

75g/3oz/¾ cup coarsely chopped spring onions (scallions), with some of the green stems

475ml/16fl oz/2 cups mild-flavoured chicken stock

5ml/1 tsp salt

hot pepper sauce (optional)

natural (plain) yogurt or cream, to serve

1 ▼ Halve the avocados, pull out the stones (pits) and peel. Roughly chop the flesh and place in a food processor or blender. Add the lemon juice and process until very smooth.

2 ▲ Add the cucumber, sherry and most of the spring onions. Process again until smooth.

3 ▲ In a large bowl, combine the avocado mixture with the chicken stock. Whisk until well blended. Season with the salt and a few drops of hot pepper sauce, if you like. Cover the bowl and chill well.

4 ▲ To serve, fill individual bowls with the soup. Place a spoonful of yogurt or cream in the centre of each bowl and swirl with a spoon. Sprinkle with the reserved spring onions.

Shrimp and Corn Bisque

SERVES 4

30ml/2 tbsp olive oil

1 onion, finely chopped

50g/2oz/¼ cup butter or margarine

25g/1oz/¼ cup plain (all-purpose) flour

750ml/1¼ pints/3 cups fish or chicken
    stock, or clam juice

250ml/8fl oz/1 cup milk

150g/5oz/1 cup peeled cooked small
    prawns, (shrimp), deveined if necessary

250g/9oz/1½ cups corn kernels (fresh,
    frozen or canned)

2.5ml/½ tsp finely chopped fresh dill
    or thyme

salt

hot pepper sauce

120ml/4fl oz/½ cup single (light) cream

1 Heat the olive oil in a large heavy
pan. Add the onion and cook over a a
low heat until softened, 8–10 minutes.

2 Meanwhile, melt the butter or
margarine in a medium heavy pan.
Add the flour and stir with a wire
whisk until blended. Cook for
1–2 minutes. Pour in the stock and
milk and stir to blend. Bring to the
boil over a medium heat and cook for
5–8 minutes, stirring frequently.

3 ▲ Cut each prawn into two or three
pieces and add to the onion with the
corn and dill or thyme. Cook for
2–3 minutes, stirring occasionally.
Remove the pan from the heat.

4 ▼ Add the sauce mixture to the
prawn and corn mixture and mix
well. Remove 750ml/1¼ pints/3 cups of
the soup and purée in a blender or food
processor. Return it to the rest of the
soup in the pan and stir well. Season
with salt and hot pepper sauce to taste.

5 ▲ Add the cream and stir to blend.
Heat the soup almost to boiling point,
stirring frequently. Serve hot.

Palm Beach Papaya and Avocado Salad

SERVES 4

2 ripe avocados

1 ripe papaya

1 large sweet orange

1 small red onion

115g/4oz/2 cups small rocket
  (arugula) leaves

FOR THE DRESSING

50ml/2fl oz/¼ cup olive oil

30ml/2 tbsp fresh lemon or lime juice

salt and pepper

1 ▼ Halve the avocados and remove
the stones (pits). Carefully peel off the
skin. Cut each avocado in half lengthways into four thick slices.

2 ▲ Peel the papaya. Cut it in half
lengthways and scoop out the seeds
with a spoon. Set aside 5ml/1 tsp of
the seeds for the dressing. Cut each
papaya half lengthways into eight slices.

3 ▲ Peel the orange. Using a sharp
paring knife, cut out the sections,
cutting on either side of the dividing
membranes. Cut the onion into very
thin slices and separate into rings.

4 ▲ Combine the dressing
ingredients in a bowl and mix well.
Stir in the reserved papaya seeds.

5 Assemble the salad on four
individual serving plates. Alternate
slices of papaya and avocado and add
the orange sections and a small mound
of rocket topped with onion rings.
Spoon on the dressing.

Warm Salad of Black-eyed Beans

SERVES 4

2 small red (bell) peppers

2.5ml/½ tsp Dijon-style mustard

30ml/2 tbsp wine vinegar

1.5ml/¼ tsp salt

pinch of pepper

90ml/6 tbsp olive oil

30ml/2 tbsp finely chopped fresh chives

350g/12oz/3 cups fresh black-eyed
   beans (peas)

1 bay leaf

8 lean bacon rashers (strips)

1 Preheat the grill (broiler).

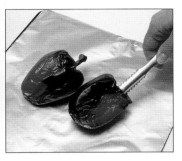

2 ▲ Grill (broil) the peppers until the skins blacken and blister, turning the peppers so that all sides are charred. Remove from the grill and place the peppers in a paper or plastic bag to steam. Leave to cool for 10 minutes.

3 Peel off the skins. Cut the peppers in half, discard the seeds, white membranes and stem, and slice into 1 × 5cm/½ × 2in strips. Set aside.

~ **COOK'S TIP** ~

If preferred, chop the roasted red (bell) peppers rather than cutting them into strips and mix into the warm black-eyed beans (peas).

4 ▼ Combine the mustard and vinegar in a small bowl. Add the salt and pepper. Beat in the oil until well blended. Add the chives.

5 Add the black-eyed beans to a pan of boiling salted water, with the bay leaf. Boil until just tender, 13–15 minutes.

6 Meanwhile, cook the bacon until crisp. Drain on kitchen paper. Cut or break into small pieces.

7 ▲ When the black-eyed beans are done, drain them and discard the bay leaf. While they are still warm, toss them with the chive dressing.

8 Make a mound of beans on a serving dish. Sprinkle with the bacon pieces and garnish with the strips of red pepper. Serve warm.

Fromajardis

MAKES ABOUT 40

225g/8oz/2 cups plain (all-purpose) flour

1.5ml/¼ tsp grated nutmeg

2.5ml/½ tsp salt

150g/5oz/10 tbsp cold butter, lard or
   white cooking fat, diced

45–60ml/4–5 tbsp iced water

FOR THE FILLING

2 eggs

115g/4oz mature (sharp) Cheddar
   cheese, grated

hot pepper sauce, to taste

15ml/1 tbsp finely chopped mixed fresh
   herbs, such as thyme, chives and sage

1 For the pastry, sift the flour, nutmeg
and salt into a bowl. Using your
fingertips, rub the butter, lard or white
cooking fat into the dry ingredients as
quickly as possible until the mixture is
crumbly and resembles breadcrumbs.

2 ▲ Sprinkle 60ml/4 tbsp of the iced
water over the flour mixture. Combine
with a fork until the pastry holds
together. If the pastry is too crumbly,
add a little more water, 5ml/1 tsp at a
time. Gather the pastry into a ball.

3 ▲ Divide the pastry in half and pat
each portion into a disk. Wrap in clear
film (plastic wrap); chill for 20 minutes.

4 Preheat the oven to 220°C/425°F/
Gas 7.

5 ▲ For the filling, put the eggs in a
mixing bowl and beat well with a fork.
Add the cheese, hot pepper sauce to
taste and the herbs.

6 ▲ On a lightly floured surface, roll
out the dough to a thickness of 3mm/
⅛in or less. Cut out rounds using a
7.5cm/3in drinking glass or cutter.

7 ▲ Place 5ml/1 tsp of the filling in
the centre of each pastry round. Fold
over to make half-moon shapes, and
press the edges together with the tines
of a fork. A bit of filling may ooze
through the seam.

8 ▲ Cut a few small slashes in the
top of each pastry with the point of a
sharp knife. Place on ungreased baking
sheets. Bake until the pastries start to
darken slightly, 18–20 minutes. To test
if they are cooked, cut one in half; the
pastry should be cooked through. Serve
warm with drinks.

~ COOK'S TIP ~

The fromajardis may be made
ahead of time. Leave them to cool
on a wire rack and then store in
an airtight container. Just before
serving, reheat the pastries in a
preheated 190°C/375°F/Gas 5 oven
for 5–10 minutes.

Crab Bayou

SERVES 6

450g/1lb fresh crab meat

3 hard-boiled egg yolks

5ml/1 tsp Dijon-style mustard

75g/3oz/6 tbsp butter or margarine,
    at room temperature

1.5ml/¼ tsp cayenne pepper

45ml/3 tbsp sherry

30ml/2 tbsp finely chopped fresh parsley

120ml/4fl oz/½ cup whipping cream

50g/2oz/½ cup thinly sliced spring onions
    (scallions), including some of the
    green stems

salt and black pepper

30g/1¼oz/½ cup dried breadcrumbs

1 Preheat oven to 180°C/350°F/Gas 4.

2 ▼ Pick over the crab meat and remove any shell or cartilage, keeping the pieces of crab as big as possible.

3 ▲ In a medium bowl, crumble the egg yolks with a fork. Add the mustard, 60ml/4 tbsp of the butter or margarine, and the cayenne, and mash together to form a paste. Mash in the sherry and parsley.

4 ▲ Mix in the cream and spring onions. Stir in the crab meat. Season with salt and pepper.

5 ▲ Divide the mixture equally among six greased scallop shells or other individual baking dishes. Sprinkle with the breadcrumbs and dot with the remaining butter or margarine.

6 Bake until bubbling hot and golden brown, about 20 minutes.

Cajun "Popcorn" with Basil Mayonnaise

SERVES 8

900g/2lb raw crayfish tails, peeled, or
    small prawns (shrimp), peeled
    and deveined

2 eggs

250ml/8fl oz/1 cup dry white wine

50g/2oz/½ cup fine cornmeal, or plain
    (all-purpose) flour if not available

50g/2oz/½ cup plain flour

15ml/1 tbsp finely chopped fresh chives

1 garlic clove, finely chopped

2.5ml/½ tsp fresh thyme leaves

1.5ml/¼ tsp salt

1.5ml/¼ tsp cayenne pepper

1.5ml/¼ tsp black pepper

oil for deep-frying

FOR THE MAYONNAISE

1 egg yolk

10ml/2 tsp Dijon-style mustard

15ml/1 tbsp white wine vinegar

salt and pepper

250ml/8fl oz/1 cup olive or vegetable oil

25g/1oz/½ cup finely chopped fresh
    basil leaves

1 ▲ Rinse the crayfish tails or
prawns in cool water. Drain well and
set aside in a cool place.

2 Mix together the eggs and wine in a
small bowl.

3 ▼ In a mixing bowl, combine the
cornmeal and/or flour, chives, garlic,
thyme, salt, cayenne and pepper.
Gradually whisk in the egg mixture,
blending well. Cover the batter and
leave to stand for 1 hour.

4 For the mayonnaise, combine the
egg yolk, mustard and vinegar in a
mixing bowl. Add salt and pepper to
taste. Add the oil in a thin stream,
beating vigorously with a wire whisk.
When the mixture is thick and
smooth, stir in the basil. Cover and
chill until ready to serve.

5 Heat 5–7.5cm/2–3in oil in a large
frying pan or deep-fryer to 188–190°C/
365–370°F. Dip the seafood into the
batter and fry in small batches until
golden brown, 2–3 minutes. Turn as
necessary for even colouring. Remove
with a slotted spoon and drain on
kitchen paper. Serve hot, with the
basil mayonnaise.

Crayfish or Prawn Etouffée

SERVES 6

1.2kg/2½lb raw crayfish or prawns
  (shrimp) in shell

750ml/1¼ pints/3 cups water

75ml/2½ fl oz/⅓ cup vegetable oil or lard

40g/1½oz/⅓ cup plain (all-purpose) flour

1½ onions, finely chopped

50g/2oz/¼ cup finely chopped green
  (bell) pepper

25g/1oz/¼ cup finely chopped celery

1 garlic clove, finely chopped

120ml/4fl oz/½ cup dry white wine

25g/1oz/2 tbsp butter or margarine

25g/1oz/½ cup finely chopped
  fresh parsley

15g/½oz/¼ cup finely chopped
  fresh chives

salt

hot pepper sauce

rice, to serve

1 ▲ Peel and devein the crayfish or prawns; reserve the heads and shells. Keep the seafood in a covered bowl in the refrigerator; put the heads and shells in a large pot with the water.

2 Bring the pot to the boil, cover and simmer for 15 minutes. Strain and reserve 350ml/12fl oz/1½ cups of this stock. Set aside.

3 To make the Cajun roux, heat the oil or lard in a heavy cast iron frying pan or steel pan.

4 ▲ When the oil is hot, add the flour, a little at a time, and blend to a smooth paste using a long-handled flat-bottomed wooden spoon.

5 ▲ Cook over a medium-low heat, stirring constantly, until the Cajun roux reaches the desired colour, 25–40 minutes. It will gradually deepen in colour from light beige to tan, to a deeper, redder brown. When it reaches the colour of peanut butter, remove the pan from the heat and immediately mix in the onions, pepper and celery. Continue stirring to prevent any further darkening.

6 ▲ Return the pan to a low heat. Add the garlic and cook for 1–2 minutes, stirring. Add the seafood stock and blend well with a wire whisk. Whisk in the white wine.

7 ▲ Bring to the boil, stirring, and simmer until the sauce is thick, 3–4 minutes. Remove from the heat.

8 ▲ In a large heavy pan, melt the butter or margarine. Add the crayfish or prawns, stir and cook until pink, 2–3 minutes. Stir in the parsley and chives.

9 Add the sauce and stir well to combine. Season with salt and hot pepper sauce to taste. Simmer over a medium heat for 3–4 minutes more. Serve hot with rice.

~ COOK'S TIP ~

When making the Cajun roux, take great care not to burn the flour. If the mixture starts to smoke, immediately remove the pan from the heat and stir until the mixture cools slightly. If the flour mixture should burn, or if black specks appear, throw it away and start again, or the étouffée will have a bitter burned taste. Do not use a nonstick pan.

Prawn-stuffed Aubergines

SERVES 4

2 large firm aubergines (eggplants)

30ml/2 tbsp fresh lemon juice

40g/1½oz/3 tbsp butter or margarine

225g/8oz raw prawns (shrimp), peeled and deveined

40g/1½oz/½ cup thinly sliced spring onions (scallions), including some green stems

350g/12oz/1½ cups chopped fresh tomatoes

1 garlic clove, finely chopped

15g/½oz/¼ cup chopped fresh parsley

15g/½oz/¼ cup chopped fresh basil

pinch of grated nutmeg

salt and pepper

hot pepper sauce, to taste

30g/1¼oz/½ cup dried breadcrumbs

rice, to serve (optional)

1 Preheat oven to 190°C/375°F/Gas 5.

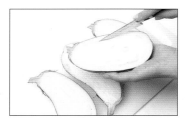

2 ▲ Cut the aubergines in half lengthways. With a small sharp knife, cut around the inside edge of each aubergine half, about 1cm/½in from the skin. Carefully scoop out the flesh, leaving a shell 1cm/½in thick.

3 Immerse the shells, skin side up, in cold water to prevent them from discolouring.

~ COOK'S TIP ~

This can also be served cold for an unusual summer dish.

4 ▲ Chop the scooped-out aubergine flesh coarsely, toss with the lemon juice and set aside.

5 ▲ Melt 25g/1oz/2 tbsp of the butter or margarine in a frying pan. Add the prawns and sauté until pink, 2–3 minutes, turning so they cook evenly. Remove the prawns with a slotted spoon and set aside.

6 ▲ Add the spring onions to the pan and cook over a medium heat for about 2 minutes, stirring constantly. Add the tomatoes, garlic and parsley and cook for 5 minutes more.

7 Add the chopped aubergines, basil and nutmeg. If necessary, add a little water to prevent the vegetables sticking. Mix well. Cover and simmer for 8–10 minutes. Remove from the heat.

8 ▲ Cut each prawn into two or three pieces. Stir into the vegetable mixture. Season with salt, pepper and hot pepper sauce to taste.

9 Lightly oil a shallow baking tin (pan) large enough to hold the aubergine halves in one layer. Drain and dry the aubergine shells and arrange in the pan.

10 ▲ Sprinkle a layer of breadcrumbs into each shell. Spoon in a layer of the prawn mixture. Repeat, finishing with a layer of breadcrumbs.

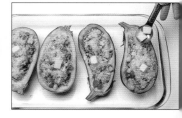

11 ▲ Dot with the remaining butter or margarine. Bake until bubbling hot and golden brown on top, about 20–25 minutes. Serve immediately, accompanied by rice, if you wish.

Prawns Creole

SERVES 4

675g/1½lb raw prawns (shrimp) in shell, with heads, if available

475ml/16fl oz/2 cups water

45ml/3 tbsp olive or vegetable oil

3 onions, finely chopped

50g/2oz/½ cup finely chopped celery

115g/4oz/½ cup finely chopped green (bell) pepper

25g/1oz/½ cup chopped fresh parsley

1 garlic clove, finely chopped

15ml/1 tbsp Worcestershire sauce

1.5ml/¼ tsp cayenne pepper

120ml/4fl oz/½ cup dry white wine

225g/8oz/1 cup chopped peeled plum tomatoes

5ml/1 tsp salt

1 bay leaf

5ml/1 tsp granulated sugar

rice, to serve

1 ▲ Peel and devein the prawns; reserve the heads and shells. Keep the prawns in a covered bowl in the refrigerator while you make the sauce.

2 Put the prawn heads and shells in a pan with the water. Bring to the boil and simmer for 15 minutes. Strain and reserve 350ml/2fl oz/1½ cups of this stock. Set the stock aside.

3 ▲ Heat the oil in a heavy pan. Add the onions and cook over a low heat until softened, 8–10 minutes. Add the celery and pepper and cook for 5 minutes more. Stir in the parsley, garlic, Worcestershire sauce and cayenne. Cook for another 5 minutes, stirring occasionally.

4 Raise the heat to medium. Stir in the wine and simmer for 3–4 minutes. Add the tomatoes, prawns, stock, salt, bay leaf and sugar and bring to the boil. Stir well, then reduce the heat to low and simmer until the tomatoes have fallen apart and the sauce has reduced slightly, about 30 minutes. Remove from the heat and leave to cool slightly.

5 Discard the bay leaf. Pour the sauce into a food processor or blender and process until quite smooth. Taste and adjust the seasoning.

6 ▲ Return the sauce to the pan and bring to the boil. Add the prawns and simmer until they turn pink, 4–5 minutes only. Serve with rice.

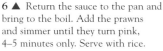

Fried Catfish Fillets with Piquant Sauce

SERVES 4

1 egg

50ml/2fl oz/¼ cup olive oil

squeeze of lemon juice

2.5ml/½ tsp finely chopped fresh dill
  or parsley

salt and pepper

4 catfish fillets

50g/2oz/½ cup plain (all-purpose) flour

25g/1oz/2 tbsp butter or margarine

FOR THE SAUCE

1 egg yolk

30ml/2 tbsp Dijon-style mustard

30ml/2 tbsp white wine vinegar

10ml/2 tsp paprika

300ml/½ pint/1¼ cups olive or
  vegetable oil

30ml/2 tbsp prepared horseradish

2.5ml/½ tsp finely chopped garlic

25g/1oz/¼ cup finely chopped celery

30ml/2 tbsp tomato ketchup

2.5ml/½ tsp pepper

2.5ml/½ tsp salt

1 ▲ For the sauce, combine the egg yolk, mustard, vinegar and paprika in a mixing bowl. Add the oil in a thin stream, beating vigorously with a wire whisk to blend it in.

2 ▲ When the mixture is smooth and thick, beat in all the other sauce ingredients. Cover and chill until ready to serve.

3 ▲ Combine the egg, 15ml/1 tbsp of the olive oil, the lemon juice, herbs and a little salt and pepper in a shallow dish. Beat until well combined.

4 ▼ Dip both sides of each catfish fillet in the egg and herb mixture, then coat lightly with flour, shaking off the excess.

5 Heat the butter or margarine with the remaining olive oil in a large heavy frying pan. Add the fillets and fry until golden brown on both sides and cooked, 8–10 minutes. To test if it is done, insert the point of a sharp knife into the fish: it should still be just opaque in the centre.

6 Serve the catfish fillets hot, with the piquant sauce.

~ VARIATION ~

If preferred, serve the catfish fillets with lime or lemon wedges.

Seafood and Sausage Gumbo

SERVES 10–12

1.3kg/3lb raw prawns (shrimp) in shell, with heads, if available

1.65 litres/2¾ pints/7 cups water

1 onion, quartered

4 bay leaves

175ml/6fl oz/¾ cup vegetable oil

115g/4oz/1 cup plain (all-purpose) flour

50g/2oz/¼ cup margarine or butter

6 onions, finely chopped

450g/1lb/2 cups finely chopped green (bell) pepper

225g/8oz/2 cups finely chopped celery

675g/1½lb kielbasa (Polish) or andouille sausage, cut into 1cm/½in rounds

450g/1lb fresh okra, cut into 1cm/½in slices

3 garlic cloves, finely chopped

2.5ml/½ tsp fresh or dried thyme leaves

10ml/2 tsp salt

2.5ml/½ tsp black pepper

2.5ml/½ tsp white pepper

5ml/1 tsp cayenne pepper

hot pepper sauce (optional)

450g/1lb/2 cups chopped peeled fresh or canned plum tomatoes

450g/1lb fresh crab meat

rice, to serve

1 Peel and devein the prawns; reserve the heads and shells. Keep the prawns in a covered bowl in the refrigerator while you make the sauce.

2 Put the prawn heads and shells in a pan with the water, quartered onion and one of the bay leaves. Bring to the boil, then partly cover and simmer for 20 minutes. Strain and set aside.

3 Heat the oil in a heavy cast iron or steel pan. (Do not use a non-stick pan.) When the oil is hot, add the flour, a little at a time, and blend to a smooth paste using a long-handled flat-bottomed wooden spoon.

4 ▲ Cook over a medium-low heat, stirring constantly, until the Cajun roux reaches the desired colour, about 25–40 minutes. The roux will gradually deepen in colour from light beige to tan, to a deeper, redder brown. When it reaches the colour of peanut butter, remove the pan from the heat and continue stirring until the roux has cooled and stopped cooking.

5 ▲ Melt the margarine or butter in a large heavy pan. Add the finely chopped onions, bell pepper and celery. Cook over a medium-low heat until the onions are softened, 6–8 minutes, stirring occasionally.

6 ▲ Add the sausage and mix well. Cook for 5 minutes more. Add the okra and garlic, stir and cook until the okra stops producing white "threads".

7 ▲ Add the remaining bay leaves, the thyme, salt, both peppers, cayenne and hot pepper sauce to taste, if you like. Mix well. Stir in 1.3 litres/2¼ pints/ 6 cups of the prawn stock and the tomatoes. Bring to the boil, then partly cover the pan, lower the heat and simmer for about 20 minutes.

8 Whisk in the Cajun roux. Raise the heat and bring to the boil, whisking well. Lower the heat again and simmer, uncovered, for 40–50 minutes more, stirring occasionally.

9 ▲ Gently stir in the prawns and crabmeat. Cook until the prawns turn pink, 3–4 minutes. To serve, put a mound of hot rice in each serving bowl and ladle on the gumbo, making sure each person gets some seafood and some sausage.

~ COOK'S TIP ~

Heavy pans retain their heat. When making a Cajun roux, do not let it get too dark, as the roux will continue cooking off the heat.

Smothered Rabbit

SERVES 4

90ml/6 tbsp soy sauce

hot pepper sauce, to taste

2.5ml/½ tsp white pepper

5ml/1 tsp sweet paprika

5ml/1 tsp dried basil

0.9–1.3kg/2–3lb rabbit, cut into pieces

45ml/3 tbsp peanut or olive oil

90g/3½oz/¾ cup plain (all-purpose) flour

4 onions, finely sliced

250ml/8fl oz/1 cup dry white wine

250ml/8fl oz/1 cup chicken or meat stock

5ml/1 tsp salt

5ml/1 tsp finely chopped garlic

25g/1oz/½ cup finely chopped fresh parsley

mashed potatoes or rice, to serve

1 ▼ Combine the soy sauce, hot pepper sauce to taste, white pepper, paprika and basil in a medium bowl. Add the rabbit pieces and rub them with the mixture. Leave to marinate for at least 1 hour.

2 ▲ Heat the oil in a high-sided ovenproof frying pan or large saucepan. Coat the rabbit pieces lightly in the flour, shaking off the excess. Brown the rabbit in the hot oil, turning frequently, for 5–6 minutes. Remove and set aside.

3 Preheat the oven to 180°C/350°F/ Gas 4.

4 ▲ Add the onions to the pan and cook over a low heat until softened, 8–10 minutes. Raise the heat to medium, add the wine and stir well to mix in all the cooking juices.

5 Return the rabbit to the pan. Add the stock, salt, garlic and parsley. Mix well and turn the rabbit to coat with the sauce.

6 Cover the frying pan and place it in the oven. Cook until the rabbit is tender, about 1 hour, stirring occasionally. Serve with mashed potatoes or rice.

Pork Jambalaya

SERVES 6

1.2kg/2½lb boneless pork shoulder

50ml/2fl oz/¼ cup olive oil

3 onions, finely chopped

115g/4oz/1 cup finely chopped celery

350g/12oz/1½ cups finely chopped green or red (bell) peppers

250g/9oz/1½ cups smoked ham, such as tasso, cut into 1cm/½in cubes

5ml/1 tsp black pepper

5ml/1 tsp white pepper

2.5ml/½ tsp cayenne

5ml/1 tsp salt

1 garlic clove, finely chopped

350g/12oz/1½ cups chopped peeled fresh or canned tomatoes

1 bay leaf

2.5ml/½ tsp fresh or dried thyme leaves

hot pepper sauce

250ml/8fl oz/1 cup dry white wine

400g/14oz/2 cups long-grain rice

0.75–1 litre/1¼–1¾ pints/3–4 cups chicken stock, heated

1 Remove any visible fat or gristle from the pork, and cut the meat into 1cm/½in cubes.

2 ▲ Heat the oil in a large casserole or pan. Brown the cubes of pork, in batches, stirring to colour evenly. Remove the pork with a slotted spoon and set aside.

3 ▼ Add the onions, celery and peppers to the casserole and cook, stirring, for 3–4 minutes. Add the ham, black and white peppers, cayenne and salt. Cook over a medium heat, stirring frequently, until the onions are soft and golden, about 12 minutes.

4 Add the garlic, tomatoes, herbs and hot pepper sauce to taste. Cook for 5 minutes more. Add the pork and wine and mix well, then cover the casserole and cook gently over a low heat for about 45 minutes.

5 Add the rice and stir well. Cook for 3–4 minutes.

6 Pour in 750ml/1¼ pints/3 cups of the chicken stock and stir to blend. Bring to the boil. Cover, reduce the heat to low and simmer until the rice is tender, about 15 minutes. Stir the mixture occasionally and add more chicken stock if necessary. The rice should be moist, not dry and fluffy. Serve straight from the casserole or in a large heated serving dish.

Pecan-stuffed Pork Chops

SERVES 4

4 pork chops, at least 2.5cm/1in thick, trimmed of almost all fat

25g/1oz/½ cup fresh breadcrumbs

40g/1½oz/½ cup finely chopped spring onions (scallions)

1 apple, finely chopped

50g/2oz/½ cup chopped pecans

1 garlic clove, finely chopped

15g/½oz/¼ cup finely chopped fresh parsley

1.5ml/¼ tsp cayenne

1.5ml/¼ tsp black pepper

2.5ml/½ tsp dry mustard

pinch of ground cumin

30ml/2 tbsp olive oil

120ml/4fl oz/½ cup meat or chicken stock

120ml/4fl oz/½ cup dry white wine

1 bay leaf

1 Preheat the oven to 180°C/350°F/Gas 4.

2 ▲ Make a pocket in each chop by cutting horizontally from the fatty side straight to the bone.

3 ▲ Combine all the other ingredients except the stock, wine and bay leaf. Mix well. Divide the mixture among the chops, filling each pocket with as much stuffing as it will comfortably hold.

4 ▲ Place the chops in a greased baking dish large enough to hold them in one layer.

5 ▲ Pour the stock and wine over them and add the bay leaf and any leftover stuffing. Cover tightly. Bake until tender, about 1 hour, basting occasionally with the pan juices. Serve with the cooking juices spooned over.

Ham with Red-eye Gravy

SERVES 1

15ml/1 tbsp butter or margarine

1 slice of ham, 5–10mm/¼–½in thick, preferably uncooked country-style ham, with some fat left on it

120ml/4fl oz/½ cup strong coffee, heated

mashed potatoes, to serve (optional)

~ COOK'S TIP ~

Try ham cooked this way for breakfast, accompanied by grits.

---

1 ▼ Melt the butter or margarine in a small frying pan. Add the ham and sauté until golden brown on both sides. Remove to a warm plate.

2 ▲ Pour the coffee into the pan and stir to mix with the cooking juices. When the gravy is boiling, pour it over the ham. Serve the ham with mashed potatoes, if you like.

Pecan-stuffed Pork Chops (top), Ham with Red-Eye Gravy

Oven "Fried" Chicken

SERVES 4

4 large chicken pieces

50g/2oz/½ cup plain (all-purpose) flour

2.5ml/½ tsp salt

1.5ml/¼ tsp pepper

1 egg

30ml/2 tbsp water

30ml/2 tbsp finely chopped mixed fresh herbs, such as parsley, basil and thyme

65g/2½oz/1 cup dried breadcrumbs

20g/¾oz/¼ cup freshly grated Parmesan cheese

lemon wedges, to garnish

1 Preheat the oven to 200°C/400°F/ Gas 6. Rinse the chicken pieces in cool water. Pat dry with kitchen paper.

2 ▼ Combine the flour, salt and pepper on a plate and stir with a fork to mix. Coat the chicken pieces on both sides with the seasoned flour and shake off the excess.

3 Sprinkle a little water on to the chicken pieces, and coat again lightly with the seasoned flour.

4 ▲ Beat the egg with the water in a shallow dish. Stir in the herbs. Dip the chicken pieces into the egg mixture, turning to coat them evenly.

5 ▲ Combine the breadcrumbs and the grated Parmesan cheese on a plate. Roll the chicken pieces in the crumbs, patting with your fingers to help them to stick.

6 ▲ Place the chicken pieces in a greased shallow pan large enough to hold them in one layer. Bake until thoroughly cooked and golden brown, 20–30 minutes. To test if they are done, prick with a fork; the juices that run out should be clear, not pink. Serve hot, with lemon wedges.

Blackened Chicken Breasts

SERVES 6

6 medium-size skinless chicken
  breast fillets

75g/3oz/6 tbsp butter or margarine

5ml/1 tsp garlic powder

10ml/2 tsp onion powder

5ml/1 tsp cayenne pepper

10ml/2 tsp sweet paprika

7.5ml/1½ tsp salt

2.5ml/½ tsp white pepper

5ml/1 tsp black pepper

1.5ml/¼ tsp ground cumin

5ml/1 tsp dried thyme leaves

1 ▲ Slice each chicken piece in half horizontally, making two pieces of about the same thickness. Flatten slightly with the heel of the hand.

2 Melt the butter or margarine in a small pan.

~ **VARIATION** ~

For Blackened Catfish Fillets, substitute six medium catfish fillets for the chicken. Do not slice them in half, but season as chicken and cook for 2 minutes on the first side and 1½–2 minutes on the other, or until the fish flakes easily.

3 ▼ Combine all the remaining ingredients in a shallow bowl and stir to blend well. Brush the chicken pieces on both sides with melted butter or margarine, then sprinkle evenly with the seasoning mixture.

4 Heat a large heavy frying pan over high heat until a drop of water sprinkled on the surface sizzles. This will take 5–8 minutes.

5 ▲ Drizzle 5ml/1 tsp melted butter on each chicken piece. Place them in the frying pan in an even layer, two or three at a time. Cook until the underside begins to blacken, 2–3 minutes. Turn and cook the other side for 2–3 minutes more. Serve hot.

Corn Maque Choux

SERVES 4

30ml/2 tbsp groundnut (peanut) or olive oil

1 onion, finely chopped

40g/1½oz/⅓ cup finely chopped celery

65g/2½oz/⅓ cup finely chopped red (bell) pepper

475g/18oz/3 cups corn kernels (fresh, frozen or canned)

2.5ml/½ tsp cayenne pepper

120ml/4fl oz/½ cup dry white wine or water

1 medium tomato, diced

5ml/1 tsp salt

black pepper

45ml/3 tbsp whipping cream

30ml/2 tbsp shredded fresh basil

1 Heat the oil in a heavy frying pan. Add the onion and cook over a low heat until softened, about 8–10 minutes, stirring occasionally.

2 ▲ Raise the heat to medium, add the celery and pepper and cook for 5 minutes more, stirring.

3 ▲ Stir in the corn kernels and the cayenne pepper and cook until the corn begins to stick to the bottom of the pan, about 10 minutes.

4 ▲ Pour in the wine or water and scrape up the corn from the bottom of the pan. Add the tomato, salt and pepper to taste. Mix well. Cover and cook over a low heat until the tomato has softened, 8–10 minutes.

5 ▲ Remove from the heat, stir in the cream and basil and serve.

Spring Greens and Rice

SERVES 4

475ml/16fl oz/2 cups chicken or meat stock

200g/7oz/1 cup long grain rice

15ml/1 tbsp butter or margarine

2.5ml/½ tsp salt

175g/6oz/3 cups chopped spring greens (collard leaves), loosely packed

pepper

1 ▼ Bring the stock to the boil in a medium pan. Add the rice, butter or margarine and salt. Stir.

2 ▲ Add the greens, a handful at a time, stirring well after each addition.

3 Bring back to the boil, then cover, reduce the heat and cook until the rice is tender, 15–20 minutes. Season with pepper before serving.

Corn Maque Choux (top), Spring Greens and Rice

Dirty Rice

SERVES 4

90ml/6 tbsp olive or vegetable oil

2 onions, finely chopped

225g/8oz pork mince

1 garlic clove, finely chopped

225g/8oz chicken gizzards, chopped

50g/2oz/½ cup finely chopped celery

115g/4oz/½ cup finely chopped red or
   green (bell) pepper

2.5ml/½ tsp white pepper

5ml/1 tsp cayenne

1 bay leaf

2.5ml/½ tsp fresh or dried thyme leaves

5ml/1 tsp salt

750ml/1¼ pints/3 cups chicken stock

225g/8oz chicken livers, chopped

200g/7oz/1 cup long grain rice

45ml/3 tbsp chopped fresh parsley

1 Heat the oil in a large frying pan over a low heat. Add the onion and cook until softened, 8–10 minutes.

2 ▼ Add the pork mince. Raise the heat to medium-high and stir with a fork or wooden spoon to break up the lumps. When the meat has lost its pink, raw colour, add the garlic and gizzards. Stir well. Cover the pan, lower the heat to medium and cook for about 10 minutes, stirring occasionally.

3 ▲ Add the celery and pepper and cook for 5 minutes more. Stir in the white pepper, cayenne, bay leaf, thyme and salt. Add the chicken stock, stirring to scrape up the cooking juices in the bottom of the frying pan. Cook for about 10 minutes, stirring occasionally.

4 ▲ Add the chicken livers and cook for 2 minutes, stirring.

5 ▲ Stir in the rice. Reduce the heat to low, cover the pan, and cook until the rice is tender, 15–20 minutes. Stir in the parsley before serving.

Spoonbread

SERVES 4

550ml/18fl oz/2½ cups milk

115g/4oz/1 cup yellow cornmeal

75g/3oz/6 tbsp butter or margarine

5ml/1 tsp salt

7.5ml/1½ tsp baking powder

3 eggs, separated

1 Preheat the oven to 190°C/375°F/ Gas 5.

2 ▲ Heat the milk in a heavy pan. Just before it boils, beat in the corn- meal with a wire whisk. Cook over a low heat for about 10 minutes, stirring constantly.

3 ▲ Remove from the heat and beat in the butter or margarine, salt and baking powder.

4 ▼ Add the egg yolks and beat until the mixture is smooth.

~ **COOK'S TIP** ~

The beaten egg whites give a light texture a bit like a soufflé.

5 ▲ In a large bowl, whisk the egg whites until they form stiff peaks. Fold them into the cornmeal mixture.

6 Pour into a well-greased 1.5 litre/ 2½ pint baking dish. Bake until puffed and brown, 30–40 minutes. Serve with a spoon from the baking dish, and pass butter on the side.

Charleston Cheese Corn Bread

SERVES 8

90g/3½oz/¾ cup yellow cornmeal

90g/3½oz/¾ cup plain (all-purpose) flour

10ml/2 tsp baking powder

5ml/1 tsp salt

3 eggs

175ml/6fl oz/¾ cup buttermilk

130g/4½oz/¾ cup chopped corn kernels
(fresh, frozen or canned)

75ml/2½fl oz/⅓ cup melted lard, white
cooking fat or vegetable oil

115g/4oz/1 cup grated mature (sharp)
Cheddar cheese

25g/1oz/2 tbsp butter or margarine

1 Preheat the oven to 200°C/400°F/
Gas 6.

~ VARIATION ~

For a spicier version, add one mild
chilli, seeded and finely chopped,
to the mixture.

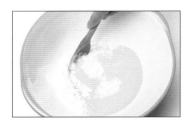

2 ▲ In a large bowl, combine the
cornmeal, flour, baking powder and
salt. Stir to mix.

3 ▲ In a medium bowl, beat the eggs
until blended. Stir in the buttermilk,
corn, lard, white cooking fat or oil and
half the grated cheese.

4 Put the butter or margarine in a
20–23cm/ 8–9in frying pan (with
a heatproof handle) and place in the
oven. Heat until melted. Remove from
the oven and swirl the fat around to
coat the bottom and sides of the pan.

5 ▲ Add the liquid ingredients to the
dry ones and mix until just blended.
Pour the batter into the hot frying pan
and sprinkle with the remaining cheese.

6 Bake until the bread is golden brown
and shrinks slightly from the edges of
the frying pan, 25–30 minutes. Cut
into wedges and serve hot, with butter
or margarine.

Hush Puppies

SERVES 6

115g/4oz/1 cup plain (all-purpose) flour

10ml/2 tsp baking powder

5ml/1 tsp salt

115g/4oz/1 cup cornmeal, preferably
stoneground

40g/1½oz/½ cup finely chopped
spring onions (scallions)

1 egg, beaten

250ml/8fl oz/1 cup buttermilk

oil for deep-frying

1 Sift the flour, baking powder and
salt into a medium bowl. Stir in the
cornmeal and spring onions.

2 ▲ In a separate bowl, beat the egg
and buttermilk together. Stir rapidly
into the dry ingredients. Let the batter
rest for 20–30 minutes.

3 Heat oil in a deep-fryer or large,
heavy pan to 190°C/375°F (or when a
cube of bread browns in 40 seconds).

4 ▼ Drop the cornmeal mixture by
tablespoonfuls into the hot oil. If the
mixture seems too thick, add a little
more buttermilk. Fry until golden
brown. Drain on kitchen paper. Serve
the hush puppies hot.

Charleston Cheese Corn Bread (top), Hush Puppies

Cornmeal Scones

MAKES ABOUT 12

150g/5oz/1¼ cups plain (all-purpose) flour

12.5ml/2½ tsp baking powder

4ml/¾ tsp salt

50g/2oz/½ cup cornmeal, plus more for sprinkling

150g/5oz/⅓ cup cold butter, lard or white cooking fat, diced

175ml/6fl oz/¾ cup milk

1 Preheat the oven to 230°C/450°F/ Gas 8.

2 ▼ Sift the flour, baking powder and salt into a bowl. Stir in the cornmeal. Using your fingertips, rub the butter, lard or white cooking fat into the dry ingredients as quickly as possible until the mixture is crumbly and resembles breadcrumbs.

3 ▲ Make a well in the centre and pour in the milk. Stir in quickly with a wooden spoon until the dough begins to pull away from the sides of the bowl, about 1 minute.

4 ▲ Turn the dough onto a lightly floured surface and knead lightly 8–10 times only. Roll out to a thickness of 1cm/½in. Cut into rounds with a floured 5cm/2in pastry (cookie) cutter. Do not twist the cutter as you cut.

5 ▲ Sprinkle an ungreased baking sheet lightly with cornmeal. Arrange the scones on the sheet, about 2.5cm/1in apart. Sprinkle the tops of the scones with more cornmeal.

6 Bake until golden brown, about 10–12 minutes. Serve the scones hot, with butter or margarine.

French Quarter Beignets

MAKES ABOUT 20

225g/8oz/2 cups plain (all-purpose) flour

5ml/1 tsp salt

15ml/1 tbsp baking powder

5ml/1 tsp ground cinnamon

2 eggs

50g/2oz/¼ cup granulated sugar

175ml/6fl oz/¾ cup milk

2.5ml/½ tsp vanilla extract

oil for deep-frying

icing (confectioners') sugar, for sprinkling

1 ▲ To make the pastry, sift the flour, salt, baking powder and ground cinnamon into a medium mixing bowl.

2 ▲ In a separate bowl, beat together the eggs, granulated sugar, milk and vanilla. Pour the egg mixture into the dry ingredients and mix together quickly to form a ball.

3 Turn the pastry out on to a lightly floured surface and knead until it is smooth and elastic.

4 Heat the oil in a deep-fryer or large, heavy pan to 190°C/375°F.

5 ▼ Roll out the pastry to a round 5mm/¼in thick. Slice diagonally into diamonds about 7.5cm/3in long.

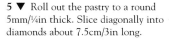

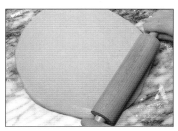

6 ▲ Fry in the hot oil, turning once, until golden brown on both sides. Remove with tongs or a slotted spoon and drain well on kitchen paper. Sprinkle the beignets with icing sugar before serving.

Georgia Peanut Butter Pie

SERVES 8

115g/4oz/2 cups fine digestive biscuit (graham cracker) crumbs

50g/2oz/¼ cup soft light brown sugar

75g/3oz/6 tbsp butter or margarine, melted

whipped cream or ice cream, to serve

FOR THE FILLING

3 egg yolks

90g/3½oz/½ cup granulated sugar

50g/2oz/¼ cup soft light brown sugar

25g/1oz/¼ cup cornflour (cornstarch)

pinch of salt

550ml/18fl oz/2½ cups evaporated milk

25g/1oz/2 tbsp butter or margarine

7.5ml/1½ tsp vanilla extract

115g/4oz/½ cup chunky peanut butter

90g/3½oz/¾ cup icing (confectioners') sugar

1 Preheat the oven to 180°C/350°F/Gas 4.

2 ▲ Combine the biscuit crumbs, sugar and butter or margarine in a bowl and blend well. Spread the mixture in a well-greased 23cm/9in pie tin (pan), pressing evenly over the bottom and sides with your fingertips.

3 Bake the biscuit case for 10 minutes. Remove from the oven and leave to cool. Leave the oven on.

4 ▲ Combine the egg yolks, granulated and brown sugars, cornflour and salt in a heavy pan.

5 Slowly whisk in the milk. Cook over a medium heat, stirring constantly, until the mixture thickens, about 8–10 minutes. Reduce the heat to very low and cook until very thick, about 3–4 minutes more.

6 ▲ Beat in the butter or margarine. Stir in the vanilla. Remove from the heat. Cover the surface closely with clear film (plastic wrap) and cool.

~ VARIATIONS ~

If preferred, use an equal amount of finely crushed vanilla wafers or ginger nut biscuits (ginger snaps) in place of digestive biscuits for the base. Or make the pie with a ready-to-use digestive biscuit case.

7 ▲ In a small bowl combine the peanut butter with the icing sugar, working with your fingers to blend the ingredients to the consistency of small breadcrumbs.

8 ▲ Sprinkle all but 45ml/3 tbsp of the peanut butter crumbs evenly over the bottom of the biscuit case.

9 ▲ Pour in the filling, spreading it into an even layer. Sprinkle with the remaining crumbs. Bake for 15 minutes.

10 Leave the pie to cool for 1 hour. Serve with whipped cream or ice cream.

Mississippi Mud Cake

SERVES 8–10

225g/8oz/2 cups plain (all-purpose) flour

pinch of salt

5ml/1 tsp baking powder

300ml/½ pint/1¼ cups strong coffee

50ml/2fl oz/¼ cup whisky or brandy

150g/5oz plain (semisweet) chocolate

225g/8oz/1 cup butter or margarine

400g/14oz/2 cups granulated sugar

2 eggs, at room temperature

7.5ml/1½ tsp vanilla extract

unsweetened cocoa powder

sweetened whipped cream or ice cream,
   to serve (optional)

1 Preheat the oven to 140°C/275°F/
Gas 1.

2 Sift together the flour, salt and
baking powder.

3 ▼ Combine the coffee, whisky or
brandy, chocolate and butter or
margarine in the top of a double
boiler. Heat until the chocolate and
butter have melted and the mixture is
smooth, stirring occasionally.

4 ▲ Pour the chocolate mixture into
a large bowl. Using an electric mixer
on low speed, gradually beat in the
sugar. Continue beating until the
sugar has dissolved.

5 Raise the speed to medium and add
the sifted dry ingredients. Mix well,
then beat in the eggs and vanilla until
thoroughly blended.

6 Pour the mixture into a well-greased
3.5 litre/6 pint decorative ring mould
that has been dusted lightly with cocoa
powder. Bake until a skewer inserted in
the centre of the cake comes out clean,
about 1 hour 20 minutes.

7 ▲ Leave to cool in the pan for
15 minutes, then turn out on to a wire
rack. Leave to cool completely.

8 When the cake is cold, dust it
lightly with cocoa powder. Serve with
sweetened whipped cream or ice
cream, if you wish.

Banana Lemon Layer Cake

SERVES 8–10

250g/9oz/2¼ cups self-raising
(self-rising) flour

6ml/1¼ tsp baking powder

2.5ml/½ tsp salt

115g/4oz/½ cup butter, softened

200g/7oz/1 cup granulated sugar

115g/4oz/½ cup soft light brown sugar

2 eggs

2.5ml/½ tsp grated lemon rind

3 very ripe bananas, mashed

5ml/1 tsp vanilla extract

50ml/2fl oz/¼ cup milk

75g/3oz/¾ cup chopped walnuts

FOR THE ICING

115g/4oz/½ cup butter, softened

500g/1¼lb/4½ cups icing
(confectioners') sugar

4ml/¾ tsp grated lemon rind

45–75ml/3–5 tbsp fresh lemon juice

1 Preheat the oven to 180°C/350°F/
Gas 4. Grease two 23cm/9in round cake
tins (pans) and line the bottom of each
with a disk of greased baking parchment.

2 Sift the flour with the baking
powder and salt.

3 ▲ In a large mixing bowl, cream
the butter with the sugars until light
and fluffy. Beat in the eggs, one at a
time. Stir in the lemon rind.

4 ▲ In a small bowl, mix the mashed
bananas with the vanilla and milk.
Add the banana mixture and the dry
ingredients to the butter mixture
alternately in two or three batches and
stir until just blended. Fold in the nuts.

5 Divide the mixture between the cake
tins and spread it out evenly. Bake until
a skewer inserted in the centre comes
out clean, 30–35 minutes. Leave to
stand for 5 minutes before turning out
on to a wire rack. Peel off the baking
parchment and leave to cool.

6 For the icing, cream the butter until
smooth, then gradually beat in the
sugar. Stir in the lemon rind and
enough juice to make a spreadable
consistency.

7 ▼ Set one of the cake layers on a
serving plate. Cover with about one-
third of the icing. Top with the second
cake layer. Spread the remaining icing
evenly over the top and around the
sides of the cake.

Southern Ambrosia

SERVES 6

4 large sweet oranges

1 fresh ripe pineapple

1 coconut

icing (confectioners') sugar (optional)

strips of fresh coconut or lime wedges, to garnish

1 Using a sharp knife, cut the peel and pith off the oranges, working over a bowl to catch the juices. Slice each orange into very thin rounds and place in the bowl with the juice.

2 ▲ Peel the pineapple. Cut into quarters lengthways, and cut away the core. Cut into thin slices.

3 Pierce the "eyes" of the coconut with a screwdriver or ice pick. Drain off the liquid. Using a heavy hammer, crack the shell until it can be opened. Prise out the white meat with a blunt knife. Peel the dark brown skin from the coconut meat and shred the meat using the coarse blade of a grater or food processor.

4 To assemble the dessert, layer the fruits and coconut alternately in a glass serving bowl. Sprinkle the layers occasionally with a small amount of icing sugar, if you like, to increase the sweetness. Serve at once or chill before eating. Garnish with strips of fresh coconut or lime wedges before serving.

Pecan Pralines

MAKES ABOUT 30

350g/12oz/1½ cups soft light brown sugar

350g/12oz/1½ cups soft dark brown sugar

1.5ml/¼ tsp salt

120ml/4fl oz/½ cup milk

120ml/4fl oz/½ cup single (light) cream

25g/1oz/2 tbsp butter or margarine

5ml/1 tsp vanilla extract

175g/6oz/1 cup pecan pieces or halves

1 ▲ In a heavy pan mix together the sugars, salt, milk and cream. Stir constantly until the mixture comes to the boil. Cover the pan and cook, without stirring, until crystals no longer form on the sides of the pan, about 3 minutes.

2 Uncover the pan and cook over a medium heat, without stirring, to the soft ball stage, 119°C/238°F on a sugar thermometer.

3 Remove from the heat and beat in the butter or margarine with a wooden spoon. Continue beating until the mixture is smooth and creamy and the temperature of the mixture comes down to 56°C/110°F. Beat in the vanilla and the nuts.

4 ▼ Using two spoons, drop the praline mixure by the spoonful on to a baking sheet lined with buttered baking parchment. When cool, store the pralines in an airtight container with parchment between each of the layers.

~ COOK'S TIP ~

To test for the soft ball stage without a sugar thermometer, drop a small amount of the caramel into iced water. It should form a ball that will hold its shape and flatten readily when picked up between the fingers.

Southern Ambrosia (top), Pecan Pralines

Pink Grapefruit Sorbet

SERVES 8

175g/6oz/¾ cup granulated sugar

120ml/4fl oz/½ cup water

1 litre/1¾ pints/4 cups strained freshly
    squeezed pink grapefruit juice

15–30ml/1–2 tbsp fresh lemon juice

icing (confectioners') sugar, to taste

1 In a small heavy pan, dissolve the
granulated sugar in the water over a
medium heat, without stirring. When
the sugar has dissolved, boil for about
3–4 minutes. Remove from the heat
and leave to cool.

2 ▼ Pour the cooled sugar syrup into
the grapefruit juice. Stir well. Taste
the mixture and adjust the flavour by
adding some lemon juice or a little
icing sugar, if necessary, but do not
over-sweeten.

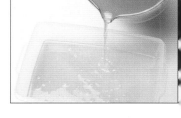

3 ▲ Pour the mixture into a metal or
plastic freezer container and freeze
until softly set, about 3 hours.

4 ▲ Remove from the container and
chop roughly into 7.5cm/3in pieces.
Place in a food processor and process
until smooth. Return the mixture to
the freezer container and freeze again
until set. Repeat this freezing and
chopping process two or three times,
until a smooth consistency is obtained.

5 Alternatively, freeze the sorbet in
an ice cream maker, following the
manufacturer's instructions.

> ### ~ VARIATION ~
>
> For Orange Sorbet, substitute an
> equal amount of orange juice for
> the grapefruit juice and increase
> the lemon juice to 45–60ml/
> 3–4 tbsp, or to taste. For additional
> flavour, add 15ml/1 tbsp finely
> grated orange rind. If blood oranges
> are available, their deep red colour
> gives a dramatic effect, and the
> flavour is exciting as well.

Key Lime Sorbet

SERVES 4

250g/9oz/1¼ cups granulated sugar

550ml/18fl oz/2½ cups water

grated rind of 1 lime

175ml/6fl oz/¾ cup freshly squeezed
   lime juice

15–30ml/1–2 tbsp fresh lemon juice

icing (confectioners') sugar, to taste

1 ▲ In a small heavy pan, dissolve
the granulated sugar in the water,
without stirring, over a medium heat.
When the sugar has dissolved, boil for
5–6 minutes. Remove from the heat
and leave to cool.

2 ▲ Combine the cooled sugar syrup
and lime rind and juice in a measuring
jug (cup) or bowl. Stir well. Taste and
adjust the flavour by adding lemon
juice or some icing sugar, if necessary.
Do not over-sweeten.

3 ▲ Freeze the sorbet in an ice cream
maker, following the manufacturer's
instructions.

4 If you do not have an ice cream
maker, pour the mixture into a metal
or plastic freezer container and freeze
until softly set, about 3 hours.

5 Remove from the container and
chop roughly into 7.5cm/3in pieces.
Place in a food processor and process
until smooth. Return the mixture to
the freezer container and freeze again
until set. Repeat this freezing and
chopping process two or three times,
until a smooth consistency is obtained.

~ COOK'S TIP ~

If using an ice cream maker for
these sorbets, check the
manufacturer's instructions to
find out the freezing capacity.
If necessary, halve the
recipe quantities.

THE
MIDWEST

THE HEARTLAND OF AMERICA
CONTRIBUTES SIGNIFICANTLY TO
THE FOOD SUPPLY OF THE ENTIRE
COUNTRY, WITH GREAT FIELDS OF
WHEAT AND CORN, ORCHARDS AND
VERDANT FARMLAND. THE SYSTEM
OF WATERWAYS, INCLUDING THE
GREAT LAKES AND THE MISSISSIPPI,
HAS HISTORICALLY MOVED
PRODUCE TO OTHER REGIONS
WHILE PROVIDING A RICH SOURCE
OF FOOD AND BEAUTY.

Onion Soup with Mini Dumplings

SERVES 6

50g/2oz/¼ cup butter or margarine

30ml/2 tbsp olive oil

675g/1½lb onions, finely sliced

15ml/1 tbsp soft light brown sugar

5ml/1 tsp salt

2.5 litres/4 pints good beef stock or
   bouillon, homemade if possible

250ml/8fl oz/1 cup dry white wine

FOR THE MINI DUMPLINGS

1 egg

90g/3½oz/¾ cup–115g/4oz/1 cup plain
   (all-purpose) flour

2.5ml/½ tsp salt

pepper

1 Heat the butter or margarine with the oil in a large heavy pan. Add the onions and stir to coat well with the fats. Cover the pan and cook over a a low heat about 15 minutes, stirring occasionally.

2 ▲ Uncover the pan, add the sugar and salt, and continue cooking until the onions turn a rich brown colour. Stir often or the onions may burn.

3 ▲ Stir in the stock or bouillon and wine and bring to the boil. Lower the heat and simmer, partly covered, while you prepare the mini dumplings.

4 ▲ Beat the egg into a medium bowl. Add the flour, salt and pepper to taste and mix with a wooden spoon. Finish mixing with your fingers, rubbing to blend the egg and flour together. The pieces of dough should be pea-size or smaller.

5 ▲ Bring the soup back to the boil. Sprinkle in the pieces of dough, stirring gently. Reduce the heat and simmer for about 6 minutes, until the mini dumplings are slightly swollen and cooked through. Serve at once.

Split Pea Soup

SERVES 8

450g/1lb dried green split peas

2.5 litres/4 pints water

1 ham bone with some meat left on it, or 1 ham hock

2 onions, finely chopped

115g/4oz/1 cup sliced leeks

50g/2oz/½ cup finely sliced celery

15g/½oz/¼ cup fresh parsley sprigs

5ml/1 tsp salt

6 black peppercorns

2 bay leaves

1 ▲ Rinse the split peas under cold running water. Discard any discoloured peas. Place the peas in a large pan and add water to cover. Bring to the boil and boil for 2 minutes. Remove from the heat and leave to soak for 1 hour. Drain.

2 ▲ Put the peas back in the pan and add the measured water, ham bone or hock, onion, leeks, celery, parsley, salt, peppercorns and bay leaves. Bring to the boil. Reduce the heat, cover and simmer gently until the peas are tender, 1–1½ hours. Skim occasionally.

3 ▼ Remove the bay leaves and the ham bone or hock from the soup. Cut the meat off the bone, discarding any fat, and chop the meat finely. Set aside. Discard the ham bone and the bay leaves.

4 ▲ Purée the soup in batches in a food processor or blender. Pour into a clean pan and add the chopped ham. Check the seasoning. Simmer the soup for 3–4 minutes to heat right through before serving.

Spiced Pumpkin Soup

SERVES 6

45ml/3 tbsp olive oil

1 onion, sliced

6 spring onions (scallions), bulbs and
  greens sliced separately

pinch of cayenne pepper

1.5ml/¼ tsp ground cumin

pinch of ground nutmeg or mace

1.2 litres/2 pints/5 cups chicken stock

800g/1¾lb/2½ cups pumpkin purée

2.5ml/½ tsp salt

250ml/8fl oz/1 cup single (light) cream

1 Heat the oil in a large heavy pan.
Add the onion and spring onion bulbs
and cook over a low heat until softened, 8–10 minutes.

2 ▲ Add the spices and stir well to
coat the onions. Cook for 3–4 minutes.
Add the pumpkin purée, stock and
salt. Raise the heat to medium; cook
for 15 minutes, stirring occasionally.

3 Let the soup cool slightly. Purée it
in a food processor or blender.

4 ▼ Return the soup to the pan.
Taste and add more cayenne, if
you like. Heat to simmering. Stir in
most of the cream and simmer
for 2–3 minutes more. Serve hot, with
a swirl of cream and some sliced
spring onion greens.

Indian Beef and Berry Soup

SERVES 4

30ml/2 tbsp vegetable oil

450g/1lb tender beef steak

3 onions, finely sliced

25g/1oz/2 tbsp butter

1 litre/1¾ pints/4 cups good beef stock
  or bouillon

2.5ml/½ tsp salt

1 cup fresh huckleberries, blueberries or
  blackberries, lightly mashed

15ml/1 tbsp honey

1 Heat the oil in a heavy pan until
almost smoking. Add the steak and
brown on both sides over medium-high
heat. Remove the steak and set aside.

2 Reduce the heat to low and add the
onions and butter to the pan. Stir well,
scraping up the meat juices. Cook
over a low heat until the onions are
softened, 8–10 minutes.

3 ▲ Add the stock or bouillon and
salt and bring to the boil, stirring well.
Mix in the berries and honey. Simmer
for 20 minutes.

4 Meanwhile, cut the steak into thin,
bitesize slivers.

5 ▼ Taste the soup and add more salt
or honey if necessary. Add the steak
and its juices to the pan. Stir, cook for
30 seconds and serve.

Spiced Pumpkin Soup (top), Indian Beef and Berry Soup

Dandelion Salad with Hot Bacon Dressing

SERVES 6

115g/4oz/about 2½ cups young tender
dandelion leaves or other sharp-flavoured
leaves such as rocket (arugula)

1 head of Boston, cos or romaine lettuce

4 spring onions (scallions), thinly sliced

8 bacon rashers (strips), cut across in
thin strips

50ml/2fl oz/¼ cup fresh lemon juice

30ml/2 tbsp granulated sugar

5ml/1 tsp Dijon-style mustard

pepper

1 Carefully pick over the dandelion
leaves and wash thoroughly in several
changes of water. Pat or spin dry.
Wash and dry the lettuce leaves.

2 ▼ Tear each lettuce and dandelion
leaf into two or three pieces. Arrange a
mixture of leaves on individual
serving plates. Sprinkle with the
sliced spring onions.

3 ▲ In a small frying pan, cook the
bacon until crisp. Remove the bacon
pieces with a slotted spoon and drain
on kitchen paper.

4 ▲ Add the lemon juice, sugar and
mustard to the bacon fat in the pan.
Heat the mixture gently for about
3–4 minutes, scraping up the browned
bits in the cooking juices and blending
in the mustard with a wooden spoon.

5 Spoon the hot dressing over the
salads and sprinkle with the bacon
pieces and freshly ground black
pepper. Serve at once.

~ COOK'S TIP ~

Commercially grown dandelion
leaves are sometimes available
from specialist grocers. If picking
your own, choose leaves from
spring plants that have not yet
flowered, and use them fresh. After
flowering, the leaves of dandelions
become bitter and tough.

Vegetable Chilli

SERVES 8

50ml/2fl oz/¼ cup olive or vegetable oil

4 onions, chopped

50g/2oz/½ cup finely sliced celery

2–3 carrots, cut into 1cm/½ in cubes

2 garlic cloves, finely chopped

2.5ml/½ tsp celery seeds

1.5ml/¼ tsp cayenne pepper

5ml/1 tsp ground cumin

45ml/3 tbsp chilli powder

450g/1lb/2 cups canned chopped plum
    tomatoes with their juice

250ml/8fl oz/1 cup vegetable stock
    or water

7.5ml/1½ tsp salt

2.5ml/½ tsp fresh or dried thyme leaves

1 bay leaf

150g/5oz/2 cups cauliflower florets

250g/9oz/2 cups 1cm/½ in cubes of
    courgette (zucchini)

kernels from 1 corn on the cob

275g/10oz/2 cups cooked or canned
    kidney or pinto beans

hot pepper sauce (optional)

2 Stir in the celery seed, cayenne, cumin and chilli powder. Mix well. Add the tomatoes, stock or water, salt, thyme and bay leaf. Stir. Cook for 15 minutes, uncovered.

3 ▼ Add the cauliflower, courgette and corn. Cover and cook for a further 15 minutes.

4 ▲ Add the kidney or pinto beans, stir well and cook for 10 minutes more, uncovered. Check the seasoning, and add a dash of hot pepper sauce if you like. This is good with freshly boiled rice or baked potatoes.

1 ▲ Heat the oil in a large flameproof casserole or heavy pan and add the onions, celery, carrots and garlic. Cover the casserole and cook over a low heat, stirring from time to time, until the onions are softened, 8–10 minutes.

Stuffed Devilled Eggs

SERVES 6

6 hard-boiled eggs, peeled

40g/1½oz/¼ cup finely chopped
    cooked ham

6 walnut halves, finely chopped

15ml/1 tbsp finely chopped spring onion
    (scallion)

15ml/1 tbsp Dijon-style mustard

15ml/1 tbsp mayonnaise

10ml/2 tsp vinegar

1.5ml/¼ tsp salt

1.5ml/¼ tsp black pepper

1.5ml/¼ tsp cayenne pepper (optional)

paprika and a few slices of dill pickle,
    to garnish

1 Cut each egg in half lengthways. Place the yolks in a bowl and set the whites aside.

2 ▲ Mash the yolks well with a fork, or push them through a strainer. Add all the remaining ingredients and mix well with the yolks. Taste and adjust the seasoning if necessary.

3 ▼ Spoon the filling into the egg white halves, or pipe it in with a pastry bag and nozzle. Garnish the top of each stuffed egg with a little paprika and a small star or other shape cut from the pickle slices. Serve the stuffed eggs at room temperature.

Stuffed Celery Sticks

SERVES 4–6

12 crisp, tender celery sticks

25g/1oz/¼ cup crumbled blue cheese

115g/4oz/½ cup cream cheese

45ml/3 tbsp sour cream

50g/2oz/½ cup chopped walnuts

2 ▼ In a small bowl, combine the crumbled blue cheese, cream cheese and sour cream. Stir together with a wooden spoon until smoothly blended. Fold in all but 15ml/1 tbsp of the chopped walnuts.

3 ▲ Fill the celery pieces with the cheese mixture. Chill before serving, garnished with the reserved walnuts.

1 ▲ Trim the celery sticks and cut into 10cm/4in pieces.

~ VARIATION ~

Use the same filling to stuff
scooped-out cherry tomatoes.

Stuffed Devilled Eggs, Stuffed Celery Stick

Chicago Deep-pan Pizza

MAKES A 35CM/14IN PIZZA

1½ packets active dried yeast

250ml/8fl oz/1 cup lukewarm water

15ml/1 tbsp caster (superfine) sugar

440g/15½oz/3¾ cups plain
   (all-purpose) flour

5ml/1 tsp salt

45ml/3 tbsp olive oil

FOR THE TOPPING

45ml/3 tbsp olive oil

275g/10oz/2½ cups diced
   mozzarella cheese

500g/1¼lb/2½ cups peeled and chopped
   tomatoes, preferably plum-type

40g/1½oz/½ cup freshly grated
   Parmesan cheese

salt and pepper

25g/1oz/½ cup fresh basil leaves,
   loosely packed

1 In a small bowl, mix the yeast with
half the warm water. Stir in the sugar.
Leave for 10 minutes.

2 Put the flour in a food processor
with the steel blade. Add the salt. Pour
in the yeast mixture, olive oil and the
remaining warm water. Process until the
dough begins to form a ball. If the dough
is too sticky, add a little more flour. If
it will not mass together, add a little
more warm water and process again.

3 Turn the dough on to a lightly
floured surface. Knead until smooth,
about 5 minutes. Form into a ball and
place in a lightly oiled large bowl.
Cover with a damp dish towel. Leave
to rise in a warm place until the dough
doubles its volume, about 1½ hours.

4 Preheat the oven to 240°C/475°F/
Gas 9.

5 ▲ Knock back (punch down) the
dough and knead it lightly for about
2–3 minutes. Set it in the centre of an
oiled 35cm/14in diameter pizza pan.
Using your fingertips, stretch and pat
out the dough to line the pan evenly.

6 ▲ Prick the dough evenly all over
with a fork. Bake for 5 minutes.

7 ▲ Brush the pizza dough base with
15ml/1 tbsp of the olive oil. Sprinkle
with the mozzarella, leaving the rim
clear. Spoon the tomatoes over the
mozzarella and sprinkle with the
Parmesan. Season and drizzle over the
remaining olive oil.

8 Bake until the crust is golden
brown and the topping is bubbling
hot, 25–30 minutes. Scatter over the
basil leaves and serve.

Pirozhki with Ham Filling

MAKES 12

25g/1oz/2 tbsp butter or margarine

½ onion, finely chopped

175g/6oz/1½ cups finely chopped ham

120ml/4fl oz/½ cup whipping cream

30ml/2 tbsp finely chopped fresh parsley

15ml/1 tbsp Worcestershire sauce

salt and pepper

FOR THE PASTRY

225g/8oz/2 cups plain (all-purpose) flour

5ml/1 tsp salt

12.5ml/2½ tsp baking powder

115g/4oz/½ cup cold butter, lard or white
   cooking fat, diced

45–60ml/3–4 tbsp milk, plus more
   for brushing

1 ▲ Melt the butter or margarine in a small frying pan. Add the onions and cook over a low heat until soft and golden, 10–12 minutes. Add the ham and cook for 2–3 minutes more, stirring.

2 ▲ Turn the onion and ham mixture into a bowl. Leave to cool slightly, then stir in the cream, parsley and Worcestershire sauce. Season with salt and pepper.

3 Preheat oven to 230°C/450°F/Gas 8.

4 ▲ For the pastry, sift the flour, salt and baking powder into a bowl. With a pastry blender, cut in the butter, lard or white cooking fat until the mixture resembles breadcrumbs, or rub in with your fingertips.

5 Make a well in the centre and add the milk. Stir with a fork until the mixture begins to pull away from the sides of the bowl, no more than 1 minute. (If overmixed, the pastry will not be as light and tender.)

6 Turn the pastry on to a lightly floured surface and knead lightly for less than 1 minute. Roll out to 6mm/¼in thick. Cut into 7.5cm/3in squares.

7 ▲ Place a spoonful of the ham filling in the centre of each pastry square. Brush the edges with milk and fold the pastry over to form a triangular shape. Press the edges together with a fork to seal.

8 Arrange the triangles on a baking sheet and brush them with milk. Bake until the pastry is golden and cooked, about 30 minutes.

Pan-fried Honey Chicken Drumsticks

SERVES 4

120ml/4fl oz/½ cup honey

juice of 1 lemon

30ml/2 tbsp soy sauce

15ml/1 tbsp sesame seeds

2.5ml/½ tsp fresh or dried thyme leaves

12 chicken drumsticks

2.5ml/½ tsp salt

2.5ml/½ tsp pepper

90g/3½oz/¾ cup plain (all-purpose) flour

45ml/3 tbsp butter or margarine

45ml/3 tbsp vegetable oil

120ml/4fl oz/½ cup white wine

120ml/4fl oz/½ cup chicken stock

1 In a large bowl, combine the honey, lemon juice, soy sauce, sesame seeds and thyme. Add the drumsticks and mix to coat them well. Leave to marinate in a cool place for 2 hours or more, turning occasionally.

2 ▲ Mix the salt, pepper and flour in a shallow bowl. Drain the drumsticks, reserving the marinade. Roll them in the seasoned flour to coat all over.

3 Heat the butter or margarine with the oil in a large heavy frying pan. When hot and sizzling, add the drumsticks. Brown on all sides. Reduce the heat to medium-low and cook until the chicken is done, 12–15 minutes.

4 Test with a fork to see if the chicken is done; the juices should be clear. Remove the drumsticks to a serving dish and keep hot.

5 ▲ Pour off most of the fat from the pan. Add the wine, stock and reserved marinade and stir well to mix in the cooking juices on the bottom of the pan. Bring to the boil and simmer until reduced by half. Check for seasoning, then spoon this sauce over the drumsticks and serve.

Oatmeal Pan-fried Trout

SERVES 4

135g/4¾oz/1½ cups rolled oats

salt and pepper

4 medium river trout, cleaned, heads and tails left on if desired

75g/3oz/6 tbsp butter or margarine

lemon halves, to serve

1 Grind the oats in a food processor or blender until they are the texture of fine meal. Turn into a shallow dish and spread out evenly. Season with salt and pepper.

2 Rinse the trout and dry well with kitchen paper.

3 Melt the butter or margarine in a large frying pan over a low heat.

4 ▲ Dip both sides of each trout in the butter or margarine, then roll in the ground oats, patting with your fingers to help the oats stick.

5 ▼ Put the fish in the frying pan in one layer. Increase the heat to medium and cook until golden brown, about 3–4 minutes on each side. (Cook in batches, if necessary, using more butter or margarine.) Serve hot, with lemon halves on the side.

Pan-fried Honey Chicken Drumsticks (top), Oatmeal Pan-fried Trout

Savoury Sausage Scones

200g/7oz/1¾ cups plain (all-purpose) flour

5ml/1 tsp salt

12.5ml/2½ tsp baking powder

50g/2oz/¼ cup cold butter, lard or
   white cooking fat, diced

175ml/6fl oz/¾ cup plus 45ml/3 tbsp milk

FOR THE GRAVY

40g/1½oz/3 tbsp butter or margarine

45ml/3 tbsp finely chopped onion

350g/12oz lean pork sausage meat
   (bulk sausage)

25g/1oz/¼ cup plain (all-purpose) flour

475ml/16fl oz/2 cups milk, warmed

1.5ml/¼ tsp paprika

15ml/1 tbsp chopped fresh parsley

1　Preheat oven to 230°C/450°F/Gas 8.

2　For the savoury scones, sift the flour, salt and baking powder into a mixing bowl. Using your fingertips, rub the butter, lard or white cooking fat into the dry ingredients until the mixture is crumbly and resembles breadcrumbs.

3　Make a well in the centre and add the 175ml/6fl oz/¾ cup milk. Stir with a wooden spoon until the dough begins to come away from the sides of the bowl, less than 1 minute. (Do not overmix the dough or the scones will not be light and tender.)

4　Turn the dough on to a lightly floured surface and knead gently for about ½ minute, making 8–10 folds only. Roll out to about 2cm/¾in thick. Cut out rounds using a 6cm/2½in pastry (cookie) cutter. Do not twist the cutter.

5　▲　Brush the tops of the rounds with the 45ml/3 tbsp of milk. Arrange on a lightly greased baking sheet. Bake until puffed and lightly golden, 12–15 minutes.

6　While the scones are baking, make the sausage sauce. Melt the butter or margarine in a heavy pan. Add the onion and cook for 3–4 minutes. Add the sausage meat and cook over a medium-low heat until lightly browned and crumbly. Do not overcook. Drain off the excess fat in the pan, leaving about 30–45ml/2–3 tbsp.

7　▲　Sprinkle the flour over the sausage mixture in the pan. Stir well to blend thoroughly.

8　Slowly add the warmed milk, blending it in well and scraping up the pan juices. Simmer until thickened. Add the paprika and parsley.

9　Split the scones and place on individual serving plates. Spoon the sauce on top and serve at once.

Twin Cities Meatballs

SERVES 6

25g/1oz/2 tbsp butter or margarine

½ onion, finely chopped

350g/12oz rump (round) steak mince

115g/4oz veal mince

225g/8oz lean pork mince

1 egg

40g/1½oz/½ cup mashed potatoes

30ml/2 tbsp finely chopped fresh dill
  or parsley

1 garlic clove, finely chopped

5ml/1 tsp salt

2.5ml/½ tsp pepper

2.5ml/½ tsp ground allspice

1.5ml/¼ tsp ground nutmeg

40g/1½oz/¾ cup fresh breadcrumbs

175ml/6fl oz/¾ cup milk

25g/1oz/¼ cup plus 15ml/1 tbsp plain
  (all-purpose) flour

30ml/2 tbsp olive oil

175ml/6fl oz/¾ cup pouring (half-and-
  half) cream or evaporated milk

buttered noodles, to serve

1 Melt the butter or margarine in a large frying pan. Add the onion and cook over a low heat until softened, 8–10 minutes. Remove from the heat. Using a slotted spoon, transfer the onion to a large mixing bowl.

2 ▲ Add the minced meats, egg, mashed potatoes, dill or parsley, garlic, salt, pepper, allspice and nutmeg to the bowl.

3 Put the breadcrumbs in a small bowl and add the milk. Stir until well moistened, then add to the other ingredients. Mix well.

4 ▲ Shape the mixture into balls about 2.5cm/1in in diameter. Roll them in 25g/1oz/¼ cup of the flour to coat all over.

5 Add the olive oil to the pan and heat over a a medium heat. Add the meatballs and brown on all sides, 8–10 minutes. Shake the pan occasionally to roll the balls so that they colour evenly. With a slotted spoon, remove the meatballs to a serving dish. Cover with foil and keep warm.

6 ▲ Stir the 15ml/1 tbsp of flour into the fat in the pan. Add the pouring cream or evaporated milk and mix in with a small whisk. Simmer for 3–4 minutes. Check the seasoning.

7 Pour the sauce over the meatballs. Serve hot with noodles.

~ COOK'S TIP ~

The meatballs are also good for a buffet or cocktail party. To serve with drinks, omit the sauce.

Country Meat Loaf

25g/1oz/2 tbsp butter or margarine

1 onion, finely chopped

2 garlic cloves, finely chopped

50g/2oz/½ cup finely chopped celery

450g/1lb lean ground beef

225g/8oz veal mince

225g/8oz lean pork mince

2 eggs

50g/2oz/1 cup fine fresh breadcrumbs

25g/1oz/½ cup chopped fresh parsley

30ml/2 tbsp chopped fresh basil

2.5ml/½ tsp fresh or dried thyme leaves

2.5ml/½ tsp salt

2.5ml/½ tsp pepper

30ml/2 tbsp Worcestershire sauce

50ml/2fl oz/¼ cup chilli sauce or
   tomato ketchup

6 bacon rashers (strips)

1 Preheat oven to 180°C/350°F/Gas 4.

2 ▼ Melt the butter or margarine in a small frying pan over a low heat. Add the onion, garlic and celery and cook until softened, 8–10 minutes. Remove from the heat and leave to cool slightly.

3 ▲ In a large mixing bowl, combine the onion, garlic and celery with all the other ingredients except the bacon. Mix together lightly, using a fork or your fingers. Do not overwork or the meat loaf will be too compact.

4 ▲ Form the meat mixture into an oval loaf. Carefully transfer it to a shallow baking tin (pan).

5 ▲ Lay the bacon slices across the meat loaf. Bake for 1¼ hours, basting occasionally with the juices and bacon fat in the pan.

6 Remove from the oven and drain off the fat. Leave the meat loaf to stand for 10 minutes before serving.

Spareribs with Sauerkraut

SERVES 4

1.3–1.8kg/3–4lb spareribs, cut in
   individual portions

½ onion, finely chopped

50ml/2fl oz/¼ cup Worcestershire sauce

15ml/1 tbsp dry mustard

2.5ml/½ tsp paprika

5ml/1 tsp salt

750ml/1¼ pints/3 cups flat beer

45ml/3 tbsp olive or vegetable oil

1.75 litres/3 pints sauerkraut, canned
   or bulk

1 tart-sweet apple, peeled, cored
   and sliced

5ml/1 tsp caraway seeds

parsley, for garnishing

1 Arrange the ribs in a single layer in
a large baking dish.

2 ▲ In a large measuring jug (cup),
combine the onion, Worcestershire
sauce, mustard, paprika, salt and beer.
Mix well. Pour the mixture evenly
over the ribs. Leave to marinate for at
least 2 hours, basting occasionally.

3 Preheat the oven to 190°C/375°F/
Gas 5.

4 Remove the ribs from the dish and
pat dry with kitchen paper. Reserve
the marinade.

5 ▲ Heat the oil in a flameproof
casserole. Brown the ribs, turning to
sear them on all sides. Work in batches,
if necessary. Pour in the marinade.
Transfer the casserole to the oven.
Bake for 35–40 minutes, turning the
ribs occasionally.

6 Rinse the sauerkraut, if desired,
and drain well. Mix with the apple
and caraway seeds.

7 ▼ Remove the casserole from the
oven. Holding the ribs to one side,
distribute the sauerkraut mixture
evenly in the bottom of the casserole.
Arrange the ribs on top of the kraut,
pushing them down evenly.

8 Return to the oven and bake until
the meat on the ribs is tender, about
45–60 minutes more. Serve the ribs on
a large heated platter, on a bed of
sauerkraut, garnished with parsley.

Baked Pork Loin with Red Cabbage and Apples

SERVES 8

2kg/4½lb boned loin of pork

2.5ml/½ tsp ground ginger

salt and pepper

60ml/4 tbsp melted butter

about 350ml/12fl oz/1½ cups sweet apple
cider or dry white wine

FOR THE CABBAGE

40g/1½oz/3 tbsp butter or margarine

3 onions, finely sliced

5ml/1 tsp caraway seeds

3 tart-sweet apples, quartered, cored
and sliced

15ml/1 tbsp soft dark brown sugar

1.6kg/3½lb head of red cabbage, cored
and shredded

90ml/6 tbsp cider vinegar, or
50ml/2fl oz/¼ cup wine vinegar and
30ml/2 tbsp water

120ml/4fl oz/½ cup beef stock

120ml/4fl oz/½ cup sweet apple cider
or white wine

5ml/1 tsp salt

1.5ml/¼ tsp fresh or dried thyme leaves

1 Preheat oven to 180°C/350°F/Gas 4.

2 ▲ Trim any excess fat from the
pork roast. Tie it into a neat shape, if
necessary. Sprinkle with the ginger, salt
and pepper.

3 ▲ Place the pork, fat side down, in
a large casserole. Cook over a medium
heat, turning frequently, until browned
on all sides, about 15 minutes. Add a
little of the melted butter if the roast
starts to stick.

4 Cover, transfer to the oven and
roast for 1 hour, basting frequently
with the pan drippings, melted butter
and cider or wine.

5 ▲ Meanwhile, to prepare the
cabbage, melt the butter or margarine
in a large frying pan and add the
onions and caraway seeds. Cook over a
low heat until softened, 8–10 minutes.
Stir in the apple slices and brown
sugar. Cover the pan and cook for
4–5 minutes more.

6 Stir in the cabbage. Add the
vinegar. Cover and cook for 10 minutes.
Pour in the stock and cider or wine,
add the salt and thyme leaves, and stir
well. Cover again and cook over a
medium-low heat for 30 minutes.

7 ▲ After this time, remove the pot
from the oven. Transfer the roast to a
plate and keep hot. Tilt the casserole
and spoon off and discard all but 30ml/
2 tbsp of the fat.

8 ▲ Transfer the cabbage mixture
from the frying pan to the casserole
and stir well to mix thoroughly with
the roasting juices.

9 ▲ Place the pork roast on top of the
layer of cabbage. Cover and return to
the oven. Cook for another hour,
basting occasionally with cider or wine.

Spicy Sauerbraten with Ginger Nut Gravy

SERVES 8

1.8kg/4lb beef chuck roast or boneless
  venison shoulder roast

10ml/2 tsp salt

pepper

2 onions, sliced

100g/3½oz/½ cup sliced carrots

2 bay leaves

5ml/1 tsp black peppercorns

12 juniper berries

6 whole cloves

5ml/1 tsp dry mustard

a few blades of mace

475ml/2 cups wine vinegar

475ml/2 cups boiling water

50ml/2fl oz/¼ cup vegetable oil or butter

15ml/1 tbsp soft dark brown sugar

65g/2½oz/¾ cup crushed ginger nut
  biscuits (gingersnaps)

noodles, to serve (optional)

1 ▲ Rub the roast with the salt and some freshly ground black pepper.

~ COOK'S TIP ~

In braising, meat is browned or seared in hot fat on all sides to seal in the juices before being cooked slowly in liquid. Check the sauerbraten after about 30 minutes of baking to make sure that the cooking liquid is simmering slowly, not boiling. If necessary, lower the oven temperature slightly.

2 ▲ In a deep earthenware or non-metallic bowl, combine the onions, carrots, bay leaves, peppercorns, juniper berries, cloves, mustard, mace and vinegar. Mix well. Stir in the boiling water.

3 ▲ Set the meat in the bowl and add more water if necessary: the meat should be at least half covered. Cover tightly and chill for at least 48 hours and up to 4 days. Turn the meat once a day.

4 Preheat the oven to 180°C/350°F/ Gas 4.

5 ▲ Remove the meat, reserving the marinade. Pat it dry with kitchen paper. Heat the oil or butter in a large flameproof casserole and brown the meat on all sides. This will take about 15 minutes.

6 ▲ Add the onions and carrots from the marinade, as well as 475ml/16fl oz/ 2 cups of the liquid. Reserve the remaining marinade. Cover the casserole and transfer to the oven. Cook for 4 hours.

7 ▲ Remove the meat to a hot serving dish. Press the vegetables and liquids from the casserole through a fine strainer. There should be about 600ml/1 pint/2½ cups strained liquid; if necessary, add a little more of the marinade liquid. Pour into a pan.

8 ▲ Boil until slightly reduced and thickened, about 5 minutes. Stir in the brown sugar and ginger nut crumbs. Adjust the seasoning if necessary.

9 Slice the meat. Serve with the hot ginger nut gravy and boiled noodles, if you like.

Mashed Carrots and Parsnips

SERVES 6

450g/1lb parsnips, cut into 1cm/½in slices

450g/1lb carrots, cut into 1cm/½in slices

1 onion, chopped

1 bay leaf

10ml/2 tsp granulated sugar

1.5ml/¼ tsp salt

250ml/8fl oz/1 cup water

30ml/2 tbsp butter or olive oil

finely chopped fresh chives, to garnish

1 Put the parsnip and carrot slices in a medium pan with the chopped onion, bay leaf, sugar and salt. Add the water.

2 ▼ Cover the pan tightly and cook over a medium heat, stirring occasionally, until the vegetables are just tender, about 20 minutes. Check from time to time to make sure the water has not evaporated, adding a little more if necessary.

3 ▲ Drain most of the water from the vegetables and discard the bay leaf. Purée the vegetables in a food processor or food mill. Beat in the butter or oil and turn into a warmed serving dish. Sprinkle with the chives and serve at once.

Baked Acorn Squash with Herbs

SERVES 4

2 acorn squash

90ml/6 tbsp mixed finely chopped fresh chives, thyme, basil and parsley

50g/2oz/¼ cup butter or margarine

salt and pepper

1 ▲ Cut each squash in half crossways and scoop out the seeds and stringy fibres. If necessary, cut a small slice off the base of each squash half so that it sits level.

2 Preheat oven to 190°C/375°F/Gas 5.

3 ▼ Divide the herbs in four, and spoon into the squash half hollows.

~ VARIATION ~

For Caramel-baked Acorn Squash, replace the herbs with 45ml/3 tbsp soft dark brown sugar. Melt the butter or margarine, dissolve the brown sugar in it and fill squashes.

4 ▲ Top each half with 15ml/1 tbsp butter or margarine and season with salt and pepper.

5 ·Arrange the squash halves in a shallow baking dish large enough to hold them in one layer. Pour boiling water into the bottom of the dish, to a depth of about 2.5cm/1in. Cover the squash loosely with a piece of foil.

6 Bake until the squash is tender when tested with a fork, ¾–1 hour. Serve hot, keeping the halves upright.

Mashed Carrots and Parsnips (top), Baked Acorn Squash with Herbs

Wisconsin Cheddar and Chive Biscuits

MAKES ABOUT 20

200g/7oz/1¾ cups plain (all-purpose) flour

10ml/2 tsp baking powder

2.5ml/½ tsp bicarbonate of soda
(baking soda)

1.5ml/¼ tsp salt

1.5ml/¼ tsp pepper

65g/2½oz/5 tbsp cold unsalted butter, diced

50g/2oz/½ cup grated mature (sharp)
Cheddar cheese

30ml/2 tbsp finely chopped fresh chives

175ml/6fl oz/¾ cup buttermilk

~ VARIATION ~

For Cheddar and Bacon Biscuits,
substitute 45ml/3 tbsp crumbled
cooked bacon for the chives.

1 Preheat oven to 200°C/400°F/Gas 6.

2 ▲ Sift the flour, baking powder,
bicarbonate of soda, salt and pepper
into a large bowl. Using your fingertips, rub the butter into the dry ingredients until the mixture is crumbly and
resembles breadcrumbs. Add the
cheese and chives and stir to blend.

3 Make a well in the centre of the
mixture. Add the buttermilk and stir
vigorously until the mixture comes away
from the sides of the bowl, 1 minute.

4 ▼ Drop 30ml/2 tbsp mounds spaced
5–7.5cm/2–3in apart on a lightly
greased baking sheet. Bake until
golden brown, 12–15 minutes.

Corn Oysters

MAKES ABOUT 8

150g/5oz/1 cup grated fresh corn

1 egg, separated

30ml/2 tbsp plain (all-purpose) flour

1.5ml/¼ tsp salt

1.5ml/¼ tsp pepper

30–60ml/2–4 tbsp butter or margarine

30–60ml/2–4 tbsp vegetable oil

1 Combine the corn, egg yolk and
flour in a bowl. Mix well. Add the salt
and pepper.

~ COOK'S TIP ~

Thawed frozen or canned corn
kernels can also be used. Drain
them well and chop.

2 ▲ In a separate bowl, whisk the egg
white until it forms stiff peaks. Fold it
carefully into the corn mixture.

3 Heat 30ml/2 tbsp of the butter or
margarine with 30ml/2 tbsp of the oil
in a frying pan. When the fats are very
hot and almost smoking, drop
tablespoonfuls of the corn mixture
into the pan. Fry until crisp and
brown on the bases.

4 ▼ Turn the "oysters" over and
cook for 1–2 minutes on the other
side. Drain on kitchen paper and keep
hot. Continue frying the "oysters",
adding more fat as necessary.

5 Serve hot as an accompaniment to
meat or chicken dishes, or by
themselves as a light dish with a
mixed salad.

Wisconsin Cheddar and Chive Biscuits (top), Corn Oysters

Milwaukee Onion Tart

SERVES 6

30ml/2 tbsp butter or olive oil

5 onions, thinly sliced

2.5ml/½ tsp salt

2.5ml/½ tsp fresh or dried thyme leaves

1.5ml/¼ tsp pepper

1 egg

120ml/4fl oz/½ cup sour cream or natural
(plain) yogurt

10ml/2 tsp poppy seeds

1.5ml/¼ tsp ground mace or nutmeg

FOR THE PASTRY

115g/4oz/1 cup plain (all-purpose) flour

6ml/1¼ tsp baking powder

2.5ml/½ tsp salt

40g/1½oz/3 tbsp cold butter, lard or
white cooking fat, diced

30–45ml/2–3 tbsp milk

1 ▲ Heat the butter or oil in a
medium frying pan. Add the onions
and cook over a low heat until soft and
golden, 10–12 minutes. Season with
the salt, thyme and pepper. Remove
from the heat and leave to cool.

2 Preheat the oven to 220°C/425°F/
Gas 7.

3 ▲ For the pastry, sift the flour,
baking powder and salt into a bowl.
Using your fingertips, rub the butter,
lard or white cooking fat into the dry
ingredients until the mixture is crumbly
and resembles breadcrumbs. Add the
milk and stir in lightly with a wooden
spoon to make a dough.

4 Turn the pastry out on to a floured
surface and knead lightly for 30 seconds.

5 Pat out the pastry into a disc about
20cm/8in in diameter. Transfer to a
20cm/8in baking tin (pan) that is at
least 5cm/2in deep. Press the pastry into
an even layer. Cover with the onions.

6 ▲ Beat together the egg and sour
cream or yogurt. Spread evenly over
the onions. Sprinkle with the poppy
seeds and mace or nutmeg. Bake until
the egg topping is puffed and golden,
25–30 minutes.

7 Leave to cool in the pan for
10 minutes. Slip a knife between the
tart and the tin to loosen, then turn
out on to a plate. Cut the onion tart
into wedges and serve warm.

Huckleberry Cake

SERVES 10

225g/8oz/2 cups plain (all-purpose) flour

15ml/1 tbsp baking powder

5ml/1 tsp salt

65g/2½oz/⅓ cup butter or margarine, at room temperature

150g/5oz/¾ cup granulated sugar

1 egg

250ml/8fl oz/1 cup milk

2.5ml/½ tsp grated lemon rind

225g/8oz/2 cups fresh or frozen huckleberries, well drained

115g/4oz/1 cup icing (confectioners') sugar

30ml/2 tbsp fresh lemon juice

1 Preheat the oven to 180°C/350°F/ Gas 4.

2 ▲ Sift the flour with the baking powder and salt.

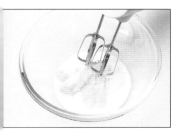

3 ▲ In a large bowl, beat the butter or margarine with the granulated sugar until light and fluffy. Beat in the egg and milk. Fold in the flour mixture, mixing well until evenly blended. Mix in the lemon rind.

4 ▼ Spread half the mixture in a greased 15 × 3½ × 5cm/13 × 9 × 2in baking dish. Sprinkle with 250ml/8fl oz/ 1 cup of the berries. Top with the remaining mixture and sprinkle with the rest of the berries. Bake until golden brown and a skewer inserted in the centre comes out clean, 35–45 minutes.

5 ▲ Mix the icing sugar gradually into the lemon juice to make a smooth glaze with a pourable consistency. Drizzle the glaze over the top of the cake and allow it to set before serving, still warm or at room temperature.

Pickled Eggs and Beetroot

SERVES 8

900g/2lb small beetroot, cooked
 and peeled

350ml/12fl oz/1½ cups cider vinegar

350ml/12fl oz/1½ cups beetroot cooking
 liquid or water

90g/3½oz/½ cup granulated sugar

1 bay leaf

5ml/1 tsp salt

15ml/1 tbsp whole allspice berries

5ml/1 tsp whole cloves

2.5ml/½ tsp ground ginger

2.5ml/½ tsp caraway seeds

8 hard-boiled eggs, shelled

1 ▲ Place the beetroot in a very large
glass jar, or in several smaller jars.

2 Combine the vinegar, beetroot
liquid or water, sugar, bay leaf, salt and
spices in a pan. Heat, stirring to dissolve
the sugar. Simmer for 5 minutes.

3 Pour the mixture over the beetroot.
Leave to cool completely.

4 ▼ Add the eggs to the jar(s) of
beetroot. Cover and chill for 2–3 days
before serving. The pickle will keep for
up to a week in the refrigerator.

Pickled Cucumber and Onion

MAKES ABOUT 1 LITRE/1¾ PINTS/4 CUPS

900g/2lb cucumbers, scrubbed and cut
 into 6mm/¼in slices

4 onions, very thinly sliced

30ml/2 tbsp salt

350ml/12fl oz/1½ cups cider vinegar

300g/11oz/1½ cups granulated sugar

30ml/2 tbsp mustard seeds

30ml/2 tbsp celery seeds

1.5ml/¼ tsp turmeric

1.5ml/¼ tsp cayenne pepper

1 ▲ Put the sliced cucumbers and
onions in a large bowl and sprinkle
with the salt. Mix well. Cover loosely
and leave to stand for 3 hours.

2 Drain the vegetables. Rinse well
under cold water and drain again.

3 Prepare some heatproof glass jars
(such as bottling jars). Wash them
well in warm soapy water and rinse
thoroughly in warm water. Put them in
a 150°C/300°F/Gas 2 oven and heat
for 30 minutes to sterilize them. Keep
the jars hot until ready to use.

4 ▼ Combine the remaining
ingredients in a large non-metallic pan
and bring to the boil. Add the cucumbers and onions. Reduce the heat and
simmer for 2–3 minutes. Do not boil or
the pickles will be limp.

5 ▲ Spoon the hot vegetables into
the hot jars. Add enough of the hot
liquid to come to 1cm/½in from the
top. Carefully wipe the jar rims with a
clean damp cloth.

6 To seal, cover the surface of the
pickles with a waxed disc, wax side
down, then put on the jar lid. The
pickles should be sealed immediately.
If the lid does not have a rubber
seal, first cover the top of the jar with
clear film (plastic wrap) or cellophane
and then screw a plastic top down over
it. Avoid using metal, as it may rust.
Store in a cool dark place for at least
4 weeks before serving.

Pickled Eggs and Beetroot (centre), Pickled Cucumber and Onion

Rhubarb Pie

SERVES 6

175g/6oz/1½ cups plain (all-purpose) flour

2.5ml/½ tsp salt

10ml/2 tsp granulated sugar

75g/3oz/6 tbsp cold butter, lard or
  white cooking fat, diced

30–45ml/2–3 tbsp iced water

30ml/2 tbsp whipping cream

FOR THE FILLING

900g/2lb fresh rhubarb, cut into
  1–2.5cm/½–1in slices

30ml/2 tbsp cornflour (cornstarch)

1 egg

300g/11oz/1½ cups granulated sugar

15ml/1 tbsp grated orange rind

1 ▲ For the pastry, sift the flour, salt
and sugar into a bowl. With a pastry
blender, cut in the butter, lard or
white cooking fat until the mixture
resembles breadcrumbs, or rub in
with your fingertips.

2 Sprinkle with 30ml/2 tbsp of the iced
water and mix until the pastry holds
together. If the pastry is too crumbly, add
a little more water, 5ml/1 tsp at a time.

~ COOK'S TIP ~

Be sure to cut off and discard the
green rhubarb leaves from the
pink stalks, as they are toxic
and not edible.

3 ▲ Gather the pastry into a ball,
flatten into a disk, wrap in clear film
(plastic wrap) and chill for 20 minutes.

4 ▲ Roll out the pastry between two
sheets of clear film to a thickness of
about 3mm/⅛in. Use to line a 23cm/
9in pie tin (pan). Trim all around,
leaving a 1cm/½in overhang. Fold the
overhang under the edge and flute.
Chill the pastry case (pie shell) and
trimmings for 30 minutes.

5 ▲ For the filling, put the rhubarb
in a bowl and sprinkle with the
cornflour. Toss to coat.

6 Preheat oven to 220°C/425°F/Gas 7.

7 In a small bowl, beat the egg with
the sugar. Mix in the orange rind.

8 ▲ Stir the sugar mixture into the
rhubarb and mix well. Spoon the fruit
into the pastry case.

9 ▲ Roll out the pastry trimmings.
Stamp out decorative shapes with a
pastry (cookie) cutter or cut shapes
with a small knife, using a cardboard
template as a guide, if you like.

10 Arrange the shapes on top of the
pie. Brush the trimmings and the edge
of the pastry case with cream.

11 Bake for 30 minutes. Reduce the
heat to 160°C/325°F/Gas 3 and
continue baking until the pastry is
golden brown and the rhubarb is tender,
about 15–20 minutes more.

Brown Sugar Tart

SERVES 8

175g/6oz/1½ cups plain (all-purpose) flour

2.5ml/½ tsp salt

10ml/2 tsp granulated sugar

75g/3oz/6 tbsp cold butter or lard, diced

30–45ml/2–3 tbsp iced water

FOR THE FILLING

25g/1oz/¼ cup plain (all-purpose)
flour, sifted

225g/8oz/1 cup soft light brown sugar

2.5ml/½ tsp vanilla extract

350ml/12fl oz/1½ cups whipping cream

40g/1½oz/3 tbsp butter, finely diced

pinch of grated nutmeg

1 Sift the flour, salt and sugar into a bowl. Using your fingertips, rub the butter or lard into the dry ingredients until the mixture resembles breadcrumbs.

2 ▲ Sprinkle with 30ml/2 tbsp of the water and mix until the pastry holds together. If it is too crumbly, add more water, 5ml/1 tsp at a time. Gather into a ball and flatten. Wrap in clear film (plastic wrap) and chill for 20 minutes.

3 Roll out the pastry to about 3mm/⅛in thick and line a 23cm/9in tart tin (pan). Trim all around, leaving a 1cm/½in overhang. Fold it under and flute the edge. Chill for 30 minutes.

4 Preheat oven to 220°C/425°F/Gas 7.

5 Line the pastry case (pie shell) with a piece of baking parchment 5cm/2in larger all around than the diameter of the tin. Fill the case with dried beans. Bake until the pastry has just set, 8–10 minutes. Remove from the oven and carefully lift out the paper and beans. Prick the bottom of the case all over with a fork. Return to the oven and bake for 5 minutes more. Let the pastry case cool slightly before filling. Turn the oven down to 190°C/375°F/Gas 5.

6 ▲ In a small bowl, mix together the flour and sugar using a fork. Spread this mixture in an even layer on the bottom of the pastry case.

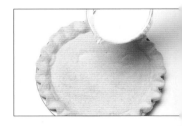

7 ▲ Stir the vanilla into the cream. Pour the flavoured cream over the flour and sugar mixture and gently swirl with a fork to mix. Dot with the butter. Sprinkle the nutmeg on top.

8 Cover the edge of the tart with foil strips to prevent overbrowning. Set on a baking sheet and bake until the filling is golden brown and set to the touch, about 45 minutes. Serve the tart at room temperature.

Apple Maple Dumplings

SERVES 8

475g/18oz/4½ cups plain
(all-purpose) flour

10ml/2 tsp salt

350g/12oz/1½ cups butter or lard, diced

90–105ml/6–7 tbsp iced water

8 firm, tart-sweet apples

1 egg white

130g/4½oz/⅔ cup granulated sugar

45ml/3 tbsp whipping cream

2.5ml/½ tsp vanilla extract

250ml/8fl oz/1 cup maple syrup

whipped cream, to serve

1 Sift the flour and salt into a large bowl. Using your fingertips, rub the butter or lard into the flour until the mixture resembles breadcrumbs. Sprinkle with 90ml/6 tbsp of the water and mix until it holds together. If it is too crumbly, add more water, 5ml/1 tsp at a time. Gather into a ball. Wrap in clear film (plastic wrap) and chill for 20 minutes.

2 Preheat oven to 220°C/425°F/Gas 7.

3 Peel the apples. Remove the cores, cutting from the stem end, without cutting through the base.

4 ▲ Roll out the pastry thinly. Cut squares almost large enough to enclose the apples. Brush the squares with egg white. Set an apple in the centre of each pastry square.

5 Combine the sugar, cream and vanilla in a small bowl. Spoon some into the hollow in each apple.

6 ▼ Pull the points of the pastry squares up around the apples and moisten the edges where they overlap. Mold the pastry around the apples, pleating the top. Do not cover the centre hollows. Crimp the edges tightly to seal.

7 Place the apples in a large greased baking dish, at least 2cm/¾in apart. Bake for 30 minutes. Lower the oven temperature to 180°C/350°F/Gas 4 and continue baking until the pastry is golden brown and the apples are tender, about 20 minutes more.

8 Transfer the dumplings to a serving dish. Mix the maple syrup with the juices in the baking dish and drizzle over the dumplings.

9 Serve the dumplings hot with whipped cream.

Apple Fritters

SERVES 4–6

165g/5½oz/1⅓ cups plain
(all-purpose) flour

10ml/2 tsp baking powder

1.5ml/¼ tsp salt

150ml/¼ pint/⅔ cup milk

1 egg, beaten

oil for deep-frying

150g/5oz/¾ cup granulated sugar

5ml/1 tsp ground cinnamon

2 large tart-sweet apples, peeled, cored
and cut into 5mm/¼in slices

icing (confectioners') sugar, for dusting

1 Sift the flour, baking powder and
salt into a bowl. Beat in the milk and
egg with a wire whisk.

2 Heat at least 7.5cm/3in oil in a
heavy frying pan to 185°C/360°F.

3 ▲ Mix the granulated sugar and
cinnamon in a shallow bowl or plate.
Toss the apple slices in the sugar
mixture to coat all over.

4 Dip the apple slices in the batter,
using a fork or slotted spoon. Drain off
the excess batter. Fry, in batches, in
the hot oil until golden brown on both
sides, about 4–5 minutes. Drain the
fritters on kitchen paper.

5 ▼ Sprinkle with icing sugar, and
serve hot.

Cherry Compote

SERVES 6

120ml/4fl oz/½ cup water

120ml/4fl oz/½ cup red wine

50g/2oz/¼ cup soft light brown sugar

50g/2oz/¼ cup granulated sugar

15ml/1 tbsp honey

2 × 2.5cm/1in strips of orange rind

1.5ml/¼ tsp almond extract

675g/1½lb sweet cherries, pitted

ice cream or whipped cream, to serve

~ VARIATION ~

Sour cherries may be used for the
compote instead of sweet. If using
sour cherries, increase the amount
of the sugars to 75g/3oz/⅓ cup each,
or to taste.

1 ▼ Combine all the ingredients
except the cherries in a pan. Stir over
a medium heat until the sugar
dissolves. Raise the heat and boil until
the liquid reduces slightly.

2 ▲ Add the cherries. Bring back to
the boil. Reduce the heat slightly and
simmer for 8–10 minutes. If necessary,
skim off any foam.

3 Leave to cool to lukewarm. Spoon
warm over vanilla ice cream, or chill
and serve cold with whipped cream,
if you like.

Apple Fritters (top), Cherry Compote

Black Walnut Layer Cake

SERVES 8

225g/8oz/2 cups self-raising (self-rising) flour

15ml/1 tbsp baking powder

2.5ml/½ tsp salt

115g/4oz/½ cup butter or margarine

200g/7oz/1 cup granulated sugar

2 eggs

5ml/1 tsp grated orange rind

5ml/1 tsp vanilla extract

115g/4oz/1 cup finely chopped black walnut pieces

175ml/6fl oz/¾ cup milk

black walnut halves, for decoration

FOR THE ICING

115g/4oz/½ cup butter

175g/6oz/¾ cup soft light brown sugar

45ml/3 tbsp maple syrup

50ml/2fl oz/¼ cup milk

200g/7oz/1¼ cups–225g/8oz/2 cups icing (confectioners') sugar, sifted

1 ▲ Grease two 20 × 5cm/8 × 2in cake tins (pans) and line each with a disk of greased baking parchment. Preheat the oven to 190°C/ 375°F/Gas 5.

2 Sift together the flour, baking powder and salt.

~ VARIATION ~

If black walnuts are unavailable, substitute regular walnuts, or use pecans instead.

3 ▲ Beat the butter or margarine to soften, then gradually beat in the granulated sugar until light and fluffy. Beat in the eggs, one at a time. Add the orange rind and vanilla and beat to mix well.

4 ▲ Stir in the finely chopped walnuts. Add the flour alternately with the milk, stirring only enough to blend after each addition.

5 ▲ Divide the mixture between the prepared cake tins. Bake until a skewer inserted in the centre comes out clean, about 25 minutes. Cool in the tins for 5 minutes before turning out on to a wire rack.

6 ▲ For the icing, melt the butter in a medium pan. Add the brown sugar and maple syrup and boil for 2 minutes, stirring constantly.

7 ▲ Add the milk. Bring back to the boil and stir in 25g/1oz/¼ cup of the icing sugar. Remove from the heat and leave to cool to lukewarm. Gradually beat in the remaining icing sugar. Set the pan in a bowl of iced water and stir until the icing is thick enough to spread over the cake.

8 ▲ Spread some of the icing on one of the cake layers. Set the other layer on top. Spread the remaining icing over the top and sides of the cake. Decorate with the walnut halves.

Apple Sauce Cookies

MAKES 36

90g/3½oz/½ cup granulated sugar

50g/2oz/¼ cup butter, lard or white cooking fat, at room temperature

175ml/6fl oz/¾ cup thick apple sauce

pinch of grated lemon rind

115g/4oz/1 cup plain (all-purpose) flour

2.5ml/½ tsp baking powder

1.5ml/¼ tsp bicarbonate of soda (baking soda)

1.5ml/¼ tsp salt

2.5ml/½ tsp ground cinnamon

50g/2oz/½ cup chopped walnuts

~ COOK'S TIP ~

If the apple sauce is runny, put it in a strainer over a bowl and let it drain for 10 minutes.

1 Preheat oven to 190°C/375°F/Gas 5.

2 In a medium bowl, beat together the sugar and butter, lard or white cooking fat until well mixed. Beat in the apple sauce and lemon rind.

3 ▲ Sift the flour, baking powder, bicarbonate of soda, salt and cinnamon into the mixture, and stir to blend. Fold in the chopped walnuts.

4 ▲ Drop teaspoonfuls of the mixture on to a lightly greased baking sheet, spacing them about 5cm/2in apart.

5 Bake the cookies in the centre of the oven until they are golden brown, 8–10 minutes. Transfer the cookies to a wire rack to cool.

Toffee Bars

MAKES 32

450g/1lb/2 cups soft light brown sugar

450g/1lb/2 cups butter or margarine, at room temperature

2 egg yolks

7.5ml/1½ tsp vanilla extract

450g/1lb/4 cups plain (all-purpose) or wholemeal (whole-wheat) flour

2.5ml/½ tsp salt

225g/8oz milk chocolate, broken in pieces

115g/4oz/1 cup chopped walnuts or pecans

1 Preheat the oven to 180°C/350°F/Gas 4.

2 Beat together the sugar and butter or margarine until light and fluffy. Beat in the egg yolks and vanilla. Stir in the flour and salt.

3 ▼ Spread the shortbread in a greased 15 × 3½ × 5cm/13 × 9 × 2in baking tin (pan). Bake until lightly browned, 25–30 minutes. The texture will be soft.

4 ▲ Remove from the oven and immediately place the chocolate pieces on the hot shortbread base. Leave until the chocolate softens, then spread it evenly with a spatula. Sprinkle with the nuts.

5 While still warm, cut into bars of about 5 × 4cm/2 × 1½in.

Apple Sauce Cookies (top), Toffee Bars

THE
SOUTHWEST

THE POPULAR TASTE FOR "TEX-MEX" HAS SPREAD FAR AND WIDE, BUT THE ROOTS OF THIS CUISINE ARE IN NATIVE AMERICAN HERITAGE. THE FOOD OF THIS REGION FEATURES PRODUCTS CULTIVATED BY THE ORIGINAL AMERICANS – CORN IN MANY FORMS, TOMATOES, BEANS – COMBINED WITH INFLUENCES FROM SOUTH OF THE BORDER AND FROM THE RIGOURS OF FARMING IN A DESERT.

Tortilla Soup

SERVES 4–6

15ml/1 tbsp vegetable oil

1 onion, finely chopped

1 large garlic clove, finely chopped

2 medium tomatoes, peeled, seeded, chopped

2.5ml/½ tsp salt

2.5 litres/4 pints chicken stock

1 carrot, diced

1 small courgette (zucchini), diced

1 skinless chicken breast fillet,
 cooked and shredded

40g/1½oz/¼ cup canned green chillies,
 chopped

TO GARNISH

4 corn tortillas

oil for frying

1 small ripe avocado

2 spring onions (scallions), chopped

chopped fresh coriander (cilantro)

grated Cheddar or Monterey Jack
 cheese (optional)

1 ▲ Heat the oil in a pan. Add the onion and garlic and cook over a medium heat until just softened, 5–8 minutes. Add the tomatoes and salt and cook for 5 minutes more.

2 Stir in the stock. Bring to the boil, then lower the heat and simmer, covered, for about 15 minutes.

3 ▲ Meanwhile, for the garnish, trim the tortillas into squares, then cut them into strips.

4 ▲ Put a 1cm/½in layer of oil in a frying pan and heat until hot but not smoking. Add the tortilla strips, in batches, and fry until just beginning to brown, turning occasionally. Remove with a slotted spoon and drain on kitchen paper.

5 Add the carrot to the soup. Cook, covered, for 10 minutes. Add the courgette, chicken and chillies and continue cooking, uncovered, until the vegetables are just tender, about 5 minutes more.

6 Meanwhile, peel and stone (pit) the avocado. Chop into fine dice.

7 Divide the tortilla strips among four soup bowls. Sprinkle with the avocado. Ladle in the soup, then scatter spring onions and coriander on top. Serve at once, with grated cheese if you like.

Spicy Bean Soup

SERVES 6–8

175g/6oz/1 cup dried black beans,
 soaked overnight and drained

175g/6oz/1 cup dried kidney beans,
 soaked overnight and drained

2 bay leaves

90ml/6 tbsp sea salt

30ml/2 tbsp olive or vegetable oil

3 carrots, chopped

1 onion, chopped

1 celery stick

1 garlic clove, finely chopped

5ml/1 tsp ground cumin

1.5–2.5ml/¼ –½ tsp cayenne pepper

2.5ml/½ tsp dried oregano

salt and pepper

75ml/2½fl oz/⅓ cup red wine

1.2 litres/2 pints beef stock

250ml/8fl oz/1 cup water

TO GARNISH

sour cream

chopped fresh coriander (cilantro)

3 Heat the oil in a large flameproof casserole. Add the carrots, onion, celery and garlic and cook over a low heat, stirring, until softened, about 8–10 minutes. Stir in the cumin, cayenne, oregano and salt to taste.

4 ▼ Add the wine, stock and water and stir to mix. Add the beans. Bring to the boil, reduce the heat, then cover and simmer for about 20 minutes, stirring occasionally.

5 ▲ Transfer half the soup (including most of the solids) to a food processor or blender. Process until smooth. Return to the pan and stir to combine well.

6 Reheat the soup if necessary and taste for seasoning. Serve hot, garnished with sour cream and chopped fresh coriander.

1 ▲ Put the black beans and kidney beans in two separate pans. To each, add a bay leaf and fresh cold water to cover. Bring to the boil, then cover and simmer for 30 minutes.

2 Add half the sea salt to each pan and continue simmering until the beans are tender, about 30 minutes more. Drain and leave to cool slightly. Discard the bay leaves.

Desert Nachos

SERVES 2

175g/6oz blue corn tortilla chips or ordinary tortilla chips

30–60ml/2–4 tbsp chopped pickled jalapeños, according to taste

25g/1oz/⅓ cup sliced black olives

250g/8oz/2 cups grated Monterey Jack or Cheddar cheese

TO SERVE

guacamole

tomato salsa

sour cream

1 Preheat the oven to 180°C/350°F/ Gas 4.

2 ▲ Put the tortilla chips in a 33 × 23cm/13 × 9in baking dish and spread them out evenly. Sprinkle the jalapeños, olives and cheese evenly over the tortilla chips.

3 ▼ Place in the top of the oven and bake until the cheese melts, 10–15 minutes. Serve the nachos at once, with the guacamole, tomato salsa and sour cream for dipping.

Huevos Rancheros

SERVES 4

460g/17oz can refried beans

300ml/½ pint/1¼ cups enchilada sauce

oil for frying

4 corn tortillas

4 eggs

salt and pepper

150g/5oz/1¼ cups grated Monterey Jack or Cheddar cheese

1 ▼ Heat the beans in a pan. Cover and set aside.

2 Heat the enchilada sauce in a small pan. Cover and set aside.

3 Preheat oven to 160°C/325°F/Gas 3.

4 ▲ Put a 6mm/¼in layer of oil in a small non-stick frying pan and heat. When hot, add the tortillas, one at a time, and fry until just crisp, about 30 seconds per side. Drain the tortillas on kitchen paper and keep them warm on a baking sheet in the oven. Discard the oil used for frying.

5 Leave the frying pan to cool slightly, then wipe it with kitchen paper to remove all but a film of oil. Heat the pan over a low heat. Break in 2 eggs and cook until the whites are just set. Season with salt and pepper, then transfer to the oven to keep warm. Repeat to cook the remaining eggs.

6 ▼ To serve, place a tortilla on each of four plates. Spread a layer of refried beans over each tortilla, then top each with an egg. Spoon over the warm enchilada sauce, then sprinkle with the cheese. Serve hot.

Desert Nachos (top), Huevos Rancheros

Arizona Jalapeño and Onion Quiche

SERVES 6

15ml/1 tbsp butter

2 onions, sliced

4 spring onions (scallions), cut into
   1cm/½in pieces

2.5ml/½ tsp ground cumin

15–30ml/1–2 tbsp chopped
   canned jalapeños

4 eggs

300ml/½ pint/1¼ cups milk

2.5ml/½ tsp salt

65g/2½oz/⅔ cup grated Monterey Jack
   or Cheddar cheese

FOR THE PASTRY

175g/6oz/1½ cups plain
   (all-purpose) flour

1.5ml/¼ tsp salt

1.5ml/¼ tsp cayenne pepper

75g/3oz/6 tbsp cold butter or margarine

30–45ml/2–3 tbsp iced water

1 For the pastry, sift the flour, salt and cayenne into a bowl. Using your fingertips, rub the butter and margarine into the dry ingredients until the mixture is crumbly and resembles breadcrumbs. Sprinkle with 30ml/2 tbsp of the iced water and mix until the pastry holds together. If the pastry is too crumbly, add a little more water, 5ml/1 tsp at a time. Gather the pastry into a ball and flatten into a disk. Wrap in clear film (plastic wrap) and chill for at least 30 minutes.

2 Preheat the oven to 190°C/375°F/ Gas 5.

3 Roll the pastry out to about 3mm/⅛in thick. Use to line a 23cm/9in fluted tart tin (pan) with a removable base. Line the case with baking parchment and fill with dried beans.

4 Bake until the pastry has just set, 12–15 minutes. Remove from the oven and carefully lift out the paper and beans. Prick the bottom of the pastry case all over. Return to the oven and bake until golden, 5–8 minutes more. Leave the oven on.

5 ▲ Melt the butter in a non-stick frying pan. Add the onions and cook over a medium heat until softened, about 5 minutes. Add the spring onions and cook for 1 minute more. Stir in the cumin and jalapeños and set aside.

6 In a mixing bowl, combine the eggs, milk and salt and whisk until thoroughly blended.

7 ▲ Spoon the onion mixture into the pastry case. Sprinkle with the cheese, then pour in the egg mixture.

8 Bake until the filling is golden and set, 30–40 minutes. Serve hot or at room temperature.

San Antonio Tortilla

SERVES 4

15ml/1 tbsp vegetable oil

½ onion, sliced

1 small green (bell) pepper,
   seeded and sliced

1 garlic clove, finely chopped

1 tomato, chopped

6 black olives, chopped

3 small potatoes (about 275g/10oz
   total), cooked and sliced

50g/2oz sliced chorizo, cut into strips

15ml/1 tbsp chopped canned jalapeños,
   or to taste

50g/2oz/½ cup grated Cheddar cheese

6 large (US extra large) eggs

45ml/3 tbsp milk

2.5–6ml/½–¾ tsp salt

1.5ml/¼ tsp ground cumin

1.5ml/¼ tsp dried oregano

1.5ml/¼ tsp paprika

black pepper

1 Preheat the oven to 190°C/375°F/
Gas 5.

2 ▲ Heat the oil in a non-stick frying
pan. Add the onion, green pepper and
garlic and cook over a medium heat
until softened, 5–8 minutes.

3 Transfer the vegetables to a 23cm/9in
round non-stick springform tin (pan).
Add the tomato, olives, potatoes,
chorizo and jalapeños. Sprinkle with
the cheese and set aside.

4 ▲ In a bowl, combine the eggs and
milk and whisk until frothy. Add the
salt, cumin, oregano, paprika and
pepper to taste. Whisk to blend.

5 Pour the egg mixture into the
vegetable mixture, tilting the pan to
spread it evenly.

6 ▲ Bake until set and lightly golden,
about 30 minutes. Serve hot or cold.

Santa Fe Prawn Salad

SERVES 4

450g/1lb cooked peeled prawns

2 spring onions (scallions), chopped

30ml/2 tbsp fresh lemon juice

30ml/2 tbsp extra virgin olive oil

5ml/1 tsp salt

350g/12oz/6 cups shredded lettuce

1 large ripe avocado

225g/8oz/1 cup tomato salsa

TO GARNISH

fresh coriander (cilantro) sprigs

lime slices

1 ▲ In a bowl, combine the prawns, spring onions, lemon juice, oil and salt. Mix well and set aside.

2 ▲ Line four plates (or a large serving dish) with the shredded lettuce.

3 ▲ Halve the avocado and remove the stone (pit). With a small melon baller, scoop out balls of avocado and add to the prawn mixture. Scrape the remaining avocado flesh into the salsa and stir. Add the salsa to the prawn mixture and stir gently to blend.

4 ▲ Divide the prawn mixture among the plates, piling it up in the centre. Garnish each salad with fresh coriander sprigs and slices of lime, and serve at once.

Pinto Bean Salad

SERVES 4

260g/9½oz/1½ cups dried pinto beans, soaked overnight and drained

1 bay leaf

45ml/3 tbsp sea salt

2 ripe tomatoes, diced

4 spring onions (scallions), finely chopped

FOR THE DRESSING

50ml/2fl oz/¼ cup fresh lemon juice

5ml/1 tsp salt

pepper

90ml/6 tbsp olive oil

1 garlic clove, finely chopped

45ml/3 tbsp chopped fresh coriander (cilantro)

1 ▲ Put the beans in a large pan. Add fresh cold water to cover and the bay leaf. Bring to the boil, then cover and simmer for 30 minutes. Add the salt and continue simmering until tender, about 30 minutes more. Drain and leave to cool slightly. Discard the bay leaf.

2 ▲ For the dressing, mix the lemon juice and salt with a fork until dissolved. Gradually stir in the oil until thick. Add the garlic, coriander and pepper to taste.

3 ▲ While the beans are still warm, place them in a medium bowl. Add the dressing and toss to coat. Let the beans cool completely.

4 ▼ Add the tomatoes and spring onions and toss to coat evenly. Leave to stand for at least 30 minutes, then serve.

Chillies Rellenos

SERVES 4

8 large green (bell) peppers or fresh green chillies such as poblano

15–30ml/1–2 tbsp vegetable oil, plus more for frying

450g/1lb/4 cups grated Monterey Jack or Cheddar cheese

4 eggs, separated

75g/3oz/⅔ cup plain (all-purpose) flour

FOR THE SAUCE

15ml/1 tbsp vegetable oil

1 small onion, finely chopped

1.5ml/¼ tsp salt

5–10ml/1–2 tsp red pepper flakes

2.5ml/½ tsp ground cumin

250ml/8fl oz/1 cup beef or chicken stock

450g/1lb canned peeled tomatoes

1 ▲ For the sauce, heat the oil in a frying pan. Add the onion and cook over a low heat until just soft, about 8 minutes. Stir in the salt, pepper flakes, cumin, stock and tomatoes. Cover and simmer gently for 5 minutes, stirring occasionally.

2 Transfer to a food processor or blender and process until smooth. Strain into a clean pan. Taste for seasoning, and set aside.

~ COOK'S TIP ~

If necessary, work in batches, but do not coat the peppers until you are ready to fry them.

3 Preheat the grill (broiler).

4 ▲ Brush the peppers or chillies lightly all over with oil. Lay them on a baking sheet. Grill (broil) as close to the heat as possible until blackened all over, 5–8 minutes. Cover with a clean dish towel and set aside.

5 ▲ When cool enough to handle, remove the charred skin. Carefully slit the peppers or chillies and scoop out the seeds. If using chillies, wear rubber gloves. For less chilli-heat, gently remove the white veins.

6 ▲ With your hands, form the cheese into eight cylinders that are slightly shorter than the peppers. Place the cheese cylinders inside the peppers. Secure the slits with wooden toothpicks. Set aside.

7 ▲ Beat the egg whites until just stiff. Add the egg yolks, one at a time, beating on low speed just to incorporate them. Beat in 15ml/1 tbsp of the flour.

8 Put a 2.5cm/1in layer of oil in a frying pan. Heat until hot but not smoking. (To test, drop a scrap of batter in the oil: if the oil sizzles, it is hot enough for frying.)

9 ▲ Coat the peppers lightly in flour all over; shake off any excess. Dip into the egg batter, then place in the hot oil. Fry until brown on one side, about 2 minutes. Turn carefully and brown the other side.

10 Reheat the sauce and serve with the chillies rellenos.

~ VARIATION ~

If using peppers rather than green chillies, mix the grated cheese with 7.5–15ml/½–1 tbsp hot chilli powder for a more authentic Southwest taste.

Black Bean Burritos

SERVES 4

185g/6½oz/1 cup dried black beans, soaked overnight and drained

1 bay leaf

45ml/3 tbsp sea salt

1 small red onion, finely chopped

225g/8oz/2 cups grated Monterey Jack or Cheddar cheese

15–45ml/1–3 tbsp chopped pickled jalapeños

15ml/1 tbsp chopped fresh coriander (cilantro)

800g/1¾lb/3½ cups tomato salsa

8 flour tortillas

diced avocado, to serve

1 ▲ Place the beans in a large pan. Add fresh cold water to cover and the bay leaf. Bring to the boil, then cover and simmer for 30 minutes. Add the salt and continue simmering until tender, about 30 minutes more. Drain and leave to cool slightly. Discard the bay leaf.

2 Preheat the oven to 180°C/350°F/ Gas 4. Grease a rectangular baking dish.

3 ▲ In a bowl, combine the beans, onion, half the cheese, the jalapeños, coriander and 250g/8oz/1 cup of salsa. Stir to blend and taste for seasoning.

4 ▲ Place a tortilla on a work surface. Spread a large spoonful of the filling down the middle, then roll up to enclose the filling. Place the burrito in the prepared dish, seam side down. Repeat with the remaining tortillas.

5 ▲ Sprinkle the remaining cheese over the burritos, in a line down the middle. Bake until the cheese melts, about 15 minutes.

6 Serve the burritos at once, with the avocado and remaining salsa.

Black Bean Chilli

SERVES 6

375g/13oz/2 cups dried black beans,
   soaked overnight and drained

30ml/2 tbsp sea salt

30ml/2 tbsp vegetable oil

2 onions, chopped

1 green (bell) pepper, seeded and chopped

4 garlic cloves, finely chopped

900g/2lb steak mince

25ml/1½ tbsp ground cumin

2.5ml/½ tsp cayenne pepper, or to taste

12.5ml/2½ tsp paprika

30ml/2 tbsp dried oregano

5ml/1 tsp salt

45ml/3 tbsp tomato purée (paste)

675g/1½lb/3 cups chopped peeled fresh
   or canned tomatoes

120ml/4fl oz/½ cup red wine

1 bay leaf

TO SERVE

chopped fresh coriander (cilantro)

sour cream

grated Monterey Jack or
   Cheddar cheese

1 Put the beans in a large pan. Add fresh cold water to cover. Bring to the boil, then cover and simmer for 30 minutes. Add the sea salt and continue simmering until the beans are tender, about 30 minutes or longer. Drain and set aside.

2 Heat the oil in a large pan or flame-proof casserole. Add the onions and pepper. Cook the vegetables over a medium heat until just softened, about 5 minutes, stirring occasionally. Stir in the garlic and continue cooking for 1 minute more.

3 Add the mince and cook over a high heat, stirring frequently, until browned and crumbly. Reduce the heat and stir in the cumin, cayenne, paprika, oregano and salt.

4 ▼ Add the tomato purée, tomatoes, drained black beans, wine and bay leaf and stir well. Simmer for 20 minutes, stirring occasionally.

5 ▲ Taste for seasoning. Remove the bay leaf and serve at once, with chopped fresh coriander, sour cream and grated cheese on the side.

Red Snapper with Coriander Salsa

SERVES 4

4 red snapper fillets, about 175g/6oz each

25ml/1½ tbsp vegetable oil

15g/½oz/1 tbsp butter

salt and pepper

FOR THE SALSA

115g/4oz/2 cups fresh coriander
   (cilantro) leaves

250ml/8fl oz/1 cup olive oil

2 garlic cloves, chopped

2 tomatoes, cored and chopped

30ml/2 tbsp fresh orange juice

15ml/1 tbsp sherry vinegar

5ml/1 tsp salt

1 ▲ For the salsa, place the coriander, oil and garlic in a food processor or blender. Process until almost smooth. Add the tomatoes and pulse on and off several times; the mixture should be slightly chunky.

2 ▲ Transfer to a bowl. Stir in the orange juice, vinegar and salt. Set the salsa aside.

3 ▲ Rinse the fish fillets and pat dry. Sprinkle on both sides with salt and pepper. Heat the oil and butter in a large non-stick frying pan. When hot, add the fish and cook until opaque throughout, 2–3 minutes on each side. Work in batches, if necessary.

4 ▲ Carefully transfer the fillets to warmed dinner plates. Top each with a spoonful of salsa. Serve additional salsa on the side.

Cornmeal-coated Gulf Prawns

SERVES 4

75g/3oz/¾ cup cornmeal

5–10ml/1–2 tsp cayenne pepper

2.5ml/½ tsp ground cumin

5ml/1 tsp salt

30ml/2 tbsp chopped fresh coriander
(cilantro) or parsley

900g/2lb large raw Gulf or king prawns
(jumbo shrimp), peeled and deveined

flour, for dredging

50ml/2fl oz/¼ cup vegetable oil

115g/4oz/1 cup grated Monterey Jack or
Cheddar cheese

TO SERVE

lime wedges

tomato salsa

1 Preheat the grill (broiler).

2 ▲ In a medium bowl, combine the
cornmeal, cayenne, cumin, salt and
coriander or parsley.

3 ▲ Coat the prawns lightly in flour,
then dip in water and roll in the
cornmeal mixture to coat.

4 ▼ Heat the oil in a non-stick
frying pan. When hot, add the prawns,
in batches if necessary. Cook until they
are opaque throughout, 2–3 minutes
on each side. Drain on kitchen paper.

5 ▲ Place the prawns in a large
baking dish, or individual dishes.
Sprinkle the cheese evenly over the
top. Grill (broil) about 7.5cm/3in
from the heat until the cheese melts,
2–3 minutes. Serve at once, with lime
wedges and tomato salsa.

Galveston Chicken

SERVES 4

1.6kg/3½lb chicken

juice of 1 lemon

4 garlic cloves, finely chopped

15ml/1 tbsp cayenne pepper

15ml/1 tbsp paprika

15ml/1 tbsp dried oregano

2.5ml/½ tsp coarsely ground black pepper

10ml/2 tsp olive oil

5ml/1 tsp salt

~ COOK'S TIP ~

Roasting chicken in an oven that
has not been preheated produces
a particularly crispy skin.

1 ▼ With a sharp knife or poultry
shears, remove the backbone from the
chicken. Turn it breast side up. With
the heel of your hand, press down to
break the breastbone, and open the
chicken flat like a book. Insert a
skewer through the chicken, at the
thighs, to keep it flat during cooking.

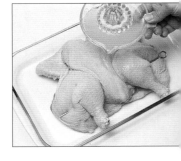

2 ▲ Place the chicken in a shallow
dish and pour over the lemon juice.

3 ▲ In a small bowl, combine the
garlic, cayenne, paprika, oregano,
pepper and oil. Mix well. Rub evenly
over the surface of the chicken.

4 Cover and leave to marinate for
2–3 hours at room temperature, or
chill overnight (return to room temperature before roasting).

5 Season the chicken with salt on
both sides. Transfer to a shallow
roasting pan.

6 Put the pan in a cold oven and set
the temperature to 200°C/400°F/Gas 6.
Roast until the chicken is done, about
1 hour, turning occasionally and basting
with the pan juices. To test if the
chicken is done, prick with a skewer:
the juices that run out should be clear.

Turkey Breasts with Tomato-Corn Salsa

SERVES 4

4 skinless turkey breast fillets, about
    175g/6oz each

30ml/2 tbsp fresh lemon juice

30ml/2 tbsp olive oil

2.5ml/½ tsp ground cumin

2.5ml/½ tsp dried oregano

5ml/1 tsp coarsely ground black pepper

salt

FOR THE SALSA

1 hot green chilli pepper

450g/1lb tomatoes, seeded and chopped

250g/9oz/1½ cups corn kernels, cooked,
    canned or thawed frozen

3 spring onions (scallions), chopped

15ml/1 tbsp chopped fresh parsley

30ml/2 tbsp chopped fresh
    coriander (cilantro)

30ml/2 tbsp fresh lemon juice

45ml/3 tbsp olive oil

5ml/1 tsp salt

1 ▲ With a meat mallet, pound the
turkey fillets between two sheets of
baking parchment until thin.

~ VARIATION ~

Use the cooked turkey, thinly
sliced and combined with the salsa,
as a filling for warmed flour tortillas.

2 ▲ In a shallow dish, combine the
lemon juice, oil, cumin, oregano and
pepper. Add the turkey and turn to
coat. Cover and leave to stand for at
least 2 hours, or chill overnight.

3 For the salsa, roast the chilli over a
gas flame, holding it with tongs, until
charred on all sides. (Alternatively,
char the skin under the grill/broiler.)
Leave to cool for 5 minutes. Wearing
rubber gloves, carefully rub off the
charred skin. For a less hot flavour,
discard the seeds. Chop the chilli finely
and place in a bowl.

4 ▲ Add the remaining salsa
ingredients to the chilli and toss well
to blend. Set aside.

5 Remove the turkey from the
marinade. Season lightly on both sides
with salt to taste.

6 Heat a ridged frying pan. When hot,
add the turkey breasts and cook until
browned, about 3 minutes. Turn and
cook the meat on the other side until it
is cooked through, 3–4 minutes more.
Serve the turkey at once, accompanied
by the salsa.

Spicy New Mexico Pork Stew

SERVES 6

250ml/8fl oz/1 cup water

15ml/1 tbsp tomato purée (paste)

4 garlic cloves, finely chopped

10ml/2 tsp dried oregano

12.5ml/2½ tsp ground cumin

10ml/2 tsp salt

15–45ml/1–3 tbsp red pepper flakes

900g/4lb boneless pork shoulder, cubed

2 onions, thickly sliced

warm flour tortillas, for serving

1 In a large casserole, combine the water, tomato purée, garlic, oregano, cumin and salt. Add red pepper flakes to taste and stir to mix.

2 ▲ Add the pork cubes and toss to coat them evenly. Cover and allow to marinate for 6–8 hours, or overnight, in the refrigerator.

3 Preheat oven to 150°C/300°F/Gas 2.

4 ▼ Cover the casserole and put in the oven. Cook for 1½ hours. Add the onions and cook for 1½ hours more. Serve with flour tortillas.

Turkey and Chorizo Tacos

SERVES 4

15ml/1 tbsp vegetable oil

450g/1lb turkey mince

5ml/1 tsp salt

5ml/1 tsp ground cumin

12 taco shells

75g/3oz chorizo, finely chopped

3 spring onions (scallions), chopped

2 tomatoes, chopped

150g/5oz/2½ cups shredded lettuce

250g/8oz/2 cups grated Monterey Jack or Cheddar cheese

TO SERVE

tomato salsa

guacamole

1 Preheat oven to 180°C/350°F/Gas 4.

2 ▲ Heat the oil in a non-stick frying pan. Add the turkey, salt and cumin and sauté over a medium heat until the turkey is cooked through, 5–8 minutes. Stir frequently to prevent large lumps from forming.

3 Meanwhile, arrange the taco shells in one layer on a large baking sheet and heat in the oven for about 10 minutes, or according to the directions on the packet.

4 Add the chorizo and spring onions to the turkey and stir to mix. Cook until just warmed through, stirring the mixture occasionally.

5 ▲ To assemble each taco, place 1–2 spoonfuls of the turkey mixture in the bottom of a warmed taco shell. Top with a generous sprinkling of chopped tomato, shredded lettuce and grated cheese.

6 Serve at once, with tomato salsa and guacamole.

~ **VARIATION** ~

For Chicken Tacos, use finely chopped chicken instead of turkey.

Spicy New Mexico Pork Stew (top), Turkey and Chorizo Tacos

Pork Chops with Sour Green Chilli Salsa

SERVES 4

30ml/2 tbsp vegetable oil

15ml/1 tbsp fresh lemon juice

10ml/2 tsp ground cumin

5ml/1 tsp dried oregano

salt and pepper

8 pork loin chops, about 2cm/¾in thick

FOR THE SALSA

2 hot green chilli peppers

2 green (bell) peppers, seeded
and chopped

1 tomato, peeled and seeded

½ onion, coarsely chopped

4 spring onions (scallions)

1 pickled jalapeño, stem removed

30ml/2 tbsp olive oil

30ml/2 tbsp fresh lime juice

45ml/3 tbsp cider vinegar

5ml/1 tsp salt

1 In a small bowl, combine the vegetable oil, lemon juice, cumin and oregano. Add pepper to taste and stir to blend.

2 ▼ Arrange the pork chops in one layer in a shallow dish. Brush each with the oil mixture on both sides. Cover and leave to stand for 2–3 hours, or chill overnight.

3 ▲ For the salsa, roast the chillies over a gas flame, holding them with tongs, until charred on all sides. (Alternatively, char the skins under the grill/broiler.) Leave to cool for 5 minutes. Wearing rubber gloves, remove the charred skin. For a milder flavour, discard the seeds.

4 Place the chillies in a food processor or blender. Add the remaining salsa ingredients. Process until finely chopped but do not purée.

5 Transfer the salsa to a heavy pan and simmer for 15 minutes, stirring occasionally. Set aside.

6 ▲ Season the pork chops. Heat a ridged frying pan. (Alternatively, preheat the grill/broiler.) When hot, add the pork chops and cook until browned, about 5 minutes. Turn and continue cooking until done, 5–7 minutes more. Work in batches, if necessary.

7 Serve at once, with the sour green chilli salsa.

Pork Fajitas

SERVES 6

juice of 3 limes

90ml/6 tbsp olive oil

5ml/1 tsp dried oregano

5ml/1 tsp ground cumin

2.5ml/½ tsp red pepper flakes

675g/1½lb pork tenderloin, cut across
    into 7.5cm/3in pieces

salt and pepper

2 large onions, halved and thinly sliced

1 large green (bell) pepper, seeded and
    thinly sliced lengthways

TO SERVE

12–15 flour tortillas, warmed

tomato salsa

guacamole

sour cream

1 ▲ In a shallow dish, combine the
lime juice, 45ml/3 tbsp of the oil, the
oregano, cumin and red pepper flakes
and mix well. Add the pork pieces and
turn to coat. Cover and leave to stand
for 1 hour, or chill overnight.

2 Remove the pieces of pork from the
marinade. Pat them dry and season
with salt and pepper.

3 Heat a ridged frying pan. When hot,
add the pork and cook over a high
heat, turning occasionally, until
browned on all sides and cooked
through, about 10–12 minutes.

4 ▼ Meanwhile, heat the remaining
oil in a large frying pan. Add the
onions and pepper. Stir in 2.5ml/½ tsp
salt and cook until the vegetables are
very soft, about 15 minutes. Stir
occasionally. Remove from the heat
and set aside.

5 ▲ Slice the pork pieces into thin
strips. Add to the onion mixture and
reheat briefly if necessary.

6 Spoon a little of the pork mixture on
to each tortilla. Add salsa, guacamole
and sour cream, and roll up.
Alternatively, the fajitas may be
assembled at the table.

Lamb Stew with Cornmeal Dumplings

SERVES 6

15ml/1 tbsp vegetable oil

1 large onion, chopped

1 large celery stick, chopped

1 red (bell) pepper, seeded and chopped

675g/1½lb boneless lamb, cubed

5ml/1 tsp salt, or to taste

3 medium tomatoes, cored and chopped

5ml/1 tsp ground cumin

pinch of ground cinnamon

1.5ml/¼ tsp cayenne, or to taste

1.2 litres/2 pints/5 cups beef stock

2 courgettes (zucchini), about 225g/8oz,
    quartered and chopped

FOR THE DUMPLINGS

115g/4oz/1 cup cornmeal

30ml/2 tbsp plain (all-purpose) flour

10ml/2 tsp baking powder

2.5ml/½ tsp salt

1 large (US extra large) egg, beaten

30ml/2 tbsp melted butter

75ml/2½fl oz/⅓ cup milk

1 Heat the oil in a large flameproof casserole. Add the onion and celery and cook over a medium heat until just soft, about 5 minutes.

2 ▲ Add the pepper, lamb and salt. Cook until the cubes of lamb are browned, 5–7 minutes more. Stir to brown them evenly.

3 Stir in the tomatoes, spices and stock. Bring to the boil, skimming off any foam that rises to the surface. Reduce the heat, cover and simmer gently for 25 minutes. From time to time, skim off any surface fat.

4 Meanwhile, for the dumplings, heat about 5cm/2in water in the bottom of a steamer.

5 ▲ Combine the cornmeal, flour, baking powder and salt in a large bowl. Make a well in the centre and add the egg, butter and milk. Stir with a fork until blended.

6 With your hands, shape the mixture into six balls, each about 5cm/2in in diameter.

7 ▲ When the water in the steamer is hot, place the dumplings in the steamer basket. Cover and steam for about 20 minutes. (If necessary, add boiling water to replenish the bottom of the steamer.)

8 About 5 minutes before the stew has finished cooking, add the courgette and stir to mix.

9 Ladle the stew into shallow bowls. Place a dumpling in the centre of each and serve at once.

Tamale Pie

SERVES 8

115g/4oz bacon, chopped

1 onion, finely chopped

450g/1lb lean steak mince

10–15ml/2–3 tsp chilli powder

5ml/1 tsp salt

300g/11oz peeled fresh or canned tomatoes

25g/1oz/⅓ cup chopped black olives

175g/6oz/1 cup corn kernels, freshly
   cooked, canned or thawed frozen

120ml/4fl oz/½ cup sour cream

115g/4oz/1 cup grated Monterey Jack cheese

FOR THE TAMALE CRUST

250–300ml/8–10fl oz/1–1¼ cups
   chicken stock

salt and pepper

175g/6 oz/1½ cups cornmeal

75g/3 oz/6 tbsp margarine or lard

2.5ml/½ tsp baking powder

50ml/2fl oz/¼ cup milk

1 Preheat the oven to 190°C/375°F/
Gas 5.

2 Cook the bacon in a large frying pan
until the fat is rendered, 2–3 minutes.
Pour off the excess fat, leaving 15–30ml/
1–2 tbsp. Add the onion and cook
until just softened, about 5 minutes.

3 ▲ Add the beef, chilli powder and
salt and cook for 5 minutes, stirring to
break up the meat. Stir in the tomatoes
and cook for 5 minutes more, breaking
them up with a spoon.

4 ▲ Add the olives, corn and sour
cream and mix well. Transfer to a
38cm/15in long rectangular or oval
baking dish. Set aside.

5 For the crust, bring the stock to the
boil in a pan; season it with salt and
pepper if necessary.

6 In a food processor, combine the
cornmeal, margarine or lard, baking
powder and milk. Process until
combined. With the machine on,
gradually pour in the hot stock until
a smooth, thick mixture is obtained.
If the mixture is too thick to spread,
add additional hot stock or water,
a little at a time.

7 Pour the mixture over the top of the
beef mixture, spreading it evenly with
a metal spatula.

8 Bake until the top is just browned,
about 20 minutes. Sprinkle the surface
evenly with the grated cheese and continue baking until melted and bubbling,
10–15 minutes more. Serve at once.

Beef Enchiladas

SERVES 4

900g/2lb chuck steak

15ml/1 tbsp vegetable oil,
    plus more for frying

5ml/1 tsp salt

5ml/1 tsp dried oregano

2.5ml/½ tsp ground cumin

1 onion, quartered

2 garlic cloves, crushed

1 litre/1¾pints/4 cups enchilada sauce

12 corn tortillas

115g/4oz/1 cup grated Monterey Jack cheese

TO SERVE

1 chopped spring onion (scallion)

sour cream

1 Preheat oven to 160°C/325°F/Gas 3.

2 ▲ Place the meat on a sheet of foil. Rub all over with the oil. Sprinkle both sides with the salt, oregano and cumin and rub in well. Add the onion and garlic. Top with another sheet of foil and roll up to seal the edges, leaving room for some steam expansion during cooking.

~ COOK'S TIP ~

Allow extra tortillas because some will break when dipping in the oil or sauce.

3 ▲ Place in a baking dish. Bake until the meat is tender enough to shred, about 3 hours. Remove the meat from the foil and shred with a fork. (This can be prepared 1–2 days in advance.)

4 ▲ Add 120ml/4fl oz/½ cup of the enchilada sauce to the beef. Stir well. Spoon a thin layer of enchilada sauce on the bottom of a rectangular baking dish, or into four individual baking dishes.

5 ▲ Place the remaining enchilada sauce in a frying pan and warm gently.

6 ▲ Put a 1cm/½in layer of vegetable oil in a second frying pan and heat until hot but not smoking. With tongs, lower a tortilla into the oil; the temperature is correct if it just sizzles. Cook for 2 seconds, then turn and cook the other side for 2 seconds. Lift out, drain over the frying pan, and then transfer to the frying pan of sauce. Dip into the sauce just to coat both sides.

7 ▲ Transfer the softened tortilla immediately to a plate. Spread 2–3 spoonfuls of the beef mixture down the centre of the tortilla. Roll up and place seam-side down in the prepared dish. Repeat the process for the remaining tortillas.

8 Spoon the remaining sauce from the frying pan over the enchiladas, spreading it to the ends. Sprinkle the cheese down the centre.

9 Bake until the cheese just melts, 10–15 minutes. Sprinkle with chopped spring onions and serve at once, with sour cream on the side.

Lone Star Steak and Potato Dinner

SERVES 4

45ml/3 tbsp olive oil

5 large garlic cloves, finely chopped

5ml/1 tsp coarsely ground black pepper

2.5ml/½ tsp ground allspice

5ml/1 tsp ground cumin

2.5ml/½ tsp chilli powder

10ml/2 tsp dried oregano

15ml/1 tbsp cider vinegar

4 boneless sirloin steaks,
    about 2cm/¾in thick

salt

FOR THE POTATOES

50ml/2fl oz/¼ cup vegetable oil

1 onion, chopped

5ml/1 tsp salt

900g/2lb potatoes, boiled and diced

30–75ml/2–5 tbsp chopped canned green
    chillies, according to taste

TO SERVE

tomato salsa

freshly cooked corn on the cob (optional)

1 ▲ Heat the olive oil in a heavy frying pan. When hot, add the garlic and cook, stirring often, until tender and just brown, about 3 minutes; do not let the garlic burn.

2 Transfer the garlic and oil to a shallow dish large enough to hold the steaks in one layer.

3 ▲ Add the pepper, spices, herbs and vinegar to the garlic and stir to blend thoroughly. If necessary, add just enough water to obtain a moderately thick paste.

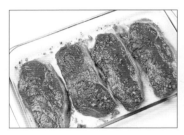

4 ▲ Add the steaks to the dish and turn to coat evenly on both sides with the spice mixture. Cover and leave to stand for 2 hours, or chill the steaks overnight. (Bring them back to room temperature before cooking.)

~ **VARIATION** ~

The steaks can also be cooked on a barbecue (charcoal grill). Prepare the fire, and when the coals are glowing red and covered with grey ash, spread them in a single layer. Cook the steaks in the centre of an oiled grill (broiling) rack set about 13cm/5in above the coals for 1 minute per side to sear them. Move them away from the centre and cook for 10–12 minutes longer for medium rare, turning once.

5 ▲ For the potatoes, heat the oil in a large non-stick frying pan. Add the onion and salt. Cook over a medium heat until softened, about 5 minutes. Add the potatoes and chillies. Cook, stirring occasionally, until well browned, 15–20 minutes.

6 ▲ Season the steaks on both sides with salt to taste. Heat a ridged frying pan. When hot, add the steaks and cook, turning once, until done to your taste. Allow about 2 minutes on each side for medium-rare, and 3–4 minutes for well done.

7 ▲ If necessary, briefly reheat the potatoes. Serve at once, with the tomato salsa and corn, if using.

Guacamole

MAKES 475ML/16FL OZ/2 CUPS

3 large ripe avocados

3 spring onions (scallions), finely chopped

1 garlic clove, finely chopped

15ml/1 tbsp olive oil

15ml/1 tbsp sour cream

2.5ml/½ tsp salt

30ml/2 tbsp fresh lemon or lime juice

1 ▲ Halve the avocados and remove the stones (pits). Peel the halves. Put the avocado flesh in a large bowl.

2 ▲ With a fork, mash the avocado flesh coarsely.

3 Add the spring onions, garlic, olive oil, sour cream, salt and lemon or lime juice. Mash until well blended, but do not overwork the mixture. Small chunks of avocado should still remain. Taste the guacamole and adjust the seasoning if necessary, with more salt or lemon or lime juice.

4 ▼ Transfer to a serving bowl. Serve at once.

~ COOK'S TIP ~

Guacamole does not keep well, but, if necessary, it can be stored in the refrigerator for a few hours. Cover the surface with clear film (plastic wrap) to prevent discolouring.

Tomato Salsa

MAKES 900ML/1½ PINTS/3¾ CUPS

1 hot green chilli pepper, seeded if desired, chopped

1 garlic clove

½ red onion, coarsely chopped

3 spring onions (scallions), chopped

15g/½oz/¼ cup fresh coriander (cilantro) leaves

675g/1½lb ripe tomatoes, seeded and coarsely chopped

1–3 canned green chillies

15ml/1 tbsp olive oil

30ml/2 tbsp fresh lime or lemon juice

2.5ml/½ tsp salt, or to taste

30–45ml/2–3 tbsp tomato juice or cold cold water

1 Place the green chilli, garlic, red onion, spring onions and coriander in a food processor or blender. Process until finely chopped.

2 ▼ Add the tomatoes, canned chillies, olive oil, lime or lemon juice, salt and tomato juice or water. Pulse on and off until just chopped; the salsa should be chunky.

3 ▲ Transfer to a bowl and taste for seasoning. Leave to stand for at least 30 minutes before serving. This salsa is best served the day it is made.

~ COOK'S TIP ~

For less heat, remove the seeds from the fresh and canned chillies.

Guacamole (top), Tomato Salsa

Tomato Rice

SERVES 4

475ml/16fl oz/2 cups unsalted chicken
  or beef stock

7.5ml/1½ tbsp vegetable oil

1 small onion, finely chopped

200g/7oz/1 cup long grain rice

5ml/1 tsp salt

2.5ml/½ tsp ground cumin

1 tomato, peeled, seeded and chopped

15ml/1 tbsp tomato purée (paste)

15ml/1 tbsp chopped fresh
  coriander (cilantro)

1 Place the stock in a pan and heat until just simmering. Remove from the heat, cover and set aside.

2 ▼ Heat the oil in a large heavy pan. Add the onion and rice and cook over a medium heat until the onion is just softened, about 5 minutes. Stir in the salt, cumin, tomato and tomato purée and then cook for 1 minute more, stirring frequently.

3 ▲ Gradually add the warm stock, stirring to blend. Bring to the boil, then lower the heat, cover and cook until the rice is tender and all the liquid is absorbed, 30–40 minutes.

4 Fluff the rice with a fork and stir in the coriander. Serve at once.

Enchilada Sauce

MAKES ABOUT 1.3 LITRES/2¼ PINTS/6 CUPS

4 x 450g/16oz cans peeled plum
  tomatoes, drained

3 garlic cloves, coarsely chopped

1 onion, coarsely chopped

30–60ml/2–4 tbsp ground red chilli

5ml/1 tsp cayenne pepper, or to taste

5ml/1 tsp ground cumin

2.5ml/½ tsp dried oregano

2.5ml/½ tsp salt

~ COOK'S TIP ~

Ground red chilli is not the same thing as chilli powder. If ground red chilli is unavailable, use hot red pepper flakes and strain the sauce before using.

1 ▼ Place the tomatoes, garlic and onion in a food processor or blender. Process until smooth.

2 Pour and scrape the mixture into a heavy pan.

3 ▲ Add the remaining ingredients and stir to blend. Bring to the boil, stirring occasionally. Boil for 2–3 minutes. Reduce the heat, cover and simmer for 15 minutes.

4 Dilute with 120–250ml/4–8fl oz/ ½–1 cup water, as necessary, to obtain a pouring consistency. Taste for seasoning; if a hotter sauce is wanted, add more cayenne, not ground chilli.

Tomato Rice (top), Enchilada Sauce

Navajo Fried Bread

MAKES 8 BREAD ROUNDS

225g/8oz/2 cups plain (all-purpose) flour

10ml/2 tsp baking powder

2.5ml/½ tsp salt

250ml/8fl oz/1 cup lukewarm water

oil for frying

1 Sift the flour, baking powder and salt into a bowl. Pour in the water and stir quickly with a fork until the dough gathers into a ball.

2 ▼ With floured hands, gently knead the dough by rolling it around the bowl. Do not overknead; the dough should be very soft.

3 ▲ Divide the dough into eight pieces. With floured hands, pat each piece into a round about 13cm/5in in diameter. Place the rounds on a floured baking sheet.

4 Put a 2.5cm/1in layer of oil in a heavy frying pan and heat until hot but not smoking. To test the temperature, drop in a small piece of dough; if it bubbles at once, the oil is ready.

5 ▲ Add the dough rounds to the hot oil and press down with a slotted spoon to submerge them. Release the dough and cook until puffed and golden on both sides, 3–5 minutes total, turning for even browning. Fry in batches, if necessary.

6 Drain the bread on kitchen paper and serve at once. They are good as an accompaniment for chilli or with grated cheese and an assortment of southwestern salsas. (Fried bread will not keep.)

Bean Dip

MAKES 750ML/1¼ PINTS/3 CUPS

275g/10oz/1½ cups dried pinto beans, soaked overnight and drained

1 bay leaf

45ml/3 tbsp sea salt

15ml/1 tbsp vegetable oil

1 small onion, sliced

1 garlic clove, finely chopped

2–4 canned hot green chillies (optional)

75ml/2½fl oz/⅓ cup sour cream, plus more for garnishing

2.5ml/½ tsp ground cumin

hot pepper sauce

15ml/1 tbsp chopped fresh coriander (cilantro)

tortilla chips, to serve

1 ▲ Place the beans in a large pan. Add fresh cold water to cover and the bay leaf. Bring to the boil, then cover and simmer for 30 minutes.

2 Add the sea salt and continue simmering until the beans are tender, about 30 minutes or more.

3 Drain the beans, reserving 120ml/4fl oz/½ cup of the cooking liquid. Leave to cool slightly. Discard the bay leaf.

4 Heat the oil in a non-stick frying pan. Add the onion and garlic and cook over a low heat until just softened, 8–10 minutes, stirring occasionally.

5 ▲ Place the beans, onion mixture, chillies, if using, and the reserved cooking liquid in a food processor or blender. Process until the mixture resembles a coarse purée.

6 ▼ Transfer to a bowl and stir in the sour cream, cumin and hot pepper sauce to taste. Stir in the coriander, garnish with sour cream and serve warm, with tortilla chips.

Chocolate Cinnamon Cake with Banana Sauce

SERVES 6

115g/4oz semisweet chocolate, chopped

115g/4oz/½ cup unsalted butter,
    at room temperature

15ml/1 tbsp instant coffee powder

5 eggs, separated

200g/7oz/1 cup granulated sugar

115g/4oz/1 cup plain (all-purpose) flour

10ml/2 tsp ground cinnamon

For the sauce

4 ripe bananas

50g/2oz/¼ cup soft light brown sugar

15ml/1 tbsp fresh lemon juice

175ml/6fl oz/¾ cup whipping cream

15ml/1 tbsp rum (optional)

---

1 Preheat the oven to 180°C/350°F/
Gas 4. Grease a 20cm/8in round cake
tin (pan).

2 ▲ Combine the chocolate and
butter in the top of a double boiler or
in a heatproof bowl set over hot water.
Stir until melted. Remove from the
heat and stir in the coffee. Set aside.

3 Beat the egg yolks with the
granulated sugar until thick and
lemon-coloured. Add the chocolate
mixture and beat on low speed just to
blend the mixtures evenly.

4 Sift together the flour and
cinnamon into a bowl.

5 ▲ In another bowl, beat the egg
whites until they hold stiff peaks.

6 ▲ Fold a dollop of whites into the
chocolate mixture to lighten it. Fold in
the remaining whites in three batches,
alternating with the sifted flour.

7 ▲ Pour the mixture into the
prepared tin. Bake until a skewer
inserted in the centre comes out clean,
40–50 minutes. Turn out the cake on
to a wire rack.

8 Preheat the broiler (grill).

9 ▲ For the sauce, slice the bananas
into a shallow, heatproof dish. Add
the brown sugar and lemon juice and
stir to blend. Place under the grill
(broiler) and cook, stirring occasionally
until the sugar is caramelized and
bubbling, about 8 minutes.

10 ▲ Transfer the bananas to a bowl
and mash with a fork until almost
smooth. Stir in the cream and rum, if
using. Serve the cake and sauce warm.

~ VARIATION ~

For a special occasion, top the cake
slices with a scoop of ice cream
(rum and raisin, chocolate or vanilla)
before adding the banana sauce.
With this addition, the dessert
will make at least 8 portions.

Mexican Hot Fudge Sundaes

SERVES 4

600ml/1 pint vanilla ice cream

600ml/1 pint coffee ice cream

2 large ripe bananas, sliced

whipped cream

toasted sliced almonds

FOR THE SAUCE

50ml/2fl oz/¼ cup soft light brown sugar

185g/6½oz/½ cup light corn syrup

45ml/3 tbsp strong black coffee

5ml/1 tsp ground cinnamon

150g/5oz bittersweet chocolate,
  broken up

75ml/2½fl oz/⅓ cup whipping cream

45ml/3 tbsp coffee liqueur (optional)

1 ▼ For the sauce, combine the brown sugar, corn syrup, coffee and cinnamon in a heavy pan. Bring to the boil. Boil the mixture, stirring constantly, for about 5 minutes.

2 ▲ Remove from the heat and stir in the chocolate. When melted and smooth, stir in the cream and liqueur, if using. Leave the sauce to cool just to lukewarm, or, if made ahead, reheat gently while assembling the sundaes.

3 ▲ Fill sundae dishes with one scoop each of vanilla and coffee ice cream.

4 ▲ Arrange the bananas on the top of each dish. Pour the warm sauce over the bananas, then top each sundae with a generous rosette of whipped cream. Top with toasted almonds and serve at once.

New Mexico Christmas Biscochitos

MAKES 24

175g/6oz/1½ cups plain
  (all-purpose) flour

5ml/1 tsp baking powder

pinch of salt

50g/2oz/½ cup unsalted butter, softened

90g/3½oz/½ cup granulated sugar

1 egg

5ml/1 tsp whole aniseed

15ml/1 tbsp brandy

50g/2oz/¼ cup granulated sugar mixed
  with 2.5ml/½ tsp ground cinnamon,
  for sprinkling

1 Sift together the flour, baking powder and salt. Set aside.

2 ▲ In a bowl, beat the butter with the sugar until soft and fluffy. Add the egg, aniseed and brandy and beat until incorporated. Fold in the dry ingredients just until blended to a dough. Chill for 30 minutes.

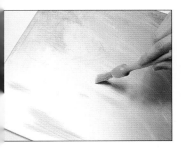

3 ▲ Preheat the oven to 180°C/350°F/Gas 4. Grease two baking sheets.

4 On a lightly floured surface, roll out the chilled biscuit essential to about 3mm/⅛in thickness.

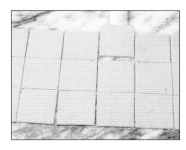

5 ▲ With a cutter, pastry wheel or knife, cut the mixture into squares, diamonds or other shapes. The traditional shape for biscochitos is a fleur-de-lis.

6 ▲ Place on the prepared baking sheets and sprinkle lightly with the cinnamon sugar.

7 Bake until just barely golden, about 10 minutes. Cool on the sheet for 5 minutes before transferring to a wire rack to cool completely. The biscuits can be kept in an airtight container for up to 1 week.

Pueblo Pastelitos

MAKES 16

450g/1lb/2 cups dried fruit, such as apricots or prunes

115g/4oz/1/2 cup soft light brown sugar

65g/21/2oz/1/2 cup raisins

50g/2oz/1/2 cup pine nuts or chopped almonds

2.5ml/1/2 tsp ground cinnamon

oil for frying

45ml/3 tbsp granulated sugar mixed with 5ml/1 tsp ground cinnamon, for sprinkling

FOR THE PASTRY

225g/8oz/2 cups plain (all-purpose) flour

1.5ml/1/4 tsp baking powder

1.5ml/1/4 tsp salt

10ml/2 tsp granulated sugar

50g/2oz/1/4 cup unsalted butter, chilled

25g/1oz/2 tbsp lard or white cooking fat

60–75ml/4–5 tbsp iced water

1 ▲ For the pastry, sift the flour, baking powder, salt and sugar into a bowl. With a pastry blender, cut in the butter until the mixture resembles breadcrumbs, or rub in with your fingertips. Sprinkle with 60ml/4 tbsp of the iced water and mix until the pastry holds together. If the pastry is too crumbly, add a little more water, 5ml/1 tsp at a time.

2 Gather the pastry into a ball and flatten into a disk. Wrap the pastry in clear film (plastic wrap) and chill for at least 30 minutes.

3 ▲ Place the dried fruit in a medium pan and add cold water to cover. Bring to the boil, then simmer gently until the fruit is soft enough to purée, about 30 minutes.

4 ▲ Drain the fruit and place in a food processor or blender. Process until smooth. Return the fruit purée to the pan. Add the brown sugar and cook, stirring constantly, until thick, about 5 minutes. Remove from the heat and stir in the raisins, pine nuts or almonds and cinnamon. Allow the mixture to cool.

5 Roll out the chilled pastry to about 3mm/1/8in thick. Stamp out rounds with a 10cm/4in pastry (cookie) cutter. (Roll and cut out in two batches if it is more convenient.)

~ COOK'S TIP ~

If you prefer, the pastry and the filling can both be made up to 2 days in advance and chilled.

6 ▲ Place a spoonful of the fruit filling in the centre of each round.

7 ▲ Moisten the edge with a brush dipped in water, then fold over the dough to form a half-moon shape. With a fork, crimp the rounded edge.

8 ▲ Put a 1cm/1/2in layer of oil in a heavy frying pan and heat until hot but not smoking. (To test, drop a scrap of dough in the oil; if the oil sizzles, it is hot enough.) Add the pastelitos, a few at a time, and fry until golden on both sides, about 1 1/2 minutes per side.

9 Drain briefly on kitchen paper, then sprinkle with the cinnamon sugar. Serve the pastelitos warm.

Flan

SERVES 8–10

800ml/1⅓ pints/3½ cups milk

120ml/4fl oz/½ cup whipping cream

200g/7oz/1 cup granulated sugar

1 cinnamon stick

8 large (US extra large) eggs

5ml/1 tsp vanilla extract

FOR THE CARAMEL

130g/4½oz/⅔ cup granulated sugar

50ml/2fl oz/¼ cup water

1 In a medium pan, combine the milk, cream, sugar and cinnamon. Scald over a medium heat, stirring. Remove, cover and leave to stand for 30 minutes.

2 For the caramel, combine the sugar and water in a small, heavy pan over medium-high heat.

3 Bring to the boil, then simmer until the syrup begins to colour; do not stir. When the syrup is a deep golden brown, dip the base of the pan in cold water to stop it cooking.

4 ▲ Quickly pour the caramel syrup into a 3 litre/5 pint/2½ quart dish and tilt the dish to coat the bottom evenly.

5 Preheat oven to 180°C/350°F/Gas 4.

6 ▲ Reheat the milk mixture just to warm. Remove the cinnamon stick.

7 In a large bowl, combine the eggs and vanilla and mix together. Pour the milk mixture over the egg mixture, stirring constantly.

8 ▲ Place the caramel-coated dish in a large baking dish and add just enough hot water to come about 5cm/2in up the side of the dish. Pour the egg mixture through a strainer into the dish. Cover with foil.

9 Bake until the custard is just set, 40–50 minutes. Leave to cool in the water, then chill for at least 4 hours.

10 To turn out, run a knife around the inside of the dish. Place an inverted plate on top and flip over to release the flan. Scrape any remaining caramel on to the flan. Serve cold.

Southwestern Rice Pudding

SERVES 4–6

40g/1½oz/¼ cup raisins

475ml/16fl oz/2 cups water

200g/7oz/1 cup short-grain rice

1 cinnamon stick

25g/1oz/2 tbsp granulated sugar

475ml/16fl oz/2 cups milk

250ml/8fl oz/1 cup canned sweetened
  coconut cream

2.5ml/½ tsp vanilla extract

15ml/1 tbsp butter

25g/1oz/⅓ cup grated fresh coconut

ground cinnamon, for sprinkling

1 ▲ Put the raisins in a small bowl
and add water to cover. Leave to soak.

2 ▲ In a medium pan, bring the
measurement water to the boil. Add
the rice, cinnamon stick and sugar and
stir. Return to the boil, then lower the
heat, cover and simmer gently until
the liquid is absorbed, 15–20 minutes.

3 ▼ Meanwhile, combine the milk,
coconut cream and vanilla in a bowl.
Drain the raisins.

4 Remove the cinnamon stick from
the pan. Add the milk mixture and
drained raisins to the rice and stir to
mix. Continue cooking, covered and
stirring often, until the mixture is just
thick, about 20 minutes. Do not
overcook the rice.

5 Preheat the grill (broiler).

6 Transfer the mixture to a heatproof
serving dish. Dot with the butter and
sprinkle the grated coconut evenly
over the surface. Grill (broil) about
13cm/5in from the heat until the top is
just browned, 3–5 minutes. Sprinkle
with cinnamon. Serve warm or cold.

CALIFORNIA

TRENDS, CULINARY AND
OTHERWISE, SEEM TO BEGIN HERE.
THE LIFESTYLE – WEST COAST
INFORMALITY, WITH ITS EMPHASIS
ON OUTDOOR LIVING AND DINING –
DICTATES A UNIQUE CUISINE. FOOD
GURUS AND THEIR BOUTIQUE FARMS
BRING DIVERSE AGRICULTURAL
PRODUCTS INCLUDING FRUIT,
BERRIES, NUTS, AVOCADOS AND
ARTICHOKES TO OUR TABLES YEAR
ROUND, AND CALIFORNIA WINE IS
APPRECIATED WORLDWIDE.

Tomato Sandwiches with Olive Mayonnaise

SERVES 6

1 garlic clove, finely chopped

30ml/2 tbsp olive oil

5ml/1 tsp red wine vinegar

2 beefsteak tomatoes

25g/1oz/½ cup fresh basil leaves or
  parsley, chopped

1.5ml/¼ tsp salt

black pepper

7 brine-cured black olives, pitted and
  finely chopped

90ml/6 tbsp mayonnaise

12 slices of sourdough bread,
  lightly toasted

6 large lettuce leaves

1 ▼ Combine the garlic, oil and vinegar in a small bowl and mix together. Alternatively, shake the ingredients in a screwtop jar until blended. Set the dressing aside.

2 ▲ Core the tomatoes. With a sharp knife, cut six shallow lengthways slits in the skin of each to make the tomatoes easier to eat; do not cut too deeply into the flesh. Cut the tomatoes crossways into thin slices.

3 Place the tomato slices in a shallow dish. Add the oil and vinegar dressing, basil or parsley, salt and pepper to taste. Leave to marinate for at least 30 minutes.

4 ▲ In another bowl, stir together the olives and mayonnaise.

5 ▲ Spread six slices of bread with the olive mayonnaise. Arrange the tomato slices on top and drizzle over any remaining dressing from the bowl. Top each with a lettuce leaf. Cover with the remaining bread and serve.

Gazpacho

SERVES 4

½ cucumber (about 225g/8oz),
   coarsely chopped

½ green (bell) pepper, seeded and
   coarsely chopped

½ red (bell) pepper, seeded and
   coarsely chopped

1 large tomato, coarsely chopped

2 spring onions (scallions), chopped

hot pepper sauce (optional)

45ml/3 tbsp chopped fresh parsley or
   coriander (cilantro)

croutons, for serving

FOR THE SOUP BASE

450g/1lb ripe tomatoes, peeled, seeded
   and chopped

15ml/1 tbsp tomato ketchup

30ml/2 tbsp tomato purée (paste)

1.5ml/¼ tsp granulated sugar

3.5ml/¾ tsp salt

5ml/1 tsp pepper

50ml/2fl oz/¼ cup sherry vinegar

175ml/6fl oz/¾ cup olive oil

350ml/12fl oz/1½ cups tomato juice

2 Add the tomato ketchup, tomato purée, sugar, salt, pepper, vinegar and oil and pulse on and off three or four times, just to blend. Transfer to a large bowl. Stir in the tomato juice.

3 ▼ Place the cucumber and peppers in the food processor or blender and pulse on and off until finely chopped; do not overmix.

4 ▲ Reserve about 30ml/2 tbsp of the chopped vegetables for garnishing; stir the remainder into the soup base. Taste for seasoning. Mix in the chopped tomato, spring onions and a dash of hot pepper sauce, if you like. Chill well.

5 To serve, ladle into bowls and sprinkle with the reserved chopped vegetables, chopped fresh parsley or coriander, and croutons.

1 ▲ For the soup base, put the tomatoes in a food processor or blender and pulse on and off until just smooth, scraping the sides of the container occasionally.

Individual Goat's Cheese Tarts

SERVES 6

6–8 sheets filo pastry (about 115g/4oz)

50g/2oz/¼ cup butter, melted

350g/12oz firm log-shaped goat's cheese, rind removed

9 cherry tomatoes, quartered

120ml/4fl oz/½ cup milk

2 eggs

30ml/2 tbsp whipping cream

pinch of ground white pepper

mixed green salad, to serve (optional)

~ COOK'S TIP ~

Keep the filo pastry under a damp cloth while working to prevent the sheets from drying out.

1 Preheat oven to 190°C/375°F/Gas 5. Grease six 10cm/4in tart tins (pans).

2 ▲ For each tart, cut out four circles of filo pastry, each about 12cm/4½in in diameter. Place one circle in the tin and brush with some melted butter. Top with another filo circle and brush with butter. Continue until there are four layers of filo pastry; do not butter the last layer. Repeat the procedure for the remaining three tins.

3 ▲ Place the pastry-lined tins on a baking sheet. Cut the goat's cheese log into six slices. Place a slice in each of the pastry cases.

4 ▲ Arrange the tomato quarters around the cheese slices.

5 ▲ Combine the milk, eggs, cream and pepper in a measuring jug (cup) or bowl and whisk to mix. Pour into the pastry cases, filling them almost to the top.

6 Bake until puffed and golden, 30–40 minutes. Serve hot or warm, with a mixed green salad if you like.

Turkey and Avocado Pitta Bread Pizzas

SERVES 4

8 plum tomatoes, quartered

45–60ml/3–4 tbsp olive oil

salt and pepper

1 large ripe avocado

8 pitta bread rounds

6–7 slices of cooked turkey, chopped

1 onion, thinly sliced

275g/10oz/2½ cups grated Monterey Jack or Cheddar cheese

30ml/2 tbsp chopped fresh coriander (cilantro)

1 Preheat oven to 230°C/450°F/Gas 8.

2 ▲ Place the tomatoes in a baking dish. Drizzle over 15ml/1 tbsp of the olive oil and season with salt and pepper. Bake for 30 minutes; do not stir.

3 Remove the baking dish from the oven and mash the tomatoes with a fork, removing the skins as you mash. Set aside.

4 ▲ Peel and stone (pit) the avocado. Cut into 16 thin slices.

5 Brush the edges of the pitta breads with oil. Arrange the breads on two baking sheets.

6 ▼ Spread each pitta with mashed tomato, almost to the edges.

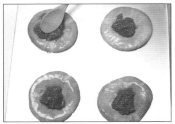

7 ▲ Top each with two avocado slices. Sprinkle with the turkey, then add a few onion slices. Season with salt and pepper. Sprinkle on the cheese.

8 Place one sheet in the middle of the oven and bake until the cheese begins to melt, 15–20 minutes. Sprinkle with half the coriander and serve. Meanwhile, bake the second batch of pizzas to serve them hot.

Crab Louis

SERVES 4

225g/8oz/4 cups Little Gem (Bibb)
  lettuce leaves

350g/12oz/2 cups fresh crab meat

4 hard-boiled eggs, sliced

4 tomatoes, quartered

½ green (bell) pepper, seeded and thinly sliced

50g/2oz/½ cup pitted black olives, sliced

FOR THE DRESSING

250ml/8fl oz/1 cup mayonnaise

10ml/2 tsp fresh lemon juice

50ml/2fl oz/¼ cup chilli sauce

½ green (bell) pepper, seeded and
  finely chopped

5ml/1 tsp prepared horseradish

5ml/1 tsp Worcestershire sauce

1 ▲ For the dressing, combine all
the ingredients in a bowl and mix
well. Set aside.

2 Line four salad plates with the
lettuce leaves. Heap the crab meat in
the centre. Arrange hard-boiled eggs
and tomatoes around the outside.

3 ▼ Spoon some of the dressing over
the crab. Arrange the green pepper
slices on top and sprinkle with the
olives. Serve at once, with the
remaining dressing.

Poolside Tuna Salad

SERVES 4–6

175g/6oz radishes

1 cucumber

3 celery sticks

1 yellow (bell) pepper

175g/6oz cherry tomatoes, halved

4 spring onions (scallions), thinly sliced

2.5ml/½ tsp salt, or to taste

50ml/2fl oz/¼ cup fresh lemon juice

50ml/2fl oz/¼ cup olive oil

black pepper

2 x 200g/7oz cans tuna, drained

30ml/2 tbsp chopped fresh parsley

lettuce leaves, to serve

twisted lemon peel, to garnish

1 Cut the radishes, cucumber, celery
and pepper into pea-size dice. Place in
a large, shallow dish. Add the tomatoes
and spring onions.

2 ▼ In a small bowl, stir together the
salt and lemon juice with a fork until
dissolved. Pour this over the vegetable
mixture. Add the oil and pepper to
taste. Stir to blend. Cover and leave to
stand for 1 hour.

3 Add the tuna and parsley and toss
gently until combined.

4 ▲ Arrange the lettuce leaves on a
serving dish and heap the salad in the
centre. Garnish with the lemon peel.

~ **VARIATION** ~

Prepare the vegetables as above
and add the parsley. Arrange
lettuce leaves on individual plates
and divide the vegetable mixture
between them. Place a mound of
tuna on top of each and finish
with a dollop of mayonnaise.

Crab Louis (top), Poolside Tuna Salad

Goat's Cheese Salad

<u>SERVES 4</u>

30ml/2 tbsp olive oil

4 slices of French bread, 1cm/½in thick

450g/1lb/8 cups mixed salad greens, such as curly endive, radicchio and red oak leaf, torn into small pieces

4 firm goat's cheese rounds, about 50g/2oz each, rind removed

1 yellow or red (bell) pepper, seeded and finely diced

1 small red onion, thinly sliced

45ml/3 tbsp chopped fresh parsley

30ml/2 tbsp chopped fresh chives

<u>FOR THE DRESSING</u>

30ml/2 tbsp wine vinegar

1.5ml/¼ tsp salt

5ml/1 tsp wholegrain mustard

75ml/5 tbsp olive oil

black pepper

1 For the dressing, mix the vinegar and salt with a fork until dissolved. Stir in the mustard. Gradually stir in the oil until blended. Season with pepper and set aside.

2 Preheat the grill (broiler).

3 ▲ Heat the oil in a frying pan. When hot, add the bread slices and cook until golden, about 1 minute. Turn and cook the other side, for about 30 seconds more. Drain on kitchen paper and set aside.

4 ▲ Place the salad greens in a bowl. Add 45ml/3 tbsp of the dressing and toss to coat. Divide the dressed leaves between four salad plates.

5 ▲ Put the goat's cheeses, cut side up, on a baking sheet and grill (broil) until bubbling and golden, 1–2 minutes.

6 Set one goat's cheese on each slice of bread and place in the centre of each plate. Scatter the diced pepper, red onion, parsley and chives over the salad. Drizzle with the remaining dressing and serve.

~ VARIATION ~

For a more substantial main course salad, increase the amount of greens and make double the quantity of dressing. Add 300g/11oz/ 2 cups sliced cooked green beans and 300g/11oz/2 cups diced ham to the greens, and toss with half the dressing. Top with the grilled goat's cheeses and remaining dressing.

Three-bean and Lentil Salad

SERVES 6

1 cup dried chickpeas, soaked overnight and drained

1 cup dried red kidney beans, soaked overnight and drained

3 bay leaves

30ml/2 tbsp sea salt

50g/2oz/½ cup lentils

225g/8oz fresh green beans, cut in 2.5cm/1in slices and cooked

1 small red onion, finely chopped

3 spring onions (scallions), chopped

15ml/1 tbsp chopped fresh parsley

FOR THE DRESSING

75–90ml/5–6 tbsp red wine vinegar

5ml/1 tsp salt

10ml/2 tsp Dijon-style mustard

90ml/6 tbsp olive oil

1 garlic clove, finely chopped

black pepper

3 Halfway through the beans' cooking time, put the lentils in a large pan and add cold water to cover and the remaining bay leaf. Bring to the boil, then cover and simmer until just tender, 30–40 minutes.

4 ▼ As the lentils and the beans finish cooking, drain thoroughly in a colander and place them in a large bowl. Discard the bay leaves.

5 ▲ Add the green beans, red onion, spring onions and parsley to the bowl. Add the dressing and toss well.

6 Taste the salad and adjust the seasoning, adding more vinegar, salt and pepper if you want. Serve the salad at room temperature.

1 ▲ For the dressing, in a bowl mix 60ml/4 tbsp of the vinegar and the salt with a fork until dissolved. Stir in the mustard. Gradually stir in the oil until blended. Add the garlic and pepper to taste. Set aside.

2 Put the chickpeas and kidney beans in separate large pans. To each, add fresh cold water to cover and a bay leaf. Bring to the boil, then cover and simmer for 30 minutes. Add half the sea salt to each pan and continue simmering until tender, 30 minutes– 1½ hours more.

Artichoke Pasta Salad

SERVES 4

105ml/7 tbsp olive oil

1 red (bell) pepper, quartered, seeded and thinly sliced

1 onion, halved and thinly sliced

5ml/1 tsp dried thyme

salt and pepper

45ml/3 tbsp sherry vinegar

450g/1lb pasta shapes, such as penne or fusilli

2 x 175g/6oz jars marinated artichoke hearts, drained and thinly sliced

150g/5oz cooked broccoli, chopped

20–25 salt-cured black olives, pitted and chopped

30ml/2 tbsp chopped fresh parsley

1 ▼ Heat 30ml/2 tbsp of the oil in a non-stick frying pan. Add the red pepper and onion and cook over a low heat until just soft, 8–10 minutes, stirring occasionally.

2 ▲ Stir in the thyme, 1.5ml/¼ tsp salt and the vinegar. Cook, stirring, for 30 seconds more, then set aside.

3 ▲ Bring a large pan of salted water to the boil. Add the pasta and cook until just tender (following the packet instructions for timing). Drain, rinse with hot water then drain again well. Transfer to a large bowl. Add 30ml/2 tbsp of the oil and toss well to coat.

4 ▲ Add the artichokes, broccoli, olives, parsley, onion mixture and remaining oil to the pasta. Season with salt and pepper. Stir to blend. Leave to stand for at least 1 hour before serving, or chill overnight. Serve at room temperature.

Asparagus with Creamy Raspberry Vinaigrette

SERVES 4

675g/1½lb thin asparagus spears

30ml/2 tbsp raspberry vinegar

2.5ml/½ tsp salt

5ml/1 tsp Dijon-style mustard

75ml/5 tbsp sunflower oil

30ml/2 tbsp sour cream or natural (plain) yogurt

white pepper

175g/6oz/1 cup raspberries, to garnish

1 Fill a large wide pan, frying pan or wok with water about 10cm/4in deep and bring to the boil.

2 ▲ Trim the tough ends of the asparagus spears. If you want, remove the "scales" using a vegetable peeler.

4 ▼ With a slotted fish slice or metal spatula, carefully remove the asparagus bundles from the boiling water and immerse in cold water to stop them cooking. Drain and untie the bundles. Pat dry with kitchen paper. Chill the asparagus for at least 1 hour.

5 ▲ Combine the vinegar and salt in a bowl and stir with a fork until dissolved. Stir in the mustard. Gradually stir in the oil until blended. Add the sour cream or yogurt and pepper to taste.

6 To serve, place the asparagus on individual plates and drizzle the dressing across the middle of the spears. Garnish with the fresh raspberries and serve.

3 ▲ Tie the asparagus spears into two bundles. Lower into the boiling water and cook, keeping the bundles upright, until just tender, about 2 minutes.

California Taco Salad with Beef

Serves 4

10ml/2 tsp vegetable oil
450g/1lb lean beef mince
1 small onion, chopped
2.5ml/½ tsp salt
1.5ml/¼ tsp cayenne pepper, or to taste
175g/6oz/1 cup corn kernels (fresh, frozen or canned)
150g/5oz/1 cup cooked or canned kidney beans
15ml/1 tbsp chopped fresh coriander (cilantro), plus more coriander leaves to garnish
1 small head of romaine lettuce
3 tomatoes, quartered
225g/8oz/2 cups grated Monterey Jack or Cheddar cheese
1 avocado
40g/1½oz/⅓ cup pitted black olives, sliced
4 spring onions (scallions), chopped
tortilla chips, to serve

For the dressing

45ml/3 tbsp white wine vinegar
2.5ml/½ tsp salt
5ml/1 tsp Dijon-style mustard
30ml/2 tbsp buttermilk
150ml/¼ pint/⅔ cup vegetable oil
1 small garlic clove, finely chopped
5ml/1 tsp ground cumin
5ml/1 tsp dried oregano
1.5ml/¼ tsp pepper

~ VARIATIONS ~

For California Taco Salad with Chicken, substitute 450g/1lb skinless chicken breast fillets, finely diced, for the minced beef. Chickpeas may be used in place of the kidney beans. Although frozen or canned corn is convenient, freshly cooked corn kernels scraped from the cob give added moisture and extra flavour.

1 ▲ For the dressing, mix the vinegar and salt with a fork until dissolved. Stir in the mustard and buttermilk. Gradually stir in the oil until blended. Add the garlic, cumin, oregano and pepper and set aside.

2 ▲ Heat the oil in a non-stick frying pan. Add the beef, onion, salt and cayenne and cook until just browned, 5–7 minutes. Stir frequently to break up the lumps. Drain and leave to cool.

3 ▲ In a large bowl, combine the beef, corn, kidney beans and chopped coriander and toss to blend.

4 ▲ Stack the lettuce leaves on top of one another and slice thinly, crossways, into shreds. Place in another bowl and toss with 50ml/2fl oz/¼ cup of the dressing. Divide the shredded lettuce between four dinner plates.

5 ▲ Heap the meat mixture in the centre of each plate. Arrange the tomatoes at the edge. Sprinkle with the grated cheese.

6 ▲ Peel, stone (pit) and dice the avocado. Scatter on top of the salad with the olives and spring onions.

7 Pour the remaining dressing over the salads. Garnish with coriander. Serve with tortilla chips.

Cheesy Courgette Casserole

SERVES 4

1 garlic clove, crushed with a knife

30ml/2 tbsp olive oil or melted butter

900g/2lb courgettes (zucchini)

salt and pepper

2 cups grated Monterey Jack or Cheddar cheese

2 eggs

350ml/12fl oz/1½ cups milk

~ VARIATIONS ~

For a spicier version, replace the cheese with a chilli-flavoured cheese, such as Jalapeño Jack, and toss the courgettes in 10ml/2 tsp chilli powder.

1 Preheat oven to 190°C/375°F/Gas 5.

2 ▼ Rub the garlic clove around the inside of a baking dish, pressing hard to extract the juice; discard the garlic. Grease the dish with half the oil or melted butter.

3 ▲ Cut the courgettes across into 6mm/¼in slices. Place them in a bowl and toss with the remaining oil or melted butter and salt to taste.

4 ▲ Arrange half the courgette slices in an even layer in the baking dish. Sprinkle with half the cheese. Add the remaining courgette slices, spreading them evenly over the top.

5 ▲ Combine the eggs, milk, 2.5ml/½ tsp salt and pepper to taste in a bowl and whisk together. Pour over the courgettes. Sprinkle with the remaining grated cheese.

6 Cover with foil and bake for about 30 minutes. Remove the foil and continue baking until the top is browned, 30–40 minutes more. Serve hot, warm or cold.

San Francisco Chicken Wings

SERVES 4

75ml/2½fl oz/⅓ cup soy sauce

15ml/1 tbsp soft light brown sugar

15ml/1 tbsp rice vinegar

30ml/2 tbsp dry sherry

juice of 1 orange

5cm/2in strip of orange peel

1 star anise

5ml/1 tsp cornflour (cornstarch)

50ml/2fl oz/¼ cup water

15ml/1 tbsp finely chopped fresh
   root ginger

1.5–5ml/¼–1 tsp Oriental chilli-garlic
   sauce, to taste

1.6kg/3½lb chicken wings (22–24),
   tips removed

1 Preheat oven to 200°C/400°F/Gas 6.

2 ▲ Combine the soy sauce, brown sugar, vinegar, sherry, orange juice and peel and star anise in a pan. Bring to the boil over a medium heat.

3 ▲ Combine the cornflour and water in a small bowl and stir until blended. Add to the boiling soy sauce mixture, stirring well. Boil for 1 minute more, stirring constantly.

4 ▼ Remove the soy sauce mixture from the heat and stir in the finely chopped ginger and chilli-garlic sauce.

5 ▲ Arrange the chicken wings, in one layer, in a large baking dish. Pour over the soy sauce mixture and stir to coat the wings evenly.

6 Bake until tender and browned, 30–40 minutes, basting occasionally. Serve the wings hot or warm.

Swordfish with Pepper and Orange Relish

SERVES 4

75ml/5 tbsp olive oil

1 large fennel bulb, cut into 6mm/
¼in dice

1 red (bell) pepper, seeded and cut into
6mm/¼in dice

1 yellow (bell) pepper, seeded and cut
into 6mm/¼in dice

1 orange or green (bell) pepper, seeded
and cut into 6mm/¼in dice

1 small onion, cut into 6mm/¼ in dice

5ml/1 tsp grated orange rind

50ml/2fl oz/¼ cup fresh orange juice

salt

4 pieces of swordfish steak, about
150g/5oz each

1 ▼ Heat 45ml/3 tbsp of the oil in a large non-stick frying pan. Add the fennel, peppers and onion and cook over a medium heat until just tender, about 5 minutes (they should retain some crunch).

2 ▲ Stir in the orange rind and juice and cook for 1 minute more. Stir in 2.5ml/½ tsp salt. Cover and set aside.

3 Bring some water to the boil in the bottom of a steamer.

4 ▲ Meanwhile, brush the fish steaks on both sides with the remaining oil and season with salt.

5 ▲ Place the fish steaks in the top part of the steamer. Cover the pan and steam until the steaks are opaque throughout, about 5 minutes.

6 Transfer the fish to dinner plates. Serve at once, accompanied by the pepper and orange relish.

Tangerine-Soy Marinated Salmon

SERVES 4

250ml/8fl oz/1 cup soy sauce

25ml/1½ tsp soft light brown sugar

50ml/2fl oz/¼ cup rice vinegar

15ml/1 tbsp finely chopped fresh
   root ginger

2 garlic cloves, finely chopped

grated rind and juice of 1 tangerine

120ml/4fl oz/½ cup water

4 pieces of salmon fillet, about
   175g/6oz each

1 ▲ Combine the soy sauce, sugar,
vinegar, ginger, garlic, orange rind
and juice and water in a bowl. Stir
until well blended.

2 ▲ Arrange the fish, in one layer, in
a large shallow dish. Pour over the soy
sauce mixture and turn the fish so that
both sides are coated. Cover and leave
to marinate at room temperature for
1 hour, or chill overnight.

3 Preheat oven to 180°C/350°F/Gas 4.

4 ▼ Remove the fish from the
marinade, leaving on any pieces of
ginger that cling to the fish. Place in a
baking dish, in one layer.

5 ▲ Cover the dish with foil. Bake
until the fish is opaque throughout,
20–30 minutes. Transfer to four dinner
plates and serve at once. This dish is
good served with steamed broccoli.

Cioppino

SERVES 4

300ml/2 tbsp olive oil

1 onion, halved and thinly sliced

several saffron threads, crushed

5ml/1 tsp dried thyme

pinch of cayenne pepper

salt and pepper

2 garlic cloves, finely chopped

2 x 400g/14oz cans peeled tomatoes,
    drained and chopped

175ml/6fl oz/¾ cup dry white wine

2.5 litres/4 pints fish stock

350g/12oz skinless fish fillets,
    cut into pieces

450g/1lb monkfish, membrane removed,
    cut into pieces

450g/1lb mussels in shell,
    thoroughly scrubbed

225g/8oz small squid bodies, cleaned
    and cut into rings

30ml/2 tbsp chopped fresh parsley

thickly sliced sourdough bread,
    to serve

1 ▼ Heat the oil in a large, heavy pan. Add the onion, saffron, thyme, cayenne and 2.5ml/½ tsp salt. Stir well and cook over a low heat until soft, 8–10 minutes. Add the garlic and cook for 1 minute more.

~ COOK'S TIP ~

Do not prepare mussels more than a few hours in advance of cooking or they will spoil and die.

2 ▲ Stir in the tomatoes, wine and fish stock. Bring to the boil and boil for 1 minute, then reduce the heat to medium-low and simmer for 15 minutes.

3 ▲ Add the fish fillet and monkfish pieces to the pan and simmer gently for 3 minutes.

4 ▲ Add the mussels and squid and simmer until the mussel shells open, about 2 minutes more. Stir in the parsley. Season with salt and pepper.

5 Ladle into warmed soup bowls and serve at once, with bread.

Prawn Kebabs with Plum Sauce

SERVES 6

15ml/1 tbsp vegetable oil

1 onion, finely chopped

1 garlic clove, finely chopped

450g/1lb purple plums, stoned (pitted)
  and chopped

15ml/1 tbsp rice vinegar

30ml/2 tbsp fresh orange juice

5ml/1 tsp Dijon-style mustard

30ml/2 tbsp soy sauce

15ml/1 tbsp soft light brown sugar

1 point of a star anise

120ml/4fl oz/½ cup water

675g/1½lb medium-size raw prawns,
  peeled (tails left on if desired)
  and deveined

boiled rice, to serve

1 ▲ Heat the oil in a pan. Add the onion, garlic and plums and cook over a low heat, stirring occasionally, until softened, about 10 minutes.

2 Stir in the vinegar, orange juice, mustard, soy sauce, sugar, star anise and water. Bring to the boil. Lower the heat, cover and simmer, stirring occasionally, for 20 minutes.

3 Uncover the pan and simmer the sauce for 10 minutes more to thicken, stirring frequently.

4 ▼ Remove the star anise. Transfer to a food processor or blender and purée until smooth.

5 Press the sauce through a fine strainer to remove all the fibres and plum skins.

6 Preheat the grill (broiler).

7 ▲ Thread the prawns, flat, on to six skewers. Brush them all over with three-quarters of the plum sauce.

8 Place the prawn kebabs on a foil-lined grill (broiling) pan. Grill (broil) until opaque throughout, 5–6 minutes. Turn the kebabs once.

9 Meanwhile, reheat the remaining plum sauce. Serve the kebabs with rice and the sauce.

Lemon Chicken with Guacamole Sauce

SERVES 4

juice of 2 lemons

45ml/3 tbsp olive oil

2 garlic cloves, finely chopped

salt and pepper

4 chicken breasts, about 200g/7oz each

2 beefsteak tomatoes, cored and cut in half

chopped fresh coriander (cilantro), to garnish

FOR THE SAUCE

1 ripe avocado

50ml/2fl oz/¼ cup sour cream

45ml/3 tbsp fresh lemon juice

2.5ml/½ tsp salt

50ml/2fl oz/¼ cup water

1 ▲ Combine the lemon juice, oil, garlic, 2.5ml/½ tsp salt and a little pepper in a bowl. Stir to mix.

~ VARIATION ~

To grill the chicken, prepare the fire, and when the coals are glowing red and covered with grey ash, spread them in a single layer. Set an oiled grill rack about 13cm/5in above the coals and cook the chicken breasts until lightly charred and cooked through, about 15–20 minutes. Allow extra olive oil for basting.

2 ▲ Arrange the chicken breasts, in one layer, in a shallow glass or ceramic dish. Pour over the lemon mixture and turn to coat evenly. Cover and leave to stand for at least 1 hour at room temperature, or chill overnight.

3 ▲ For the sauce, cut the avocado in half, remove the stone (pit) and scrape the flesh into a food processor or blender.

4 ▲ Add the sour cream, lemon juice and salt and process until smooth. Add the water and process just to blend. If necessary, add more water to thin the sauce. Transfer to a bowl, taste and adjust the seasoning, if necessary. Set aside.

5 ▲ Preheat the grill (broiler). Heat a ridged frying pan. Remove the chicken from the marinade and pat dry.

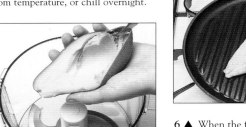

6 ▲ When the frying pan is hot, add the chicken breasts and cook, turning often, until they are cooked through, about 10 minutes.

7 ▲ Meanwhile, arrange the tomato halves, cut-sides up, on a baking sheet and season lightly with salt and pepper. Grill (broil) until hot and bubbling, about 5 minutes.

8 To serve, place a chicken breast, tomato half and a dollop of avocado sauce on each plate. Sprinkle with coriander and serve.

Poussins with Raisin and Walnut Stuffing

SERVES 4

250ml/8fl oz/1 cup port

100g/3¾oz/⅔ cup raisins

15ml/1 tbsp walnut oil

75g/3oz mushrooms, finely chopped

1 large celery stick, finely chopped

1 small onion, chopped

salt and pepper

50g/2oz/1 cup fresh breadcrumbs

50g/2oz/½ cup chopped walnuts

15ml/1 tbsp each chopped fresh basil
   and parsley, or 30ml/2 tbsp
   chopped parsley

2.5ml/½ tsp dried thyme

75g/3oz/6 tbsp butter, melted

4 poussins

1 Preheat oven to 180°C/350°F/Gas 4.

2 In a small bowl, combine the port and raisins and leave to soak for about 20 minutes.

3 ▲ Meanwhile, heat the oil in a non-stick frying pan. Add the mushrooms, celery, onion and 1.5ml/¼ tsp salt and cook over a low heat until softened, 8–10 minutes. Leave to cool slightly.

4 ▲ Drain the raisins, reserving the port. Combine the raisins, breadcrumbs, walnuts, basil, parsley and thyme in a bowl. Stir in the onion mixture and 60ml/4 tbsp of the melted butter. Add 2.5ml/½ tsp salt and pepper to taste.

5 ▲ Fill the cavity of each poussin with the stuffing mixture, but do not pack it down. Tie the legs together, looping the tail with the string to enclose the stuffing securely.

6 Brush the poussins with the remaining butter and place in a baking dish that is just large enough to hold the birds comfortably. Pour over the reserved port.

7 Roast, basting occasionally, for about 1 hour. To test if the birds are done, pierce the thigh with a skewer; the juices should run clear. Serve at once, pouring some of the pan juices over each bird.

Fusilli with Turkey, Tomatoes and Broccoli

SERVES 4

675g/1½lb ripe but firm plum
tomatoes, quartered

90ml/6 tbsp olive oil

5ml/1 tsp dried oregano

salt and pepper

350g/12oz broccoli florets

1 small onion, sliced

5ml/1 tsp dried thyme

450g/1lb skinless boneless
turkey breast, cubed

3 garlic cloves, finely chopped

15ml/1 tbsp fresh lemon juice

450g/1lb fusilli

1 Preheat oven to 200°C/400°F/Gas 6.

2 ▲ Place the tomatoes in a baking dish. Add 15ml/1 tbsp of the oil, the oregano and 2.5ml/½ tsp salt and stir to blend.

3 Bake until the tomatoes are just browned, 30–40 minutes; do not stir.

4 Meanwhile, bring a large pan of salted water to the boil. Add the broccoli and cook until just tender, about 5 minutes. Drain and set aside. (Alternatively, steam the broccoli until tender.)

5 ▲ Heat 30ml/2 tbsp of the oil in a large non-stick frying pan. Add the onion, thyme, cubes of turkey and 2.5ml/½ tsp salt. Cook over a high heat, stirring often, until the meat is cooked and beginning to brown, 5–7 minutes. Add the garlic and cook for 1 minute more, stirring frequently.

6 Remove from the heat. Stir in the lemon juice and season with pepper. Set aside and keep warm.

7 Bring another large pan of salted water to the boil. Add the fusilli and cook until just tender (follow the packet instructions for timing). Drain and place in a large bowl. Toss with the remaining oil.

8 ▼ Add the broccoli to the turkey mixture. Add to the fusilli. Add the tomatoes and stir gently to blend. Serve at once.

Chicken with White Wine, Olives and Garlic

SERVES 4

1.6kg/3½lb chicken,
    cut into serving pieces

1 onion, sliced

salt and pepper

3–6 garlic cloves, to taste, finely chopped

5ml/1 tsp dried thyme

475ml/16fl oz/2 cups dry white wine

175g/6oz/1 cup green olives
    (16–18), pitted

1 bay leaf

15ml/1 tbsp lemon juice

15–25g/½–1oz/1–2 tbsp butter

1 Heat a deep, heavy cast iron frying pan. When hot, add the chicken pieces, skin side down, and cook over a medium heat until browned, about 10 minutes. Turn and brown the other side, 5–8 minutes more. (Work in batches if necessary.)

2 Transfer the chicken pieces to a serving dish and set aside.

3 Drain the excess fat from the frying pan, leaving about 15ml/1 tbsp. Add the onion and 2.5ml/½ tsp salt and cook until just soft, about 5 minutes. Add the garlic and thyme and cook for 1 minute more.

4 ▼ Add the wine and stir, scraping up any bits that cling to the pan. Bring to the boil and boil for 1 minute. Stir in the green olives.

5 ▲ Return the chicken pieces to the pan. Add the bay leaf and season lightly with pepper. Lower the heat, cover and simmer until the chicken is cooked through, 20–30 minutes.

6 Transfer the chicken pieces to a warmed serving dish. Stir the lemon juice into the sauce. Whisk in the butter to thicken the sauce slightly. Spoon over the chicken and serve at once.

Turkey Meat Loaf

SERVES 4

15ml/1 tbsp olive oil

1 onion, chopped

1 green (bell) pepper, seeded and
    finely chopped

1 garlic clove, finely chopped

450g/1lb turkey mince

50g/2oz/1 cup fresh breadcrumbs

1 egg, beaten

75g/3oz/½ cup pine nuts

12 sun-dried tomatoes in oil, drained
    and chopped

75ml/2½fl oz/⅓ cup milk

10ml/2 tsp chopped fresh rosemary, or
    2.5ml/½ tsp dried rosemary

5ml/1 tsp ground fennel

2.5ml/½ tsp dried oregano

2.5ml/½ tsp salt

1 Preheat oven to 190°C/375°F/Gas 5.

2 ▼ Heat the oil in a frying pan. Add the onion, pepper and garlic and cook over a low heat, stirring often, until just softened, 8–10 minutes. Remove from the heat and leave to cool.

3 Place the turkey in a large bowl. Add the onion mixture and the remaining ingredients and mix thoroughly together.

4 ▲ Transfer to a 21 × 12cm/8½ × 4½in loaf tin (pan), packing the mixture down firmly. Bake until golden brown, about 1 hour. Serve hot or cold.

Chicken with White Wine, Olives and Garlic (top), Turkey Meat Loaf

Pork Chops with Chilli and Nectarine Relish

SERVES 4

250ml/8fl oz/1 cup fresh orange juice

45ml/3 tbsp olive oil

2 garlic cloves, finely chopped

5ml/1 tsp ground cumin

15ml/1 tbsp coarsely ground black pepper

8 pork loin chops, about 2cm/¾in thick, well trimmed

salt

FOR THE RELISH

1 small fresh green chilli

30ml/2 tbsp honey

juice of ½ lemon

250ml/8fl oz/1 cup chicken stock

2 nectarines, stoned (pitted) and chopped

1 garlic clove, finely chopped

½ onion, finely chopped

5ml/1 tsp finely chopped fresh root ginger

1.5ml/¼ tsp salt

15ml/1 tbsp chopped fresh coriander (cilantro)

1 For the relish, roast the chilli over a gas flame, holding it with tongs, until charred on all sides. (Alternatively, char the skin under the grill/broiler.) Leave to cool for 5 minutes.

2 ▼ Wearing rubber gloves, carefully remove the charred skin of the chilli. Discard the seeds if a less hot flavour is desired. Finely chop the chilli and place in a heavy pan.

3 ▲ Add the honey, lemon juice, chicken stock, nectarines, garlic, onion, ginger and salt. Bring to a boil, then simmer, stirring occasionally, for about 30 minutes. Stir in the coriander and set aside.

4 In a small bowl, combine the orange juice, oil, garlic, cumin and pepper. Stir to mix.

5 ▲ Arrange the pork chops, in one layer, in a shallow dish. Pour over the orange juice mixture and turn to coat. Cover and leave to stand for at least 1 hour, or chill overnight.

6 Remove the pork from the marinade and pat dry with kitchen paper. Season lightly with salt.

7 Heat a ridged frying pan. When hot, add the pork chops and cook until browned, about 5 minutes. Turn and cook on the other side until done, about 10 minutes more. (Work in batches if necessary.) Serve at once, with the relish.

Roast Leg of Lamb with Pesto

SERVES 6

115g/4oz/2 cups fresh basil leaves

4 garlic cloves, coarsely chopped

45ml/3 tbsp pine nuts

150ml/¼ pint/⅔ cup olive oil

50g/2oz/⅔ cup freshly grated
  Parmesan cheese

5ml/1 tsp salt, or to taste

2.25–2.75kg/5–6lb leg of lamb

1 ▲ To make the pesto, combine the basil, garlic and pine nuts in a food processor, and process until finely chopped. With the motor running, slowly add the oil in a steady stream.

2 Scrape the mixture into a bowl. Stir in the Parmesan and salt.

3 ▲ Place the lamb in a roasting dish. Make several slits in the meat with a sharp knife and spoon some pesto into each slit.

4 Rub more pesto over the surface of the lamb.

5 ▲ Continue patting on the pesto in a thick, even layer. Cover and leave to stand for 2 hours at room temperature, or chill overnight.

6 Preheat the oven to 180°C/350°F/Gas 4.

7 Place the lamb in the oven and roast, allowing about 20 minutes per 450g/1lb for rare meat and 25 minutes for medium-rare. Turn the lamb occasionally during roasting.

8 Remove the leg of lamb from the oven, cover it loosely with foil and leave it to rest for about 15 minutes before carving and serving.

Beef and Aubergine Stir-fry with Ginger

SERVES 4–6

600g/1lb 6oz boneless beef, such as flank
   steak, thinly sliced

30ml/2 tbsp soy sauce,
   plus extra for serving

450g/1lb aubergine (eggplant)

45ml/3 tbsp water

30ml/2 tbsp rice vinegar

15ml/1 tbsp dry sherry

5ml/1 tsp honey

5ml/1 tsp red pepper flakes

50ml/2fl oz/¼ cup vegetable oil

15ml/1 tbsp sesame oil

1 garlic clove, finely chopped

15ml/1 tbsp finely chopped fresh
   root ginger

boiled rice, to serve

1 ▲ Combine the beef and soy sauce
in a shallow dish. Stir to coat evenly.
Cover and leave to marinate for 1 hour,
or chill overnight.

~ VARIATIONS ~

For Turkey and Aubergine Stir-fry,
substitute thinly sliced turkey
breast for the beef. If time is short,
it is not essential to precook the
aubergine, but microwaving or
steaming the aubergine before stir-
frying helps to eliminate any
bitterness and also prevents the
aubergine from soaking up too
much oil.

2 ▲ Cut the aubergine into eighths
lengthways. Trim away the inner part
with the seeds, leaving a flat edge.
Cut the aubergine slices on the diagonal
into diamond shapes that are about
2.5cm/1in wide.

3 ▲ Place the aubergine in a large
microwaveable dish. Stir in the water.
Cover and microwave on high (650
watt) for 3 minutes. Stir gently, then
microwave for 3 minutes more. Set
aside, still covered. (Alternatively,
steam the aubergine over boiling water
until tender, if preferred.)

4 ▲ In a small bowl, combine the
vinegar, sherry, honey and red pepper
flakes. Stir to mix. Set aside.

5 ▲ Heat 15ml/1 tbsp vegetable oil
and 5ml/1 tsp sesame oil in a large
non-stick frying pan or wok. Add half
the beef, garlic and ginger. Cook
over a high heat, stirring frequently,
until the beef is just cooked through,
2–3 minutes. Remove to a bowl. Cook
the remaining beef, garlic and ginger
in the same way. Add to the bowl and
set aside.

6 ▲ Heat the remaining vegetable
and sesame oils in the frying pan or
wok. Add the aubergine and cook over
moderate heat until just browned and
tender, about 5 minutes. (Work in two
batches if necessary.)

7 Return the beef to the frying pan or
wok. Stir in the vinegar mixture and
cook just until the liquid is absorbed,
2–3 minutes more. Taste for seasoning.
Serve at once, with rice and extra
soy sauce.

Berry Salsa

MAKES 675G/1½LB/3 CUPS

1 fresh jalapeño pepper
½ red onion, finely chopped
2 spring onions (scallions), chopped
1 tomato, finely diced
1 small yellow (bell) pepper, seeded and finely chopped
15g/½oz/¼ cup chopped fresh coriander (cilantro)
1.5ml/¼ tsp salt
15ml/1 tbsp raspberry vinegar
15ml/1 tbsp fresh orange juice
5ml/1 tsp honey
15ml/1 tbsp olive oil
300ml/½ pint strawberries, hulled
300ml/½ pint blueberries or blackberries
300ml/½ pint raspberries

1 ▼ Wearing rubber gloves, finely chop the jalapeño pepper (discarding the seeds and membrane if a less hot flavour is desired). Place the pepper in a medium bowl.

2 ▲ Add the red onion, spring onions, tomato, pepper and coriander and stir to blend.

3 ▲ In a small measuring jug (cup), whisk together the salt, vinegar, orange juice, honey and oil. Pour over the jalapeño mixture and stir well.

4 ▲ Coarsely chop the strawberries. Add to the jalapeño mixture with the other berries and stir to blend. Leave to stand at room temperature for 3 hours.

5 Serve the salsa at room temperature, with grilled fish or poultry.

Fresh Pineapple and Mint Chutney

MAKES 675G/1½LB/3 CUPS

250ml/8fl oz/1 cup raspberry vinegar

250ml/8fl oz/1 cup dry white wine

1 small pineapple, skin removed and
   flesh chopped

2 medium oranges, peeled and chopped

1 apple, peeled and chopped

1 red (bell) pepper, seeded and diced

1½ onions, finely chopped

50g/2oz/¼ cup honey

pinch of salt

1 clove

4 black peppercorns

30ml/2 tbsp chopped fresh mint

1 ▲ In a pan, combine the vinegar
and wine and bring to the boil. Boil for
3 minutes.

2 ▲ Add the remaining ingredients,
except the mint, and stir to blend.
Simmer gently for about 30 minutes,
stirring occasionally.

3 Transfer to a strainer set over a
bowl and drain, pressing down to
extract the liquid. Remove and
discard the clove and peppercorns.
Set the fruit mixture aside.

4 ▼ Return the strained juice to the
pan and boil until reduced by two-
thirds. Pour over the fruit mixture.

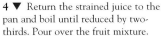

5 ▲ Stir in the mint. Leave the
chutney to stand for 6–8 hours before
serving, with pork or lamb dishes.

~ COOK'S TIP ~

The chutney will keep about
1 week in the refrigerator.

Aubergine Ratatouille

SERVES 6

1.6kg/3½lb aubergines (about 4)

45ml/3 tbsp olive oil

1 large onion, sliced

salt and pepper

3 garlic cloves, finely chopped

2 x 400g/14oz cans peeled plum tomatoes, drained and chopped

30ml/2 tbsp chopped fresh basil, or 5ml/1 tsp dried basil

fresh basil leaves, for garnishing

1 Cut the aubergines into large cubes. Bring a large pan of salted water to the boil. Add the aubergine and cook for 3–4 minutes. Drain thoroughly.

2 ▼ Heat 30ml/2 tbsp of the oil in a large frying pan. Add the onion and 1.5ml/¼ tsp salt and cook over a low heat until just soft, 8–10 minutes.

3 Add the garlic, aubergine and remaining oil and stir to mix. Cook gently for about 5 minutes.

4 ▲ Stir in the tomatoes and basil. Season with salt and pepper. Cover and cook over a low heat until the aubergine is very tender, about 30 minutes, stirring occasionally.

5 Sprinkle the ratatouille with fresh basil leaves and serve.

Garlicky Sautéed Courgettes

SERVES 4

6 medium courgettes (zucchini)

30ml/2 tbsp olive oil

2.5ml/½ tsp salt

4–6 garlic cloves, finely chopped

5ml/1 tsp dried thyme

15ml/1 tbsp fresh lemon juice

black pepper

~ VARIATION ~

For Pasta with Courgette Sauce, add 2 x 400g/14oz cans peeled plum tomatoes, roughly chopped, to the browned courgettes instead of the lemon juice.
Simmer until thickened, 5–10 minutes longer. Serve with boiled pasta shapes and sprinkle with grated Parmesan cheese, if you like.

1 ▼ Trim the ends of the courgettes, then halve and quarter them lengthways. Cut into slices about 2cm/¾in thick.

2 Heat the oil in a large non-stick frying pan. Add the courgette and toss to coat evenly. Add the salt and stir, then leave to cook until browned on one side, about 5 minutes.

3 ▲ Add the garlic and thyme. Shake the pan and turn the courgette with the aid of a wooden spatula. Continue cooking until golden brown on both sides and tender, about 5 minutes more. Do not let the garlic burn; if necessary, reduce the heat and increase the cooking time slightly.

4 Stir in the lemon juice, season liberally with black pepper and serve.

Aubergine Ratatouille (top), Garlicky Sautéed Courgettes

Herbed Goat's Cheese Dip

MAKES ABOUT 450G/1LB/2 CUPS

275g/10oz soft mild goat's cheese

120ml/4fl oz/½ cup single (light) or pouring (half-and-half) cream

10ml/2 tsp fresh lemon juice

15ml/1 tbsp chopped fresh chives

15ml/1 tbsp chopped fresh parsley

30ml/2 tbsp chopped fresh basil

black pepper

raw or briefly cooked cold vegetables, crisps (US potato chips) or savoury biscuits (crackers), to serve

1 ▼ In a food processor or blender, combine the goat's cheese and cream and process to blend. Add the lemon juice and process until smooth.

2 ▲ Scrape into a bowl. Stir in the chives, parsley, basil and pepper to taste. Serve cold, as a dip for vegetables, crisps or savoury biscuits.

Avocado Dressing

MAKES ABOUT 350ML/12FL OZ/1½ CUPS

30ml/2 tbsp wine vinegar

2.5ml/½ tsp salt, or to taste

2.5ml/¾ tsp white pepper

½ red onion, coarsely chopped

45ml/3 tbsp olive oil

1 large ripe avocado, halved and stone (pit) removed

15ml/1 tbsp fresh lemon juice

45ml/3 tbsp natural (plain) yogurt

45ml/3 tbsp water, or as needed

30ml/2 tbsp chopped fresh coriander (cilantro)

raw or briefly cooked cold vegetables, for serving

1 ▲ In a bowl, combine the vinegar and salt and stir with a fork to dissolve. Stir in the pepper, chopped red onion and olive oil.

3 ▲ Add the yogurt and water and process until smooth. If you like, add more water to thin. Taste and adjust the seasoning if necessary.

2 ▲ Scoop the avocado flesh into a food processor or blender. Add the lemon juice and onion dressing and process just to blend.

4 ▲ Scrape into a bowl. Stir in the coriander. Serve at once, as a dressing for salads, or use as a dip for raw or briefly cooked cold vegetables.

~ COOK'S TIP ~

This versatile dressing need not be limited to serving with salads and crudités. Serve it as a sauce with grilled chicken or fish, or use it on sandwiches in place of mayonnaise or mustard, or to provide a cool contrast to any sort of spicy food.

Herbed Goat's Cheese Dip (top), Avocado Dressing

Zinfandel Poached Pears

SERVES 4

1 bottle of red Zinfandel wine

150g/5oz/¾ cup granulated sugar

45ml/3 tbsp honey

juice of ½ lemon

1 cinnamon stick

1 vanilla pod (bean),
    split open lengthways

5cm/2in piece of orange peel

1 clove

1 black peppercorn

4 firm, ripe pears

whipped cream or sour cream,
    to serve

1 ▼ In a pan just large enough to hold the pears standing upright, combine the wine, sugar, honey, lemon juice, cinnamon, vanilla pod, orange peel, clove and peppercorn. Heat gently, stirring occasionally, until the sugar has dissolved.

2 ▲ Meanwhile, peel the pears, leaving the core and stem intact. Slice a small piece off the base of each pear so it will stand upright.

3 ▲ Gently place the pears in the wine mixture. Simmer, uncovered, until the pears are just tender, about 20–35 minutes depending on size and ripeness; do not overcook.

4 ▲ With a slotted spoon, gently transfer the pears to a bowl. Continue to boil the poaching liquid until reduced by about half. Leave to cool.

5 Strain the cooled liquid over the pears and chill for at least 3 hours.

6 Place the pears in serving dishes and spoon over the liquid. Serve with whipped cream or sour cream.

Baked Peaches with Raspberry Sauce

SERVES 6

40g/1½oz/3 tbsp unsalted butter,
  at room temperature

50g/2oz/¼ cup granulated sugar

1 egg, beaten

50g/2oz/½ cup ground almonds

6 ripe peaches

FOR THE SAUCE

175g/6oz/1 cup raspberries

15ml/1 tbsp icing (confectioners') sugar

15ml/1 tbsp fruit-flavoured
  brandy (optional)

1 Preheat the oven to 180°C/350°F/
Gas 4.

2 ▲ Beat the butter with the sugar
until soft and fluffy. Beat in the egg.
Add the ground almonds and beat just
to blend well together.

3 ▲ Halve the peaches and remove
the stones (pits). With a spoon, scrape
out some of the flesh from each peach
half, slightly enlarging the hollow left
by the stone. Reserve the excess peach
flesh to use in the sauce.

4 ▼ Place the peach halves on a
baking sheet (if necessary, secure with
crumpled foil to keep them steady).
Fill the hollow in each peach half with
the almond mixture.

5 Bake until the almond filling is
puffed and golden and the peaches are
very tender, about 30 minutes.

6 ▲ Meanwhile, for the sauce,
combine all the ingredients in a food
processor or blender. Add the reserved
peach flesh. Process until smooth.
Press through a strainer set over a
bowl to remove fibres and seeds.

7 Let the peaches cool slightly. Place
two peach halves on each plate and
spoon over some of the sauce. Serve
at once.

Chocolate, Coconut and Macadamia Parfait

SERVES 10

250g/8oz white chocolate, chopped

600ml/1 pint/2½ cups whipping cream

120ml/4fl oz/½ cup milk

10 egg yolks

15ml/1 tbsp granulated sugar

40g/1½oz/½ cup desiccated (dry unsweetened shredded) coconut, plus more to garnish

120ml/4fl oz/½ cup canned sweetened coconut cream

150g/5oz unsalted macadamia nuts

FOR THE GLAZE

225g/8oz dark (bittersweet) chocolate

75g/3oz/6 tbsp butter

20ml/4 tsp golden (light corn) syrup

175ml/6fl oz/¾ cup whipping cream

1 ▲ Line the bottom and sides of a 25 × 10cm/10 × 4in terrine dish with clear film (plastic wrap).

2 ▲ Combine the white chocolate and 50ml/2fl oz/¼ cup of the cream in the top of a double boiler or in a heat-proof bowl set over hot water. Stir until melted and smooth. Set aside.

3 Put 250ml/8fl oz/1 cup of the cream and the milk in a heavy pan and scald over a medium heat.

4 ▲ Meanwhile, in a large bowl, beat the egg yolks and sugar together until thick and pale.

5 ▲ Add the hot cream mixture to the yolks, beating constantly. Pour back into the pan and cook over a low heat until thickened, 2–3 minutes. Stir constantly and do not boil. Remove from the heat.

6 Stir in the melted chocolate, desiccated coconut and coconut cream until blended. Leave to cool.

7 Whip the remaining cream until thick. Fold into the chocolate and coconut mixture.

8 Put 475ml/16fl oz/2 cups of the parfait mixture in the prepared dish and spread evenly. Cover and freeze until just firm, about 2 hours. Cover the remaining mixture and chill.

9 ▲ Arrange the macadamia nuts evenly over the frozen parfait layer. Pour in the remaining parfait mixture. Cover the dish and freeze until the parfait is firm, 6–8 hours or overnight.

10 ▲ For the glaze, combine the dark chocolate, butter, and golden syrup in the top of a double boiler and stir occasionally until melted.

11 In a pan, heat the cream until just simmering. Stir into the chocolate mixture. Remove from the heat and leave to cool to lukewarm.

12 To turn out the parfait, wrap the dish in a hot towel and set it upside down on a plate. Peel off the clear film. Set the parfait on a rack over a baking sheet. Pour the glaze evenly over the top. Working quickly, smooth the glaze down the sides with a palette knife. Leave to set slightly, then sprinkle with desiccated coconut. Freeze for about 3–4 hours more.

13 To serve the parfait, slice it with a knife dipped in hot water.

Lemon Pound Cake

SERVES 8–10

275g/10oz/1¼ cups unsalted butter, at room temperature

375g/13oz/1¾ cups granulated sugar

6 eggs

grated rind and juice of 1 large lemon

265g/9½oz/2⅓ cups sifted self-raising (self-rising) flour

2.5ml/½ tsp salt

icing (confectioners') sugar, for dusting

1 Preheat the oven to 180°C/350°F/Gas 4. Grease a 2.25 litre/3¾ pint/9 cup bundt tin (pan).

2 Beat the butter until it is soft and creamy. Gradually add the sugar and continue beating until fluffy.

3 ▼ Beat in the eggs, one at a time, beating well after each addition. Beat in the lemon rind and juice. Fold in the flour and salt in three batches.

4 Pour the mixture into the prepared tin and smooth the surface.

5 ▲ Bake until a skewer inserted in the centre comes out clean, 40–50 minutes. Leave to cool for 10 minutes before turning out on to a wire rack.

6 When the cake is cold, dust it with icing sugar.

Piña Colada Fruit Salad

SERVES 4

1 large pineapple

2 kiwi fruit

15g/½oz/¼ cup slivered fresh coconut

30ml/2 tbsp fresh lime juice

5ml/1 tsp granulated sugar

15–30ml/1–2 tbsp rum

8 large strawberries, halved

1 ▲ Cut a thick slice off one long side of the pineapple, not cutting into the crown of leaves.

2 ▼ Using a sharp spoon or a grapefruit knife, scoop out the flesh, taking care not to puncture the skin. Cut out and discard the core. Set the pineapple boat aside.

3 Chop the scooped-out flesh into bitesize pieces, keeping any juice, and place in a bowl.

4 Peel the kiwi fruit and chop into bitesize pieces. Add the kiwi fruit and coconut to the pineapple pieces.

5 ▲ In a small bowl, combine the lime juice, sugar and rum to taste. Stir to blend, then pour over the fruit. Toss well. Cover and chill the fruit salad for 1 hour.

6 To serve, spoon the fruit mixture into the pineapple boat. Garnish with the strawberries and serve at once.

Lemon Pound Cake (top), Piña Colada Fruit Salad

THE NORTHWEST & MOUNTAIN STATES

AN AREA THAT ENCOMPASSES SOME OF THE MOST MODERN CITIES AND WILDEST TERRAIN ALSO PROVIDES CULINARY CONTRASTS. MUCH OF IT OFFERS GOOD HUNTING AND FISHING TERRITORY, WHICH ARE COMPLEMENTED BY ORCHARDS AND AGRICULTURAL CULTIVATION, AS WELL AS ARTISANAL WINE AND CHEESEMAKING.

Salmon Chowder

SERVES 4

20g/¾ oz/1½ tbsp butter or margarine

1 onion, finely chopped

1 leek, finely chopped

50g/2oz/½ cup finely chopped
 fennel bulb

25g/1oz/¼ cup plain (all-purpose) flour

1.75 litres/3 pints fish stock

2 potatoes, cut into 1cm/½in cubes

salt and pepper

450g/1lb skinless salmon fillet,
 cut into 2cm/¾in cubes

175ml/6fl oz/¾ cup milk

120ml/4fl oz/½ cup whipping cream

30ml/2 tbsp chopped fresh dill

1 ▲ Melt the butter or margarine in a large pan. Add the onion, leek and fennel and cook over a medium heat until softened, 5–8 minutes, stirring the vegetables occasionally.

2 Stir in the flour. Reduce the heat to low and cook, stirring occasionally, for 3 minutes.

3 ▲ Add the stock and potatoes. Season with salt and pepper. Bring to the boil, then reduce the heat, cover and simmer until the potatoes are tender, about 20 minutes.

4 ▲ Add the salmon and simmer until just cooked, 3–5 minutes.

5 ▲ Stir in the milk, cream and dill. Cook just until warmed through; do not boil. Taste and adjust the seasoning, if necessary, then serve.

Smoked Turkey and Lentil Soup

SERVES 4

25g/1oz/2 tbsp butter

1 large carrot, chopped

1 onion, chopped

1 celery stick, chopped

1 leek, white part only, chopped

115g/4oz mushrooms, chopped

50ml/2fl oz/¼ cup dry white wine

1 litre/1¾ pints/4 cups chicken stock

10ml/2 tsp dried thyme

1 bay leaf

115g/4oz/½ cup lentils

225g/8oz smoked turkey meat, diced

salt and pepper

chopped fresh parsley, to garnish

1 ▲ Melt the butter in a large pan. Add the carrot, onion, leek, celery and mushrooms. Cook until golden, 3–5 minutes.

2 ▲ Stir in the wine and chicken stock. Bring to the boil and skim any foam that rises to the surface. Add the thyme and bay leaf. Lower the heat, cover and simmer gently for 30 minutes.

3 ▼ Add the lentils and continue cooking, covered, until they are just tender, 30–40 minutes more. Stir the soup from time to time.

4 ▲ Stir in the turkey and season to taste with salt and pepper. Cook until just heated through. Ladle into bowls and garnish with parsley.

Tomato and Blue Cheese Soup with Bacon

SERVES 4

1.3kg/3lb ripe tomatoes, peeled, quartered and seeded

2 garlic cloves, finely chopped

salt and pepper

30ml/2 tbsp vegetable oil or butter

1 leek, chopped

1 carrot, chopped

1.2 litres/2 pints unsalted chicken stock

115g/4oz blue cheese, such as Oregon Blue, crumbled

45ml/3 tbsp whipping cream

several large fresh basil leaves, or 1–2 fresh parsley sprigs

175g/6oz bacon, cooked and crumbled

1 Preheat oven to 200°C/400°F/ Gas 6.

2 ▲ Spread the tomatoes in a baking dish. Sprinkle with the garlic and some salt and pepper. Place in the oven and bake for 35 minutes.

3 ▲ Heat the oil or butter in a large pan. Add the leek and carrot and season lightly with salt and pepper. Cook over a low heat, stirring often, until softened, about 10 minutes.

4 ▲ Stir in the stock and tomatoes. Bring to the boil, then lower the heat, cover and simmer for 20 minutes.

5 ▲ Add the blue cheese, cream and basil or parsley. Transfer to a food processor or blender and process until smooth (work in batches if necessary). Taste for seasoning.

6 If necessary, reheat the soup, but do not boil. Ladle into bowls and sprinkle with the crumbled bacon.

Macaroni and Blue Cheese

SERVES 6

450g/1lb macaroni

1.2 litres/2 pints milk

50g/2oz/¼ cup butter

90ml/6 tbsp plain (all-purpose) flour

1.5ml/¼ tsp salt

225g/8oz blue cheese, such as
    Oregon Blue, crumbled

black pepper, for serving

1 Preheat the oven to 180°C/350°F/Gas 4. Grease a 33 × 23cm/13 × 9in baking dish.

2 ▲ Bring a large pan of water to the boil. Salt to taste and add the macaroni. Cook until just tender (check the packet instructions for cooking times). Drain and rinse under cold water. Place in a large bowl. Set aside.

3 In another pan, bring the milk to the boil and set aside.

4 ▲ Melt the butter in a heavy pan over a low heat. Whisk in the flour and cook for 5 minutes, whisking constantly; do not let the mixture become brown.

5 ▼ Remove from the heat and whisk the hot milk into the butter and flour mixture. When the mixture is smoothly blended, return to a medium heat and continue cooking, whisking constantly, until the sauce is thick, about 5 minutes. Add the salt.

6 Add the sauce to the macaroni. Add three-quarters of the crumbled blue cheese and stir well. Transfer the macaroni mixture to the prepared baking dish and spread in an even layer.

7 Sprinkle the remaining cheese evenly over the surface. Bake until bubbling hot, about 25 minutes.

8 If you like, lightly brown the top of the macaroni cheese under a hot grill (broiler) for 3–4 minutes. Serve hot, sprinkled with black pepper.

Smoked Trout Pasta Salad

SERVES 6

15g/½oz/1 tbsp butter

115g/4oz/1 cup finely chopped
    fennel bulb

6 spring onions (scallions),
    2 finely chopped and 4 thinly sliced

salt and pepper

225g/8oz skinless smoked trout
    fillets, flaked

45ml/3 tbsp chopped fresh dill

120ml/4fl oz/½ cup mayonnaise

10ml/2 tsp fresh lemon juice

30ml/2 tbsp whipping cream

450g/1lb small pasta shapes,
    such as shells

fresh dill sprigs, to garnish (optional)

1 ▼ Melt the butter in a small non-stick frying pan. Add the fennel and finely chopped spring onions and season lightly with salt and pepper. Cook over a medium heat until just softened, 3–5 minutes. Transfer to a large bowl and leave to cool slightly.

2 ▲ Add the sliced spring onions, trout, dill, mayonnaise, lemon juice and cream. Mix gently until well blended.

3 ▲ Bring a large pan of water to the boil. Salt to taste and add the pasta. Cook until just tender (check the packet intructions for cooking times). Drain thoroughly and leave to cool.

4 ▲ Add the pasta to the vegetable and trout mixture and toss to coat evenly. Taste for seasoning. Serve the salad lightly chilled or at room temperature, garnished with dill, if you like.

Trout and Bacon Hash

SERVES 2

3–4 potatoes, cut into 1cm/½in cubes

salt and pepper

40g/1½oz/3 tbsp unsalted butter

½ onion, finely chopped

½ green (bell) pepper, seeded and finely chopped

1 garlic clove, finely chopped

50g/2oz Canadian bacon or other back bacon, chopped

200g/7oz skinless trout fillets, cut into 1cm/½in pieces

5ml/1 tsp dried oregano

15ml/1 tbsp chopped fresh parsley (optional)

3 ▼ Add the remaining butter and the potatoes to the frying pan. Cook over a high heat, stirring occasionally, until the potatoes are lightly browned, about 5 minutes longer.

4 ▲ Add the trout, oregano and parsley, if using. Season with salt and pepper. Continue cooking, smashing down with a wooden spoon, until the trout is cooked through, 3–4 minutes more. Serve at once.

1 ▲ Put the potatoes in a pan, add cold water to cover, and bring to the boil. Add 5ml/1 tsp salt and simmer until just tender, 8–10 minutes. Drain and set aside.

2 ▲ Melt 25g/1oz/2 tbsp of the butter in a large non-stick frying pan. Add the onion, pepper, garlic and bacon and cook over a medium heat until the onion is just softened, 5–8 minutes.

Seattle Fish Fritters

SERVES 4

½ fennel bulb, finely chopped

1 medium leek, finely chopped

1 green (bell) pepper, seeded and diced

2 garlic cloves

15g/½oz/1 tbsp butter

pinch of red pepper flakes

salt and pepper

175g/6oz skinless salmon fillet,
    cut into pieces

90g/3½oz skinless rockfish fillet or
    ling cod, cut into pieces

75g/3oz cooked peeled prawns (shrimp)

115g/4oz/1 cup plain (all-purpose) flour

6 eggs, beaten

350–475ml/12–16fl oz/1½–2 cups milk

15ml/1 tbsp chopped fresh basil

60–90ml/4–6 tbsp oil, for greasing

sour cream, for serving

1 ▲ Combine the fennel, leek, pepper and garlic in a food processor and process until finely chopped.

~ **VARIATION** ~

For Seattle Salmon Fritters, increase the amount of salmon to 350g/12oz, and omit the rockfish or ling cod and prawns. Use dill in place of the basil. Serve with a tossed green salad, if you like.

2 ▲ Melt the butter in a frying pan until sizzling. Add the vegetable mixture and red pepper flakes. Season with salt and pepper. Cook over a low heat until softened, 8–10 minutes. Remove from the heat and set aside.

3 ▲ Place the salmon, rockfish or ling cod and prawns in the food processor. Process, using the pulse button and scraping the sides of the container several times, until the mixture is coarsely chopped. Scrape into a large bowl and set aside.

4 ▲ Sift the flour into another bowl and make a well in the centre.

5 ▲ Gradually whisk in the eggs alternately with 350ml/12fl oz/1½ cups milk to make a smooth batter. Strain the batter to remove lumps, If necessary.

6 ▲ Stir the seafood, vegetables and basil into the batter. If it seems too thick, add a little more milk.

7 ▲ Lightly oil a griddle or non-stick frying pan and place over a medium heat. Ladle in the batter, adding around 75ml/2½fl oz/⅓ cup at a time. Cook the fritters until both sides are golden around the edges, 2–3 minutes per side. Work in batches, keeping the cooked fritters warm.

8 Serve hot, with sour cream.

Scalloped Oysters

SERVES 4

90g/3½oz/7 tbsp butter

1 shallot, finely chopped

115g/4oz mushrooms, finely chopped

10ml/2 tsp plain (all-purpose) flour

dash of hot pepper sauce

salt and pepper

24 oysters, shucked and drained

75ml/2½fl oz/⅓ cup dry white wine

150ml/¼ pint/⅔ cup whipping cream

30ml/2 tbsp chopped fresh parsley

90ml/6 tbsp fresh breadcrumbs

1 Preheat the oven to 190°C/375°F/ Gas 5. Grease a 15 × 20cm/6 × 8in baking dish.

2 Melt the butter in a large frying pan. Add the shallot and mushrooms and cook until softened, about 3 minutes.

3 ▼ Add the flour and hot pepper sauce. Season with salt and pepper. Cook, stirring constantly, for 1 minute.

4 ▲ Stir in the oysters and wine, scraping the bottom of the frying pan. Add the cream. Transfer the mixture to the prepared baking dish.

5 ▲ In a small bowl, combine the chopped parsley, fresh breadcrumbs and salt to taste. Stir to mix.

6 ▲ Sprinkle the crumbs evenly over the oyster mixture. Bake until the top is golden and the sauce bubbling, 15–20 minutes. Serve at once.

Penn Cove Steamed Mussels

SERVES 2

675g/1½lb mussels in shell

½ fennel bulb, finely chopped

1 shallot, finely chopped

45ml/3 tbsp dry white wine

45ml/3 tbsp whipping cream

30ml/2 tbsp chopped fresh parsley

black pepper

1 ▲ Scrub the mussels under cold running water. Remove any barnacles with a small knife, and remove the beards. Rinse once more.

2 ▲ Place the mussels in a large casserole with a lid. Sprinkle them with the fennel, shallot and wine. Cover the casserole and place over a medium-high heat. Steam until the mussels open, 3–5 minutes.

3 Lift out the mussels with a slotted spoon and remove the top shells. Discard any mussels that did not open. Arrange the mussels, on their bottom shells, in one layer in a shallow serving dish. Keep warm.

4 ▼ Place a double layer of dampened muslin (cheesecloth) in a strainer set over a bowl. Strain the mussel cooking liquid through the muslin. Return the strained liquid to a clean pan and bring to the boil.

5 ▲ Add the cream, stir well and boil for 3 minutes to reduce slightly. Stir in the parsley. Spoon the sauce over the mussels and sprinkle with freshly ground black pepper. Serve the mussels at once.

Stuffed Potato Skins

3 baking potatoes, about 350g/12oz
  each, scrubbed and patted dry

15ml/1 tbsp vegetable oil

40g/1½oz/3 tbsp butter

1 onion, chopped

salt and pepper

1 green (bell) pepper, seeded and
  coarsely chopped

5ml/1 tsp paprika

115g/4oz/1 cup grated Monterey Jack or
  Cheddar cheese

1 Preheat oven to 230°C/450°F/Gas 8.

2 ▲ Brush the potatoes all over with
the oil. Prick them in several places
on all sides with a fork.

3 ▲ Place in a baking dish. Bake
until tender, about 1½ hours.

4 ▲ Meanwhile, heat the butter in a
large non-stick frying pan. Add the
onion and a little salt and cook over a
medium heat until softened, about
5 minutes. Add the pepper and
continue cooking until just tender but
still crunchy, 2–3 minutes more. Stir in
the paprika and set aside.

5 ▲ When the potatoes are done,
halve them lengthways. Scoop out the
flesh, keeping the pieces coarse. Keep
the potato skins warm.

6 Preheat the grill (broiler).

~ VARIATION ~

For Bacon-stuffed Potato Skins, add
130g/4½oz/¾ cup chopped cooked
bacon to the cooked potato flesh
and vegetables. Stuff as above.

7 ▲ Add the potato flesh to the
frying pan and cook over a high heat,
stirring, until the potato is lightly
browned. Season with pepper.

8 ▲ Divide the vegetable mixture
between the potato skins.

9 ▲ Sprinkle the cheese on top.
Grill until the cheese just melts,
3–5 minutes. Serve at once.

Pasta with Scallops

SERVES 4

450g/1lb pasta, such as fettucine
   or linguine

30ml/2 tbsp olive oil

2 garlic cloves, finely chopped

450g/1lb scallops,
   sliced in half horizontally

salt and pepper

FOR THE SAUCE

30ml/2 tbsp olive oil

½ onion, finely chopped

1 garlic clove, finely chopped

2.5ml/½ tsp salt

2 × 400g/14oz cans peeled tomatoes
   in juice

30ml/2 tbsp chopped fresh basil

1 For the sauce, heat the oil in a non-stick frying pan. Add the onion, garlic and a little salt, and cook over a medium heat until just softened, about 5 minutes, stirring occasionally.

2 ▲ Add the tomatoes, with their juice, and crush with the tines of a fork. Bring to the boil, then reduce the heat and simmer gently for 15 minutes. Remove from the heat and set aside.

3 ▲ Bring a large pan of salted water to the boil. Add the pasta and cook until just tender to the bite (check the packet instructions for cooking times).

4 ▲ Meanwhile, combine the oil and garlic in another non-stick frying pan and cook until just sizzling, about 30 seconds. Add the scallops and 2.5ml/½ tsp salt and cook over a high heat, tossing, until the scallops are cooked through, about 3 minutes.

5 ▲ Add the scallops to the tomato sauce. Season with salt and pepper, stir and keep warm.

6 Drain the pasta, rinse under hot water and drain again. Place in a large warmed serving bowl. Add the scallop sauce and the basil and toss thoroughly. Serve at once.

Clam and Sausage Chilli

Serves 4

185g/6½oz/1 cup dried black kidney
  beans, soaked overnight and drained

1 bay leaf

2.5ml/½ tsp sea salt

225g/½lb lean pork sausage meat
  (bulk sausage)

15ml/1 tbsp vegetable oil

1 onion, finely chopped

1 garlic clove, finely chopped

5ml/1 tsp fennel seeds

5ml/1 tsp dried oregano

1.5ml/¼ tsp red pepper flakes, or to taste

10–15ml/2–3 tsp chilli powder, or to taste

5ml/1 tsp ground cumin

2 × 400g/14oz cans canned chopped
  tomatoes in juice

120ml/4fl oz/½ cup dry white wine

2 × 275g/10oz cans clams, drained and
  liquid reserved

salt and pepper

1 Put the beans in a large pan. Add fresh cold water to cover and the bay leaf. Bring to the boil, then cover and simmer for 30 minutes. Add the salt and continue simmering until tender, about 30 minutes more. Drain the beans and discard the bay leaf.

2 ▲ Put the sausage meat in a large flameproof casserole. Cook over a medium heat until just beginning to brown, 2–3 minutes. Stir frequently to break up the lumps. Add the oil, onion and garlic.

3 Continue cooking until the vegetables are softened, about 5 minutes more, stirring occasionally.

4 ▼ Stir in the herbs and spices, tomatoes, wine and 150ml/¼ pint/⅔ cup of the reserved clam juice. Bring to the boil, then lower the heat and cook, stirring occasionally, for 15 minutes.

5 ▲ Add the black beans and clams and stir to combine. Taste and adjust the seasoning if necessary. Continue cooking until the clams are just heated through. Serve at once.

Pan-fried Trout with Horseradish Sauce

SERVES 4

4 whole rainbow trout, about 175g/6oz
  each, cleaned

salt and pepper

25g/1oz/¼ cup plain (all-purpose) flour

25g/1oz/2 tbsp butter

15ml/1 tbsp vegetable oil

FOR THE SAUCE

120ml/4fl oz/½ cup mayonnaise

120ml/4fl oz/½ cup sour cream

3.5ml/¾ tsp grated horseradish

1.5ml/¼ tsp paprika

30ml/2 tbsp tomato or lemon juice

15ml/1 tbsp chopped fresh herbs, such
  as chives, parsley or basil

1 ▼ For the sauce, combine the
mayonnaise, sour cream, horseradish,
paprika, tomato or lemon juice and
herbs. Season with salt and pepper
and mix well. Set the sauce aside.

2 ▲ Rinse the trout and pat dry.
Season the cavities in the fish
generously with salt and pepper.

3 ▲ Combine the flour, 2.5ml/½ tsp
salt and a little pepper in a shallow
dish. Coat the trout on both sides
with the seasoned flour, shaking off
any excess.

4 ▲ Heat the butter and oil in a large
non-stick frying pan over a medium-
high heat. When sizzling, add the trout
and cook until opaque throughout,
4–5 minutes on each side. Serve
at once, with the sauce.

Salmon with Sizzling Herbs

SERVES 4

4 salmon steaks, 175–200g/6–7oz each

salt and pepper

75ml/2½fl oz/⅓ cup olive oil

25g/1 oz/½ cup chopped fresh
    coriander (cilantro)

45ml/3 tbsp finely chopped fresh root ginger

40g/1½oz/½ cup chopped spring
    onions (scallions)

50ml/2fl oz/¼ cup soy sauce, plus extra
    for serving

1 Bring some water to the boil in the bottom of a steamer.

2 ▲ Season the fish steaks on both sides with salt and pepper.

3 ▲ Place the fish steaks in the top part of the steamer. Cover the pan and steam until the fish is opaque throughout, 7–8 minutes.

4 ▼ Meanwhile, heat the oil in a small heavy pan until very hot. (To test the temperature, drop in a piece of chopped spring onion; if it sizzles, the oil is hot enough.)

5 Place the steamed salmon steaks on warmed plates.

6 ▲ Divide the chopped coriander among the salmon steaks, heaping it on top of the fish. Sprinkle with the ginger and then the spring onions. Drizzle 15ml/1 tbsp of the soy sauce over each salmon steak.

7 Spoon the hot oil over each salmon steak and serve at once, with additional soy sauce.

Pork Chops with Cider and Apples

SERVES 4

450g/1lb tart cooking apples (3–4), peeled, quartered and cored

4 pork chops, about 2.5cm/1in thick

5ml/1 tsp dried thyme

1.5ml/¼ tsp ground allspice

salt and pepper

15g/½oz/1 tbsp butter

15ml/1 tbsp vegetable oil

1 bay leaf

120ml/4fl oz/½ cup apple cider

30ml/2 tbsp whipping cream

potato pancakes, for serving

1 Preheat the oven to 190°C/375°F/Gas 5. Grease a casserole large enough to hold the pork chops in one layer.

2 ▲ Spread the apples in an even layer in the prepared dish. Set aside.

3 Sprinkle the pork chops on both sides with the thyme, ground allspice and a little salt and pepper.

4 Heat the butter and oil in a frying pan. When hot, add the pork chops and cook over a medium-high heat until browned, 2–3 minutes. Turn and cook the other side, 2–3 minutes more. Remove from the heat.

5 ▲ Arrange the pork chops on top of the apples. Add the bay leaf and pour over the cider. Cover and bake for 15 minutes.

6 ▲ Turn the chops over. Continue baking until they are cooked through, about 15 minutes more.

7 Transfer the pork chops to warmed plates. Remove the apple quarters with a slotted spoon and divide them equally among the plates.

8 Stir the cream into the sauce and heat just until warmed through. Taste for seasoning. Spoon the sauce over the pork chops and serve at once, with potato pancakes.

Pork Braised in Beer

SERVES 6

1.8–2.25kg/4–5lb pork loin, boned,
    trimmed of excess fat and tied into a
    neat shape

salt and pepper

15ml/1 tbsp butter

15ml/1 tbsp vegetable oil

3 large onions, halved and thinly sliced

1 garlic clove, finely chopped

750ml/1¼ pints/3 cups beer

1 bay leaf

15ml/1 tbsp plain (all-purpose) flour
    blended with 30ml/2 tbsp water

1 ▲ Season the pork loin on all
sides with salt and pepper. Heat the
butter and oil in a flameproof casserole
just large enough to hold the pork
loin. When hot, add the meat and
brown on all sides, 5–7 minutes,
turning it to colour evenly. Remove
from the casserole and set aside.

2 ▲ Drain the excess fat from the
pan, leaving about 15ml/1 tbsp. Add
the onions and garlic and cook just
until softened, about 5 minutes.

3 ▲ Stir in the beer, scraping to
remove any bits on the bottom of the
pan. Add the bay leaf.

4 Return the pork to the casserole.
Cover and cook over a low heat for
about 2 hours, turning the pork
halfway through the cooking time.

5 ▼ Remove the pork. Cut it into
serving slices and arrange on a serving
dish. Cover and keep warm.

6 Discard the bay leaf. Add the flour
to the cooking juices and cook over a
high heat, stirring constantly, until
thickened. Taste for seasoning. Pour
the sauce over the pork slices and
serve at once.

Chicken and Mushroom Pie

SERVES 6

15g/½ oz dried porcini mushrooms

50g/2oz/¼ cup butter

30ml/2 tbsp plain (all-purpose) flour

250ml/8fl oz/1 cup chicken stock, warmed

50ml/2fl oz/¼ cup whipping cream or milk

salt and pepper

1 onion, coarsely chopped

2 carrots, sliced

2 celery sticks, coarsely chopped

50g/2oz mushrooms, quartered

450g/1lb cooked chicken meat, cubed

50g/2oz/½ cup shelled fresh or frozen peas

beaten egg, for glazing

FOR THE PASTRY

225g/8oz/2 cups plain (all-purpose) flour

1.5ml/¼ tsp salt

75g/3oz/6 tbsp cold butter, diced

25g/1oz/2 tbsp lard or white cooking
    fat, diced

45–60ml/3–4 tbsp iced water

1 ▲ For the pastry, sift the flour and salt into a bowl. With a pastry blender, cut in the butter and lard or white cooking fat until the mixture resembles breadcrumbs, or rub in with your fingertips. Sprinkle with 45ml/3 tbsp of the iced water and mix until the pastry holds together. If it is too crumbly, add a little more water, 5ml/1 tsp at a time. Gather the pastry into a ball and flatten into a disk.Wrap in clear film (plastic wrap) and chill for at least 30 minutes.

2 Place the porcini mushrooms in a small bowl. Add hot water to cover and soak until soft, about 30 minutes. Lift out of the water with a slotted spoon to leave any grit behind and drain. Discard the soaking water.

3 Preheat oven to 190°C/375°F/Gas 5.

4 ▲ Melt half the butter in a heavy pan. Whisk in the flour and cook until bubbling, whisking constantly. Add the warm chicken stock and cook over a medium heat, whisking, until the mixture boils. Cook for 2–3 minutes more. Whisk in the whipping cream or milk. Season with salt and pepper. Set aside.

5 ▲ Heat the remaining butter in a large non-stick frying pan until foamy. Add the onion and carrots and cook until softened, about 5 minutes. Add the celery and fresh mushrooms and cook for 5 minutes more. Stir in the chicken, peas and drained porcini mushrooms.

6 Add the chicken mixture to the cream sauce and stir to mix. Taste for seasoning. Transfer to a 2.5 litre/4 pint/10 cup rectangular baking dish.

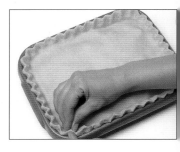

7 ▲ Roll out the pastry to about 3mm/⅛in thick. Cut out a rectangle about 2.5cm/1in larger all around than the dish. Lay the rectangle of pastry over the filling. Make a decorative edge, crimping the pastry by pushing the index finger of one hand between the thumb and index finger of the other.

8 Cut several vents in the pastry to allow steam to escape. Brush with the egg glaze.

9 ▲ Press together the dough trimmings, then roll out again. Cut into strips and lay them over the top crust. Glaze again. If desired, roll small balls of dough and set them in the "windows" in the lattice.

10 Bake until the pastry is browned, about 30 minutes. Serve the pie hot from the dish.

Oregon Blue Cheese Burgers

SERVES 4

900g/2lb lean beef mince

1 garlic clove, finely chopped

30ml/2 tbsp chopped fresh parsley

30ml/2 tbsp chopped fresh chives

2.5ml/½ tsp salt

pepper

225g/8oz Oregon Blue cheese, crumbled

4 hamburger buns, split and toasted

TO SERVE

tomato slices and lettuce

mustard or ketchup

1 ▼ In a bowl, combine the beef, garlic, parsley, chives, salt and a little pepper. Mix lightly together, then form into four thick burgers.

2 ▲ Make a slit in the side of each burger, poking well into the beef to form a pocket. Fill each pocket with 50g/2oz of the blue cheese.

3 ▲ Close the holes to seal the blue cheese inside the burgers.

4 Heat a ridged frying pan or preheat the grill (broiler).

5 Cook the burgers for 4–5 minutes on each side for medium-rare, about 6–7 minutes for well done.

6 ▲ Place the burgers in the split hamburger buns. Serve at once, with sliced tomatoes and lettuce leaves, and mustard or ketchup if you like.

Steak with Mushrooms and Leeks in Red Wine

SERVES 4

6–8 leeks (about 500g/1¼lb), white and
   light green parts only

50ml/2fl oz/¼ cup olive oil

675g/1½lb mushrooms, quartered

475ml/16fl oz/2 cups dry red wine, such
   as a pinot noir or merlot

salt and pepper

4 × 225g/8oz boneless sirloin steaks,
   about 2cm/¾in thick

15ml/1 tbsp chopped fresh parsley

4 Remove the lid, raise the heat and
cook until the wine has reduced
slightly, about 5 minutes. Set aside.

5 ▼ Brush the steaks with the
remaining 15ml/1 tbsp oil and sprinkle
generously on both sides with salt
and pepper.

6 Heat a ridged frying pan or preheat
the grill (broiler). When hot, add the
steaks and cook for 3–4 minutes on
each side for medium-rare.

7 Meanwhile, stir the parsley into the
leek mixture and reheat.

8 Place the steaks on four warmed
plates. Heap the leek mixture on top
and serve.

~ VARIATION ~

If available, use fresh wild
mushrooms for extra flavour.

1 ▲ Trim the leeks and cut into
2.5cm/1in slices on the diagonal.

2 ▲ Heat 45ml/3 tbsp of the oil in
a large frying pan. When hot, add the
leeks and mushrooms and cook over a
medium heat, stirring often, until
lightly browned.

3 Stir in the wine, scraping the
bottom of the pan. Season with salt
and pepper. Bring to the boil and boil
for 1 minute. Reduce the heat to low,
then cover and cook for 5 minutes.

Idaho Beef Stew

SERVES 6

50ml/2fl oz/¼ cup vegetable oil

2 onions, chopped

4 large carrots, thickly sliced

1.3kg/3lb chuck steak, cubed

salt and pepper

45ml/3 tbsp plain (all-purpose) flour

750ml/1¼ pints/3 cups unsalted beef stock

250ml/8fl oz/1 cup strong black coffee

10ml/2 tsp dried oregano

1 bay leaf

115g/4oz/1 cup shelled fresh or frozen peas

mashed potatoes, for serving

1 ▼ Heat 30ml/2 tbsp of the oil in a large flameproof casserole. Add the onions and carrots and cook over a medium heat until lightly browned, about 8 minutes. Remove them with a slotted spoon, transfer to a plate or dish and reserve.

2 ▲ Add another 15ml/1 tbsp of the oil to the casserole and then add the beef cubes. Raise the heat to medium-high and cook until browned all over. (Work in batches if necessary.) Season with salt and pepper.

3 ▲ Return the vegetables to the casserole. Add the flour and the remaining 15ml/1 tbsp of oil. Cook, stirring constantly, for 1 minute. Add the stock, coffee, oregano and bay leaf. Bring to the boil and cook, stirring often, until thickened. Reduce the heat to low, then cover the casserole and simmer gently until the beef is tender, about 45 minutes.

4 ▲ Add the peas and simmer for 5–10 minutes more. Discard the bay leaf and taste for seasoning. Serve hot, with mashed potatoes.

Pot-Roasted Veal Chops with Carrots

SERVES 4

15ml/1 tbsp vegetable oil

15g/½oz/1 tbsp butter

4 veal chops, about 2cm/¾in thick

salt and pepper

1 onion, halved and thinly sliced

120ml/4fl oz/½ cup dry white wine

675g/1½lb carrots, cut into 1cm/½in slices

1 bay leaf

120ml/4fl oz/½ cup whipping cream

1 Preheat the oven to 180°C/350°F/Gas 4.

2 ▲ Heat the oil and butter in a flameproof casserole large enough to hold the veal chops in one layer. Add the chops and cook over a medium heat until well browned on both sides, 6–8 minutes. Transfer to a plate, season with salt and pepper and set aside.

3 ▲ Add the onion to the pan and cook until it is just softened, about 5 minutes. Stir in the wine.

4 ▼ Return the veal chops to the pan. Add the carrots. Season with salt and pepper and add the bay leaf.

5 Cover the casserole and transfer it to the oven. Cook until the chops are tender, about 30 minutes.

6 Remove the chops and carrots to warm plates and keep warm. Discard the bay leaf. Stir the cream into the cooking liquid and bring to the boil. Simmer until the sauce is slightly thickened, 2–3 minutes.

7 Taste the sauce and adjust the seasoning if necessary, then spoon it over the chops. Serve at once.

Cauliflower au Gratin

SERVES 4

1.2kg/2½lb cauliflower florets
(about 1 large head)

40g/1½oz/3 tbsp butter

45ml/3 tbsp plain (all-purpose) flour

475ml/16fl oz/2 cups milk

50g/2oz/½ cup grated mature (sharp)
Cheddar cheese

salt and pepper

3 bay leaves

1 ▲ Preheat the oven to 180°C/350°F/
Gas 4. Grease a 30cm/12in baking dish.

2 Bring a large pan of salted water
to the boil. Add the cauliflower and
cook until just tender but still firm,
7–8 minutes. Drain well.

3 ▲ Melt the butter in a heavy pan.
Whisk in the flour until thoroughly
blended and cook until bubbling.
Gradually add the milk. Bring to the
boil and continue cooking, stirring
constantly, until thick.

4 ▲ Remove from the heat and stir
in the grated cheese. Season the sauce
with salt and pepper.

5 ▲ Place the bay leaves on the
bottom of the prepared dish. Arrange
the cauliflower florets on top in an
even layer. Pour the cheese sauce
evenly over the cauliflower.

6 Bake until browned, 20–25 minutes.
Serve at once.

Wild Rice Pilaff

SERVES 6

200g/7oz/1 cup wild rice

salt and pepper

40g/1½oz/3 tbsp butter

½ onion, finely chopped

200g/7oz/1 cup long grain rice

475ml/16fl oz/2 cups chicken stock

65g/2½oz/⅔ cup flaked (sliced) almonds

90g/3½oz/⅔ cup sultanas (golden raisins)

30ml/2 tbsp chopped fresh parsley

1 ▲ Bring a large pan of water to the boil. Add the wild rice and 15ml/1 tsp salt. Cover and simmer gently until the rice is tender, 45–60 minutes. When done, drain well.

2 ▲ Meanwhile, melt 15g/½oz/1 tbsp of the butter in another pan. Add the onion and cook over a medium heat until it is just softened, about 5 minutes. Stir in the long grain rice and cook for 1 minute more.

3 Stir in the stock and bring to the boil. Cover and simmer gently until the rice is tender and the liquid has been absorbed, 30–40 minutes.

4 ▼ Melt the remaining butter in a small frying pan. Add the almonds and cook, stirring, until they are just golden, 2–3 minutes. Set aside.

5 ▲ In a large bowl, combine the wild rice, long grain rice, sultanas, almonds and parsley. Stir to mix. Taste and adjust the seasoning, if necessary. Transfer to a warmed serving dish and serve at once.

Blue Cheese and Chive Pennies

MAKES 48

225g/8oz blue cheese, such as
    Oregon Blue, crumbled

115g/4oz/½ cup unsalted butter,
    at room temperature

1 egg plus 1 egg yolk

45ml/3 tbsp chopped fresh chives

black pepper

225g/8oz/2 cups plain (all-purpose)
    flour, sifted

1 ▼ The day before serving, beat the
cheese and butter together until well
blended. Add the egg, egg yolk, chives
and a little pepper and beat just until
the ingredients are blended.

2 ▲ Add the flour in three batches,
folding in well between each addition.

3 ▲ Divide the mixture in half
and shape each half into a log about
5cm/2in in diameter. Wrap in baking
parchment and chill overnight.

4 Preheat the oven to 190°C/375°F/
Gas 5. Lightly grease two baking sheets.

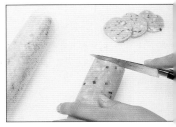

5 ▲ Cut the logs across into slices
about 3mm/⅛in thick. Place on the
prepared sheets.

6 Bake until just golden around the
edges, about 10 minutes. Transfer to a
wire rack to cool.

~ COOK'S TIP ~

The cheese pennies will keep for up
to 10 days in an airtight container.

Smoked Salmon and Dill Spread

MAKES 750ML/1¼ PINTS/3 CUPS

225g/8oz/1 cup ricotta cheese

225g/8oz/1 cup cream cheese,
    at room temperature

175g/6oz smoked salmon,
    finely chopped

115g/4oz cooked salmon, flaked

15g/½oz/¼ cup chopped fresh dill

45–60ml/3–4 tbsp fresh lemon juice

salt and pepper

vegetables, such as cucumber slices,
    Belgian endive leaves, (bell) pepper
    strips, or small toasts, for serving

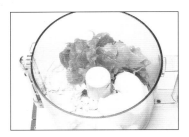

1 ▲ Place the ricotta cheese, cream
cheese and smoked salmon in a food
processor or blender and process until
light and fluffy. Scrape the mixture
into a bowl.

2 ▼ Stir in the cooked salmon, dill
and 45ml/3 tbsp of the lemon juice.
Season with salt and pepper. Taste
and add the remaining lemon juice, if
you like. Serve the spread cold.

Blue Cheese and Chive Pennies (top), Smoked Salmon and Dill Spread

Winter Warmer (Hot White Chocolate)

SERVES 4

175g/6oz white chocolate

1.75 litres/3 pints/½ quarts milk

5ml/1 tsp coffee extract, or 10ml/2 tsp instant coffee powder

10ml/2 tsp orange-flavoured liqueur (optional)

TO SERVE

whipped cream

ground cinnamon

~ COOK'S TIP ~

If you prefer, use milk chocolate or plain (semisweet) chocolate instead of white chocolate, but taste before serving in case a little sugar is needed.

1 ▼ With a sharp knife, finely chop the white chocolate. (Try not to handle it too much or it will soften and stick together.)

2 Pour the milk into a medium heavy pan and bring just to the boil (bubbles will form around the edge of the pan).

3 ▲ Add the chopped white chocolate, coffee extract or powder and orange-flavoured liqueur, if using. Stir until the chocolate has melted.

4 Divide the hot chocolate between four coffee mugs. Top each with a rosette or spoonful of whipped cream and a sprinkling of ground cinnamon. Serve at once.

Easy Hazelnut Fudge

MAKES 16 SQUARES

150ml/¼ pint/⅔ cup evaporated milk

375g/13oz/1¾ cups granulated sugar

pinch of salt

50g/2oz/½ cup halved hazelnuts

350g/12oz/2 cups plain (semisweet) chocolate chips

5ml/1 tsp hazelnut liqueur (optional)

1 Generously grease a 20cm/8in square cake tin (pan).

~ VARIATION ~

For Easy Peanut Butter Fudge, substitute peanut butter chips for the chocolate chips and replace the hazelnuts with peanuts.

2 Combine the evaporated milk, sugar and salt in a heavy pan. Bring to the boil over a medium heat, stirring constantly. Simmer gently, stirring, for about 5 minutes.

3 ▼ Remove from the heat and add the hazelnuts, chocolate chips and liqueur, if using. Stir until the chocolate has completely melted.

4 ▲ Quickly pour the fudge mixture into the prepared pan and spread it out evenly. leave to cool.

5 When the fudge is set, cut it into 2.5cm/1in squares. Store in an airtight container, separating the layers with baking parchment.

Winter Warmer (top), Easy Hazelnut Fudge

Northwestern Brown Betty

SERVES 6

1kg/2¼lb pears (about 8)

50ml/2fl oz/¼ cup lemon juice

175g/6oz/3 cups fresh breadcrumbs

75g/3oz/6 tbsp butter, melted

90g/3½oz/⅔ cup dried cherries

65g/2½oz/⅔ cup coarsely
    chopped hazelnuts

90g/3½oz/½ cup soft light brown sugar

15–25g/½–1oz/1–2 tbsp butter,
    finely diced

whipped cream, for serving

1 Preheat the oven to 190°C/375°F/Gas 5. Grease a 20cm/8in square cake tin (pan).

2 ▼ Peel, core and dice the pears. Sprinkle them with the lemon juice to prevent discolouration.

3 ▲ Combine the breadcrumbs and melted butter in a bowl. Spread a scant one-third of the crumb mixture over the bottom of the prepared dish.

4 ▲ Top with half the pears. Sprinkle over half the dried cherries, half the hazelnuts and half the sugar. Repeat the layers, then finish with a layer of buttered breadcrumbs.

5 ▲ Dot with the pieces of butter. Bake until golden, 30–35 minutes. Serve hot, with whipped cream.

Rhubarb and Strawberry Crisp

SERVES 4

225g/8oz strawberries, hulled

450g/1lb rhubarb, diced

90g/3½oz/½ cup granulated sugar

15ml/1 tbsp cornflour (cornstarch)

75ml/2½fl oz/⅓ cup fresh orange juice

115g/4oz/1 cup plain (all-purpose) flour

90g/3½oz/1 cup rolled oats

90g/3½oz/½ cup soft light brown sugar

2.5ml/½ tsp ground cinnamon

50g/2oz/½ cup ground almonds

150g/5oz/10 tbsp cold butter, diced

1 egg, lightly beaten

1 Preheat oven to 180°C/350°F/Gas 4.

2 ▲ If the strawberries are large, cut them in half. Combine the strawberries, rhubarb and granulated sugar in a 2.5 litre/4 pint baking dish.

3 ▲ In a small bowl, blend the cornflour with the orange juice. Pour this mixture over the fruit and stir gently to coat. Set the baking dish aside while making the topping.

4 ▼ In a bowl, toss together the flour, oats, brown sugar, cinnamon and almonds. With a pastry blender, cut in the butter until the mixture resembles breadcrumbs, or rub in with your fingertips. Stir in the beaten egg.

5 ▲ Spoon the oat mixture evenly over the fruit and press down gently. Bake until browned, 50–60 minutes. Serve the crisp warm.

Blackberry Cobbler

SERVES 8

800g/1¾lb/6 cups blackberries

200g/7oz/1 cup granulated sugar

45ml/3 tbsp plain (all-purpose) flour

grated rind of 1 lemon

30ml/2 tbsp granulated sugar mixed with 1.5ml/¼ tsp grated nutmeg

FOR THE TOPPING

225g/8oz/2 cups plain (all-purpose) flour

200g/7oz/1 cup granulated sugar

15ml/1 tbsp baking powder

pinch of salt

250ml/8fl oz/1 cup milk

115g/4oz/½ cup butter, melted

1 Preheat oven to 180°C/350°F/Gas 4.

2 ▼ In a bowl, combine the blackberries, sugar, flour and lemon rind. Stir gently to blend. Transfer to a 2.5 litre/4 pint baking dish.

3 ▲ For the topping, sift the flour, sugar, baking powder and salt into a large bowl. Set aside. In a measuring jug (cup), combine the milk and butter.

4 ▲ Gradually stir the milk mixture into the dry ingredients and stir until the mixture is just smooth.

5 ▲ Spoon the mixture over the berries, spreading to the edges.

6 Sprinkle the surface with the sugar and nutmeg mixture. Bake until the topping is set and lightly browned, about 50 minutes. Serve hot.

Baked Apples

SERVES 6

115g/4oz/½ cup chopped dried apricots

25g/1oz/½ cup chopped walnuts

5ml/1 tsp grated lemon rind

1.5ml/¼ tsp ground cinnamon

90g/3½oz/½ cup soft light brown sugar

25g/1oz/2 tbsp butter,
   at room temperature

6 baking apples

15ml/1 tbsp melted butter

1 Preheat oven to 190°C/375°F/Gas 5.

2 ▲ In a bowl, combine the apricots, walnuts, lemon rind and cinnamon. Add the sugar and butter and stir until thoroughly combined.

3 ▲ Core the apples, without cutting all the way through to the base. With a small knife, slightly widen the top of each opening by about 4cm/1½in to make room for the filling.

4 Spoon the apricot and walnut filling into the opening in the apples, packing it down lightly.

5 ▼ Place the apples in a baking dish just large enough to hold them comfortably side by side.

6 ▲ Brush the apples with the melted butter. Bake until they are tender, 40–45 minutes. Serve hot.

Blueberry and Hazelnut Cheesecake

SERVES 6–8

350g/12oz blueberries

15ml/1 tbsp honey

75g/3oz/6 tbsp granulated sugar

5ml/1 tsp plus 15ml/1 tbsp fresh
    lemon juice

175g/6oz cream cheese,
    at room temperature

1 egg

5ml/1 tsp hazelnut liqueur (optional)

120ml/4fl oz/½ cup whipping cream

FOR THE BISCUIT CASE

185g/6½oz/1⅔ cups ground hazelnuts

75g/3oz/⅔ cup plain (all-purpose) flour

pinch of salt

50g/2oz/¼ cup butter,
    at room temperature

65g/2½oz/⅓ cup soft light brown sugar

1 egg yolk

1 ▲ For the crust, put the hazelnuts
in a large bowl. Sift in the flour and
salt, and stir to mix. Set aside.

~ COOK'S TIP ~

The cheesecake can be prepared
1 day in advance, but add the fruit
shortly before serving. Instead of
covering the top completely, leave
spaces to make a design, if you wish.

2 Beat the butter with the brown
sugar until light and fluffy. Beat in the
egg yolk. Gradually fold in the nut
mixture, in three batches.

3 ▲ Press the biscuit mixture into a
greased 23cm/9in pie dish, spreading it
evenly against the sides. Form a rim
around the top edge that is slightly
thicker than the sides. Cover and chill
for at least 30 minutes.

4 Preheat oven to 180°C/350°F/Gas 4.

5 ▲ Meanwhile, for the topping,
combine the blueberries, honey,
15ml/1 tbsp of the granulated sugar
and 5ml/1 tsp lemon juice in a heavy
pan. Cook the mixture over a low
heat, stirring occasionally, until the
berries have given off some liquid but
still retain their shape, 5–7 minutes.
Remove from the heat and set aside.

6 Place the base in the oven and
bake for 15 minutes. Remove and leave
to cool while making the filling.

7 ▲ Beat together the cream cheese
and remaining granulated sugar until
light and fluffy. Add the egg,
remaining lemon juice, the liqueur,
if using, and the cream and beat until
thoroughly incorporated.

8 ▲ Pour the cheese mixture into
the crust and spread evenly. Bake
until just set, 20–25 minutes.

9 Let the cheesecake cool completely
on a wire rack, then cover and chill for
at least 1 hour.

10 Spread the blueberry mixture
evenly over the top of the cheesecake.
Serve at cool room temperature.

Mocha Vanilla Deserts

SERVES 6

285g/10½oz/1½ cups granulated sugar

90ml/6 tbsp cornflour (cornstarch)

1 litre/1¾ pints/4 cups milk

3 egg yolks

75g/3oz/6 tbsp unsalted butter,
  at room temperature

20ml/4 tsp instant coffee powder

10ml/2 tsp vanilla extract

30ml/2 tbsp unsweetened cocoa powder

whipped cream, for serving

1 ▲ For the coffee layer, combine 90g/
3½oz/½ cup of the sugar and 30ml/2 tbsp
of the cornflour in a heavy pan. Gradually
add 325ml/11fl oz/1⅓ cups of the milk,
whisking until well blended. Over a
medium heat, whisk in one egg yolk
and bring to the boil, whisking constantly.
Boil for 1 minute, still whisking.

2 ▲ Remove from the heat. Stir in
30ml/2 tbsp of the butter and the
coffee powder. Leave to cool slightly.

3 ▲ Divide the coffee mixture
among six wine glasses. Smooth the
tops before the mixture sets.

4 ▲ Wipe any dribbles on the insides
and outsides of the glasses with damp
kitchen paper.

5 ▲ For the vanilla layer, combine 90g/
3½oz/½ cup of the sugar and 30ml/ 2 tbsp
of the cornflour in a heavy pan. Gradually
whisk in 325ml/11fl oz/1⅓ cups of the milk
until well blended. Over a medium heat,
whisk in one egg yolk and bring to the
boil, whisking. Boil for 1 minute.

6 Remove from the heat and stir in
25g/1oz/2 tbsp of the butter and the
vanilla. Leave to cool slightly, then
spoon into the glasses on top of the
coffee layer. Smooth the tops and wipe
the glasses with kitchen paper.

7 ▲ For the chocolate layer, combine
the remaining sugar and cornflour in a
heavy pan. Gradually whisk in the
remaining milk until well blended.
Over a moderate heat, whisk in the
last egg yolk and bring to the boil,
whisking constantly. Boil for 1 minute.
Off the heat, stir in the remaining
butter and the cocoa powder. Leave to
cool slightly, then spoon into the
glasses on top of the vanilla layer.
Chill until set.

8 ▲ Pipe or spoon whipped cream on
top of each pudding before serving.

~ COOK'S TIP ~

For a special occasion, prepare the
vanilla layer using a fresh vanilla
pod (bean). Choose a plump, supple
pod and split it down the centre
with a sharp knife. Add to the
mixture with the milk and discard
the pod before spooning into the
glasses. The flavour will be more
pronounced and the pudding will
have pretty brown speckles from
the vanilla seeds.

GREAT AMERICAN BAKING

Nothing equals the satisfaction of home baking. No commercial cake mix or store-bought biscuit can match one that is made from the best fresh ingredients with all the added enjoyment that baking at home provides – the enticing aromas that fill the house and stimulate appetites, the delicious straight-from-the-oven flavour, as well as the pride of having created such wonderful goodies yourself.

This section of the book is filled with familiar favourites as well as many other lesser known recipes. Explore the wealth of biscuits, buns, tea breads, yeast breads, pies, tarts, and cakes within these pages. Even if you are a novice baker, the easy-to-follow and clear step-by-step photographs will help you achieve good results. For the more experienced home baker, this book will provide some new recipes to add to your repertoire.

Baking is an exact science and needs to be approached in an ordered way. First read through the recipe from beginning to end. Set out all the required ingredients before you begin. Medium eggs are assumed unless specified otherwise, and they should be at room temperature for best results. Sift the flour after you have measured it, and incorporate other dry ingredients as specified in the individual recipes. If you sift the flour from a fair height, it will have more chance to aerate and lighten.

When a recipe calls for folding one ingredient into another, it should be done in a way that incorporates as much air as possible into the mixture. Use either a large metal spoon or a long rubber or plastic scraper. Gently plunge the spoon or scraper deep into the centre of the mixture and, scooping up a large amount of the mixture, fold it over. Turn the bowl slightly so each scoop folds over another part of the mixture.

No two ovens are alike. Buy a reliable oven thermometer and test the temperature of your oven. When possible bake in the centre of the oven where the heat is more likely to be constant. If using a fan-assisted oven, follow the manufacturer's guidelines for baking. Good quality baking tins can improve your results, as they conduct heat more efficiently.

Practice, patience and enthusiasm are the keys to confident and successful baking. The recipes that follow will inspire you to start sifting flour, breaking eggs and stirring up all sorts of delectable homemade treats – all guaranteed to bring great satisfaction to both the baker and those lucky enough to enjoy the results.

BISCUITS & BARS

KEEP THE BISCUIT TIN FILLED WITH
THIS WONDERFUL ARRAY OF
BISCUITS AND BARS – SOME SOFT
AND CHEWY, SOME CRUNCHY AND
NUTTY, SOME RICH AND SINFUL,
AND SOME PLAIN AND WHOLESOME.
ALL ARE IRRESISTIBLE.

Farmhouse Cookies

Makes 18

115g/4oz/¹/² cup butter or margarine, at room temperature

90g/3¹/² oz/generous 1 cup light brown sugar

65g/2¹/² oz/¹/⁴ cup crunchy peanut butter

1 egg

50g/2oz/¹/² cup plain (all-purpose) flour

2.5ml/¹/² tsp baking powder

2.5ml/¹/² tsp ground cinnamon

pinch of salt

175g/6oz/1¹/² cups muesli (granola)

50g/2oz/¹/³ cup raisins

50g/2oz/¹/² cup chopped walnuts

1 Preheat the oven to 180°C/350°F/ Gas 4. Grease a baking sheet.

2 With an electric mixer, cream the butter or margarine and sugar until light and fluffy. Beat in the peanut butter. Beat in the egg.

3 ▲ Sift the flour, baking powder, cinnamon and salt over the peanut butter mixture and stir to blend. Stir in the muesli, raisins and walnuts. Taste the mixture to see if it needs more sugar, as muesli varies.

4 ▲ Drop rounded tablespoonfuls of the mixture on to the prepared baking sheet about 2.5cm/1in apart. Press gently with the back of a spoon to spread each mound into a circle.

5 Bake until lightly coloured, about 15 minutes. With a metal spatula, transfer to a rack to cool. Store in an airtight container.

Crunchy Oatmeal Cookies

MAKES 14

175g/6oz/³/⁴ cup butter or margarine, at room temperature

175g/6oz/scant 1 cup caster (superfine) sugar

1 egg yolk

175g/6oz/1¹/² cups plain (all-purpose) flour

5ml/1 tsp bicarbonate of soda (baking soda)

2.5ml/¹/² tsp salt

50g/2oz/¹/² cup rolled oats

50g/2oz/¹/² cup small crunchy nugget cereal

~ VARIATION ~

For Nutty Oatmeal Biscuits, substitute an equal quantity of chopped walnuts or pecan nuts for the cereal, and prepare as described.

1 ▲ With an electric mixer, cream the butter or margarine and sugar together until light and fluffy. Mix in the egg yolk.

2 Sift over the flour, bicarbonate of soda and salt, then stir into the butter mixture. Add the oats and cereal and stir to blend. Chill for at least 20 minutes. Meanwhile, preheat the oven to 190°C/375°F/Gas 5. Grease a baking sheet.

3 ▼ Roll the mixture into balls. Place them on the sheet and flatten with the bottom of a floured glass.

4 Bake until golden, 10–12 minutes. With a metal spatula, transfer to a rack to cool completely. Store in an airtight container.

Farmhouse Cookies (top), Crunchy Oatmeal Cookie

Oaty Coconut Cookies

MAKES 48

175g/6oz/1¾ cups quick-cooking oats

75g/3oz/1 cup desiccated (dry unsweetened) coconut

225g/8oz/1 cup butter or margarine, at room temperature

115g/4oz/generous ½ cup caster (superfine) sugar, plus 30ml/2 tbsp

50g/2oz/¼ cup soft dark brown sugar

2 eggs

60ml/4 tbsp milk

7.5ml/1½ tsp vanilla extract

115g/4oz/1 cup plain (all-purpose) flour

2.5ml/½ tsp bicarbonate of soda (baking soda)

2.5ml/½ tsp salt

5ml/1 tsp ground cinnamon

1 Preheat the oven to 200°C/400°F/ Gas 6. Lightly grease two baking sheets.

2 ▲ Spread the oats and coconut on an ungreased baking sheet. Bake until golden brown, 8–10 minutes, stirring occasionally.

3 With an electric mixer, cream the butter or margarine and both sugars until light and fluffy. Beat in the eggs, one at a time, then the milk and vanilla. Sift over the dry ingredients and fold in. Stir in the oats and coconut.

4 ▼ Drop spoonfuls of the mixture 2.5–5cm/1–2in apart on the prepared sheets and flatten with the bottom of a greased glass dipped in sugar. Bake until golden, 8–10 minutes. Transfer to a rack to cool.

Crunchy Jumbles

MAKES 36

115g/4oz/½ cup butter or margarine, at room temperature

225g/8oz/generous 1 cup caster (superfine) sugar

1 egg

5ml/1 tsp vanilla extract

150g/5oz/¾ cup plain (all-purpose) flour

2.5ml/½ tsp bicarbonate of soda (baking soda)

pinch of salt

50g/2oz crisped rice cereal

175g/6oz chocolate chips

~ VARIATION ~

For even crunchier biscuits, add 50g/2oz/⅓ cup walnuts, coarsely chopped, with the cereal and chocolate chips.

1 Preheat the oven to 180°C/350°F/ Gas 4. Lightly grease two baking sheets.

2 ▲ With an electric mixer, cream the butter or margarine and sugar until light and fluffy. Beat in the egg and vanilla. Sift over the flour, bicarbonate of soda and salt and fold in carefully.

3 ▼ Add the cereal and chocolate chips. Stir to mix thoroughly.

4 Drop spoonfuls of the mixture 2.5–5cm/1–2in apart on the sheets. Bake until golden, 10–12 minutes. Transfer to a rack to cool.

Oaty Coconut Cookies (top), Crunchy Jumble

Ginger Cookies

MAKES 36

225g/8oz/generous 1 cup caster
  (superfine) sugar

90g/3¹/₂oz/generous 1 cup soft light
  brown sugar

115g/4oz/¹/₂ cup butter, at
  room temperature

115g/4oz/¹/₂ cup margarine, at
  room temperature

1 egg

90ml/6 tbsp black treacle (molasses)

250g/9oz/2¹/₄ cups plain (all-purpose) flour

10ml/2 tsp ground ginger

2.5ml/¹/₂ tsp freshly grated nutmeg

5ml/1 tsp ground cinnamon

10ml/2 tsp bicarbonate of soda
  (baking soda)

2.5ml/¹/₂ tsp salt

1 Preheat the oven to 170°C/325°F/
Gas 3. Line two or three baking sheets
with baking parchment; grease lightly.

2 ▲ With an electric mixer, cream
half the caster sugar, the brown
sugar, butter and margarine until
light and fluffy. Add the egg and
continue beating to blend well. Add
the treacle.

3 ▲ Sift the flour, spices and
bicarbonate of soda three times,
then stir into the butter mixture.
Refrigerate for 30 minutes.

4 ▲ Place the remaining sugar in a
shallow dish. Roll tablespoonfuls of
the biscuit mixture into balls, then
roll the balls in the sugar to coat.

5 Place the balls 5cm/2in apart
on the prepared sheets and flatten
slightly. Bake until golden around the
edges but soft in the middle, 12–15
minutes. Leave to stand for 5 minutes
before transferring to a rack to cool.

~ VARIATION ~

To make Gingerbread Men, increase
the amount of flour by 25g/1oz/
¹/₄ cup. Roll out the mixture and
cut out shapes with a special cutter.
Decorate with icing, if you like.

Orange Cookies

MAKES 30

115g/4oz/^{1}/$_2$ cup butter, at room temperature
200g/7oz/1 cup caster (superfine) sugar
2 egg yolks
15ml/1 tbsp fresh orange juice
grated rind of 1 large orange
200g/7oz/scant 2 cups plain (all-purpose) flour
10g/^{1}/$_4$oz/1 tbsp cornflour (cornstarch)
2.5ml/^{1}/$_2$ tsp salt
5ml/1 tsp baking powder

1 ▲ With an electric mixer, cream the butter and sugar until light and fluffy. Add the yolks, orange juice and rind, and continue beating to blend. Set aside.

2 In another bowl, sift together the flour, cornflour, salt and baking powder. Add to the butter mixture and stir until it forms a dough.

3 ▲ Wrap the dough in baking parchment and chill for 2 hours.

4 Preheat the oven to 190°C/375°F/Gas 5. Grease two baking sheets.

5 ▲ Roll spoonfuls of the dough into balls and place 2.5–5cm/1–2in apart on the prepared sheets.

6 ▼ Press down with a fork to flatten. Bake until golden brown, 8–10 minutes. With a metal spatula transfer to a rack to cool.

Cinnamon-coated Cookies

MAKES 30

115g/4oz/½ cup butter, at
   room temperature

350g/12oz/1¾ cups caster
   (superfine) sugar

5ml/1 tsp vanilla extract

2 eggs

50ml/2fl oz/¼ cup milk

400g/14oz/3½ cups plain (all-purpose) flour

5ml/1 tsp bicarbonate of soda
   (baking soda)

50g/2oz/½ cup finely chopped walnuts

FOR THE COATING

65g/2½oz/5 tbsp sugar

30ml/2 tbsp ground cinnamon

1 Preheat the oven to 190°C/375°F/
Gas 5. Grease two baking sheets.

2 With an electric mixer, cream the
butter until light. Add the sugar and
vanilla and continue mixing until
fluffy. Beat in the eggs, then the milk.

3 ▲ Sift the flour and bicarbonate of
soda over the butter mixture and stir
to blend. Stir in the nuts. Refrigerate
for 15 minutes.

4 ▲ For the coating, mix the sugar
and cinnamon. Roll tablespoonfuls of
the mixture into walnut-size balls.
Roll the balls in the sugar mixture.
You may need to work in batches.

5 Place 5cm/2in apart on the
prepared sheets and flatten slightly.
Bake until golden, about 10 minutes.
Transfer to a rack to cool.

Chewy Chocolate Cookies

MAKES 18

4 egg whites

275g/10oz/scant 2½ cups icing
   (confectioners') sugar

115g/4oz/1 cup unsweetened cocoa powder

30ml/2 tbsp plain (all-purpose) flour

5ml/1 tsp instant coffee

15ml/1 tbsp water

115g/4oz/½ cup finely chopped walnuts

1 Preheat the oven to 180°C/350°F/
Gas 4. Line two baking sheets with
baking parchment and grease the paper.

```
~ VARIATION ~
If wished, add 75g/3oz chocolate
chips to the mixture with the nuts.
```

2 With an electric mixer, beat the
egg whites until frothy.

3 ▼ Sift the sugar, cocoa, flour and
coffee into the whites. Add the water
and continue beating on low speed to
blend, then on high for a few minutes
until the mixture thickens. With a
rubber spatula, fold in the walnuts.

4 ▲ Place generous spoonfuls of the
mixture 2.5cm/1in apart on the
prepared sheets. Bake until firm and
cracked on top but soft on the inside,
12–15 minutes. With a metal spatula,
transfer to a rack to cool.

Cinnamon-coated Cookies (top), Chewy Chocolate Cookies

Chocolate Pretzels

MAKES 28

150g/5oz/1¹/₄ cups plain
  (all-purpose) flour

pinch of salt

25g/³/₄oz/1 tbsp unsweetened cocoa powder

115g/4oz/¹/₂ cup butter, at
  room temperature

130g/4¹/₂oz/scant ³/₄ cup caster
  (superfine) sugar

1 egg

1 egg white, lightly beaten, for glazing

sugar crystals, for sprinkling

1 Sift together the flour, salt and cocoa powder. Set aside. Grease two baking sheets.

2 ▲ With an electric mixer, cream the butter until light. Add the sugar and continue beating until light and fluffy. Beat in the egg. Add the dry ingredients and stir to blend. Gather the dough into a ball, wrap in clear film (plastic wrap), and chill for 1 hour or freeze for 30 minutes.

3 ▲ Roll the dough into 28 small balls. Chill the balls until needed. Preheat the oven to 190°C/375°F/ Gas 5.

4 ▲ Roll each ball into a rope about 25cm/10in long. With each rope, form a loop with the two ends facing you. Twist the ends and fold back on to the circle, pressing in to make a pretzel shape. Place on the sheets.

5 ▲ Brush the pretzels with the egg white. Sprinkle sugar crystals over the tops and bake until firm, 10–12 minutes. Transfer to a rack to cool.

Cream Cheese Spirals

MAKES 32

225g/8oz/1 cup butter, at
  room temperature
225g/8oz/1 cup cream cheese
10ml/2 tsp caster (superfine) sugar
225g/8oz/2 cups plain (all-purpose) flour
1 egg white beaten with 15ml/1 tbsp
  water, for glazing
caster sugar, for sprinkling
FOR THE FILLING
115g/4oz/1 cup finely chopped walnuts
115g/4oz/1/2 cup soft light brown sugar
5ml/1 tsp ground cinnamon

1 With an electric mixer, cream the
butter, cream cheese and sugar until
soft. Sift over the flour and mix until
combined. Gather into a ball and
divide in half. Flatten each half, wrap
in baking parchment and chill for at
least 30 minutes.

2 Meanwhile, make the filling. Mix
together the chopped walnuts, the
brown sugar and the cinnamon, and
set aside.

3 Preheat the oven to 190°C/375°F/
Gas 5. Grease two baking sheets.

4 ▲ Working with one half of the
mixture at a time, roll out thinly into
a circle about 28cm/11in in diameter.
Trim the edges with a knife, using a
dinner plate as a guide.

5 ▼ Brush the surface with the egg
white glaze and then sprinkle evenly
with half the filling.

6 Cut the circle into quarters, and
each quarter into four sections, to
form 16 triangles.

7 ▲ Starting from the base of the
triangles, roll up to form spirals.

8 Place on the sheets and brush with
the remaining glaze. Sprinkle with
caster sugar. Bake until golden,
15–20 minutes. Cool on a rack.

Vanilla Crescents

MAKES 36

175g/6oz/1 cup unblanched almonds

115g/4oz/1 cup plain (all-purpose) flour

pinch of salt

225g/8oz/1 cup unsalted (sweet) butter

115g/4oz/generous ½ cup granulated sugar

5ml/1 tsp vanilla extract

icing (confectioners') sugar, for dusting

1 Grind the almonds with a few tablespoons of the flour in a food processor, blender or nut grinder.

2 Sift the remaining flour with the salt into a bowl. Set aside.

3 With an electric mixer, cream together the butter and sugar until light and fluffy.

4 ▼ Add the almonds, vanilla essence and the flour mixture. Stir to mix well. Gather the dough into a ball, wrap in baking parchment, and chill for at least 30 minutes.

5 Preheat the oven to 160°C/325°F/ Gas 3. Lightly grease two baking sheets.

6 ▲ Break off walnut-size pieces of dough and roll into small cylinders about 1cm/½in in diameter. Bend into small crescents and place on the prepared baking sheets.

7 Bake for about 20 minutes until dry but not brown. Transfer to a wire rack to cool only slightly. Set the rack over a baking sheet and dust with an even layer of icing sugar. Leave to cool completely.

Walnut Crescents

MAKES 72

115g/4oz/⅔ cup walnuts

225g/8oz/1 cup unsalted (sweet) butter

115g/4oz/generous ½ cup granulated sugar

2.5ml/½ tsp vanilla extract

225g/8oz/2 cups plain (all-purpose) flour

1.5ml/¼ tsp salt

icing (confectioners') sugar, for dusting

1 Preheat the oven to 180°C/350°F/ Gas 4.

2 Grind the walnuts in a food processor, blender or nut grinder until they are almost a paste. Transfer to a bowl.

3 Add the butter to the walnuts and mix with a wooden spoon until blended. Add the granulated sugar and vanilla, and stir to blend.

4 ▼ Sift the flour and salt into the walnut mixture. Work into a dough.

5 Shape the dough into small cylinders about 4cm/1½in long. Bend into crescents and place evenly spaced on an ungreased baking sheet.

6 ▲ Bake until lightly browned, about 15 minutes. Transfer to a rack to cool only slightly. Set the rack over a baking sheet and dust lightly with icing sugar.

Vanilla Crescents (top), Walnut Crescent

Pecan Puffs

MAKES 24

115g/4oz/¹/₂ cup unsalted (sweet) butter

25g/1oz/2 tbsp granulated sugar

pinch of salt

5ml/1 tsp vanilla extract

115g/4oz/²/₃ cup pecan nuts

115g/4oz/1 cup plain (all-purpose)
    flour, sifted

icing (confectioners') sugar, for dusting

1 Preheat the oven to 150°C/300°F/
Gas 2. Grease two baking sheets.

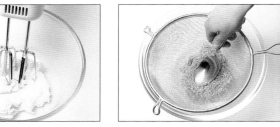

2 ▲ Cream the butter and sugar
until light and fluffy. Stir in the salt
and vanilla extract.

3 Grind the nuts in a food processor,
blender or nut grinder. Stir several
times to prevent them becoming oily.
If necessary, grind in batches.

4 ▲ Push the ground nuts through a
sieve (strainer) set over a bowl to aerate
them. Pieces too large to go through
the sieve can be ground again.

5 ▲ Stir the nuts and flour into
the butter mixture to make a firm,
springy dough.

6 Roll the dough into marble-size
balls between the palms of your
hands. Place on the prepared baking
sheets and bake for 30 minutes.

7 ▲ While the puffs are still hot,
roll them in icing sugar. Leave to cool
completely, then roll once more in
icing sugar.

Pecan Tassies

MAKES 24

115g/4oz/¹/₂ cup cream cheese

115g/4oz/¹/₂ cup butter

115g/4oz/1 cup plain (all-purpose) flour

FOR THE FILLING

2 eggs

115g/4oz/¹/₂ cup soft dark brown sugar

5ml/1 tsp vanilla extract

pinch of salt

25g/1oz/2 tbsp butter, melted

115g/4oz/²/₃ cup pecan nuts

1 Place a baking sheet in the oven and preheat to 180°C/350°F/Gas 4. Grease 24 mini-muffin tins.

2 Chop the cream cheese and butter into cubes. Put them in a mixing bowl. Sift over half the flour and mix. Add the remaining flour and continue mixing to form a dough.

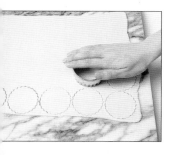

3 ▲ Roll out the dough thinly. With a floured, fluted pastry cutter, stamp out 24 6cm/2¹/₂in rounds. Line the tins with the rounds and chill.

4 To make the filling, lightly whisk the eggs in a bowl. Gradually whisk in the brown sugar, and add the vanilla extract, salt and butter. Set aside until required.

5 ▼ Reserve 24 undamaged pecan halves and chop the rest coarsely with a sharp knife.

6 ▲ Place a spoonful of chopped nuts in each muffin tin and cover with the filling. Set a pecan half on the top of each.

7 Bake on the hot baking sheet for about 20 minutes, until puffed and set. Transfer to a wire rack to cool. Serve at room temperature.

~ VARIATION ~

To make Jam Tassies, fill the cream cheese pastry shells with raspberry or blackberry jam, or other fruit jams. Bake as described.

Lady Fingers

MAKES 18

90g/3¹/₂oz/³/₄ cup plain (all-purpose) flour

pinch of salt

4 eggs, separated

115g/4oz/generous ¹/₂ cup granulated sugar

2.5ml/¹/₂ tsp vanilla extract

icing (confectioners') sugar, for sprinkling

1 Preheat the oven to 150°C/300°F/ Gas 2. Grease two baking sheets, then coat lightly with flour, and shake off the excess.

2 Sift the flour and salt together twice in a bowl.

~ COOK'S TIP ~

To make the biscuits all the same length, mark parallel lines 10cm/4in apart on the greased baking sheets.

3 With an electric mixer beat the egg yolks with half the sugar until thick enough to leave a ribbon trail when the beaters are lifted.

4 ▲ In another bowl, beat the egg whites until stiff. Beat in the remaining sugar until glossy.

5 Sift the flour over the yolks and spoon a large dollop of egg whites over the flour. Carefully fold in with a large metal spoon, adding the vanilla extract. Gently fold in the remaining whites.

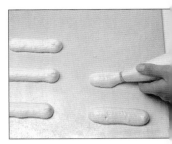

6 ▲ Spoon the mixture into a pipin (pastry) bag fitted with a large plain nozzle. Pipe 10cm/4in long lines on the prepared baking sheets about 2.5cm/1in apart. Sift over a layer of icing sugar. Turn the sheet upside down to dislodge any excess sugar.

7 Bake for about 20 minutes until crusty on the outside but soft in the centre. Cool slightly on the baking sheets before transferring to a wire rack to cool completely.

Walnut Cookies

MAKES 60

115g/4oz/¹/₂ cup butter or margarine

175g/6oz/scant 1 cup caster (superfine) sugar

115g/4oz/1 cup plain (all-purpose) flour

10ml/2 tsp vanilla extract

115g/4oz/²/₃ cup walnuts, finely chopped

~ VARIATION ~

To make Almond Cookies, use an equal amount of finely chopped unblanched almonds instead of walnuts. Replace half the vanilla with 2.5ml/ ¹/₂ tsp almond essence.

1 Preheat the oven to 150°C/300°F/ Gas 2. Grease two baking sheets.

2 ▲ With an electric mixer, cream the butter or margarine until soft. Add 50g/2oz/¹/₄ cup of the sugar and continue beating until light and fluffy. Stir in the flour, vanilla extract and walnuts.

3 Drop teaspoonfuls of the batter 2.5–5cm/1–2in apart on the prepare baking sheets and flatten slightly. Bake for about 25 minutes.

4 ▼ Transfer to a wire rack set ove a baking sheet and sprinkle with the remaining sugar.

Lady Fingers (top), Walnut Cook

Italian Almond Biscotti

MAKES 48

200g/7oz/generous 1 cup whole unblanched almonds

215g/7¹/₂oz/scant 2 cups plain (all-purpose) flour

90g/3¹/₂oz/¹/₂ cup caster (superfine) sugar

pinch of salt

pinch of saffron threads

2.5ml/¹/₂ tsp bicarbonate of soda (baking soda)

2 eggs

1 egg white, lightly beaten

~ COOK'S TIP ~

Dunk biscotti in sweet white wine, such as an Italian Vin Santo or a French Muscat de Beaumes-de-Venise.

---

1 Preheat the oven to 190°C/375°F/ Gas 5. Grease and flour two baking sheets.

2 ▲ Spread the almonds in a baking tray and bake until lightly browned, about 15 minutes. When cool, grind 50g/2oz/¹/₃ cup of the almonds in a food processor, blender, or coffee grinder until pulverized. Coarsely chop the remaining almonds into two or three pieces each. Set aside.

3 ▲ Combine the flour, sugar, salt, saffron, bicarbonate of soda and ground almonds in a bowl and mix to blend. Make a well in the centre and add the eggs. Stir to form a rough dough. Transfer to a floured surface and knead until well blended. Knead in the chopped almonds.

4 ▲ Divide the dough into three equal parts. Roll into logs about 2.5cm/1in in diameter. Place on one of the prepared sheets, brush with the egg white and bake for 20 minutes. Remove from the oven.

5 ▲ With a very sharp knife, cut into each log at an angle making 1cm ¹/₂in slices. Return the slices on the baking sheets to a 140°C/275°F/Gas 1 oven and bake for 25 minutes more. Transfer to a rack to cool.

Christmas Cookies

MAKES 30

75g/6oz/³/4 cup unsalted (sweet) butter, at room temperature

75g/10oz/scant 1¹/2 cups caster (superfine) sugar

egg

egg yolk

ml/1 tsp vanilla extract

ated rind of 1 lemon

5ml/¹/4 tsp salt

75g/10oz/2¹/2 cups plain (all-purpose) flour

OR DECORATING (OPTIONAL)

loured icing and small decorations

Preheat oven to 350°F/180°C/Gas 4.

▲ With an electric mixer, cream e butter until soft. Add the sugar aduallly and continue beating until ght and fluffy.

▲ Using a wooden spoon, slowly x in the whole egg and the egg yolk. dd the vanilla, lemon rind and salt. ir to mix well.

4 Add the flour and stir until blended. Gather the mixture into a ball, wrap in baking parchment, and chill for at least 30 minutes.

5 ▼ On a floured surface, roll out the mixture to 3mm/¹/8in thick.

6 ▲ Stamp out shapes or rounds with biscuit (cookie) cutters.

7 Bake until lightly coloured, about 8 minutes. Transfer to a rack and leave to cool completely before icing and decorating, if wished.

Toasted Oat Meringues

MAKES 12

50g/2oz/1/2 cup rolled oats

2 egg whites

pinch of salt

7.5ml/1 1/2 tsp cornflour (cornstarch)

175g/6oz/scant 1 cup caster
(superfine) sugar

1 Preheat the oven to 140°C/275°F/
Gas 1. Spread the oats on a baking
sheet and toast in the oven until
golden, about 10 minutes. Lower the
heat to 120°C/250°F/Gas 1/2. Grease
and flour a baking sheet.

~ VARIATION ~

Add 2.5ml/1/2 tsp ground cinnamon
with the oats, and fold in gently.

2 ▼ With an electric mixer, beat the
egg whites and salt until they start to
form soft peaks.

3 Sift over the cornflour and
continue beating until the whites hold
stiff peaks. Add half the sugar and
whisk until glossy.

4 ▲ Add the remaining sugar and
fold in, then fold in the oats.

5 Gently spoon the mixture on to the
prepared sheet and bake for 2 hours.

6 When done, turn off the oven. Lift
the meringues from the sheet, turn
over, and set in another place on the
sheet to prevent sticking. Leave in
the oven as they cool down.

Meringues

MAKES 24

4 egg whites

pinch of salt

275g/10oz/scant 1 1/2 cups caster
(superfine) sugar

2.5ml/1/2 tsp vanilla or almond extract
(optional)

250ml/8fl oz/1 cup whipped cream
(optional)

1 Preheat the oven to 110°C/225°F/
Gas 1/4. Grease and flour two large
baking sheets.

2 With an electric mixer, beat the
egg whites and salt in a very clean
metal bowl on low speed. When they
start to form soft peaks, add half the
sugar and continue beating until the
mixture holds stiff peaks.

3 ▲ With a large metal spoon, fold
in the remaining sugar and vanilla or
almond extract, if using.

4 ▼ Pipe the meringue mixture or
spoon it on to the prepared sheet.

5 Bake for 2 hours. Turn off the
oven. Loosen the meringues, invert,
and set in another place on the sheet
to prevent sticking. Leave in the oven
as they cool. Serve sandwiched with
whipped cream, if you wish.

Toasted Oat Meringues (top), Meringu

Chocolate Macaroons

MAKES 24

50g/2oz plain (semisweet) chocolate

175g/6oz/1 cup blanched almonds

225g/8oz/generous 1 cup caster (superfine) sugar

3 egg whites

2.5ml/½ tsp vanilla extract

1.5ml/¼ tsp almond extract

icing (confectioners') sugar, for dusting

1 Preheat the oven to 300°F/150°C/ Gas 2. Line two baking sheets with baking parchment and grease the paper.

2 ▼ Melt the chocolate in the top of a double boiler, or in a heatproof bowl set over a pan of hot water.

3 ▲ Grind the almonds finely in a food processor, blender or grinder. Transfer to a mixing bowl.

4 ▲ In a mixing bowl, whisk the egg whites until they form soft peaks. Fold in the sugar, vanilla and almond extracts, ground almonds and cooled melted chocolate Chill for 15 minutes.

5 ▲ Use a teaspoon and your hands to shape the mixture into walnut-size balls. Place on the sheets and flatten slightly. Brush each ball with a little water and sift over a thin layer of icing sugar. Bake until just firm, 20–25 minutes. With a metal spatula, transfer to a rack to cool.

~ VARIATION ~

For Chocolate Pine Nut Macaroons, spread 75g/3oz/¾ cup pine nuts in a shallow dish. Press the chocolate macaroon balls into the nuts to cover one side and bake as described, nut-side up.

Coconut Macaroons

MAKES 24

40g/1½oz/⅓ cup plain (all-purpose) flour

pinch of salt

225g/8oz/scant 3 cups desiccated (dry unsweetened) coconut

175ml/6fl oz/¾ cup sweetened condensed milk

5ml/1 tsp vanilla extract

1 Preheat the oven to 180°C/350°F/ Gas 4. Grease two baking sheets.

2 Sift the flour and salt into a bowl. Stir in the coconut.

3 ▲ Pour in the milk. Add the vanilla and stir from the centre to make a very thick mixture.

4 Drop heaped tablespoonfuls of mixture 2.5cm/1in apart on the sheets. Bake until golden brown, about 20 minutes. Cool on a rack.

Chocolate Macaroons (top), Coconut Macaroons

Almond Tuiles

MAKES 40

50g/2oz/¹/₃ cup blanched almonds
115g/4oz/generous ¹/₂ cup caster (superfine) sugar
50g/2oz/¹/₄ cup unsalted (sweet) butter
2 egg whites
40g/1¹/₂oz/¹/₃ cup plain (all-purpose) flour
2.5ml/¹/₂ tsp vanilla extract
115g/4oz/1 cup flaked (sliced) almonds

1 Grind the blanched almonds with 30ml/2 tbsp of the sugar in a food processor, blender or nut grinder. If necessary, grind in batches.

2 Preheat the oven to 220°C/425°F/ Gas 7. Grease two baking sheets.

3 ▲ Put the butter in a large bowl and mix in the remaining sugar, using a metal spoon. With an electric mixer, cream them together until light and fluffy.

4 Add the egg whites and stir until blended. Sift over the flour and fold in with a metal spoon. Fold in the ground almonds and vanilla extract.

5 ▲ Working in small batches, drop tablespoonfuls of the mixture 7.5cm/3in apart on one of the prepared sheets. With the back of a spoon, spread out into thin, almost transparent circles about 6cm/2¹/₂in in diameter. Sprinkle each circle with some of the flaked almonds.

6 Bake until the outer edges have browned slightly, about 4 minutes.

7 ▲ Remove from the oven. With a metal spatula, quickly drape the biscuits over a rolling pin to form a curved shape. Transfer to a rack when firm. If the biscuits harden too quickly to shape, reheat them briefly. Repeat the baking and shaping process until the mixture is used up. Store in an airtight container.

Florentines

MAKES 36

40g/1¹/₂oz/3 tbsp butter

120ml/4fl oz/¹/₂ cup whipping cream

130g/4¹/₂oz/scant ³/₄ cup caster
  (superfine) sugar

130g/4¹/₂oz/generous 1 cup flaked
  (sliced) almonds

60g/2oz/¹/₃ cup orange or mixed (candied)
  peel, finely chopped

40g/1¹/₂oz/¹/₄ cup glacé (candied) cherries,
  chopped

65g/2¹/₂oz/9 tbsp plain (all-purpose)
  flour, sifted

225g/8oz plain (semisweet) chocolate

5ml/1 tsp vegetable oil

1 ▲ Preheat the oven to 180°C/
350°F/Gas 4. Grease two baking
sheets. Melt the butter, cream and
sugar together and slowly bring to
the boil. Take off the heat and stir
in the almonds, orange or mixed peel,
cherries and flour until blended.

3 Drop teaspoonfuls of the batter
2.5–5cm/1–2in apart on the prepared
sheets and flatten with a fork.

4 Bake for about 10 minutes until
brown at the edges. Remove from the
oven and correct the shape whilst
they are hot by quickly pushing in any
uneven edges with a knife or a round
biscuit (cookie) cutter. If necessary,
return to the oven for a few moments
to soften. While still hot, use a metal
spatula to transfer the florentines to a
clean, flat surface.

5 Melt the chocolate in the top of a
double boiler or in a heatproof bowl
set over a pan of hot water. Add the
oil and stir to blend.

6 ▲ With a palette knife (metal
spatula), spread the smooth underside
of the cooled florentines with a thin
coating of the melted chocolate.

7 ▼ When the chocolate is about to
set, draw a serrated knife across the
surface with a slight sawing motion to
make wavy lines. Store in an airtight
container in a cool place.

Nut Lace Wafers

MAKES 18

65g/2¹/₂oz/¹/₂ cup whole blanched almonds
50g/2oz/¹/₄ cup butter
40g/1¹/₂oz/¹/₃ cup plain (all-purpose) flour
90g/3¹/₂oz/¹/₂ cup caster (superfine) sugar
30ml/2 tbsp double (heavy) cream
2.5ml/¹/₂ tsp vanilla extract

1 Preheat the oven to 190°C/375°F/ Gas 5. Grease one or two baking sheets.

2 With a sharp knife, chop the almonds as finely as possible. Alternatively, use a food processor, blender, or coffee grinder to chop the nuts very finely.

3 ▼ Melt the butter in a pan over low heat. Remove from the heat and stir in the remaining ingredients and the almonds.

4 Drop teaspoonfuls 6cm/2¹/₂in apart on the prepared sheets. Bake until golden, about 5 minutes. Cool on the baking sheets briefly, just until the wafers are stiff enough to remove.

5 ▲ With a palette knife (metal spatula), transfer to a rack to cool completely.

~ **VARIATION** ~

Add 50g/2oz finely chopped orange peel to the mixture.

Oatmeal Lace Rounds

MAKES 36

165g/5¹/₂oz/11 tbsp butter or margarine
130g/4¹/₂oz/1¹/₄ cups quick-cooking rolled oats
175g/6oz/scant 1 cup soft dark brown sugar
150g/5oz/³/₄ cup caster (superfine) sugar
40g/1¹/₂oz/¹/₃ cup plain (all-purpose) flour
1.5ml/¹/₄ tsp salt
1 egg, lightly beaten
5ml/1 tsp vanilla extract
65g/2¹/₂oz/¹/₂ cup pecan nuts or walnuts, finely chopped

1 Preheat the oven to 180°C/350°F/ Gas 4. Grease two baking sheets.

2 Melt the butter in a pan over low heat. Set aside.

3 In a mixing bowl, combine the oats, brown sugar, caster sugar, flour and salt.

4 ▲ Make a well in the centre and add the butter or margarine, egg and vanilla.

5 ▼ Mix until blended, then stir in the chopped nuts.

6 Drop rounded teaspoonfuls of the mixture about 5cm/2in apart on the prepared sheets. Bake until lightly browned on the edges and bubbling, 5–8 minutes. Leave to cool on the sheet for 2 minutes, then transfer to a rack to cool completely.

Nut Lace Wafers (top), Oatmeal Lace Rounds

Raspberry Sandwich Cookies

MAKES 32

175g/6oz/1 cup blanched almonds

175g/6oz/1½ cups plain (all-purpose) flour

175g/6oz/¾ cup butter, at room temperature

115g/4oz/generous ½ cup caster (superfine) sugar

grated rind of 1 lemon

5ml/1 tsp vanilla extract

1 egg white

pinch of salt

25g/1oz/¼ cup flaked (sliced) almonds

250ml/8fl oz/1 cup raspberry jam

15ml/1 tbsp fresh lemon juice

1 Place the blanched almonds and 20g/¾oz/3 tbsp of the flour in a food processor, blender or coffee grinder and process until finely ground. Set aside.

2 With an electric mixer, cream the butter and sugar together until light and fluffy. Stir in the lemon rind and vanilla. Add the ground almonds and remaining flour, and mix well until combined. Gather into a ball, wrap in baking parchment, and chill for at least 1 hour.

3 Preheat the oven to 160°C/325°F/ Gas 3. Line two baking sheets with baking parchment.

4 Divide the cookie mixture into four equal parts. Working with one section at a time, roll out to a thickness of 3mm/⅛in on a lightly floured surface. With a 6cm/2½in fluted pastry (cookie) cutter, stamp out circles. Gather the scraps, roll out and stamp out more circles. Repeat with the remaining sections.

5 ▲ Using a 2cm/¾in piping nozzle or pastry cutter, stamp out the centres from half the circles. Place the rings and circles 2.5cm/1in apart on the prepared sheets.

6 ▲ Whisk the egg white with the salt until just frothy. Chop the flaked almonds. Brush only the biscuit rings with the egg white, then sprinkle over the almonds. Bake until very lightly browned, 12–15 minutes. Let cool for a few minutes on the sheets before transferring to a rack.

7 ▲ In a pan, melt the jam with the lemon juice until it comes to a simmer. Brush the jam over the biscuit circles and sandwich together with the rings. Store in an airtight container with sheets of baking parchment between the layers.

Brandysnaps

MAKES 18

50g/2oz/¹/₄ cup butter, at room temperature
150g/5oz/³/₄ cup caster (superfine) sugar
15ml/1 tbsp golden (light corn) syrup
50g/1¹/₂oz/¹/₃ cup plain (all-purpose) flour
2.5ml/¹/₂ tsp ground ginger
FOR THE FILLING
250ml/8fl oz/1 cup whipping cream
30ml/2 tbsp brandy.

With an electric mixer, cream together the butter and sugar until light and fluffy, then beat in the golden syrup. Sift over the flour and ginger and mix together.

▲ Transfer the mixture to a work surface and knead until smooth. Cover and chill for 30 minutes.

Preheat the oven to 190°C/375°F/Gas 5. Grease a baking sheet.

▲ Working in batches of four, form the mixture into walnut-size balls. Place far apart on the sheet and flatten slightly. Bake until golden and bubbling, about 10 minutes.

5 ▼ Remove from the oven and let cool a few moments. Working quickly, slide a metal spatula under each one, turn over, and wrap around the handle of a wooden spoon (have four spoons ready). If they firm up too quickly, reheat for a few seconds to soften. When firm, slide the snaps off and place on a rack to cool.

6 ▲ When all the brandy snaps are cool, prepare the filling. Whip the cream and brandy until soft peaks form. Fill a piping (pastry) bag with the brandy cream. Pipe into each end of the brandy snaps just before serving.

Shortbread

MAKES 8

165g/5¹/₂oz/11 tbsp unsalted (sweet) butter, at room temperature

90g/3¹/₂oz/¹/₂ cup caster (superfine) sugar

185g/6¹/₂oz/1²/₃ cups plain (all-purpose) flour

50g/2oz/¹/₂ cup rice flour

1.5ml/¹/₄ tsp baking powder

pinch of salt

1 Preheat the oven to 170°C/325°F/ Gas 3. Grease a shallow 20cm/8in cake tin (pan), preferably with a removable base.

2 With an electric mixer, cream the butter and sugar together until light and fluffy. Sift over the flours, baking powder and salt, and mix well.

3 ▲ Press the dough neatly into the prepared tin, smoothing the surface with the back of a spoon.

4 Prick all over with a fork, then score into eight equal wedges.

5 ▲ Bake until golden, 40–45 minutes. Leave in the tin until cool enough to handle, then turn out and recut the wedges while still hot. Store in an airtight container.

Flapjacks

MAKES 8

50g/2oz/¹/₄ cup butter

15ml/1 tbsp golden (light corn) syrup

75g/3oz/¹/₃ cup soft dark brown sugar

90g/3¹/₂oz/1 cup quick-cooking rolled oats

pinch of salt

1 ▲ Preheat the oven to 180°C/ 350°F/Gas 4. Line a 20cm/8in cake tin with baking parchment and grease.

2 ▼ Place the butter, golden syrup and sugar in a pan over a low heat. Cook, stirring, until melted and combined.

~ VARIATION ~

If you like, add 5ml/1 tsp ground ginger to the melted butter.

3 ▲ Remove from the heat and add the oats and salt. Stir to blend.

4 Spoon into the prepared tin and smooth the surface. Place in the centre of the oven and bake until golden brown, 20–25 minutes. Leave in the tin until cool enough to handle, then turn out and cut into wedges while still hot.

Shortbread (top), Flapjack

Chocolate Delights

MAKES 50

25g/1oz plain (semisweet) chocolate
25g/1oz dark (bittersweet) cooking chocolate
225g/8oz/2 cups plain (all-purpose) flour
2.5ml/$\frac{1}{2}$ tsp salt
225g/8oz/1cup unsalted (sweet) butter, at room temperature
225g/8oz/generous 1 cup caster (superfine) sugar
2 eggs
5ml/1 tsp vanilla extract
115g/4oz/1 cup finely chopped walnuts

1 Melt the chocolates in the top of a double boiler, or in a heatproof bowl set over a pan of gently simmering water. Set aside.

2 ▼ In a small bowl, sift together the flour and salt. Set aside.

3 With an electric mixer, cream the butter until soft. Add the sugar and continue beating until the mixture is light and fluffy.

4 Mix the eggs and vanilla, then gradually stir into the butter mixture.

5 ▲ Stir in the chocolate, then the flour. Stir in the nuts.

6 ▲ Divide the mixture into four equal parts, and roll each into 5cm/2in diameter logs. Wrap tightly in foil and refrigerate or freeze until firm.

7 Preheat the oven to 190°C/375°F/Gas 5. Grease two baking sheets.

8 With a sharp knife, cut the logs into 5mm/$\frac{1}{4}$in slices. Place the round on the prepared sheets and bake until lightly coloured, about 10 minutes. Transfer to a rack to cool.

~ VARIATION ~

For two-tone biscuits, melt only half the chocolate. Combine all the ingredients, except the chocolate, as above. Divide the mixture in half. Add the chocolate to one half. Roll out the plain mixture on to a flat sheet. Roll out the chocolate mixture, place on top of the plain one and roll up. Wrap, slice and bake as described.

Cinnamon Treats

MAKES 50

50g/9oz/2¼ cups plain (all-purpose) flour

5ml/½ tsp salt

0ml/2 tsp ground cinnamon

25g/8oz/1 cup unsalted (sweet) butter, at room temperature

25g/8oz/generous 1 cup caster (superfine) sugar

eggs

ml/1 tsp vanilla extract

In a bowl, sift together the flour, alt and cinnamon. Set aside.

▲ With an electric mixer, cream he butter until soft. Add the sugar nd continue beating until the ixture is light and fluffy.

Beat the eggs and vanilla, then radually stir into the butter mixture.

▲ Stir in the dry ingredients.

5 ▲ Divide the mixture into four equal parts, then roll each into 5cm/2in diameter logs. Wrap tightly in foil and chill or freeze until firm.

6 Preheat the oven to 190°C/375°F/Gas 5. Grease two baking sheets.

7 ▼ With a sharp knife, cut the logs into 5mm/¼in slices. Place the rounds on the prepared sheets and bake until lightly coloured, about 10 minutes. With a metal spatula, transfer to a rack to cool.

Peanut Butter Cookies

MAKES 24

150g/5oz/1¼ cups plain
  (all-purpose) flour

2.5ml/½ tsp bicarbonate of soda
  (baking soda)

2.5ml/½ tsp salt

115g/4oz/½ cup butter,
  at room temperature

165g/5½oz/¾ cup soft light brown sugar

1 egg

5ml/1 tsp vanilla extract

265g/9½oz/1¼ cups crunchy peanut
  butter

1 Sift together the flour, bicarbonate of soda and salt, and set aside.

2 With an electric mixer, cream the butter and sugar together until light and fluffy.

3 In another bowl, mix together the egg and vanilla, then gradually beat into the butter mixture.

4 ▲ Stir in the peanut butter and blend thoroughly. Stir in the dry ingredients. Chill for at least 30 minutes, or until firm.

5 Preheat the oven to 180°C/350°F/ Gas 4. Grease two baking sheets.

6 Spoon out rounded teaspoonfuls of the dough and roll into balls.

7 ▲ Place the balls on the prepared sheets and press flat with a fork into circles about 6cm/2½in in diameter, making a criss-cross pattern. Bake until lightly coloured, 12–15 minutes. Transfer to a rack to cool.

~ **VARIATION** ~

Add 75g/3oz/½ cup peanuts, coarsely chopped, with the peanut butter.

Chocolate Chip Cookies

MAKES 24

115g/4oz/½ cup butter or margarine,
  at room temperature

50g/2oz/¼ cup caster (superfine) sugar

90g/3½oz/scant ½ cup soft dark
  brown sugar

1 egg

2.5ml/½ tsp vanilla extract

175g/6oz/1½ cups plain (all-purpose) flour

2.5ml/½ tsp bicarbonate of soda
  (baking soda)

pinch of salt

175g/6oz chocolate chips

50g/2oz/⅓ cup walnuts, chopped

1 Preheat the oven to 180°C/350°F/ Gas 4. Grease two large baking sheets.

2 ▼ With an electric mixer, cream the butter or margarine and two sugars together until light and fluffy.

3 In another bowl, mix the egg and vanilla, then gradually beat into the butter mixture. Sift over the flour, bicarbonate of soda and salt, and stir.

4 ▲ Add the chocolate chips and walnuts, and mix to combine well.

5 Place heaped teaspoonfuls of the dough 5cm/2in apart on the prepared sheets. Bake until lightly coloured, 10–15 minutes. Transfer to a rack to cool.

Peanut Butter Cookies (top), Chocolate Chip Cookies

Salted Peanut Cookies

MAKES 70

350g/12oz/3 cups plain (all-purpose) flour

2.5ml/^{1}/$_2$ tsp bicarbonate of soda (baking soda)

115g/4oz/^{1}/$_2$ cup butter

115g/4oz/^{1}/$_2$ cup margarine

250g/9oz/generous 1 cup soft light brown sugar

2 eggs

10ml/2 tsp vanilla extract

225g/8oz/1^1/$_3$ cups salted peanuts

1 Preheat the oven to 190°C/375°F/ Gas 5. Lightly grease two baking sheets. Grease the bottom of a glass and dip in sugar.

2 Sift together the flour and bicarbonate of soda. Set aside.

3 ▲ Cream the butter, margarine and sugar. Beat in the eggs and vanilla extract. Fold in the flour mixture.

4 ▲ Stir the peanuts into the butter mixture until evenly combined.

5 ▲ Drop teaspoonfuls 5cm/2in apart on the prepared sheets. Flatten with the prepared glass.

6 Bake for about 10 minutes, until lightly coloured. With a metal spatula transfer to a wire rack to cool.

> **~ VARIATION ~**
>
> To make Cashew Cookies, substitute an equal amount of salted cashew nuts for the peanuts, and add as above.

Cheddar Pennies

MAKES 20

50g/2oz/^{1}/$_4$ cup butter

115g/4oz/1^1/$_3$ cups Cheddar cheese, grated

40g/1^1/$_2$oz/^{1}/$_3$ cup plain (all-purpose) flour

pinch of salt

pinch of chilli powder

1 Put the butter in a large bowl and cut into 2.5cm/1in cubes. With an electric mixer, cream the butter until soft and fluffy.

2 ▲ Stir in the cheese, flour, salt and chilli. Gather to form a dough.

3 Transfer to a lightly floured surface. Shape into a cylinder about 3cm/ 1^1/$_4$in in diameter. Wrap in baking parchment and chill for 1–2 hours.

4 Preheat the oven to 180°C/350°F/ Gas 4. Grease one or two baking sheets.

5 ▲ Cut the dough into 5mm/^{1}/$_4$in thick slices and place on the prepared baking sheets. Bake for about 15 minutes, until golden. Transfer to a wire rack to cool.

Salted Peanut Cookies (top), Cheddar Pennies

Chocolate Chip Brownies

MAKES 24

115g/4oz plain (semisweet) chocolate

115g/4oz/¹/2 cup butter

3 eggs

200g/7oz/1 cup caster (superfine) sugar

2.5ml/¹/2 tsp vanilla extract

pinch of salt

150g/5oz/1¹/4 cups plain
(all-purpose) flour

175g/6oz chocolate chips

1 ▼ Preheat the oven to 180°C/350°F/
Gas 4. Line a 33 × 23cm/13 × 9in tin
(pan) with baking parchment and grease.

2 ▲ Melt the chocolate and butter i
the top of a double boiler, or in a
heatproof bowl set over a pan of gentl
simmering water.

3 ▲ Beat together the eggs, sugar,
vanilla and salt. Stir in the chocolate
mixture. Sift over the flour and fold
in. Add the chocolate chips.

4 ▲ Pour the mixture into the
prepared tin and spread evenly. Bake
until just set, about 30 minutes. Do
not overbake; the brownies should be
slightly moist inside. Cool in the pan

5 To turn out, run a knife all around
the edge and invert on to a baking
sheet. Remove the paper. Place
another sheet on top and invert again
so the brownies are right-side up. Cu
into squares for serving.

Marbled Brownies

MAKES 24

225g/8oz plain (semisweet) chocolate

85g/3oz/6 tbsp butter

4 eggs

300g/11oz/generous 1¹/₂ cups caster
(superfine) sugar

150g/5oz/1¹/₄ cups plain (all-purpose) flour

2.5ml/¹/₂ tsp salt

5ml/1 tsp baking powder

10ml/2 tsp vanilla extract

115g/4oz/²/₃ cups walnuts, chopped

FOR THE PLAIN MIXTURE

50g/2oz/¹/₄ cup butter, at room temperature

175g/6oz/³/₄ cup cream cheese

90g/3¹/₂oz/¹/₂ cup caster (superfine) sugar

2 eggs

25g/1oz/¹/₄ cup plain (all-purpose) flour

5ml/1 tsp vanilla extract

1 Preheat the oven to 180°C/350°F/
Gas 4. Line a 33 × 23cm/13 × 9in tin
(pan) with baking parchment and grease.

2 Melt the chocolate and butter over
very low heat, stirring constantly. Set
aside to cool.

3 Meanwhile, beat the eggs until
light and fluffy. Gradually add the
sugar and continue beating until
blended. Sift over the flour, salt and
baking powder, and fold to combine.

4 ▲ Stir in the cooled chocolate
mixture. Add the vanilla and walnuts.
Measure and set aside 475ml/16fl oz/
2 cups of the chocolate mixture.

5 ▲ For the plain mixture, cream the
butter and cream cheese with an
electric mixer.

6 Add the sugar and continue beating
until blended. Beat in the eggs, flour
and vanilla.

7 Spread the unmeasured chocolate
mixture in the tin. Pour over the
plain mixture. Drop spoonfuls of the
reserved chocolate mixture on top.

8 ▲ With a palette knife (metal
spatula), swirl the mixtures to marble.
Do not blend completely. Bake until
just set, 35–40 minutes. Turn out when
cool and cut into squares for serving.

Nutty Chocolate Squares

MAKES 16

2 eggs

10ml/2 tsp vanilla extract

pinch of salt

175g/6oz/1 cup pecan nuts,
coarsely chopped

50g/2oz/^{1}/$_2$ cup plain (all-purpose) flour

50g/2oz/^{1}/$_4$ cup caster (superfine) sugar

120ml/4fl oz/^{1}/$_2$ cup golden
(light corn) syrup

75g/3oz plain (semisweet) chocolate,
finely chopped

45ml/3 tbsp butter

16 pecan halves, for decorating

1 Preheat the oven to 160°C/325°F/
Gas 3. Line the base and sides of a
20cm/8in square baking tin (pan) with
baking parchment and grease lightly.

2 ▼ Whisk together the eggs, vanilla
and salt. In another bowl, mix
together the pecan nuts and flour.
Set both aside.

3 In a pan, bring the sugar and
golden syrup to the boil. Remove
from the heat and stir in the
chocolate and butter and blend
thoroughly with a wooden spoon.

4 ▲ Mix in the beaten eggs, then
fold in the pecan mixture.

5 Pour the mixture into the prepared
tin and bake until set, about
35 minutes. Cool in the tin for
10 minutes before turning out. Cut
into 5cm/2in squares and press pecan
halves into the tops while warm. Cool
completely on a rack.

Raisin Brownies

MAKES 16

115g/4oz/^{1}/$_2$ cup butter or margarine

50g/2oz/^{1}/$_2$ cup unsweetened cocoa
powder

2 eggs

225g/8oz/generous 1 cup caster
(superfine) sugar

5ml/1 tsp vanilla extract

40g/1^1/$_2$oz/^{1}/$_3$ cup plain (all-purpose) flour

75g/3oz/^{3}/$_4$ cup chopped walnuts

75g/3oz/^{2}/$_3$ cup raisins

1 Preheat the oven to 180°C/350°F/
Gas 4. Line the base and sides of a
20cm/8in square baking tin (pan)
with baking parchment and grease
the paper.

2 ▼ Gently melt the butter or
margarine in a small pan. Remove
from the heat and stir in the
cocoa powder.

3 With an electric mixer, beat the
eggs, sugar and vanilla together until
light. Add the cocoa mixture and stir
to blend.

4 ▲ Sift the flour over the cocoa
mixture and gently fold in. Add the
walnuts and raisins, and scrape the
mixture into the prepared tin.

5 Bake in the centre of the oven for
30 minutes. Do not overbake. Leave
in the tin to cool before cutting into
5cm/2in squares and removing. The
brownies should be soft and moist.

Nutty Chocolate Squares (top), Raisin Brownie

Chocolate Walnut Bars

MAKES 24

50g/2oz/¹/₃ cup walnuts

65g/2¹/₂oz/¹/₄ cup caster (superfine) sugar

115g/4oz/1 cup plain (all-purpose) flour, sifted

75g/3oz/6 tbsp cold unsalted (sweet) butter, cut into pieces

FOR THE TOPPING

25g/1oz/2 tbsp unsalted (sweet) butter

90ml/6 tbsp water

25g/1oz/¹/₄ cup unsweetened cocoa powder

90g/3¹/₂oz/¹/₂ cup caster sugar

5ml/1 tsp vanilla extract

pinch of salt

2 eggs

icing (confectioners') sugar, for dusting

1 Preheat the oven to 180°C/350°F/ Gas 4. Grease the base and sides of a 20cm/8in square baking tin (pan).

2 ▼ Grind the walnuts with a few tablespoons of the sugar in a food processor, blender or coffee grinder.

3 In a bowl, combine the ground walnuts, remaining sugar and flour. With your fingertips, rub in the butter until the mixture resembles coarse breadcrumbs. Alternatively, process all the ingredients in a food processor until the mixture resembles coarse breadcrumbs.

4 ▲ Pat the walnut mixture into the base of the prepared tin in an even layer. Bake for 25 minutes.

5 ▲ Meanwhile, for the topping, melt the butter with the water. Whisk in the cocoa and sugar. Remove from the heat, stir in the vanilla and salt and let cool for 5 minutes. Whisk in the eggs until blended.

6 ▲ Pour the topping over the crust when baked.

7 Return to the oven and bake until set, about 20 minutes. Set the tin on a rack to cool. Cut into 6 × 2.5cm/ 2¹/₂ × 1in bars and dust with icing sugar. Store in the refrigerator.

Pecan Squares

MAKES 36

225g/8oz/2 cups plain (all-purpose) flour

pinch of salt

115g/4oz/generous ¹/2 cup granulated sugar

225g/8oz/1 cup cold butter or
  margarine, chopped

1 egg

finely grated rind of 1 lemon

FOR THE TOPPING

175g/6oz/³/4 cup butter

75g/3oz/scant ¹/3 cup honey

50g/2oz/¹/4 cup granulated sugar

115g/4oz/¹/2 cup soft dark brown sugar

75ml/5 tbsp whipping cream

350g/11b/2²/3 cups pecan halves

1   Preheat the oven to 190°C/375°F/
Gas 5. Lightly grease a 38 × 27 × 2.5cm/
5¹/2 × 10¹/2 × 1in Swiss roll tin (jelly
roll pan).

2   ▲ Sift the flour and salt into a
mixing bowl. Stir in the sugar. Cut
and rub in the butter or margarine
until the mixture resembles coarse
breadcrumbs. Add the egg and lemon
rind and blend with a fork until the
mixture just holds together.

3   ▼ Spoon the mixture into the
prepared tin. With floured fingertips,
press into an even layer. Prick the
pastry all over with a fork and chill
for 10 minutes.

4   Bake the pastry crust for 15 minutes.
Remove the tin from the oven, but
keep the oven on while making
the topping.

5   ▲ To make the topping, melt the
butter, honey and both sugars. Bring
to the boil. Boil, without stirring, for
2 minutes. Off the heat, stir in the
cream and pecan halves. Pour over
the crust, return to the oven and bake
for 25 minutes. Leave to cool.

6   When cool, run a knife around the
edge. Invert on to a baking sheet,
place another sheet on top and invert
again. Dip a sharp knife into very hot
water and cut into squares for serving.

Figgy Bars

MAKES 48

350g/12oz/2 cups dried figs

3 eggs

175g/6oz/scant 1 cup caster (superfine) sugar

75g/3oz/²⁄₃ cup plain (all-purpose) flour

5ml/1 tsp baking powder

2.5ml/¹⁄₂ tsp ground cinnamon

1.5ml/¹⁄₄ tsp ground cloves

1.5ml/¹⁄₄ tsp freshly grated nutmeg

1.5ml/¹⁄₄ tsp salt

75g/3oz/³⁄₄ cup finely chopped walnuts

30ml/2 tbsp brandy or cognac

icing (confectioners') sugar, for dusting

1 Preheat the oven to 160°C/325°F/ Gas 3.

2 Line a 30 × 20 × 4cm/12 × 8 × 1¹⁄₂in tin (pan) with baking parchment and grease the paper.

3 ▲ With a sharp knife, chop the figs roughly. Set aside.

4 In a bowl, whisk the eggs and sugar until well blended. In another bowl, sift together the dry ingredients, then fold into the egg mixture in several batches.

5 ▼ Stir in the figs, walnuts and brandy or cognac.

6 Scrape the mixture into the prepared tin and bake until the top is firm and brown, 35–40 minutes. It should still be soft underneath.

7 Cool in the tin for 5 minutes, then turn out and transfer to a sheet of baking parchment lightly sprinkled with icing sugar. Cut into bars.

Lemon Bars

MAKES 36

50g/2oz/¹⁄₂ cup icing (confectioners') sugar

175g/6oz/1¹⁄₂ cups plain (all-purpose) flour

2.5ml/¹⁄₂ tsp salt

175g/6oz/³⁄₄ cup butter, cut in small pieces

FOR THE TOPPING

4 eggs

350g/12oz/1³⁄₄ cups caster (superfine) sugar

grated rind of 1 lemon

120ml/4fl oz/¹⁄₂ cup fresh lemon juice

175ml/6fl oz/³⁄₄ cup whipping cream

icing (confectioners') sugar, for dusting

1 Preheat the oven to 160°C/325°F/ Gas 3.

2 Grease a 33 × 23cm/13 × 9in baking tin (pan).

3 Sift the sugar, flour and salt into a bowl. With a pastry blender, cut in the butter until the mixture resembles coarse breadcrumbs.

4 ▲ Press the mixture into the base of the prepared tin (pan). Bake until golden brown, about 20 minutes.

5 Meanwhile, for the topping, whisk the eggs and sugar together until blended. Add the lemon rind and juice, and mix well.

6 ▲ Lightly whip the cream and fold into the egg mixture. Pour over the still-warm base, return to the oven, and bake until set, about 40 minutes.

7 Cool completely before cutting into bars. Dust with icing sugar.

Figgy Bars (top), Lemon Bars

Apricot Specials

MAKES 12

90g/3½oz/generous ⅓ cup soft light brown sugar

75g/3oz/⅔ cup plain (all-purpose) flour

75g/3oz/6 tbsp cold unsalted (sweet) butter, cut in pieces

FOR THE TOPPING

150g/5oz/generous ½ cup ready-to-eat dried apricots

250ml/8fl oz/1 cup water

grated rind of 1 lemon

55g/2½oz/5 tbsp caster (superfine) sugar

10ml/2 tsp cornflour (cornstarch)

50g/2oz/½ cup chopped walnuts

1 Preheat the oven to 180°C/350°F/ Gas 4.

2 ▲ In a bowl, combine the brown sugar and flour. With a pastry blender, cut in the butter until the mixture resembles coarse breadcrumbs.

3 ▲ Transfer to a 20cm/8in square baking tin (pan) and press level. Bake for 15 minutes. Remove from the oven but leave the oven on.

4 Meanwhile, for the topping, combine the apricots and water in a pan and simmer until soft, about 10 minutes. Strain the liquid and reserve. Chop the apricots.

5 ▲ Return the apricots to the pan and add the lemon rind, caster sugar, cornflour, and 60ml/4 tbsp of the soaking liquid. Cook for 1 minute.

6 ▲ Cool slightly before spreading the topping over the base. Sprinkle over the walnuts and continue baking for 20 minutes more. Leave to cool in the tin before cutting into bars.

Almond-topped Squares

MAKES 18

5g/3oz/²/³ cup butter

0g/2oz/¹/₄ cup granulated sugar

egg yolk

rated rind and juice of ¹/₂ lemon

.5ml/¹/₂ tsp vanilla extract

0ml/2 tbsp whipping cream

15g/4oz/1 cup plain (all-purpose) flour

FOR THE TOPPING

25g/8oz/generous 1 cup granulated sugar

5g/3oz/³/₄ cup flaked (sliced) almonds

egg whites

.5ml/¹/₂ tsp ground ginger

.5ml/¹/₂ tsp ground cinnamon

▲ Preheat the oven to 190°C/375°F/
Gas 5. Line a 33 × 23cm/13 × 9in
Swiss roll tin (jelly roll pan) with
baking parchment; grease the paper.

Cream the butter and sugar. Beat
in the egg yolk, lemon rind and juice,
vanilla extract and cream.

▲ Gradually stir in the flour.
Gather into a ball of dough.

4 With lightly floured fingers, press
the dough into the prepared tin. Bake
for 15 minutes. Remove from the
oven but leave the oven on.

5 ▲ To make the topping, combine
all the ingredients in a heavy pan.
Cook, stirring until the mixture
comes to the boil.

6 Continue boiling until just golden,
about 1 minute. Pour over the dough,
spreading evenly.

7 ▲ Return to the oven and bake
for about 45 minutes. Remove and
score into bars or squares. Cool
completely before cutting into
squares and serving.

Spiced Raisin Bars

MAKES 30

115g/4oz/1 cup plain (all-purpose) flour
7.5ml/1½ tsp baking powder
5ml/1 tsp ground cinnamon
2.5ml/½ tsp freshly grated nutmeg
1.5ml/¼ tsp ground cloves
1.5ml/¼ tsp ground allspsice
200g/7oz/1½ cups raisins
115g/4oz/½ cup butter or margarine, at room temperature
90g/3½oz/½ cup sugar
2 eggs
165g/5½oz/scant ½ cup black treacle (molasses)
50g/2oz/⅓ cup walnuts, chopped

1 Preheat the oven to 180°C/350°F/ Gas 4. Line a 33 × 23cm/13 × 9in tin (pan) with baking parchment; grease.

2 Sift together the flour, baking powder and spices.

3 ▲ Place the raisins in another bowl and toss with a few tablespoons of the flour mixture.

4 ▲ With an electric mixer, cream the butter or margarine and sugar together until light and fluffy. Beat in the eggs, one at a time, then the molasses. Stir in the flour mixture, raisins and walnuts.

5 Spread evenly in the tin. Bake until just set, 15–18 minutes. Cool in the tin before cutting into bars.

Toffee Meringue Bars

MAKES 12

50g/2oz/¼ cup butter
215g/7½oz/scant 1 cup soft dark brown sugar
1 egg
2.5ml/½ tsp vanilla extract
65g/2½oz/9 tbsp plain (all-purpose) flour
2.5ml/½ tsp salt
1.5ml/¼ tsp freshly grated nutmeg
FOR THE TOPPING
1 egg white
pinch of salt
15ml/l tbsp golden (light corn) syrup
90g/3½oz/½ cup caster (superfine) sugar
50g/2oz/⅓ cup walnuts, finely chopped

1 ▲ Combine the butter and brown sugar in a pan and heat until bubbling. Set aside to cool.

2 Preheat the oven to 180°C/350°F/ Gas 4. Line the base and sides of a 20cm/8in square cake tin (pan) with baking parchment and grease.

3 Beat the egg and vanilla into the cooled sugar mixture. Sift over the flour, salt and nutmeg, and fold in. Spread in the base of the tin.

4 ▲ For the topping, beat the egg white with the salt until it holds soft peaks. Beat in the golden syrup, then the sugar and continue beating until the mixture holds stiff peaks. Fold in the nuts and spread on top. Bake for 30 minutes. Cut into bars when cool.

Spiced Raisin Bars (top), Toffee Meringue Bars

BUNS & TEA BREADS

EASY TO MAKE AND SATISFYING TO
EAT, THESE BUNS AND TEA BREADS
WILL FILL THE HOUSE WITH
MOUTHWATERING SCENTS AND LURE
YOUR FAMILY AND FRIENDS TO
LINGER OVER BREAKFAST, COFFEE
OR TEA – AND THEY ARE GREAT FOR
SNACKS OR LUNCH.

Blueberry Muffins

MAKES 12

185g/6½oz/1⅔ cups plain (all-purpose) flour

65g/2½oz/5 tbsp caster (superfine) sugar

10ml/2 tsp baking powder

1.5ml/¼ tsp salt

2 eggs

50g/2oz/¼ cup butter, melted

175ml/6fl oz/¾ cup milk

5ml/1 tsp vanilla extract

5ml/1 tsp grated lemon rind

175g/6oz/1½ cups fresh blueberries

1 Preheat the oven to 200°C/400°F/ Gas 6.

2 ▼ Grease a 12-cup muffin tray.

3 ▲ Sift the flour, sugar, baking powder and salt into a bowl.

4 In another bowl, whisk the eggs until blended. Add the melted butter, milk, vanilla and lemon rind, and stir to combine.

5 Make a well in the dry ingredients and pour in the egg mixture. With a large metal spoon, stir just until the flour is moistened, not until smooth.

6 ▲ Fold in the blueberries.

7 ▲ Spoon the batter into the tray, leaving room for the muffins to rise.

8 Bake until the tops spring back when touched lightly, 20–25 minutes. Leave to cool in the tray for 5 minutes before turning out.

Apple and Cranberry Muffins

MAKES 12

0g/2oz/¹/4 cup butter or margarine
egg
0g/3¹/2oz/¹/2 cup caster (superfine) sugar
rated rind of 1 large orange
20ml/4fl oz/¹/2 cup freshly squeezed orange juice
50g/5oz/1¹/4 cups plain (all-purpose) flour
ml/1 tsp baking powder
5ml/¹/2 tsp bicarbonate of soda (baking soda)
ml/1 tsp ground cinnamon
5ml/¹/2 tsp freshly grated nutmeg
5ml/¹/2 tsp ground allspice
5ml/¹/4 tsp ground ginger
5ml/¹/4 tsp salt
–2 eating apples
50g/6oz/1¹/2 cups cranberries
0g/2oz/¹/3 cup walnuts, chopped
ing (confectioners') sugar, for dusting (optional)

Preheat the oven to 180°C/350°F/
Gas 4. Grease a 12-cup muffin tray or
se paper cases.

Melt the butter or margarine over
entle heat. Set aside to cool.

▲ Place the egg in a mixing bowl
nd whisk lightly. Add the melted
utter or margarine and whisk
o combine.

Add the sugar, orange rind and
uice. Whisk to blend, then set aside.

5 In a large bowl, sift together the
flour, baking powder, bicarbonate of
soda, cinnamon, nutmeg, allspice,
ginger and salt. Set aside.

6 ▲ Quarter, core and peel the
apples. With a sharp knife, chop
coarsely.

7 Make a well in the dry ingredients
and pour in the egg mixture. With
a spoon, stir until just blended.

8 ▲ Add the apples, cranberries and
walnuts, and stir to blend.

9 Fill the cups three-quarters full
and bake until the tops spring back
when touched lightly, 25–30 minutes.
Transfer to a rack to cool. Dust with
icing sugar, if you like.

Chocolate Chip Muffins

MAKES 10

115g/4oz/¹/₂ cup butter or margarine,
   at room temperature

65g/2¹/₂oz/5 tbsp caster (superfine) sugar

25g/1oz/2 tbsp soft dark brown sugar

2 eggs, at room temperature

215g/7¹/₂oz/scant 2 cups plain
   (all-purpose) flour

5ml/1 tsp baking powder

120ml/4fl oz/¹/₂ cup milk

175g/6oz/ plain chocolate chips

1 Preheat the oven to 190°C/375°F/
Gas 5. Grease 10 muffin cups or use
paper cases.

2 ▼ With an electric mixer, cream
the butter or margarine until soft. Add
both sugars and beat until light and
fluffy. Beat in the eggs, one at a time.

3 Sift together the flour and baking
powder, twice. Fold into the butter
mixture, alternating with the milk.

4 ▲ Divide half the mixture between
the muffin cups. Sprinkle several
chocolate chips on top, then cover
with a spoonful of the batter. To
ensure even baking, half-fill any
empty cups with water.

5 Bake until lightly coloured, about
25 minutes. Leave to stand for
5 minutes before turning out.

Chocolate Walnut Muffins

MAKES 12

175g/6oz/³/₄ cup unsalted (sweet) butter

150g/5oz plain (semisweet) chocolate

200g/7oz/1 cup caster (superfine) sugar

50g/2oz/¹/₄ cup soft dark brown sugar

4 eggs

5ml/1 tsp vanilla extract

1.5ml/¹/₄ tsp almond extract

90g/3¹/₂oz/³/₄ cup plain (all-purpose) flour

15ml/1 tbsp unsweetened cocoa powder

115g/4oz/²/₃ cup walnuts, chopped

1 Preheat the oven to 180°C/350°F/
Gas 4. Grease a 12-cup muffin tray or
use paper cases.

2 ▼ Melt the butter with the
chocolate in the top of a double boiler
or in a heatproof bowl set over a pan
of hot water. Transfer to a large
mixing bowl.

3 Stir both the sugars into the
chocolate mixture. Mix in the eggs,
one at a time, then add the vanilla
and almond extracts.

4 Sift over the flour and cocoa.

5 ▲ Fold in and stir in the walnuts.

6 Fill the prepared cups almost to the
top and bake until a skewer inserted in
the centre barely comes out clean,
30–35 minutes. Leave to stand for
5 minutes before turning out on to a
rack to cool completely.

Chocolate Chip Muffins (top), Chocolate Walnut Muffins

Raisin Bran Buns

MAKES 15

50g/2oz/¹/4 cup butter or margarine

40g/1¹/2oz/¹/3 cup plain (all-purpose) flour

50g/2oz/¹/2 cup wholemeal (whole-wheat) flour

7.5ml/1¹/2 tsp bicarbonate of soda (baking soda)

pinch of salt

5ml/1 tsp ground cinnamon

25g/1oz/¹/4 cup bran

75g/3oz/generous ¹/2 cup raisins

65g/2¹/2oz/5 tbsp soft dark brown sugar

50g/2oz/¹/4 cup caster (superfine) sugar

1 egg

250ml/8fl oz/1 cup buttermilk

juice of ¹/2 lemon

1 Preheat the oven to 200°C/400°F/ Gas 6. Grease 15 bun-tray cups.

2 ▲ Place the butter or margarine in a pan and melt over gentle heat. Set aside.

3 In a mixing bowl, sift together the flours, bicarbonate of soda, salt and cinnamon.

4 ▲ Add the bran, raisins and sugars and stir until blended.

5 In another bowl, mix together the egg, buttermilk, lemon juice and melted butter.

6 ▲ Add the buttermilk mixture to the dry ingredients and stir lightly and quickly until just moistened; do not mix until smooth.

7 ▲ Spoon the mixture into the prepared bun tray, filling the cups almost to the top. Half-fill any empty cups with water.

8 Bake until golden, 15–20 minutes. Serve warm or at room temperature.

Raspberry Crumble Buns

MAKES 12

175g/6oz/1½ cups plain (all-purpose) flour

50g/2oz/¼ cup caster (superfine) sugar

50g/2oz/¼ cup soft light brown sugar

10ml/2 tsp baking powder

pinch of salt

5ml/1 tsp ground cinnamon

115g/4oz/½ cup butter, melted

1 egg

120ml/4fl oz/½ cup milk

150g/5oz/scant 1 cup fresh raspberries

grated rind of 1 lemon

FOR THE CRUMBLE TOPPING

25g/1oz/¼ cup finely chopped pecan nuts
or walnuts

50g/2oz/¼ cup soft dark brown sugar

20g/¾oz/3 tbsp plain (all-purpose) flour

5ml/1 tsp ground cinnamon

40g/1½oz/3 tbsp butter, melted

1 ▲ Preheat the oven to 180°C/350°F/
Gas 4. Lightly grease a 12-cup bun tray
or use paper cases.

2 Sift the flour into a bowl. Add
the sugars, baking powder, salt and
cinnamon, and stir to blend.

3 ▲ Make a well in the centre.
Place the butter, egg and milk in
the well and mix until just combined.
Stir in the raspberries and lemon rind.
Spoon the mixture into the prepared
bun tray, filling the cups almost
to the top.

4 ▼ For the crumble topping, mix
the nuts, dark brown sugar, flour and
cinnamon in a bowl. Add the melted
butter and stir to blend.

5 ▲ Spoon some of the crumble over
each bun. Bake until browned, about
25 minutes. Transfer to a rack to cool
slightly. Serve warm.

Carrot Buns

MAKES 12

175g/6oz/³/4 cup margarine,
  at room temperature

90g/3¹/2oz/generous ¹/3 cup soft dark
  brown sugar

1 egg, at room temperature

15ml/1 tbsp water

225g/8oz/1 cup carrots, grated

150g/5oz/1¹/4 cups plain (all-purpose) flour

5ml/1 tsp baking powder

2.5ml/¹/2 tsp bicarbonate of soda
  (baking soda)

5ml/1 tsp ground cinnamon

1.5ml/¹/4 tsp freshly grated nutmeg

2.5ml/¹/2 tsp salt

1 Preheat the oven to 180°C/350°F/
Gas 4. Grease a 12-cup bun tray or
use paper cases.

2 With an electric mixer, cream the
margarine and sugar until light and
fluffy. Beat in the egg and water.

3 ▲ Stir in the carrots.

4 Sift over the flour, baking powder,
bicarbonate of soda, cinnamon,
nutmeg and salt. Stir to blend.

5 ▼ Spoon the mixture into the
prepared bun tray, filling the cups
almost to the top. Bake until the tops
spring back when touched lightly,
about 35 minutes. Leave to stand for
10 minutes before transferring to a rack

Dried Cherry Buns

MAKES 16

250ml/8fl oz/1 cup natural (plain) yogurt

175g/6oz/³/4 cup dried cherries

115g/4oz/¹/2 cup butter, at
  room temperature

175g/6oz/scant 1 cup caster
  (superfine) sugar

2 eggs, at room temperature

5ml/1 tsp vanilla essence (extract)

200g/7oz/1³/4 cups plain (all-purpose) flour

10ml/2 tsp baking powder

5ml/1 tsp bicarbonate of soda (baking soda)

pinch of salt

1 In a mixing bowl, combine the
yogurt and cherries. Cover and leave
to stand for 30 minutes.

2 Preheat the oven to 180°C/350°F/
Gas 4. Grease 16 bun-tray cups or use
paper cases.

3 With an electric mixer, cream the
butter and sugar together until light
and fluffy.

4 ▼ Add the eggs, one at a time,
beating well after each addition. Add
the vanilla and the cherry mixture and
stir to blend. Set aside.

5 ▲ In another bowl, sift together
the flour, baking powder, bicarbonate
of soda and salt. Fold into the cherry
mixture in three batches.

6 Fill the prepared cups two-thirds
full. For even baking, half-fill any
empty cups with water. Bake until
the tops spring back when touched
lightly, about 20 minutes. Transfer
to a rack to cool.

Carrot Buns (top), Dried Cherry Buns

Oat and Raisin Muffins

MAKES 12

75g/3oz/scant 1 cup rolled oats

250ml/8fl oz/1 cup buttermilk

115g/4oz/¹/₂ cup butter, at
room temperature

90g/3¹/₂oz/generous ¹/₃ cup soft dark
brown sugar

1 egg, at room temperature

115g/4oz/1 cup plain (all-purpose) flour

5ml/1 tsp baking powder

2.5ml/¹/₂ tsp bicarbonate of soda
(baking soda)

1.5ml/¹/₄ tsp salt

25g/1oz/2 tbsp raisins

~ COOK'S TIP ~

If buttermilk is not available, add
5ml/1 tsp lemon juice or vinegar
to milk. Let the mixture stand
for a few minutes to curdle.

1 ▲ In a bowl, combine the oats and
buttermilk, and leave to soak for 1 hour.

2 ▲ Lightly grease a 12-cup muffin
tray or use paper cases.

3 ▲ Preheat the oven to 200°C/
400°F/Gas 6. With an electric mixer,
cream the butter and sugar until light
and fluffy. Beat in the egg.

4 In another bowl, sift the flour,
baking powder, bicarbonate of soda
and salt. Stir into the butter mixture,
alternating with the oat mixture. Fold
in the raisins. Do not overmix.

5 Fill the prepared cups two-thirds
full. Bake until a skewer inserted in
the centre comes out clean, 20–25
minutes. Transfer to a rack to cool.

Pumpkin Muffins

MAKES 14

115g/4oz/¹/₂ cup butter or margarine,
at room temperature

150g/5oz/²/₃ cup soft dark brown sugar

60ml/4 tbsp black treacle (molasses)

1 egg, at room temperature, beaten

225g/8oz cooked or canned pumpkin

225g/8oz/2 cups plain (all-purpose) flour

1.5ml/¹/₄ tsp salt

5ml/1 tsp bicarbonate of soda
(baking soda)

7.5ml/1¹/₂ tsp ground cinnamon

5ml/1 tsp freshly grated nutmeg

25g/1oz/2 tbsp currants or raisins

1 Preheat the oven to 200°C/400°F/
Gas 6. Grease 14 muffin cups or use
paper cases.

2 With an electric mixer, cream the
butter or margarine until soft. Add the
sugar and molasses and beat until light
and fluffy.

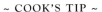

3 ▲ Add the egg and pumpkin and
stir until well blended.

4 Sift over the flour, salt, bicarbonate
of soda, cinnamon and nutmeg. Fold
just enough to blend; do not overmix.

5 ▼ Fold in the currants or raisins.

6 Spoon the mixture into the
prepared muffin cups, filling them
three-quarters full.

7 Bake until the tops spring back
when touched lightly, 12–15 minutes.
Serve warm or cold.

Prune Muffins

MAKES 12

1 egg

250ml/8fl oz/1 cup milk

120ml/4fl oz/¹/₂ cup vegetable oil

50g/2oz/¹/₄ cup caster (superfine) sugar

25g/1oz/2 tbsp soft dark brown sugar

275g/10oz/2¹/₂ cups plain (all-purpose) flour

10ml/2 tsp baking powder

2.5ml/¹/₂ tsp salt

1.5ml/¹/₄ tsp grated nutmeg

115g/4oz/¹/₂ cup cooked pitted
    prunes, chopped

1 Preheat the oven to 200°C/400°F/
Gas 6. Grease a 12-cup muffin tray.

2 Break the egg into a mixing bowl
and beat with a fork. Beat in the
milk and oil.

3 ▼ Stir in the sugars. Set aside.

4 Sift the flour, baking powder, salt
and nutmeg into a mixing bowl. Make
a well in the centre, pour in the egg
mixture and stir until moistened. Do
not overmix; the batter should be
slightly lumpy.

5 ▲ Fold in the prunes.

6 Fill the prepared cups two-thirds
full. Bake until golden brown, about
20 minutes. Leave to stand for
10 minutes before turning out. Serve
warm or at room temperature.

Yogurt and Honey Muffins

MAKES 12

50g/2oz/¹/₄ cup butter

75ml/5 tbsp clear honey

250ml/8fl oz/1 cup natural (plain) yogurt

1 large egg, at room temperature

grated rind of 1 lemon

50ml/2fl oz/¹/₄ cup lemon juice

150g/5oz/1¹/₄ cups plain (all-purpose) flour

175g/6oz/1²/₃ cups wholemeal
    (whole-wheat) flour

7.5ml/1¹/₂ tsp bicarbonate of soda
    (baking soda)

pinch of freshly grated nutmeg

~ VARIATION ~

For Walnut Yogurt Honey Muffins,
add 50g/2oz/¹/₂ cup chopped walnuts,
folded in with the flour. This
makes a more substantial muffin.

1 Preheat the oven to 190°C/375°F/
Gas 5. Grease a 12-cup muffin tray or
use paper cases.

2 In a pan, melt the butter and
honey. Remove from the heat and set
aside to cool slightly.

3 ▲ In a bowl, whisk together the
yogurt, egg, lemon rind and juice.
Add the butter and honey mixture.
Set aside.

4 ▲ In another bowl, sift together
the dry ingredients.

5 Fold the dry ingredients into the
yogurt mixture to blend.

6 Fill the prepared cups two-thirds
full. Bake until the tops spring back
when touched lightly, 20–25 minutes.
Cool in the tray for 5 minutes before
turning out. Serve warm or at room
temperature.

Prune Muffins (top), Yogurt and Honey Muffin

Banana Muffins

MAKES 10

250g/9oz/2¼ cups plain (all-purpose) flour

5ml/1 tsp baking powder

5ml/1 tsp bicarbonate of soda (baking soda)

1.5ml/¼ tsp salt

2.5ml/½ tsp ground cinnamon

1.5ml/¼ tsp freshly grated nutmeg

3 large ripe bananas

1 egg

65g/2½oz/scant ⅓ cup soft dark brown sugar

50ml/2fl oz/¼ cup vegetable oil

25g/1oz/2 tbsp raisins

1 ▼ Preheat the oven to 190°C/ 375°F/Gas 5. Lightly grease or line ten deep muffin cups with paper cases.

2 Sift together the flour, baking powder, bicarbonate of soda, salt, cinnamon and nutmeg. Set aside.

3 ▲ With an electric mixer, beat the peeled bananas at moderate speed until mashed.

4 ▲ Beat in the egg, sugar and oil.

5 Add the dry ingredients and beat in gradually, on low speed. Mix just until blended. With a wooden spoon, stir in the raisins.

6 Fill the prepared cups two-thirds full. For even baking, half-fill any empty cups with water.

7 ▲ Bake until the tops spring back when touched lightly, 20–25 minutes. Transfer to a rack to cool.

Maple Pecan Muffins

MAKES 20

175g/6oz/1 cup pecan nuts
350g/12oz/3 cups plain (all-purpose) flour
ml/1 tsp baking powder
ml/1 tsp bicarbonate of soda (baking soda)
5ml/¼ tsp salt
5ml/¼ tsp ground cinnamon
0g/3½oz/½ cup caster (superfine) sugar
5g/2½oz/scant ⅓ cup soft light brown sugar
5ml/3 tbsp maple syrup
50g/5oz/10 tbsp butter, at room temperature
eggs, at room temperature
00ml/½ pint/1¼ cups buttermilk
0 pecan halves, for decorating

Preheat the oven to 180°C/350°F/
as 4. Lightly grease 20 deep muffin
ups or use paper cases.

▲ Spread the pecan nuts on a
aking sheet and toast in the oven for
minutes. When cool, chop coarsely
nd set aside.

~ VARIATION ~

For Pecan Spice Muffins,
substitute an equal quantity of
golden (light corn) syrup for the
maple syrup. Increase the cinnamon
to 2.5ml/½ tsp, and add 5ml/1 tsp
ground ginger and 2.5ml/½ tsp
freshly grated nutmeg, sifted with
the dry ingredients.

3 In a bowl, sift together the flour,
baking powder, bicarbonate of soda,
salt and cinnamon. Set aside.

4 ▲ In a large mixing bowl, combine
the caster sugar, light brown sugar,
maple syrup and butter. Beat with an
electric mixer until light and fluffy.

5 Add the eggs, one at a time,
beating to incorporate thoroughly
after each addition.

6 ▲ Pour half the buttermilk and
half the dry ingredients into the butter
mixture, then stir until blended.
Repeat with the remaining buttermilk
and dry ingredients.

7 Fold in the chopped pecan nuts.
Fill the prepared cups two-thirds full.
Top with the pecan halves. For even
baking, half-fill any empty cups
with water.

8 Bake until puffed up and golden,
20–25 minutes. Leave to stand for
5 minutes before turning out.

Cheese Muffins

MAKES 9

50g/2oz/¼ cup butter

200g/7oz/1¾ cups plain (all-purpose) flour

10ml/2 tsp baking powder

30ml/2 tbsp sugar

1.5ml/¼ tsp salt

5ml/1 tsp paprika

2 eggs

120ml/4fl oz/½ cup milk

5ml/1 tsp dried thyme

50g/2oz/½ cup mature Cheddar cheese, cut into 1cm/½in dice

1 Preheat the oven to 190°C/375°F/ Gas 5. Thickly grease nine deep muffin cups or use paper cases.

2 Melt the butter and set aside.

3 ▼ In a mixing bowl, sift together the flour, baking powder, sugar, salt and paprika.

4 ▲ In another bowl, combine the eggs, milk, melted butter and thyme, and whisk to blend.

5 Add the milk mixture to the dry ingredients and stir until just moistened; do not mix until smooth.

6 ▲ Place a heaped spoonful of batter into the prepared cups. Drop a few pieces of cheese over each, then top with another spoonful of batter. For even baking, half-fill any empty muffin cups with water.

7 ▲ Bake until puffed and golden, about 25 minutes. Leave to stand for 5 minutes before turning out on to a rack. Serve warm or at room temperatu

Bacon and Cornmeal Muffins

MAKES 14

bacon rashers (strips)

0g/2oz/¹/₄ cup butter

0g/2oz/¹/₄ cup margarine

15g/4oz/1 cup plain (all-purpose) flour

5ml/1 tbsp baking powder

ml/1 tsp sugar

5ml/¹/₄ tsp salt

25g/8oz/2 cups cornmeal

20ml/4fl oz/¹/₂ cup milk

eggs

Preheat the oven to 200°C/400°F/
as 6. Lightly grease 14 deep muffin
ps or use paper cases.

▲ Fry the bacon until crisp. Drain
n kitchen paper, then chop into
mall pieces. Set aside.

Gently melt the butter and
margarine, and set aside.

▲ Sift the flour, baking powder,
gar, and salt into a large mixing
owl. Stir in the cornmeal, then
ake a well in the centre.

5 In a pan, heat the milk to
lukewarm. In a small bowl, lightly
whisk the eggs, then add to the milk.
Stir in the melted fats.

6 ▼ Pour the milk mixture into
the centre of the well and stir until
smooth and well blended.

7 ▲ Stir the bacon into the mixture,
then spoon the mixture into the
prepared cups, filling them half-full.
Bake until risen and lightly coloured,
about 20 minutes. Serve hot or warm.

Corn Bread

MAKES 1 LOAF

115g/4oz/1 cup plain (all-purpose) flour

65g/2¹/₂oz/5 tbsp caster (superfine) sugar

5ml/1 tsp salt

15ml/1 tbsp baking powder

175g/6oz/1¹/₂ cups cornmeal or polenta

350ml/12fl oz/1¹/₂ cups milk

2 eggs

75g/3oz/6 tbsp butter, melted

115g/4oz/¹/₂ cup margarine, melted

1 Preheat the oven to 200°C/400°F/ Gas 6. Line a 23 × 13cm/9 × 5in loaf tin (pan) with baking parchment and grease.

2 Sift the flour, sugar, salt and baking powder into a mixing bowl.

3 ▼ Add the cornmeal and stir to blend. Make a well in the centre.

4 ▲ Whisk together the milk, eggs, butter and margarine. Pour the mixture into the well. Stir until just blended; do not overmix.

5 Pour into the tin and bake until a skewer inserted into the centre come out clean, about 45 minutes. Serve hot or at room temperature.

Spicy Corn Bread

MAKES 9 SQUARES

3–4 whole canned chilli peppers, drained

2 eggs

450ml/³/₄ pint/scant 2 cups buttermilk

50g/2oz/¹/₄ cup butter, melted

50g/2oz/¹/₂ cup plain (all-purpose) flour

5ml/1 tsp bicarbonate of soda (baking soda)

10ml/2 tsp salt

175g/6oz/1¹/₂ cups cornmeal, or polenta

350g/12oz/2 cups canned corn, drained, or frozen corn, thawed

1 Preheat the oven to 200°C/400°F/ Gas 6. Line the bottom and sides of a 23cm/9in square cake tin (pan) with baking parchment and grease lightly.

2 ▲ With a sharp knife, finely chop the chillies and set aside.

3 ▲ In a large bowl, whisk the eggs until frothy, then whisk in the buttermilk. Add the melted butter.

4 In another large bowl, sift together the flour, bicarbonate of soda and salt Fold into the buttermilk mixture in three batches, then fold in the cornmeal in three batches.

5 ▲ Fold in the chillies and corn.

6 Pour the mixture into the prepare tin and bake until a skewer inserted in the middle comes out clean, 25–30 minutes. Leave to stand for 2–3 minutes before turning out. Cut into squares and serve warm.

Corn Bread (top), Spicy Corn Bre

Fruity Tea Bread

MAKES 1 LOAF

225g/8oz/2 cups plain (all-purpose) flour

115g/4oz/generous ¹/₂ cup caster (superfine) sugar

15ml/1 tbsp baking powder

2.5ml/¹/₂ tsp salt

grated rind of 1 large orange

170ml/5¹/₂fl oz/scant ³/₄ cup fresh orange juice

2 eggs, lightly beaten

75g/3oz/6 tbsp butter or margarine, melted

115g/4oz/1 cup fresh cranberries, or bilberries

50g/2oz/¹/₂ cup chopped walnuts

1 Preheat the oven to 180°C/350°F/ Gas 4. Line a 23 × 13cm/9 × 5in loaf tin (pan) with baking parchment and grease.

2 Sift the flour, sugar, baking powder and salt into a mixing bowl.

3 ▼ Stir in the orange rind.

4 ▲ Make a well in the centre and add the orange juice, eggs and melted butter or margarine. Stir from the centre until the ingredients are blended; do not overmix.

5 ▲ Add the berries and walnuts, and stir until blended.

6 Transfer the mixture to the prepared tin and bake until a skewer inserted into the centre comes out clean, 45–50 minutes.

7 ▲ Leave to cool in the tin for 10 minutes before transferring to a rack to cool completely. Serve thinly sliced, toasted or plain, with butter or cream cheese and jam.

Date and Pecan Loaf

MAKES 1 LOAF

175g/6oz/1 cup pitted dates, chopped
175ml/6fl oz/³/4 cup boiling water
50g/2oz/¹/4 cup unsalted (sweet) butter, at room temperature
50g/2oz/¹/4 cup soft dark brown sugar
50g/2oz/¹/4 cup caster (superfine) sugar
1 egg, at room temperature
30ml/2 tbsp brandy
165g/5¹/2oz/1¹/4 cups plain (all-purpose) flour
10ml/2 tsp baking powder
2.5ml/¹/2 tsp salt
4ml/³/4 tsp freshly grated nutmeg
75g/3oz/³/4 cup coarsely chopped pecan nuts or walnuts

▲ Place the dates in a bowl and pour over the boiling water. Set aside to cool.

Preheat the oven to 180°C/350°F/Gas 4. Line a 23 × 13cm/9 × 5in loaf tin (pan) with baking parchment and grease.

▲ With an electric mixer, cream the butter and sugars until light and fluffy. Beat in the egg and brandy, then set aside.

4 Sift the flour, baking powder, salt and nutmeg together, three times.

5 ▼ Fold the dry ingredients into the sugar mixture in three batches, alternating with the dates and water.

6 ▲ Fold in the nuts.

7 Pour the mixture into the prepared tin and bake until a skewer inserted into the centre comes out clean, 45–50 minutes. Leave to cool in the tin for 10 minutes before transferring to a rack to cool completely.

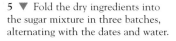

Orange and Honey Tea Bread

MAKES 1 LOAF

375g/13oz/3¹/₄ cups plain (all-purpose) flour
12.5ml/2¹/₂ tsp baking powder
2.5ml/¹/₂ tsp bicarbonate of soda (baking soda)
2.5ml/¹/₂ tsp salt
25g/1oz/2 tbsp margarine
250ml/8fl oz/1 cup clear honey
1 egg, at room temperature, lightly beaten
25ml/1¹/₂ tbsp grated orange rind
175ml/6fl oz/³/₄ cup freshly squeezed orange juice
115g/4oz/1 cup walnuts, chopped

1 Preheat the oven to 160°C/325°F/Gas 3.

2 Sift together the flour, baking powder, bicarbonate of soda and salt.

3 Line the bottom and sides of a 23 × 13cm/9 × 5in loaf tin (pan) with baking parchment and grease.

4 ▲ With an electric mixer, cream the margarine until soft. Stir in the honey until blended, then stir in the egg. Add the orange rind and stir to combine thoroughly.

5 ▲ Fold the flour mixture into the honey and egg mixture in three batches, alternating with the orange juice. Stir in the walnuts.

6 Pour into the tin and bake until a skewer inserted into the centre comes out clean, 60–70 minutes. Leave to stand for 10 minutes before turning out on to a rack to cool.

Apple Loaf

MAKES 1 LOAF

1 egg
250ml/8fl oz/1 cup bottled or homemade apple sauce
50g/2oz/¹/₄ cup butter or margarine, melted
115g/4oz/¹/₂ cup soft dark brown sugar
50g/2oz/¹/₄ cup caster (superfine) sugar
275g/10oz/2¹/₂ cups plain (all-purpose) flour
10ml/2 tsp baking powder
2.5ml/¹/₂ tsp bicarbonate of soda (baking soda)
2.5ml/¹/₂ tsp salt
5ml/1 tsp ground cinnamon
2.5ml/¹/₂ tsp freshly grated nutmeg
65g/2¹/₂oz/¹/₂ cup currants or raisins
50g/2oz/¹/₃ cup pecan nuts or walnuts, chopped

1 Preheat the oven to 180°C/350°F/Gas 4. Line a 23 × 13cm/9 × 5in loaf tin (pan) with baking parchment and grease.

2 ▲ Break the egg into a bowl and beat lightly. Stir in the apple sauce, butter or margarine and both sugars. Set aside.

3 In another bowl, sift together the flour, baking powder, bicarbonate of soda, salt, cinnamon and nutmeg. Fold the dry ingredients into the apple sauce mixture in three batches.

4 ▼ Stir in the currants or raisins, and nuts.

5 Pour into the prepared tin and bake until a skewer inserted into the centre comes out clean, about 1 hour. Leave to stand for 10 minutes. Turn out on to a rack and cool completely.

Orange and Honey Tea Bread (top), Apple Loaf

Lemon and Walnut Tea Bread

MAKES 1 LOAF

115g/4oz/^{1}/$_2$ cup butter or margarine,
    at room temperature

90g/3^1/$_2$oz/^{1}/$_2$ cup sugar

2 eggs, at room temperature, separated

grated rind of 2 lemons

30ml/2 tbsp lemon juice

225g/8oz/2 cups plain (all-purpose) flour

10ml/2 tsp baking powder

120ml/4fl oz/^{1}/$_2$ cup milk

50g/2oz/^{1}/$_3$ cup walnuts, chopped

pinch of salt

1 Preheat the oven to 180°C/350°F/
Gas 4. Line a 23 × 13cm/9 × 5in loaf
tin (pan) with baking parchment
and grease.

2 With an electric mixer, cream the
butter or margarine with the sugar
until light and fluffy.

3 ▲ Beat in the egg yolks.

4 Add the lemon rind and juice,
and stir until blended. Set aside.

5 ▲ In another bowl, sift together
the flour and baking powder, three
times. Fold into the butter mixture
in three batches, alternating with the
milk. Fold in the walnuts. Set aside.

6 ▲ Beat the egg whites and salt
until stiff peaks form. Fold a large
dollop of the egg whites into the
walnut mixture to lighten it. Fold in
the remaining egg whites carefully
until just blended.

7 ▲ Pour the batter into the
prepared tin and bake until a skewer
inserted into the centre of the loaf
comes out clean, 45–50 minutes. Leave
to stand for 5 minutes before turning
out on to a rack to cool completely.

Apricot Nut Loaf

MAKES 1 LOAF

115g/4oz/¹/₂ cup ready-to-eat dried apricots
1 large orange
75g/3oz/¹/₃ cup raisins
150g/5oz/³/₄ cup caster (superfine) sugar
85ml/3fl oz/generous ¹/₃ cup oil
2 eggs, lightly beaten
250g/9oz/2¹/₄ cups plain (all-purpose) flour
10ml/2 tsp baking powder
2.5ml/¹/₂ tsp salt
5ml/1 tsp bicarbonate of soda (baking soda)
50g/2oz/¹/₂ cup chopped walnuts

1 Preheat the oven to 180°C/350°F/
Gas 4. Line a 23 × 13cm/9 × 5in loaf
tin (pan) with baking parchment
and grease.

2 Place the apricots in a bowl, cover
with lukewarm water and leave to
stand for 30 minutes.

3 With a vegetable peeler, remove
the orange rind, leaving the pith.

4 With a sharp knife, finely chop the
orange rind strips.

5 Drain the apricots and chop
coarsely. Place in a bowl with the
orange rind and raisins. Set aside.

6 Squeeze the peeled orange. Measure
the juice and add enough hot water to
obtain 175ml/6fl oz/³/₄ cup liquid.

7 ▼ Pour the orange juice mixture
over the apricot mixture. Stir in the
sugar, oil and eggs. Set aside.

8 In another bowl, sift together
the flour, baking powder, salt and
bicarbonate of soda. Fold the flour
mixture into the apricot mixture in
three batches.

9 ▲ Stir in the walnuts.

10 Spoon the mixture into the
prepared tin and bake until a skewer
inserted into the centre comes out
clean, 55–60 minutes. If the loaf browns
too quickly, protect the top with a
sheet of foil. Leave to cool in the tin
for 10 minutes before transferring to
a rack to cool completely.

Mango Tea Bread

MAKES 2 LOAVES

275g/10oz/2¹/₂ cups plain (all-purpose) flour

10ml/2 tsp bicarbonate of soda (baking soda)

10ml/2 tsp ground cinnamon

2.5ml/¹/₂ tsp salt

115g/4oz/¹/₂ cup margarine, at room temperature

3 eggs, at room temperature

300g/11oz/generous 1¹/₂ cups caster (superfine) sugar

120ml/4fl oz/¹/₂ cup vegetable oil

1 large ripe mango, peeled and chopped

90g/3¹/₂oz/generous 1 cup desiccated (dry unsweetened) coconut

65g/2¹/₂oz/¹/₂ cup raisins

1 Preheat the oven to 180°C/350°F/ Gas 4. Line the bottom and sides of two 23 × 13cm/9 × 5in loaf tins (pans) with baking parchment and grease.

2 Sift together the flour, bicarbonate of soda, cinnamon and salt. Set aside.

3 With an electric mixer, cream the margarine until soft.

4 ▼ Beat in the eggs and sugar until light and fluffy. Beat in the oil.

5 Fold the dry ingredients into the creamed ingredients in three batches.

6 Fold in the mango, two-thirds of the coconut and the raisins.

7 ▲ Spoon the batter into the pans.

8 Sprinkle over the remaining coconut. Bake until a skewer inserted into the centre comes out clean, 50–60 minutes. Leave to stand for 10 minutes before turning out on to a rack to cool completely.

Courgette Tea Bread

MAKES 1 LOAF

50g/2oz/¹/₄ cup butter

3 eggs

250ml/8fl oz/1 cup vegetable oil

300g/11oz/generous 1¹/₂ cups sugar

2 medium unpeeled courgettes (zucchini), grated

275g/10oz/2¹/₂ cups plain (all-purpose) flour

10ml/2 tsp bicarbonate of soda (baking soda)

5ml/1 tsp baking powder

5ml/1 tsp salt

5ml/1 tsp ground cinnamon

5ml/1 tsp freshly grated nutmeg

1.5ml/¹/₄ tsp ground cloves

115g/4oz/²/₃ cup walnuts, chopped

1 Preheat the oven to 180°C/350°F/ Gas 4.

2 Line the base and sides of a 23 × 13cm/9 × 5 in loaf tin (pan) with baking parchment and grease.

3 ▲ In a pan, melt the butter over low heat. Set aside.

4 With an electric mixer, beat the eggs and oil together until thick. Beat in the sugar. Stir in the melted butter and courgettes. Set aside.

5 ▲ In another bowl, sift all the dry ingredients together three times. Carefully fold into the courgette mixture. Fold in the walnuts.

6 Pour into the tin and bake until a skewer inserted into the centre comes out clean, 60–70 minutes. Leave to stand for 10 minutes before turning out on to a wire rack to cool completely.

Mango Tea Bread (top), Courgette Tea Bread

Wholemeal Banana Nut Loaf

MAKES 1 LOAF

115g/4oz/¹/2 cup butter, at room temperature

115g/4oz/generous ¹/2 cup caster
  (superfine) sugar

2 eggs, at room temperature

115g/4oz/1 cup plain (all-purpose) flour

5ml/1 tsp bicarbonate of soda
  (baking soda)

1.5ml/¹/4 tsp salt

5ml/1 tsp ground cinnamon

50g/2oz/¹/2 cup wholemeal
  (whole-wheat) flour

3 large ripe bananas

5ml/1 tsp vanilla extract

50g/2oz/¹/3 cup chopped walnuts

1 Preheat the oven to 180°C/350°F/
Gas 4. Line the base and sides of a
23 × 13cm/9 × 5in loaf tin (pan) with
baking parchment and grease the paper.

2 With an electric mixer, cream the
butter and sugar together until light
and fluffy.

3 ▲ Add the eggs, one at a time,
beating well after each addition.

4 Sift the plain flour, bicarbonate
of soda, salt and cinnamon over the
butter mixture and stir to blend.

5 ▲ Stir in the wholemeal flour.

6 ▲ With a fork, mash the bananas
to a purée, then stir into the mixture.
Stir in the vanilla and nuts.

7 ▲ Pour the mixture into the
prepared tin and spread level.

8 Bake until a skewer inserted into
the centre comes out clean, 50–60
minutes. Leave to stand for 10 minutes
before transferring to a rack.

Dried Fruit Loaf

MAKES 1 LOAF

450g/1lb/2²/₃ cups mixed dried fruit, such as currants, raisins, chopped ready-to-eat dried apricots and dried cherries

300ml/¹/₂ pint/1¹/₄ cups cold strong tea

200g/7oz/scant 1 cup soft dark brown sugar

grated rind and juice of 1 small orange

grated rind and juice of 1 lemon

1 egg, lightly beaten

200g/7oz/1³/₄ cups plain (all-purpose) flour

15ml/1 tbsp baking powder

pinch of salt

▲ In a bowl, mix the dried fruit with the tea and soak overnight.

2 Preheat the oven to 180°C/350°F/Gas 4. Line the base and sides of a 23 × 13cm/9 × 5in loaf tin (pan) with baking parchment and grease the paper.

3 ▲ Strain the fruit, reserving the liquid. In a bowl, combine the brown sugar, grated orange and lemon rind, and fruit.

4 ▼ Pour the orange and lemon juice into a measuring jug (cup); if the quantity is less than 250ml/8fl oz/1 cup, top up with the soaking liquid.

5 Stir the citrus juices and egg into the dried fruit mixture.

6 In another bowl, sift together the flour, baking powder and salt. Stir into the fruit mixture until blended.

7 Transfer to the prepared tin and bake until a skewer inserted into the centre comes out clean, about 1¹/₄ hours. Leave to stand for 10 minutes before turning out.

Bilberry Tea Bread

MAKES 8 PIECES

50g/2oz/¹/₄ cup butter or margarine,
   at room temperature

175g/6oz/scant 1 cup caster (superfine) sugar

1 egg, at room temperature

120ml/4fl oz/¹/₂ cup milk

225g/8oz/2 cups plain (all-purpose) flour

10ml/2 tsp baking powder

2.5ml/¹/₂ tsp salt

275g/10oz/2¹/₂ cups fresh bilberries,
   or blueberries

FOR THE TOPPING

115g/4oz/generous ¹/₂ cup sugar

40g/1¹/₂oz/¹/₃ cup plain (all-purpose) flour

2.5ml/¹/₂ tsp ground cinnamon

50g/2oz/¹/₄ cup butter, cut in pieces

1 Preheat the oven to 190°C/375°F/
Gas 5. Grease a 23cm/9in baking dish.

2 With an electric mixer, cream the
butter or margarine with the sugar
until light and fluffy. Add the egg,
beat to combine, then mix in the milk
until blended.

3 ▼ Sift over the flour, baking
powder and salt, and stir just enough
to blend the ingredients.

4 ▲ Add the berries and stir.

5 Transfer to the baking dish.

6 ▲ For the topping, place the sugar,
flour, cinnamon and butter into a
mixing bowl. Cut in with a pastry
blender until the mixture resembles
coarse breadcrumbs.

7 ▲ Sprinkle the topping over the
mixture in the baking dish.

8 Bake until a skewer inserted into
the centre comes out clean, about
45 minutes. Serve warm or cold.

Chocolate Chip Walnut Loaf

MAKES 1 LOAF

90g/3¹/₂oz/¹/₂ cup caster (superfine) sugar

90g/3¹/₂oz/³/₄ cup plain (all-purpose) flour

5ml/1 tsp baking powder

60ml/4 tbsp cornflour (cornstarch)

130g/4¹/₂oz/generous ¹/₂ cup butter, at room temperature

3 eggs, at room temperature

5ml/1 tsp vanilla extract

30ml/2 tbsp currants or raisins

25g/1oz/¹/₄ cup walnuts, finely chopped

grated rind of ¹/₂ lemon

45ml/3 tbsp plain (semisweet) chocolate chips

icing (confectioners') sugar, for dusting

1 Preheat the oven to 180°C/350°F/ Gas 4. Grease and line a 21 × 12cm/ 8¹/₂ × 4¹/₂in loaf tin (pan).

2 ▲ Sprinkle 25ml/1¹/₂ tbsp of the caster sugar into the pan and tilt to distribute the sugar in an even layer over the base and sides. Shake out any excess.

~ VARIATION ~

For the best results, the eggs should be at room temperature. If they are too cold when folded into the creamed butter mixture, they may separate. If this happens, add a spoonful of the flour to help stabilize the mixture.

3 ▼ Sift together the flour, baking powder and cornflour into a mixing bowl, three times. Set aside.

4 With an electric mixer, cream the butter until soft. Add the remaining sugar and continue beating until light and fluffy. Add the eggs, one at a time, beating to incorporate thoroughly after each addition.

5 Gently fold the dry ingredients into the butter mixture, in three batches; do not overmix.

6 ▲ Fold in the vanilla, currants or raisins, walnuts, lemon rind, and chocolate chips until just blended.

7 Pour the mixture into the prepared tin and bake until a skewer inserted into the centre comes out clean, 45–50 minutes. Leave to cool in the tin for 5 minutes before transferring to a rack to cool completely. Dust over an even layer of icing sugar before serving.

Glazed Banana Spice Loaf

MAKES 1 LOAF

1 large ripe banana

115g/4oz/¹/₂ cup butter, at room temperature

165g/5¹/₂oz/generous ³/₄ cup caster (superfine) sugar

2 eggs, at room temperature

215g/7¹/₂oz/scant 2 cups plain (all-purpose) flour

5ml/1 tsp salt

5ml/1 tsp bicarbonate of soda (baking soda)

2.5ml/¹/₂ tsp freshly grated nutmeg

1.5ml/¹/₄ tsp ground allspice

1.5ml/¹/₄ tsp ground cloves

175ml/6fl oz/³/₄ cup sour cream

5ml/1 tsp vanilla extract

FOR THE GLAZE

115g/4oz/1 cup icing (confectioners') sugar

15–30ml/1–2 tbsp lemon juice

1 Preheat the oven to 180°C/350°F/Gas 4. Line a 21 × 11cm/8¹/₂ × 4¹/₂in loaf tin (pan) with baking parchment; grease.

2 ▼ With a fork, mash the banana in a bowl. Set aside.

3 With an electric mixer, cream the butter and sugar until light and fluffy. Add the eggs, one at a time, beating to blend well after each addition.

4 Sift together the flour, salt, bicarbonate of soda, nutmeg, allspice and cloves. Add to the butter mixture and stir to combine well.

5 ▲ Add the sour cream, banana, and vanilla and mix just enough to blend. Pour into the prepared tin.

6 ▲ Bake until the top springs back when touched lightly, 45–50 minutes. Leave to cool in the pan for 10 minutes. Turn out on to a wire rack to cool.

7 ▲ For the glaze, combine the icing sugar and lemon juice, then stir until smooth.

8 To glaze, place the cooled loaf on a rack set over a baking sheet. Pour the glaze over the top of the loaf and allow to set.

Sweet Sesame Loaf

MAKES 1 OR 2 LOAVES

5g/3oz/6 tbsp sesame seeds
75g/10oz/2¹/₂ cups plain (all-purpose) flour
ml/1 tsp salt
2.5ml/2¹/₂ tsp baking powder
0g/2oz/¹/₄ cup butter or margarine, at room temperature
30g/4¹/₂oz/scant ³/₄ cup sugar
eggs, at room temperature
ated rind of 1 lemon
50ml/12fl oz/1¹/₂ cups milk

Preheat the oven to 180°C/350°F/
as 4. Line a 23 × 13cm/9 × 5in loaf tin
an) with baking parchment and grease.

▲ Reserve 30ml/2 tbsp of the
same seeds. Spread the remainder
a baking sheet and bake until
ghtly toasted, about 10 minutes.

Sift the flour, salt and baking
owder into a bowl.

▲ Stir in the toasted sesame seeds
d set aside.

5 With an electric mixer, cream the butter or margarine and sugar together until light and fluffy. Beat in the eggs, then stir in the lemon rind and milk.

6 ▼ Pour the milk mixture over the dry ingredients and fold in with a large metal spoon until just blended.

7 ▲ Pour into the tin and sprinkle over the reserved sesame seeds.

8 Bake until a skewer inserted into the centre comes out clean, about 1 hour. Leave to cool in the tin for about 10 minutes. Turn out on to a wire rack to cool completely.

Wholemeal Scones

MAKES 16

175g/6oz/³/4 cup cold butter

350g/12oz/3 cups wholemeal
  (whole-wheat) flour

150g/5oz/1¹/4 cups plain (all-purpose) flour

30ml/2 tbsp caster (superfine) sugar

2.5ml/¹/2 tsp salt

12.5ml/2¹/2 tsp bicarbonate of soda
  (baking soda)

2 eggs

175ml/6fl oz/³/4 cup buttermilk

35g/1¹/4oz/2¹/2 tbsp raisins

1 Preheat the oven to 200°C/400°F/
Gas 6. Grease and flour a large
baking sheet.

2 ▲ Cut the butter into small pieces.

3 Combine the dry ingredients in a
bowl. Add the butter and rub in with
your fingertips until the mixture
resembles coarse breadcrumbs.
Set aside.

4 In another bowl, whisk together
the eggs and buttermilk. Set aside
30ml/2 tbsp for glazing.

5 Stir the remaining egg mixture into
the dry ingredients until it just holds
together. Stir in the raisins.

6 Roll out the dough to about 2cm/
³/4in thick. Stamp out circles with a
biscuit (cookie) cutter. Place on the
prepared sheet and brush with the glaze

7 Bake until golden, 12–15 minutes.
Allow to cool slightly before serving.
Split in two with a fork while still
warm and spread with butter and jam
if you like.

Orange and Raisin Scones

MAKES 16

275g/10oz/2¹/2 cups plain
  (all-purpose) flour

7.5ml/1¹/2 tsp baking powder

60g/2¹/4oz/4¹/2 tbsp sugar

2.5ml/¹/2 tsp salt

65g/2¹/2oz/5 tbsp butter, diced

65g/2¹/2oz/5 tbsp margarine, diced

grated rind of 1 large orange

50g/2oz/4 tbsp raisins

120ml/4fl oz/¹/2 cup buttermilk

milk, for glazing

1 Preheat the oven to 220°C/425°F/
Gas 7. Grease and flour a large
baking sheet.

2 Combine the dry ingredients in
a large bowl. Add the butter and
margarine and rub in with your
fingertips until the mixture resembles
coarse breadcrumbs.

3 ▲ Add the orange rind and raisins.

4 Gradually stir in the buttermilk to
form a soft dough.

5 ▲ Roll out the dough to about
2cm/³/4in thick. Stamp out circles
with a biscuit (cookie) cutter.

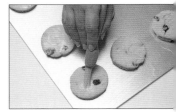

6 ▲ Place on the prepared sheet and
brush the tops with milk.

7 Bake until golden, 12–15 minutes.
Serve hot or warm, with butter, or
whipped or clotted cream, and jam

~ COOK'S TIP ~

For light, tender scones, handle
the dough as little as possible.
If you wish, split the scones when
cool and toast them under a
preheated grill (broiler). Butter
them while still hot.

Wholemeal Scones (top), Orange and Raisin Scone

Buttermilk Scones

MAKES 15

200g/7oz/1³/₄ cups plain (all-purpose) flour
5ml/1 tsp salt
5ml/1 tsp baking powder
2.5ml/¹/₂ tsp bicarbonate of soda (baking soda)
60ml/4 tbsp cold butter or margarine
175ml/6fl oz/³/₄ cup buttermilk

1 Preheat the oven to 220°C/425°F/ Gas 7. Grease and flour a baking sheet.

2 Sift the dry ingredients into a bowl. Rub in the butter or margarine with your fingertips until the mixture resembles breadcrumbs.

3 ▼ Gradually pour in the buttermilk, stirring with a fork to form a soft dough.

4 ▲ Roll out the dough to about 1cm/¹/₂in thick. Stamp out rounds with a 5cm/2in biscuit (cookie) cutter.

5 Place on the prepared baking sheet and bake until golden, 12–15 minutes. Serve warm or at room temperature.

Traditional Sweet Scones

MAKES 8

175g/6oz/1¹/₂ cups plain (all-purpose) flour
30ml/2 tbsp sugar
15ml/1 tbsp baking powder
pinch of salt
75ml/5 tbsp cold butter, cut in pieces
120ml/4fl oz/¹/₂ cup milk

1 Preheat the oven to 220°C/425°F/ Gas 7. Grease and flour a baking sheet.

2 ▲ Sift the flour, sugar, baking powder, and salt into a bowl.

3 Cut in the butter with a pastry blender until the mixture resembles coarse crumbs.

4 Pour in the milk and stir with a fork to form a soft dough.

~ VARIATION ~

To make a delicious and speedy dessert, split the scones in half while still warm. Butter one half, top with lightly sugared fresh strawberries, raspberries or blueberries, and sandwich with the other half. Serve at once with dollops of whipped cream.

5 ▲ Roll out the dough to about 5mm/¹/₄in thick. Stamp out rounds using a 6cm/2¹/₂in biscuit (cookie) cutter.

6 Place on the prepared sheet and bake until golden, about 12 minutes. Serve hot or warm, with butter and jam, to accompany tea or coffee.

Buttermilk Scones (top), Traditional Sweet Scon

Herb Popovers

MAKES 12

3 eggs

250ml/8fl oz/1 cup milk

25g/1oz/2 tbsp butter, melted

75g/3oz/²⁄₃ cup plain (all-purpose) flour

pinch of salt

1 small sprig each mixed fresh herbs, such as chives, tarragon, dill and parsley

1 Preheat the oven to 220°C/425°F/ Gas 7. Grease 12 small ramekins or individual baking cups.

2 With an electric mixer, beat the eggs until blended. Beat in the milk and melted butter.

3 Sift together the flour and salt, then beat into the egg mixture to combine thoroughly.

4 ▼ Strip the herb leaves from the stems and chop finely. Mix together and measure out 30ml/2 tbsp. Stir the herbs into the batter.

5 ▲ Fill the prepared cups half-full.

6 Bake until golden, 25–30 minutes. Do not open the oven door during baking time or the popovers may collapse. For drier popovers, pierce each one with a knife after the 30 minute baking time and bake for 5 minutes more. Serve hot.

Cheese Popovers

MAKES 12

3 eggs

250ml/8fl oz/1 cup milk

25g/1oz/2 tbsp butter, melted

75g/3oz/²⁄₃ cup plain (all-purpose) flour

1.5ml/¹⁄₄ tsp salt

1.5ml/¹⁄₄ tsp paprika

25g/1oz/¹⁄₃ cup freshly grated Parmesan cheese

~ VARIATION ~

For traditional Yorkshire Pudding, omit the cheese and paprika, and use 50–75g/2–3oz/4–6 tbsp of beef dripping to replace the butter. Put them into the oven in time to serve warm as an accompaniment for roast beef.

1 Preheat the oven to 220°C/425°F/ Gas 7.

2 ▲ Grease 12 small ramekins or individual baking cups. With an electric mixer, beat the eggs until they are blended. Beat in the milk and melted butter.

3 ▲ Sift together the flour, salt and paprika, then beat into the egg mixture. Add the cheese and stir.

4 Fill the prepared cups half-full and bake until golden, 25–30 minutes. Do not open the oven door or the popovers may collapse. For drier popovers, pierce each one with a knife after the 30 minute baking time and bake for 5 minutes more. Serve hot.

Herb Popovers (top), Cheese Popover

YEAST BREADS

THOUGH THE PACE OF TODAY'S LIFE
LEAVES LITTLE TIME FOR BAKING,
BREADMAKING CAN BE VERY
THERAPEUTIC. THE PROCESS IS
SIMPLE YET INFINITELY VARIABLE,
AS THE LOAVES THAT FOLLOW
PROVE. ROLL UP YOUR SLEEVES AND
CREATE A TRADITION.

White Bread

MAKES 2 LOAVES

50ml/2fl oz/¹/₄ cup lukewarm water
15ml/1 tbsp active dried yeast
30ml/2 tbsp sugar
450ml/16fl oz/2 cups lukewarm milk
25g/1oz/2 tbsp butter or margarine, at room temperature
10ml/2 tsp salt
850–900g/1lb 14oz–2lb/7¹/₂–8 cups strong white bread flour

1 Combine the water, dried yeast and 15ml/1 tbsp of sugar in a measuring cup and leave to stand for 15 minutes until the mixture is frothy.

2 ▼ Pour the milk into a large bowl. Add the remaining sugar, the butter or margarine, and salt. Stir in the yeast mixture.

3 Stir in the flour, 150g/5oz/1¹/₄ cups at a time, until a stiff dough is obtained. Alternatively, use a food processor.

4 ▲ Transfer the dough to a floured surface. To knead, push the dough away from you with the palm of your hand, then fold it towards you. Repeat until the dough is smooth and elastic.

5 Place the dough in a large greased bowl, cover with a plastic bag, and leave to rise in a warm place until doubled in volume, 2–3 hours.

6 Grease two 23 × 13cm/9 × 5in tins (pans).

7 ▲ Knock back (punch down) the risen dough with your fist and divide in half. Form into a loaf shape and place in the tins, seam-side down. Cover and leave to rise in a warm place until almost doubled in volume, about 45 minutes. Preheat the oven to 190°C/375°F/Gas 5.

8 Bake until firm and brown, 45–50 minutes. Turn out and tap the bottom of a loaf: if it sounds hollow the loaf is done. If necessary, return to the oven and bake a few minutes more. Leave to cool on a rack.

Country Bread

MAKES 2 LOAVES

50g/12oz/3 cups wholemeal
(whole-wheat) flour

50g/12oz/3 cups plain (all-purpose) flour

50g/5oz/1¼ cups strong white bread flour

0ml/4 tsp salt

0g/2oz/¼ cup butter, at room temperature

75ml/16fl oz/2 cups lukewarm milk

OR THE STARTER

5ml/1 tbsp active dry yeast

50ml/8fl oz/1 cup lukewarm water

50g/5oz/1¼ cups strong white bread flour

.5ml/¼ tsp caster (superfine) sugar

▲ For the starter, combine the
east, water, flour and sugar in a bowl
nd stir with a fork. Cover and leave
a warm place for 2–3 hours, or leave
vernight in a cool place.

Place the flours, salt and butter in a
od processor and process until just
lended, 1–2 minutes.

Stir together the milk and starter,
en slowly pour into the processor,
ith the motor running, until the
ixture forms a dough. If necessary,
dd more water. Alternatively, the
ough can be mixed by hand. Transfer
a floured surface and knead until
mooth and elastic.

Place in an ungreased bowl, cover
ith a plastic bag, and leave to rise in
warm place until doubled in volume,
bout 1½ hours.

5 Transfer to a floured surface and
knead briefly. Return to the bowl and
leave to rise until tripled in volume,
about 1½ hours.

6 ▲ Divide the dough in half. Cut
off one-third of the dough from each
half and shape into balls. Shape the
larger remaining portion of each half
into balls. Grease a baking sheet.

7 ▲ For each loaf, top the large ball
with the small ball, and press the
centre with the handle of a wooden
spoon to secure. Cover with a plastic
bag, slash the top, and leave to rise.

8 Preheat the oven to 200°C/400°F/
Gas 6. Dust the dough with flour and
bake until the top is browned and the
bottom sounds hollow when tapped,
45–50 minutes. Cool on a rack.

Braided Loaf

MAKES 1 LOAF

15ml/1 tbsp active dried yeast
5ml/1 tsp honey
250ml/8fl oz/1 cup lukewarm milk
50g/2oz/¹/₄ cup butter, melted
425g/15oz/3¹/₂ cups strong white bread flour
5ml/1 tsp salt
1 egg, lightly beaten
1 egg yolk beaten with 5ml/1 tsp milk, for glazing

1 ▼ Combine the yeast, honey, milk and butter. Stir and leave for 15 minutes to dissolve.

2 In a large bowl, mix together the flour and salt. Make a well in the centre and add the yeast mixture and egg. With a wooden spoon, stir from the centre, incorporating flour with each turn, to obtain a rough dough.

3 Transfer to a floured surface and knead until smooth and elastic. Place in a clean bowl, cover and leave to rise in a warm place until doubled in volume, about 1¹/₂ hours.

4 Grease a baking sheet. Knock back (punch down) the dough and divide into three equal pieces. Roll to shape each piece into a long, thin strip.

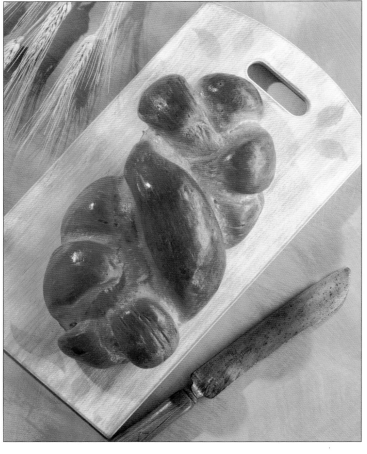

5 ▲ Begin braiding with the centre strip, tucking in the ends. Cover loosely and leave to rise in a warm place for 30 minutes.

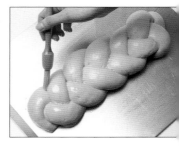

6 ▲ Preheat the oven to 190°C/375°F/Gas 5. Place the bread in a cool place while the oven heats. Brush with the glaze and bake until golden, 40–45 minutes. Turn out on to a rack to cool.

Sesame Seed Bread

MAKES 1 LOAF

0ml/2 tsp active dried yeast
00ml/¹/₂ pint/1¹/₄ cups lukewarm water
00g/7oz/1³/₄ cups strong white bread flour
00g/7oz/1³/₄ cups strong wholemeal (whole-wheat) bread flour
0ml/2 tsp salt
5g/2¹/₂oz/5 tbsp toasted sesame seeds
ilk, for glazing
5g/1oz/2 tbsp sesame seeds, for sprinkling

Combine the yeast and 75ml/5 tbsp f the water and leave to dissolve for 5 minutes. Mix the flours and salt in large bowl. Make a well in the centre nd pour in the yeast and water.

▲ With a wooden spoon, stir from he centre, incorporating flour with ach turn, to obtain a rough dough.

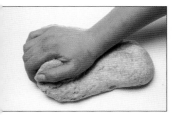

▲ Transfer to a lightly floured urface. To knead, push the dough way from you with the palm of your and, then fold it towards you and ush away again. Repeat until smooth nd elastic, then return to the bowl nd cover with a plastic bag. Leave he dough in a warm place for about ¹/₂–2 hours, until doubled in volume.

4 ▲ Grease a 23cm/9in cake tin (pan). Knock back (punch down) the dough and knead in the sesame seeds. Divide the dough into 16 balls and place in the tin. Cover with a plastic bag and leave in a warm place until risen above the rim of the tin.

5 ▼ Preheat the oven to 220°C/ 425°F/Gas 7. Brush the loaf with milk and sprinkle with the sesame seeds. Bake for 15 minutes. Lower the heat to 190°C/375°F/Gas 5 and bake until the bottom sounds hollow when tapped, about 30 minutes. Cool on a rack.

Wholemeal Bread

MAKES 1 LOAF

600g/1lb 5oz/5¼ cups strong wholemeal (whole-wheat) bread flour

10ml/2 tsp salt

20ml/4 tsp active dried yeast

425ml/15fl oz/generous 1⅔ cups lukewarm water

30ml/2 tbsp honey

45ml/3 tbsp oil

40g/1½oz wheatgerm

milk, for glazing

1 Combine the flour and salt in a bowl and place in the oven at its lowest setting until warmed, 8–10 minutes.

2 Meanwhile, combine the yeast with half of the water in a small bowl and leave to dissolve.

3 ▼ Make a well in the centre of the flour. Pour in the yeast mixture, the remaining water, honey, oil and wheatgerm. With a wooden spoon, stir from the centre until smooth.

4 Transfer the dough to a lightly floured surface and knead just enough to shape into a loaf.

5 ▲ Grease a 23 × 13cm/9 × 5in loaf tin (pan), place the dough in it and cover with a plastic bag. Leave in a warm place until the dough is about 2.5cm/1in higher than the tin rim, about 1 hour.

6 Preheat the oven to 200°C/400°F/ Gas 6. Bake until the bottom sounds hollow when tapped, 35–40 minutes. Cool.

Rye Bread

MAKES 1 LOAF

200g/7oz/1¾ cups rye flour

450ml/¾ pint/scant 2 cups boiling water

120ml/4fl oz/½ cup black treacle (molasses)

65g/2½oz/5 tbsp butter, cut in pieces

15ml/1 tbsp salt

30ml/2 tbsp caraway seeds

15ml/1 tbsp active dried yeast

120ml/4fl oz/½ cup lukewarm water

about 850g/1lb 14oz/7½ cups strong white bread flour

semolina or flour, for dusting

~ COOK'S TIP ~

To bring out the flavour of the caraway seeds, toast them lightly. Spread the seeds on a baking tray and place in a preheated 160°C/325°F/ Gas 3 oven for about 7 minutes.

1 ▲ Mix the rye flour, boiling water, treacle, butter, salt and caraway seeds in a large bowl. Leave to cool.

2 In another bowl, mix the yeast and lukewarm water and leave to dissolve. Stir into the rye flour mixture. Stir in just enough strong flour to obtain a stiff dough. If it becomes too stiff, stir with your hands.

3 Transfer to a floured surface and knead until the dough is no longer sticky and is smooth and shiny.

4 Place in a greased bowl, cover with a plastic bag, and leave in a warm place until doubled in volume. Knock back (punch down) the dough, cover, and leave to rise again for 30 minutes.

5 Preheat the oven to 180°C/350°F/ Gas 4. Dust a baking sheet with semolina.

6 ▼ Shape the dough into a ball. Place on the sheet and score several times across the top. Bake until the bottom sounds hollow when tapped, about 40 minutes. Cool on a rack.

Wholemeal Bread (top), Rye Bread

Buttermilk Graham Bread

MAKES 8

10ml/2 tsp active dried yeast

120ml/4fl oz/^{1}/$_2$ cup lukewarm water

225g/8oz/2 cups graham or strong
wholemeal (whole-wheat)
bread flour

350g/12oz/3 cups strong white
bread flour

130g/4^1/$_2$oz/generous 1 cup cornmeal

10ml/2 tsp salt

30ml/2 tbsp sugar

60ml/4 tbsp butter, at room temperature

475ml/16fl oz/2 cups lukewarm buttermilk

1 beaten egg, for glazing

sesame seeds, for sprinkling

1 Combine the yeast and water, stir, and leave for 15 minutes to dissolve.

2 ▲ Mix together the two flours, cornmeal, salt and sugar in a large bowl. Make a well in the centre and pour in the yeast mixture, then add the butter and the buttermilk.

3 ▲ Stir from the centre, mixing in the flour until a rough dough is formed. If too stiff, use your hands.

4 ▲ Transfer to a floured surface and knead until smooth. Place in a clean bowl, cover, and leave in a warm place for 2–3 hours.

5 ▲ Grease two 20cm/8in square baking tins (pans). Knock back (punch down) the dough. Divide into eight pieces and roll them into balls. Place four in each tin. Cover and leave in a warm place for about 1 hour.

6 Preheat the oven to 190°C/375°F/ Gas 5. Brush with the glaze, then sprinkle over the sesame seeds. Bake for about 50 minutes, or until the bottoms sound hollow when tapped. Cool on a wire rack.

Multi-grain Bread

MAKES 2 LOAVES

15ml/1 tbsp active dried yeast

60ml/2fl oz/¼ cup lukewarm water

65g/2½oz/⅔ cup rolled oats (not quick cook)

450ml/¾ pint/scant 2 cups milk

10ml/2 tsp salt

60ml/2fl oz/¼ cup oil

50g/2oz/¼ cup soft light brown sugar

30ml/2 tbsp honey

2 eggs, lightly beaten

25g/1oz wheatgerm

175g/6oz/1½ cups soya flour

350g/12oz/3 cups strong wholemeal
(whole-wheat) bread flour

about 450g/1lb/4 cups strong white
bread flour

1 Combine the yeast and water, stir,
and leave for 15 minutes to dissolve.

2 ▲ Place the oats in a large bowl.
Scald the milk, then pour over the
rolled oats.

3 Stir in the salt, oil, sugar and
honey. Leave until lukewarm.

4 ▲ Stir in the yeast mixture, eggs,
wheatgerm, soya and wholemeal flours.
Gradually stir in enough white flour
to obtain a rough dough.

5 Transfer the dough to a floured
surface and knead, adding flour if
necessary, until smooth and elastic.
Return to a clean bowl, cover and
leave to rise in a warm place until
doubled in volume, about 2½ hours.

6 Grease two 21 × 12cm/8½ × 4½in
bread tins (pans). Knock back (punch
down) the risen dough and knead briefly.

7 Divide the dough into quarters. Roll
each quarter into a cylinder 4cm/1½in
thick. Twist together 2 cylinders and put
in a tin; repeat for the remaining pieces.

8 Cover and leave to rise until
doubled in size, about 1 hour.

9 Preheat the oven to 190°C/375°F/
Gas 5.

10 ▲ Bake for 45–50 minutes, until
the bottoms sound hollow when
tapped lightly. Cool on a rack.

Potato Bread

MAKES 2 LOAVES

20ml/4 tsp active dried yeast

250ml/8fl oz/1 cup lukewarm milk

225g/8oz potatoes, boiled (reserve 250ml/
8fl oz/1 cup of potato cooking liquid)

30ml/2 tbsp oil

20ml/4 tsp salt

850–900g/1lb 14oz–2lb/7$^{1}/_{2}$–8 cups strong
white bread flour

1 Combine the yeast and milk in a
large bowl and leave to dissolve, about
15 minutes.

2 Meanwhile, mash the potatoes.

3 ▲ Add the potatoes, oil and salt to
the yeast mixture and mix well. Stir in
the reserved cooking water, then stir
in the flour, in six separate batches, to
form a stiff dough.

4 Transfer to a floured surface and
knead until smooth and elastic. Return
to the bowl, cover, and leave in a warm
place until doubled in size, 1–1$^{1}/_{2}$ hours
Knock back (punch down), then
leave to rise for another 40 minutes.

5 Grease two 23 × 13cm/9 × 5in loaf
tins (pans). Roll the dough into
20 small balls. Place two rows of balls
in each tin. Leave until the dough has
risen above the rim of the tins.

6 Preheat the oven to 200°C/400°F/
Gas 6. Bake for 10 minutes, then lower
the heat to 190°C/375°F/Gas 5. Bake
until the bottoms sound hollow when
tapped, 40 minutes. Cool on a rack.

Irish Soda Bread

MAKES 1 LOAF

275g/10oz/2$^{1}/_{2}$ cups plain (all-purpose)
flour

150g/5oz/1$^{1}/_{4}$ cups wholemeal
(whole-wheat) flour

5ml/1 tsp bicarbonate of soda
(baking soda)

5ml/1 tsp salt

25g/1oz/2 tbsp butter or margarine,
at room temperature

300ml/$^{1}/_{2}$ pint/1$^{1}/_{4}$ cups buttermilk

15ml/1 tbsp plain flour, for dusting

1 Preheat the oven to 200°C/400°F/
Gas 6. Grease a baking sheet.

2 Sift the flours, bicarbonate of soda
and salt together into a bowl. Make a
well in the centre and add the butter
or margarine and buttermilk. Working
outwards from the centre, stir with a
fork until a soft dough is formed.

3 ▲ With floured hands, gather the
dough into a ball.

4 ▲ Transfer to a floured surface and
knead for 3 minutes. Shape the dough
into a large round.

5 ▲ Place on the baking sheet. Cut
a cross in the top with a sharp knife.

6 ▲ Dust with flour. Bake until
brown, 40–50 minutes. Transfer to a
rack to cool.

Potato Bread (top), Irish Soda Bread

Anadama Bread

MAKES 2 LOAVES

10ml/2 tsp active dried yeast
60ml/4 tbsp lukewarm water
50g/2oz/1/2 cup cornmeal
45ml/3 tbsp butter or margarine
60ml/4 tbsp black treacle (molasses)
175ml/6fl oz/3/4 cup boiling water
1 egg
350g/12oz/3 cups strong white bread flour
30ml/2 tbsp salt

1 Combine the yeast and lukewarm water, stir well, and leave for 15 minutes to dissolve.

2 ▼ Meanwhile, combine the cornmeal, butter or margarine, black treacle and boiling water in a large bowl. Add the yeast, egg, and half the flour. Stir together to blend.

3 ▲ Stir in the remaining flour and salt. When the dough becomes too stiff, stir with your hands until it comes away from the sides of the bowl. If it is too sticky, add more flour; if too stiff, add a little water.

4 ▲ Transfer to a floured surface and knead until smooth and elastic. Place in a bowl, cover with a plastic bag, and leave in a warm place until doubled in size, 2–3 hours.

5 Grease two 18 × 7.5cm/7 × 3in bread tins (pans). Knock back (punch down) the dough. Shape into two loaves and place in the tins, seam-side down. Cover and leave in a warm place for 1–2 hours.

6 ▲ Preheat the oven to 190°C/ 375°F/Gas 5. Bake for 50 minutes. Remove and cool on a wire rack.

Oatmeal Bread

MAKES 2 LOAVES

350ml/³/₄ pint/scant 2 cups milk
25g/1oz/2 tbsp butter
50g/2oz/¹/₄ cup soft dark brown sugar
10ml/2 tsp salt
15ml/1 tbsp active dried yeast
60ml/2fl oz/¹/₄ cup lukewarm water
400g/14oz/4 cups rolled oats (not quick-cook)
700–850g/1¹/₂lb–1lb 14oz/6–7¹/₂ cups strong white bread flour

1 ▲ Scald the milk. Remove from the heat and stir in the butter, brown sugar and salt. Leave until lukewarm.

2 Combine the yeast and warm water in a large bowl and leave until the yeast is dissolved and the mixture is frothy. Stir in the milk mixture.

3 ▲ Add 270g/10oz/2¹/₄ cups of the oats and enough flour to obtain a soft dough.

4 Transfer to a floured surface and knead until smooth and elastic.

5 ▲ Place in a greased bowl, cover with a plastic bag, and leave until doubled in volume, 2–3 hours.

6 Grease a large baking sheet. Transfer the dough to a lightly floured surface and divide in half.

7 ▼ Shape into rounds. Place on the baking sheet, cover with a dish towel and leave to rise until doubled in volume, about 1 hour.

8 Preheat the oven to 200°C/400°F/Gas 6. Score the tops and sprinkle with the remaining oats. Bake until the bottoms sound hollow when tapped, 45–50 minutes. Cool on racks.

Sourdough Bread

MAKES 1 LOAF

350g/12oz/3 cups strong white bread flour
15ml/1 tbsp salt
250ml/8fl oz/1 cup Sourdough Starter
120ml/4fl oz/¹/₂ cup lukewarm water

1 ▲ Combine the flour and salt in a large bowl. Make a well in the centre and add the starter and water. With a wooden spoon, stir from the centre, incorporating more flour with each turn, to obtain a rough dough.

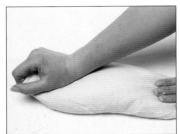

2 ▲ Transfer the dough to a floured surface. To knead, push the dough away from you with the palm of your hand, then fold it towards you, and push it away again. Repeat the process until the dough has become smooth and elastic.

3 Place in a clean bowl, cover, and leave to rise in a warm place until doubled in volume, for about 2 hours.

4 Lightly grease a 20 × 10cm/8 × 4in bread tin (pan).

5 ▼ Knock back (punch down) the dough with your fist. Knead briefly, then form into a loaf shape and place in the tin, seam-side down. Cover with a plastic bag, and leave to rise in a warm place, for about 1¹/₂ hours.

6 Preheat the oven to 220°C/425°F/ Gas 7. Dust the top of the loaf with flour, then score lengthways. Bake for 15 minutes. Lower the heat to 190°C/ 375°F/Gas 5 and bake for about 30 minutes more, or until the bottom sounds hollow when tapped.

Sourdough Starter

MAKES 750ML/1¹/₄ PINTS

5ml/1 tsp active dried yeast
175ml/6fl oz/³/₄ cup lukewarm water
50g/2oz/¹/₂ cup strong white bread flour

~ COOK'S TIP ~

After using, feed the remaining starter with a handful of flour and enough water to restore it to a thick batter. The starter can be chilled for up to 1 week, but must be brought back to room temperature before using.

1 ▲ Combine the yeast and water, stir and leave for 15 minutes to dissolve.

2 ▼ Sprinkle over the flour, and whisk until it forms a batter. Cover and leave to rise in a warm place for at least 24 hours or preferably 2–4 days, before using.

Sourdough French Loaves

MAKES 2 LOAVES

10ml/2 tsp active dried yeast
350ml/12fl oz/1½ cups lukewarm water
250ml/8fl oz/1 cup Sourdough Starter
700g/1lb 8oz/6 cups strong white bread flour
15ml/1 tbsp salt
5ml/1 tsp sugar
cornmeal, for sprinkling
5ml/1 tsp cornflour (cornstarch)
120ml/4fl oz/½ cup water

1 In a large bowl, combine the yeast and lukewarm water, stir and leave for 15 minutes to dissolve.

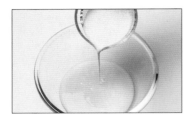

2 ▲ Pour in the Sourdough Starter. Add 450g/1lb/4 cups of the flour, the salt and the sugar. Stir until smooth. Cover the bowl with a plastic bag and leave the dough to rise in a warm place until doubled in volume, about 1½ hours.

3 Stir in just enough flour to obtain a rough dough. Transfer to a floured surface and knead until the dough is smooth and elastic. Divide in half, then shape each half into a 35cm/14in cylinder with rounded ends.

4 ▲ Place the loaves on a wooden board or tray sprinkled with cornmeal. Cover loosely with a dishtowel and leave to rise in a warm place until nearly doubled in volume.

5 Preheat the oven to 220°C/425°F/Gas 7. Place a 38 × 30cm/15 × 12in baking sheet in the oven. Half-fill a shallow baking dish with hot water and put it on the bottom of the oven.

6 Mix the cornflour and water in a small pan. Bring to the boil.

7 ▲ With a sharp knife, make several diagonal slashes across the loaves. Slide on to the hot baking sheet and brush over the cornflour mixture. Bake until the tops are golden and the bottoms sound hollow when tapped, about 25 minutes. Cool on a wire rack.

Sourdough Rye Bread

MAKES 2 LOAVES

10ml/2 tsp active dried yeast

120ml/4fl oz/¹/₂ cup lukewarm water

25g/1oz/2 tbsp butter, melted

15ml/1 tbsp salt

115g/4oz/1 cup strong wholemeal
(whole-wheat) bread flour

400–450g/14–16oz/3¹/₂–4 cups strong
white bread flour

1 egg mixed with 15ml/1 tbsp water,
for glazing

FOR THE STARTER

15ml/1 tbsp active dried yeast

350ml/12fl oz/1¹/₂ cups lukewarm water

45ml/3 tbsp black treacle (molasses)

30ml/2 tbsp caraway seeds

250g/9oz/2¹/₄ cups rye flour

1 For the starter, combine the yeast
and water, stir and leave for 15 minutes
to dissolve.

2 ▲ Stir in the black treacle,
caraway seeds and rye flour. Cover
and leave in a warm place for
2–3 days.

3 In a large bowl, combine the
yeast and water, stir and leave for
10 minutes. Stir in the melted butter,
salt, wholemeal flour and 400g/14oz/
3¹/₂ cups of the white flour.

4 ▲ Make a well in the centre and
pour in the starter.

5 Stir to obtain a rough dough, then
transfer to a floured surface and
knead until smooth and elastic.
Return to the bowl, cover and leave
to rise in a warm place until doubled
in volume, about 2 hours.

6 Grease a large baking sheet. Knock
back (punch down) the dough and
knead briefly. Cut the dough in half and
form each half into log-shaped loaves.

7 ▼ Place the loaves on the baking
sheet and score the tops with a sharp
knife. Cover and leave to rise in a
warm place until almost doubled,
about 50 minutes.

8 Preheat the oven to 190°C/375°F/
Gas 5. Brush the loaves with the egg
wash to glaze them, then bake until
the bottoms sound hollow when
tapped, about 50–55 minutes. If the
tops brown too quickly, place a sheet
of foil over the tops to protect them.
Cool on a wire rack.

Wholemeal Rolls

MAKES 12

10ml/2 tsp active dried yeast

50ml/2fl oz/¼ cup lukewarm water

5ml/1 tsp caster (superfine) sugar

175ml/6fl oz/¾ cup lukewarm buttermilk

1.5ml/¼ tsp bicarbonate of soda
  (baking soda)

5ml/1 tsp salt

40g/1½oz/3 tbsp butter,
  at room temperature

200g/7oz/1¾ cups strong wholemeal
  (whole-wheat) bread flour

150g/5oz/1¼ cups strong white
  bread flour

1 beaten egg, for glazing

1 In a large bowl, combine the yeast,
water and sugar. Stir, and leave for
15 minutes to dissolve.

2 ▲ Add the buttermilk, bicarbonate
of soda, salt and butter, and stir to
blend. Stir in the wholemeal flour.

3 Add just enough of the white flour
to obtain a rough dough.

4 Transfer to a floured surface and
knead until smooth and elastic.
Divide into three equal parts.
Roll each into a cylinder, then cut
into four.

5 ▼ Form the pieces into torpedo
shapes. Place on a greased baking
sheet, cover and leave in a warm
place until doubled in volume.

6 Preheat the oven to 200°C/400°F/
Gas 6. Brush the rolls with the glaze.
Bake until firm, 15–20 minutes. Cool
on a rack.

French Bread

MAKES 2 LOAVES

15ml/1 tbsp active dried yeast

450ml/¾ pint/scant 2 cups lukewarm water

15ml/1 tbsp salt

850g–1.2kg/1lb 14oz–2½lb/7½–10 cups
  strong white bread flour

semolina or flour, for sprinkling

1 Combine the yeast and water, stir,
and leave for 15 minutes to dissolve.
Stir in the salt.

2 Add the flour, 150g/5oz/1¼ cups at
a time. Beat in with a wooden spoon,
adding just enough flour to obtain a
smooth dough. Alternatively, use an
electric mixer with a dough hook.

3 Transfer to a floured surface and
knead until smooth and elastic.

4 Shape into a ball, place in a greased
bowl and cover with a plastic bag.
Leave to rise in a warm place until
doubled in volume, 2–4 hours.

5 ▲ Transfer to a lightly floured
board and shape into two long loaves.
Place on a baking sheet sprinkled with
semolina or flour and leave to rise for
5 minutes.

6 ▲ Score the tops in several places
with a very sharp knife. Brush with
water and place in a cold oven. Set a
pan of boiling water on the bottom of
the oven and set the oven to 200°C/
400°F/Gas 6. Bake until crusty and
golden, about 40 minutes. Cool
on a rack.

Wholemeal Rolls (top), French Bread

Pleated Rolls

MAKES 48

15ml/1 tbsp active dried yeast
475ml/16fl oz/2 cups lukewarm milk
115g/4oz/$\frac{1}{2}$ cup margarine
75ml/5 tbsp sugar
10ml/2 tsp salt
2 eggs
975g–1.2kg/2lb 3oz–2$\frac{1}{2}$lb/8$\frac{2}{3}$–10 cups strong white bread flour
50g/2oz/$\frac{1}{4}$ cup butter

1 Combine the yeast and 120ml/4fl oz/$\frac{1}{2}$ cup milk in a large bowl. Stir and leave for 15 minutes to dissolve.

2 Scald the remaining milk, cool for 5 minutes, then beat in the margarine, sugar, salt and eggs. Leave to cool to lukewarm.

3 ▲ Pour the milk mixture into the yeast mixture. Stir in half the flour with a wooden spoon. Add the remaining flour, 150g/5oz/1$\frac{1}{4}$ cups at a time, until a rough dough is obtained.

4 Transfer the dough to a lightly floured surface and knead until smooth and elastic. Place in a clean bowl, cover with a plastic bag and leave to rise in a warm place until doubled in volume, about 2 hours.

5 In a pan, melt the butter and set aside. Grease two baking sheets.

6 Knock back (punch down) the dough and divide into four equal pieces. Roll each piece into a 30 × 20cm/12 × 8in rectangle, about 5mm/$\frac{1}{4}$in thick.

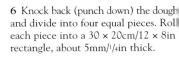

7 ▲ Cut each rectangle into four long strips. Cut each strip into three 10 × 5cm/4 × 2in rectangles.

8 ▲ Brush each rectangle with melted butter, then fold the rectangle in half, so that the top extends about 1cm/$\frac{1}{2}$in over the bottom.

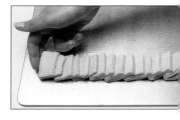

9 ▲ Place the rectangles slightly overlapping on the baking sheet, with the longer side facing up. Cover and chill for 30 minutes. Preheat the oven to 180°C/350°F/Gas 4. Bake until golden, about 18–20 minutes. Allow to cool slightly before slicing or breaking the rolls.

Clover Leaf Rolls

MAKES 24

00ml/¹/₂ pint/1¹/₄ cups milk

0ml/2 tbsp caster (superfine) sugar

0g/2oz/¹/₄ cup butter, at room temperature

0ml/2 tsp active dried yeast

egg

0ml/2 tsp salt

00–575g/1lb 2oz–1lb 4oz/4¹/₂–5 cups
   strong white bread flour

melted butter, for glazing

▲ Heat the milk until lukewarm;
est the temperature with your
nuckle. Pour into a large bowl and
ir in the sugar, butter and yeast.
eave for 15 minutes to dissolve.

Stir the egg and salt into the yeast
ixture. Gradually stir in 500g/1lb 2oz/
/₂ cups of the flour. Add just enough
xtra flour to obtain a rough dough.

▲ Transfer to a floured surface and
nead until smooth and elastic. Place
n a greased bowl, cover and leave in
warm place until doubled in volume,
bout 1¹/₂ hours.

4 Grease two 12-cup bun trays.

5 ▼ Knock back (punch down) the
dough. Cut into four equal pieces.
Roll each piece into a rope 35cm/14in
long. Cut each rope into 18 pieces,
then roll each into a ball.

6 ▲ Place three balls, side by side, in
each bun cup. Cover loosely and leave
to rise in a warm place until doubled
in volume, about 1¹/₂ hours.

7 Preheat the oven to 200°C/400°F/
Gas 6. Brush the rolls with glaze. Bake
until lightly browned, about 20 minutes.
Cool slightly before serving.

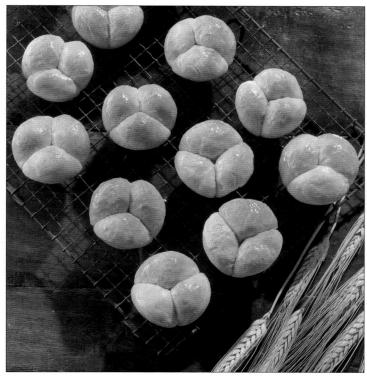

Poppyseed Knots

MAKES 12

300ml/¹/₂ pint/1¹/₄ cups lukewarm milk

50g/2oz/¹/₄ cup butter, at room temperature

5ml/1 tsp caster (superfine) sugar

10ml/2 tsp active dried yeast

1 egg yolk

10ml/2 tsp salt

500–575g/1lb 2oz–1lb 4oz/4¹/₂–5 cups
strong white bread flour

1 egg beaten with 10ml/2 tsp of water,
for glazing

poppyseeds, for sprinkling

1 In a large bowl, stir together the milk, butter, sugar and yeast. Leave for 15 minutes to dissolve.

2 Stir in the egg yolk, salt and 275g/10oz/2¹/₂ cups flour. Add half the remaining flour and stir to obtain a soft dough.

3 Transfer to a floured surface and knead, adding flour if necessary, until smooth and elastic. Place in a bowl, cover and leave in a warm place until doubled in volume, 1¹/₂–2 hours.

4 ▲ Grease a baking sheet. Knock back (punch down) the dough and cut into 12 pieces the size of golf balls.

5 ▲ Roll each piece to a rope, twist to form a knot and place 2.5cm/1in apart on the sheet. Cover and leave to rise until doubled in volume, 1–1¹/₂ hours.

6 Preheat the oven to 180°C/350°F/Gas 4.

7 ▲ Brush the knots with the egg glaze and sprinkle over the poppyseeds. Bake until the tops are lightly browned, 25–30 minutes. Cool slightly on a rack before serving.

Bread Sticks

MAKES 18–20

5ml/1 tbsp active dried yeast
00ml/¹/₂ pint/1¹/₄ cups lukewarm water
25g/15oz/3²/₃ cups strong white bread flour
0ml/2 tsp salt
ml/1 tsp caster (superfine) sugar
0ml/2 tbsp olive oil
50g/5oz/10 tbsp sesame seeds
beaten egg, for glazing
oarse salt, for sprinkling

Combine the yeast and water, stir nd leave for 15 minutes to dissolve.

▲ Place the flour, salt, sugar and live oil in a food processor. With he motor running, slowly pour in the east mixture, and process until the ough forms a ball. If sticky, add ore flour; if dry, add more water.

Transfer to a floured surface and nead until smooth and elastic. Place a bowl, cover and leave to rise in warm place for 45 minutes.

▲ Lightly toast the sesame seeds in frying pan. Grease two baking sheets.

5 ▼ Roll small handfuls of dough into cylinders, about 30cm/12in long. Place on the baking sheets.

~ VARIATION ~

If you like, use other seeds, such as poppy or caraway, or, for plain bread sticks, omit the seeds and salt.

6 ▲ Brush with egg glaze, sprinkle with the sesame seeds, then sprinkle over some coarse salt. Leave to rise, uncovered, until almost doubled in volume, about 20 minutes.

7 Preheat the oven to 200°C/400°F/ Gas 6. Bake until golden, about 15 minutes. Turn off the heat but leave the bread sticks in the oven for 5 minutes more. Serve warm or cool.

Croissants

MAKES 18

15ml/1 tbsp active dried yeast
335ml/11fl oz/generous 1¼ cups lukewarm milk
10ml/2 tsp caster (superfine) sugar
7.5ml/1½ tsp salt
425–505g/15oz–1lb 2oz/3⅔–4½ cups strong white bread flour
225g/8oz/1 cup cold unsalted (sweet) butter
1 egg beaten with 10ml/2 tsp water, for glazing

1 Stir together the yeast and warm milk in a large bowl. Leave for 15 minutes to dissolve. Stir in the sugar, salt and 150g/5oz/1¼ cups of the flour.

2 Using a dough hook, on low speed, gradually add the remaining flour. Beat on high until the dough pulls away from the sides of the bowl. Cover and let rise in a warm place until doubled, about 1½ hours.

3 On a floured surface, knead the dough until smooth. Wrap it in baking parchment and chill for 15 minutes.

4 ▲ Divide the butter into two halves and place each between two sheets of baking parchment. With a rolling pin, flatten each to form a 15 × 10cm/6 × 4in rectangle. Set aside.

5 ▲ On a floured surface, roll out the dough to 30 × 20cm/12 × 8in. Place a butter rectangle in the centre. Fold the bottom third of dough over the butter and press gently to seal. Top with the other butter rectangle, then fold over the top dough third.

6 ▲ Turn the dough so that the short side is facing you, with the long folded edge on the left and the long open edge on the right, like a book.

7 Roll the dough gently into a 30 × 20cm/12 × 8in rectangle; do not press the butter out. Fold in thirds again and mark one corner with your fingertip to indicate the first turn. Wrap and chill for 30 minutes.

8 Repeat twice more: again position the dough like a book, roll, fold in thirds, mark, wrap, and chill. After the third fold, chill for at least 2 hours (or overnight).

9 Roll out the dough about 3mm/⅛in thick to a rectangle about 33cm/13in wide. Trim the sides to neaten.

10 ▲ Cut the dough in half lengthways, then cut into triangles 15cm/6in high with a 10cm/4in base.

11 ▲ Gently go over the triangles lengthways with a rolling pin to stretch slightly. Roll up from base to point. Place point down on baking sheets and curve to form a crescent. Cover and leave to rise in a warm place until more than doubled in volume, 1–1½ hours. (Or, chill overnight and bake the next day.)

12 ▲ Preheat the oven to 240°C/475°F/Gas 9. Brush with the glaze. Bake for 2 minutes. Lower the heat to 190°C/375°F/Gas 5. Bake until golden 10–12 more minutes. Serve warm.

Dill Bread

MAKES 2 LOAVES

20ml/4 tsp active dried yeast
475ml/16fl oz/2 cups lukewarm water
30ml/2 tbsp sugar
1.05kg/2lb 5^1/$_2$oz/9^1/$_4$ cups strong white bread flour
^{1}/$_2$ onion, chopped
60ml/4 tbsp oil
1 large bunch of dill, finely chopped
2 eggs, lightly beaten
165g/5^1/$_2$oz/^{3}/$_4$ cup cottage cheese
20ml/4 tsp salt
milk, for glazing

1 Mix together the yeast, water and sugar in a large bowl and leave for 15 minutes to dissolve.

2 ▼ Stir in about half of the flour. Cover and leave to rise in a warm place for 45 minutes.

3 ▲ In a frying pan, cook the onion in 15ml/1 tbsp of the oil until soft. Set aside to cool, then stir into the yeast mixture. Stir the dill, eggs, cottage cheese, salt and remaining oil into the yeast. Gradually add the remaining flour until too stiff to stir.

4 ▲ Transfer to a floured surface and knead until smooth and elastic. Place in a bowl, cover and leave to rise until doubled in volume, 1–1^1/$_2$ hours.

5 ▲ Grease a large baking sheet. Cu[t] the dough in half and shape into two rounds. Leave to rise in a warm place for 30 minutes.

6 Preheat the oven to 190°C/375°F/ Gas 5. Score the tops, brush with the milk and bake until browned, about 50 minutes. Cool on a rack.

Spiral Herb Bread

MAKES 2 LOAVES

30ml/2 tbsp active dried yeast
600ml/1 pint/2½ cups lukewarm water
825g/15oz/3⅔ cups strong white bread flour
505g/1lb 2oz/4½ cups strong wholemeal (whole-wheat) bread flour
15ml/3 tsp salt
25g/1oz/2 tbsp butter
1 large bunch of parsley, finely chopped
1 bunch of spring onions (scallions), chopped
1 garlic clove, finely chopped
salt and ground black pepper
1 egg, lightly beaten
milk, for glazing

1 Combine the yeast and 50ml/2fl oz/¼ cup of the water, stir and leave for 15 minutes to dissolve.

2 Combine the flours and salt in a large bowl. Make a well in the centre and pour in the yeast mixture and the remaining water. With a wooden spoon, stir from the centre, working outwards to obtain a rough dough.

3 Transfer the dough to a floured surface and knead until smooth and elastic. Return to the bowl, cover with a plastic bag, and leave until doubled in volume, about 2 hours.

4 ▲ Meanwhile, combine the butter, parsley, spring onions and garlic in a large frying pan. Cook over low heat, stirring, until softened. Season and set aside.

5 Grease two 23 × 13cm/9 × 5in tins (pans). When the dough has risen, cut in half and roll each half into a rectangle about 35 × 23cm/14 × 9in.

6 ▼ Brush both with the beaten egg. Divide the herb mixture between the two, spreading just up to the edges.

7 ▲ Roll up to enclose the filling and pinch the short ends to seal. Place in the tins, seam-side down. Cover, and leave in a warm place until the dough rises above the rim of the tins.

8 Preheat the oven to 190°C/375°F/ Gas 5. Brush with milk and bake until the bottoms sound hollow when tapped, about 55 minutes. Cool on a rack.

Pizza

MAKES 2

505g/1lb 2oz/4$\frac{1}{2}$ cups strong white
 bread flour

5ml/1 tsp salt

10ml/2 tsp active dried yeast

300ml/$\frac{1}{2}$ pint/1$\frac{1}{4}$ cups lukewarm water

50–120ml/2–4fl oz/$\frac{1}{4}$–$\frac{1}{2}$ cup extra-virgin
 olive oil

tomato sauce, grated cheese, olives and
 herbs, for topping

1 Combine the flour and salt in a
large mixing bowl. Make a well in the
centre and add the yeast, water and
30ml/2 tbsp of the olive oil. Leave for
15 minutes to dissolve the yeast.

2 With your hands, stir until the
dough just holds together. Transfer
to a floured surface and knead until
smooth and elastic. Avoid adding too
much flour while kneading.

3 ▲ Brush the inside of a clean bowl
with 15ml/1 tbsp of the oil. Place the
dough in the bowl and roll around to
coat with the oil. Cover with a plastic
bag and leave to rise in a warm place
until more than doubled in volume,
about 45 minutes.

4 Divide the dough into two balls.
Preheat the oven to 200°C/400°F/Gas 6.

5 ▲ Roll each ball into a 25cm/10in
circle. Flip the circles over and on
to your palm. Set each circle on the
work surface and rotate, stretching
the dough as you turn, until it is about
30cm/12in in diameter.

6 ▲ Brush two pizza pans with oil.
Place the dough circles in the pans
and neaten the edges. Brush with oil.

7 ▲ Cover with the toppings and
bake until golden, 10–12 minutes.

Cheese Bread

MAKES 1 LOAF

15ml/1 tbsp active dried yeast
250ml/8fl oz/1 cup lukewarm milk
25g/1oz/2 tbsp butter
425g/15oz/3²/₃ cups strong white bread flour
10ml/2 tsp salt
90g/3¹/₂oz mature Cheddar cheese, grated

1 Combine the yeast and milk. Stir and leave for 15 minutes to dissolve.

2 Melt the butter, leave to cool, and add to the yeast mixture.

3 Mix the flour and salt together in a large bowl. Make a well in the centre and pour in the yeast mixture.

4 With a wooden spoon, stir from the centre, incorporating flour with each turn, to obtain a rough dough. If the dough seems too dry, add 30–45ml/2–3 tbsp water.

5 Transfer to a floured surface and knead until smooth and elastic. Return to the bowl, cover and leave to rise in a warm place until doubled in volume, 2–3 hours.

6 ▲ Grease a 23 × 13cm/9 × 5in loaf tin (pan). Knock back (punch down) the dough with your fist. Knead in the cheese, distributing it as evenly as possible.

7 ▼ Twist the dough, form into a loaf shape and place in the tin, tucking the ends under. Leave in a warm place until the dough rises above the rim of the tin.

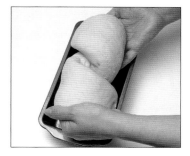

8 ▲ Preheat the oven to 200°C/400°F/Gas 6. Bake for 15 minutes, then lower to 190°C/375°F/Gas 5 and bake until the bottom sounds hollow when tapped, about 30 minutes more.

Italian Flat Bread with Sage

MAKES 1 LOAF

10ml/2 tsp active dried yeast
250ml/8fl oz/1 cup lukewarm water
350g/12oz/3 cups strong white bread flour
10ml/2 tsp salt
75ml/5 tbsp extra virgin olive oil
12 fresh sage leaves, chopped

1 Combine the yeast and water, stir and leave for 15 minutes until the yeast has completely dissolved.

2 Mix the flour and salt in a large bowl, and make a well in the centre.

3 Stir in the yeast mixture and 60ml/4 tbsp of the oil. Stir from the centre, incorporating flour with each turn, to obtain a rough dough.

4 ▲ Transfer the dough to a lightly floured surface and knead until it is smooth and elastic. Shape into a ball and place in a lightly oiled bowl. Cover and leave to rise in a warm place until doubled in volume, for about 2 hours.

5 Preheat the oven to 200°C/400°F/Gas 6 and place a baking sheet in the centre of the oven.

6 Knock back (punch down) the dough. Knead in the sage leaves, then roll into a 30cm/12in round. Leave to rise slightly.

7 ▼ Dimple the surface all over with your finger. Drizzle the remaining oil on top. Slide a floured board under the bread, carry to the oven, and slide off on the hot baking sheet. Bake for about 35 minutes, or until golden brown. Cool on a rack.

Courgette Yeast Bread

MAKES 1 LOAF

450g/1lb courgettes (zucchini), grated
30ml/2 tbsp salt
10ml/2 tsp active dried yeast
300ml/1/2 pint/11/4 cups lukewarm water
400g/14oz/31/2 cups strong white bread flour
olive oil, for brushing

1 ▼ In a colander, alternate the layers of grated courgettes and salt. Leave for 30 minutes, then squeeze out the moisture with your hands.

2 Combine yeast with 50ml/2fl oz/1/4 cup warm water. Leave for 15 minutes.

3 ▲ Place the courgettes, yeast and flour in a bowl. Stir together and add just enough of the remaining water to obtain a rough dough.

4 Transfer to a floured surface and knead until smooth and elastic. Return the dough to the bowl, cover with a plastic bag, and leave to rise in a warm place until doubled in volume, for about 11/2 hours.

5 Knock back (punch down) the risen dough with your fist and knead into a tapered cylinder. Place on a greased baking sheet, cover and leave to rise in a warm place until doubled in volume.

6 ▼ Preheat the oven to 220°C/425°F/Gas 7. Brush the bread with olive oil and bake for 40–45 minutes, or until the loaf is a golden colour.

Italian Flat Bread with Sage (top), Courgette Yeast Bread

Olive Bread

MAKES 2 LOAVES

20ml/4 tsp active dried yeast

475ml/16fl oz/2 cups warm water

400g/14oz/3½ cups strong white
  bread flour

175g/6oz/1½ cups strong wholemeal
  (whole-wheat) bread flour

65g/2½oz/generous ½ cup cornmeal

10ml/2 tsp salt

30ml/2 tbsp olive oil

115g/4oz/1 cup mixed pitted green and
  black olives, cut in half

cornmeal, for sprinkling

1 Combine the yeast and water, stir
and leave for 5 minutes to dissolve.

2 Stir in 225g/8oz/2 cups of the white
flour, cover and leave in a warm place
for 1 hour.

3 In a large mixing bowl, combine
the remaining white flour, the
wholemeal flour, cornmeal and salt.
Make a well in the centre; pour in
the olive oil and yeast mixture.

4 ▼ With a wooden spoon, stir from
the centre, incorporating flour with
each turn. When the dough becomes
stiff, stir with your hands until a rough
dough is obtained.

5 Transfer to a floured surface and
knead until smooth and elastic.
Return to the bowl, cover and leave
to rise in a warm place until doubled
in volume, about 1½ hours.

6 ▲ Knock back (punch down) the
dough. Add the olives and knead.

7 Cut the dough in half and shape
each half into a round. Sprinkle a
baking sheet with cornmeal. Place
the rounds on the sheet, seam-side
down. Cover and leave to rise until
nearly doubled in volume.

8 Place a baking tin (pan) in the
bottom of the oven and half fill it
with hot water. Preheat the oven to
220°C/425°F/Gas 7.

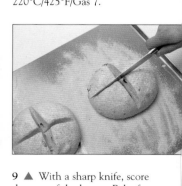

9 ▲ With a sharp knife, score
the tops of the loaves. Bake for
20 minutes. Lower the heat to
190°C/375°F/Gas 5 and bake for
25–30 minutes more, or until the
bottoms sound hollow when tapped.
Cool on a wire rack.

Pumpkin Spice Bread

MAKES 1 LOAF

30ml/2 tbsp active dried yeast
250ml/8fl oz/1 cup lukewarm water
10ml/2 tsp ground cinnamon
5ml/1 tsp ground ginger
5ml/1 tsp ground allspice
1.5ml/¼ tsp ground cloves
5ml/1 tsp salt
25g/3oz/6 tbsp dried skimmed milk
175g/6oz cooked or canned pumpkin
350g/12oz/1¾ cups sugar
115g/4oz/½ cup butter, melted
600g/1lb 6oz/5½ cups strong white bread flour
50g/2oz/⅓ cup pecan nuts, finely chopped

Using an electric mixer, combine the yeast and water, stir and leave for 5 minutes to dissolve. In another bowl, mix the spices together.

To the yeast, add the salt, milk, pumpkin, 115g/4oz/generous ½ cup of the sugar, 45ml/3 tbsp of the melted butter, 10ml/2 tsp of the spice mixture and 225g/8oz/2 cups of the flour.

▲ With the dough hook, mix on low speed until blended. Gradually add the remaining flour and mix on medium speed until a rough dough is formed. Alternatively, mix by hand.

Transfer to a floured surface and knead until smooth. Place in a bowl, cover and leave to rise in a warm place until doubled, 1–1½ hours.

5 ▼ Knock back (punch down) and knead briefly. Divide the dough into thirds. Roll each third into an 45cm/18in rope. Cut each rope into 18 equal pieces, then roll into balls.

6 Grease a 25cm/10in tube tin. Stir the remaining sugar into the remaining spice mixture. Roll the balls in the remaining melted butter, then in the sugar and spice mixture.

7 ▲ Place 18 balls in the tin and sprinkle over half the nuts. Add the remaining balls, then sprinkle over the remaining nuts. Cover and leave to rise in a warm place until almost doubled, about 45 minutes.

8 Preheat the oven to 180°C/350°F/Gas 4. Bake for 55 minutes. Cool in the tin for 20 minutes, then turn out on a rack. Serve warm.

Walnut Bread

MAKES 1 LOAF

425g/15oz/3²/₃ cups strong wholemeal (whole-wheat) bread flour

150g/5oz/1¹/₄ cups strong white bread flour

12.5ml/2¹/₂ tsp salt

550ml/18fl oz/2¹/₂ cups lukewarm water

15ml/1 tbsp honey

15ml/1 tbsp active dried yeast

150g/5oz/1 cup walnut pieces, plus extra for decorating

1 beaten egg, for glazing

1 Combine the flours and salt in a large bowl. Make a well in the centre and add 250ml/8fl oz/1 cup of the water, the honey and the yeast.

2 Set aside until the yeast dissolves and the mixture is frothy.

3 Add the remaining water. With a wooden spoon, stir from the centre, incorporating flour with each turn, to obtain a smooth dough. Add more flour if the dough is too sticky and use your hands if the dough becomes too stiff to stir.

4 Transfer to a floured board and knead, adding flour if necessary, until the dough is smooth and elastic. Place in a greased bowl and roll the dough around in the bowl to coat thoroughly on all sides.

5 ▲ Cover with a plastic bag and leave in a warm place until doubled in volume, about 1¹/₂ hours.

6 ▲ Knock back (punch down) the dough and knead in the walnuts evenly.

7 Grease a baking sheet. Shape into a round loaf and place on the baking sheet. Press in walnut pieces to decorate the top. Cover and leave to rise in a warm place until doubled, 25–30 minutes.

8 Preheat the oven to 220°C/425°F/ Gas 7.

9 ▲ With a sharp knife, score the top. Brush with the glaze. Bake for 15 minutes. Lower the heat to 190°C/ 375°F/Gas 5 and bake until the bottom sounds hollow when tapped, about 40 minutes. Cool on a rack.

Pecan Rye Bread

MAKES 2 LOAVES

5ml/1¹/2 tbsp active dried yeast
00ml/24fl oz/2³/4 cups lukewarm water
70g/1¹/2lb/6 cups strong white bread flour
05g/1lb 2oz/4¹/2 cups rye flour
0ml/2 tbsp salt
5ml/1 tbsp honey
0ml/2 tsp caraway seeds, (optional)
15g/4oz/¹/2 cup butter, at room temperature
25g/8oz/1¹/3 cups pecan nuts, chopped

Combine the yeast and 120ml/ fl oz/¹/2 cup of the water. Stir and eave for 15 minutes to dissolve.

In the bowl of an electric mixer, ombine the flours, salt, honey, araway seeds, if using, and butter. Vith the dough hook, mix on low peed until well blended.

Add the yeast mixture and the emaining water and mix on medium peed until the dough forms a ball.

▲ Transfer to a floured surface and nead in the pecan nuts.

Return the dough to a bowl, cover ith a plastic bag and leave in a warm lace until doubled, about 2 hours.

Grease two 21 × 12cm/8¹/2 × 4¹/2in read tins (pans).

7 ▲ Knock back (punch down) the risen dough.

8 Divide the dough in half and form into loaves. Place in the tins, seam-side down. Dust the tops with flour. Cover with plastic bags and leave to rise in a warm place until doubled in volume, about 1 hour.

9 Preheat the oven to 190°C/375°F/ Gas 5.

10 ▼ Bake until the bottoms sound hollow when tapped, 45–50 minutes. Cool on racks.

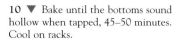

Sticky Buns

MAKES 18

170ml/5¹/₂fl oz/scant ³/₄ cup milk	
15ml/1 tbsp active dried yeast	
30ml/2 tbsp caster (superfine) sugar	
425–450g/15oz–1lb/3¹/₂–4 cups strong white bread flour	
5ml/1 tsp salt	
115g/4oz/¹/₂ cup cold butter, cut into pieces	
2 eggs, lightly beaten	
grated rind of 1 lemon	

FOR THE TOPPING AND FILLING

275g/10oz/1¹/₄ cups soft dark brown sugar	
65g/2¹/₂oz/5 tbsp butter	
120ml/4fl oz/¹/₂ cup water	
75g/3oz/¹/₂ cup pecan nuts or walnuts, chopped	
45ml/3 tbsp caster (superfine) sugar	
10ml/2 tsp ground cinnamon	
165g/5¹/₂oz/generous 1 cup raisins	

1 Heat the milk to lukewarm. Add the yeast and sugar, and leave until frothy, about 15 minutes.

2 Combine the flour and salt in a large mixing bowl. Add the butter and rub in with your fingertips until the mixture resembles coarse breadcrumbs.

3 ▲ Make a well in the centre and add the yeast mixture, eggs and lemon rind. With a wooden spoon, stir from the centre, incorporating flour with each turn. When it becomes too stiff, stir by hand to obtain a rough dough.

4 Transfer to a floured surface and knead until smooth and elastic. Return to the bowl, cover with a plastic bag and leave to rise in a warm place until doubled in volume, about 2 hours.

5 Meanwhile, for the topping, make the syrup. Combine the brown sugar, butter and water in a heavy pan. Bring to the boil and boil gently until thick and syrupy, about 10 minutes.

6 ▲ Place 15ml/1 tbsp of the syrup in the bottom of each of 18 4cm/1¹/₂in muffin cups. Sprinkle in a thin layer of chopped nuts, reserving the rest for the filling.

7 Knock back (punch down) the dough. Roll out to a 45 × 30cm/ 18 × 12in rectangle.

8 ▲ For the filling, combine the caster sugar, cinnamon, raisins and reserved nuts. Sprinkle over the dough in an even layer.

9 ▲ Roll up tightly, from the long side, to form a cylinder.

10 ▲ Cut the cylinder into 2.5cm/ 1in rounds. Place each in a prepared muffin cup, cut-side up. Leave to rise in a warm place until increased by half, about 30 minutes.

11 Preheat the oven to 180°C/350°F/ Gas 4. Place foil under the tins (pans) to catch any syrup that bubbles over. Bake until golden, about 25 minutes.

12 Remove from the oven and invert the tins on to a baking sheet. Leave for 3–5 minutes, then remove the buns from the tins. Transfer to a rack to cool. Serve sticky-side up.

~ COOK'S TIP ~

To save time and energy, make double the recipe and freeze half for another occasion.

Raisin Bread

MAKES 2 LOAVES

15ml/1 tbsp active dried yeast
475ml/16fl oz/2 cups lukewarm milk
150g/5oz/1 cup raisins
65g/2¹/₂oz/generous ¹/₄ cup currants
15ml/1 tbsp sherry or brandy
2.5ml/¹/₂ tsp freshly grated nutmeg
grated rind of 1 large orange
65g/2¹/₂oz/5 tbsp sugar
15ml/1 tbsp salt
115g/4oz/¹/₂ cup butter, melted
700–850g/1¹/₂lb–1lb 14oz/6–7¹/₂ cups strong white bread flour
1 egg beaten with 15ml/1 tbsp cream, for glazing

1 Stir together the yeast and 125ml/ 4fl oz/¹/₂ cup of the milk and leave to stand for 15 minutes to dissolve.

2 ▲ Mix the raisins, currants, sherry or brandy, nutmeg and orange rind together and set aside.

3 In another bowl, mix the remaining milk, sugar, salt and half the butter. Add the yeast mixture. With a wooden spoon, stir in half the flour, 150g/5oz/1¹/₄ cups at a time, until blended. Add the remaining flour as needed for a stiff dough.

4 Transfer to a floured surface and knead until smooth and elastic. Place in a greased bowl, cover and leave to rise in a warm place until doubled in volume, about 2¹/₂ hours.

5 Knock back (punch down) the dough, return to the bowl, cover and leave in a warm place for 30 minutes.

6 Grease two 21 × 12cm/8¹/₂ × 4¹/₂in bread tins (pans). Divide the dough in half and roll each half into a 50 × 18cm/20 × 7in rectangle.

7 ▲ Brush the rectangles with the remaining melted butter. Sprinkle over the raisin mixture, then roll up tightly, tucking in the ends slightly as you roll. Place in the prepared tins, cover, and leave to rise until almost doubled in volume.

8 ▲ Preheat the oven to 200°C/ 400°F/Gas 6. Brush the loaves with the glaze. Bake for 20 minutes. Lower to 180°C/350°F/Gas 4 and bake until golden, 25–30 minutes. Cool on rack.

Prune Bread

MAKES 1 LOAF

225g/8oz/1 cup dried prunes
5ml/1 tbsp active dried yeast
5g/3oz/²/₃ cup strong wholemeal
  (whole-wheat) bread flour
75–425g/13–15oz/3¹/₄–3²/₃ cups strong
  white bread flour
2.5ml/¹/₂ tsp bicarbonate of soda
  (baking soda)
5ml/1 tsp salt
5ml/1 tsp pepper
25g/1oz/2 tbsp butter, at room temperature
175ml/6fl oz/³/₄ cup buttermilk
50g/2oz/¹/₃ cup walnuts, chopped
milk, for glazing

1 Simmer the prunes in water to cover until soft, or soak overnight. Drain, reserving 50ml/2fl oz/¹/₄ cup of the soaking liquid. Pit and chop the prunes.

2 Combine the yeast and the reserved prune liquid. Leave for 15 minutes.

3 In a large bowl, stir together the flours, bicarbonate of soda, salt and pepper. Make a well in the centre.

4 ▲ Add the chopped prunes, butter, and buttermilk. Pour in the yeast mixture. With a wooden spoon, stir from the centre, incorporating more flour with each turn, to obtain a rough dough.

5 Transfer to a floured surface and knead until smooth and elastic. Return to the bowl, cover with a plastic bag and leave to rise in a warm place until doubled in volume, about 1¹/₂ hours.

6 Grease a baking sheet.

7 ▲ Punch down the dough with your fist, then knead in the walnuts.

8 Shape the dough into a long, cylindrical loaf. Place on the baking sheet, cover loosely, and leave to rise in a warm place for 45 minutes.

9 Preheat the oven to 220°C/425°F/Gas 7.

10 ▼ With a sharp knife, score the top deeply. Brush with milk and bake for 15 minutes. Lower to 190°C/375°F/Gas 5 and bake until the bottom sounds hollow when tapped, 35 minutes. Cool.

Braided Prune Bread

MAKES 1 LOAF

15ml/1 tbsp active dried yeast
50ml/2fl oz/¼ cup lukewarm water
50ml/2fl oz/¼ cup lukewarm milk
50g/2oz/¼ cup caster (superfine) sugar
2.5ml/½ tsp salt
1 egg
50g/2oz/¼ cup butter, at room temperature
425–505g/15oz–1lb 2oz/3⅔–4½ cups strong white bread flour
1 egg beaten with 10ml/2 tsp water, for glazing
FOR THE FILLING
200g/7oz/scant 1 cup cooked prunes, pitted
10ml/2 tsp grated lemon rind
5ml/1 tsp grated orange rind
1.5ml/¼ tsp freshly grated nutmeg
40g/1½oz/3 tbsp butter, melted
50g/2oz/¼ cup very finely chopped walnuts
25g/1oz/2 tbsp caster sugar

1 In a large bowl, combine the yeast and water, stir and leave for 15 minutes to dissolve.

2 Stir in the milk, sugar, salt, egg and butter. Gradually stir in 350g/ 12oz/3 cups of the flour to obtain a soft dough.

3 Transfer to a floured surface and knead in just enough flour to obtain a dough that is smooth and elastic. Put into a clean bowl, cover and leave to rise in a warm place until doubled in volume, about 1½ hours.

> ### ~ VARIATION ~
>
> For Plaited Apricot Bread, replace the prunes with the same amount of dried apricots. It is not necessary to cook them, but, to soften, soak them in hot tea and discard the liquid before using.

4 ▲ Meanwhile, for the filling, combine the prunes, lemon and orange rinds, nutmeg, butter, walnuts and sugar, and stir together to blend. Set aside.

5 Grease a large baking sheet. Knock back (punch down) the dough and transfer to a lightly floured surface. Knead briefly, then roll out into a 38 × 25cm/15 × 10in rectangle. Carefully transfer to the baking sheet.

6 ▲ Spread the filling in the centre.

7 ▲ With a sharp knife, cut ten strips at an angle on either side of the filling, cutting just to the filling.

8 ▲ For a braided pattern, fold up one end neatly, then fold over the strips from alternating sides until all the strips are folded over. Tuck excess dough underneath at the ends.

9 ▲ Cover loosely with a dish towel and leave to rise in a warm place until almost doubled in volume.

10 ▲ Preheat the oven to 190°C/ 375°F/Gas 5. Brush with the glaze. Bake until browned, about 30 minutes. Transfer to a rack to cool.

Kugelhopf

MAKES 1 LOAF

115g/4oz/²/₃ cup raisins

15ml/1 tbsp Kirsch or brandy

15ml/1 tbsp active dried yeast

120ml/4fl oz/¹/₂ cup lukewarm water

115g/4oz/¹/₂ cup unsalted (sweet) butter, at room temperature

90g/3¹/₂oz/¹/₂ cup sugar

3 eggs, at room temperature

grated rind of 1 lemon

5ml/1 tsp salt

2.5ml/¹/₂ tsp vanilla extract

425g/15oz/3²/₃ cups strong white bread flour

120ml/4fl oz/¹/₂ cup milk

25g/1oz/¹/₄ cup flaked (sliced) almonds

90g/3¹/₂oz/scant 1 cup whole blanched almonds, chopped

icing (confectioners') sugar, for dusting

1 ▼ In a bowl, combine the raisins and Kirsch or brandy. Set aside.

2 Combine the yeast and water, stir and leave for 15 minutes to dissolve.

3 With an electric mixer, cream the butter and sugar until thick and fluffy. Beat in the eggs, one at a time. Add the lemon rind, salt and vanilla. Stir in the yeast mixture.

4 ▲ Add the flour, alternating with the milk, until the mixture is well blended. Cover and leave to rise in a warm place until doubled in volume, about 2 hours.

5 ▲ Grease a 4¹/₂ pint Kugelhopf mould, then sprinkle the flaked almonds evenly over the bottom.

6 Work the raisins and whole almonds into the dough, then spoon into the mould. Cover with a plastic bag, and leave to rise in a warm place until the dough almost reaches the top of the mould, about 1 hour.

7 Preheat the oven to 180°C/350°F/ Gas 4.

8 Bake until golden brown, about 45 minutes. If the top browns too quickly protect with a sheet of foil. Leave to cool in the mould for 15 minutes, the turn out on to a rack. Dust the top lightly with icing sugar before serving

Panettone

MAKES 1 LOAF

150ml/¼ pint/⅔ cup lukewarm milk
15ml/1 tbsp active dried yeast
450–400g/12–14oz/3–3½ cups strong white bread flour
65g/2½oz/5 tbsp sugar
10ml/2 tsp salt
2 eggs
2 egg yolks
175g/6oz/¾ cup unsalted (sweet) butter, at room temperature
130g/4½oz/scant 1 cup raisins
grated rind of 1 lemon
65g/3oz/½ cup mixed peel

1 Combine the milk and yeast in a large warmed bowl and leave for 10 minutes to dissolve.

2 Stir in 115g/4oz/1 cup of the flour, cover loosely and leave in a warm place for 30 minutes.

3 Sift over the remaining flour and stir into the dough mixture. Make a well in the centre and add the sugar, salt, eggs and egg yolks.

4 ▲ Stir with a wooden spoon until stiff, then stir with your hands to obtain a very elastic and sticky dough. Add a little more flour if necessary, but keep the dough as soft as possible.

5 ▲ To incorporate the butter, smear it over the dough, then work it in with your hands. When the butter is evenly distributed, cover and leave to rise in a warm place until doubled in volume, 3–4 hours.

6 Grease a 2 litre/3½ pint/9 cup charlotte tin (pan) or a 1kg/2¼lb coffee tin and line the bottom with baking parchment. Grease the paper.

7 Knock back (punch down) the dough. Knead in the raisins, lemon rind and mixed peel.

8 ▲ Put the dough in the tin. Cover and leave to rise in a warm place until it is well above the top of the tin, about 2 hours.

9 Preheat the oven to 200°C/400°F/ Gas 6. Bake for 15 minutes, cover the top with foil and lower the heat to 180°C/350°F/Gas 4. Bake for 30 minutes more. Cool in the tin for 5 minutes, then transfer to a rack.

Danish Wreath

SERVES 10–12

10g/¹/₄oz active dried yeast
175ml/6fl oz/³/₄ cup lukewarm milk
50g/2oz/¹/₄ cup caster (superfine) sugar
450g/1lb/4 cups strong white bread flour
2.5ml/¹/₂ tsp salt
2.5ml/¹/₂ tsp vanilla extract
1 egg, beaten
225g/8oz/1 cup blocks unsalted (sweet) butter
1 egg yolk beaten with 10ml/2 tsp water, for glazing
115g/4oz/1 cup icing (confectioners') sugar
15–30ml/1–2 tbsp water
chopped pecan nuts or walnuts, for sprinkling

FOR THE FILLING

200g/7oz/scant 1 cup soft dark brown sugar
5ml/1 tsp ground cinnamon
50g/2oz/¹/₃ cup pecan nuts or walnuts, toasted and chopped

1 Combine the yeast, milk and 2.5ml/¹/₂ tsp of the sugar. Stir and leave for 15 minutes to dissolve.

2 Combine the flour, sugar and salt. Make a well in the centre and add the yeast mixture, vanilla and egg. Stir until a rough dough is formed.

3 Transfer to a floured surface and knead until smooth and elastic. Wrap and chill for 15 minutes.

~ VARIATION ~

For a different filling, substitute 3 tart apples, peeled and grated, the grated rind of 1 lemon, 15ml/1 tbsp lemon juice, 2.5ml/¹/₂ tsp ground cinnamon, 45ml/3 tbsp sugar, 35g/1¹/₄oz/1¹/₄ tbsp currants, and 25g/1oz/2 tbsp chopped walnuts. Combine well and use as described.

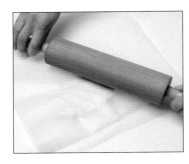

4 ▲ Meanwhile, place the butter between two sheets of baking parchment. With a rolling pin, flatten to form two 15 × 10cm/6 × 4in rectangles. Set aside.

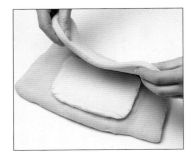

5 ▲ Roll out the dough to a 30 × 20cm/12 × 8in rectangle. Place one butter rectangle in the centre. Fold the bottom third of dough over the butter and seal the edge. Place the other butter rectangle on top and cover with the top third of the dough.

6 Turn the dough so the shorter side faces you. Roll into a 30 × 20cm/12 × 8in rectangle. Fold into thirds, and indent one edge with your finger to indicate the first turn. Wrap in clear film (plastic wrap) and chill for 30 minutes.

7 Repeat two more times; rolling, folding, marking and chilling between each turn. After the third fold chill for 1–2 hours, or longer.

8 Grease a large baking sheet. In a bowl, stir together all the filling ingredients until blended.

9 ▲ Roll out the dough to a 62 × 15cm 25 × 6in strip. Spread over the filling, leaving a 1cm/¹/₂in border.

10 Roll up the dough lengthways into a cylinder. Place on the baking sheet and form into a circle, pinching the edges together to seal. Cover with an inverted bowl and leave in a warm place to rise for 45 minutes.

11 ▲ Preheat the oven to 200°C/400°F/Gas 6. Slash the top every 5cm/2in, cutting about 1cm/¹/₂in deep Brush with the egg glaze. Bake until golden, 35–40 minutes. Cool on a rack. To serve, mix the icing sugar and water, then drizzle over the wreath. Sprinkle with the pecan nuts or walnuts.

PIES &
TARTS

HERE IS EVERY SORT OF FILLING –
FROM ORCHARD FRUITS TO AUTUMN
NUTS, TANGY CITRUS TO LUSCIOUS
CHOCOLATE – FOR THE MOST
MEMORABLE PIES AND TARTS. SOME
ARE PLAIN AND SOME ARE FANCY,
BUT ALL ARE DELICIOUS.

Plum Pie

SERVES 8

900g/2lb red or purple plums

grated rind of 1 lemon

15ml/1 tbsp lemon juice

115–175g/4–6oz/³/4–scant 1 cup caster (superfine) sugar

45ml/3 tbsp quick-cooking tapioca

pinch of salt

2.5ml/¹/2 tsp ground cinnamon

1.5ml/¹/4 tsp freshly grated nutmeg

FOR THE PASTRY

275g/10oz/2¹/2 cups plain (all-purpose) flour

5ml/1 tsp salt

75g/3oz/6 tbsp cold butter, cut in pieces

50g/2oz/¹/4 cup cold white vegetable fat (shortening), cut in pieces

50–120ml/2–4fl oz/¹/4–¹/2 cup iced water

milk, for glazing

1 ▼ For the pastry, sift the flour and salt into a bowl. Add the butter and fat and cut in with a pastry blender until the mixture resembles coarse breadcrumbs.

2 Stir in just enough water to bind the pastry. Gather into two balls, one slightly larger than the other. Wrap and chill for 20 minutes.

3 Preheat a baking sheet in the centre of a 220°C/425°F/Gas 7 oven.

4 On a lightly floured surface, roll out the larger pastry ball to about 3mm/¹/8in thick. Transfer to a 23cm/9in pie dish and trim the edge.

5 ▲ Halve the plums, discard the stones (pits), and cut into large pieces. Mix all the filling ingredients together (if the plums are tart, use extra sugar). Transfer to the pastry case (pie shell).

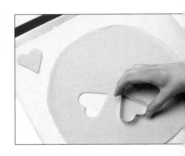

6 ▲ Roll out the remaining pastry and place on a baking tray lined with baking parchment. With a cutter, stamp out four hearts. Transfer the pastry lid to the pie using the paper.

7 Trim to leave a 2cm/³/4in overhang. Fold the top edge under the bottom and pinch to seal. Arrange the hearts on top. Brush with the milk. Bake for 15 minutes. Reduce the heat to 180°C/350°F/Gas 4 and bake for 30–35 minutes more. If the crust browns too quickly, protect with a sheet of foil.

Lattice Berry Pie

SERVES 8

450g/1lb/4 cups berries, such as bilberries, blueberries, blackcurrants etc

115g/4oz/generous $^{1}/_{2}$ cup caster (superfine) sugar

45ml/3 tbsp cornflour (cornstarch)

30ml/2 tbsp lemon juice

25g/1oz/2 tbsp butter, diced

FOR THE PASTRY

275g/10oz/2$^{1}/_{2}$ cups plain (all-purpose) flour

4ml/$^{3}/_{4}$ tsp salt

115g/4oz/$^{1}/_{2}$ cup cold butter, cut in pieces

40g/1$^{1}/_{2}$oz/3 tbsp cold white vegetable fat (shortening), cut in pieces

75–90ml/5–6 tbsp iced water

1 egg beaten with 15ml/1 tbsp water, for glazing

1 For the pastry, sift the flour and salt into a bowl. Add the butter and fat, and cut in with a pastry blender until the mixture resembles coarse breadcrumbs. With a fork, stir in just enough water to bind the pastry. Form into two balls, wrap in baking parchment, and chill for 20 minutes.

2 On a lightly floured surface, roll out one ball about 3mm/$^{1}/_{8}$in thick. Transfer to a 23cm/9in pie dish and trim to leave a 1cm/$^{1}/_{2}$in overhang. Brush the base with egg glaze.

3 ▲ Mix all the filling ingredients together, except the butter (reserve a few berries for decoration). Spoon into the pastry case and dot with the butter. Brush the egg glaze around the rim of the pastry case (pie shell).

4 Preheat a baking sheet in the centre of a 220°C/425°F/Gas 7 oven.

5 ▼ Roll out the remaining pastry on a baking tray lined with baking parchment. With a serrated pastry wheel, cut out 24 thin pastry strips. Roll out the scraps and cut out leaf shapes. Mark veins in the leaves with the point of a knife.

6 ▲ Weave the strips in a close lattice, then transfer to the pie using the paper. Press the edges to seal and trim. Arrange the pastry leaves around the rim. Brush with egg glaze.

7 Bake for 10 minutes. Reduce the heat to 180°C/350°F/Gas 4 and bake until the pastry is golden, 40–45 minutes more. Decorate with berries.

Raspberry Tart

SERVES 8

4 egg yolks
65g/2¹/₂oz/5 tbsp caster (superfine) sugar
45ml/3 tbsp plain (all-purpose) flour
300ml/¹/₂ pint/1¹/₄ cups milk
pinch of salt
2.5ml/¹/₂ tsp vanilla extract
450g/1lb/2²/₃ cups fresh raspberries
75ml/5 tbsp red currant jelly
15ml/1 tbsp fresh orange juice
FOR THE PASTRY
190g/6¹/₂oz/1²/₃ cups plain (all-purpose) flour
2.5ml/¹/₂ tsp baking powder
1.5ml/¹/₄ tsp salt
15ml/1 tbsp sugar
grated rind of ¹/₂ orange
75g/3oz/6 tbsp cold butter, cut in pieces
1 egg yolk
45–60ml/3–4 tbsp whipping cream

1 For the pastry, sift the flour, baking powder and salt into a bowl. Stir in the sugar and orange rind. Add the butter and cut in with a pastry blender until the mixture resembles coarse breadcrumbs. Stir in the egg yolk and just enough cream to bind the dough. Gather into a ball, wrap in baking parchment and chill.

2 For the custard filling, beat the egg yolks and sugar until thick and lemon-coloured. Gradually stir in the flour.

3 In a pan, bring the milk and salt just to the boil, then remove from the heat. Whisk into the egg yolk mixture, return to the pan and continue whisking over medium high heat until just bubbling. Cook for 3 minutes to thicken. Transfer immediately to a bowl. Add the vanilla and stir to blend.

4 ▲ Cover with baking parchment to prevent a skin from forming.

5 ▲ Preheat the oven to 200°C/400°F/Gas 6. On a floured surface, roll out the pastry 3mm/¹/₈in thick, transfer to a 25cm/10in pie dish and trim. Prick the base with a fork and line with crumpled baking parchment. Fill with baking beans and bake for 15 minutes. Remove the paper and beans. Continue baking until golden, 6–8 minutes more. Leave to cool.

6 ▲ Spread an even layer of the pastry cream filling in the pastry case (pie shell) and arrange the raspberries on top. Melt the jelly and orange juice in a pan and brush on top to glaze.

Rhubarb and Cherry Pie

SERVES 8

450g/1lb rhubarb, cut into
  2.5cm/1in pieces

450g/1lb canned pitted tart red or black
  cherries, drained

275g/10oz/1½ cups caster (superfine) sugar

25g/1oz quick-cooking tapioca

FOR THE PASTRY

275g/10oz/2½ cups plain (all-purpose) flour

5ml/1 tsp salt

75g/3oz/6 tbsp cold butter, cut in pieces

50g/2oz/⅓ cup cold white vegetable fat
  (shortening), cut in pieces

60–120ml/2–4fl oz/¼–½ cup iced water

milk, for glazing

1 ▲ For the pastry, sift the flour and salt into a bowl. Add the butter and fat to the dry ingredients and cut in with a pastry blender until the mixture resembles coarse breadcrumbs.

2 With a fork, stir in just enough water to bind the pastry. Gather into two balls, one slightly larger than the other. Wrap the pastry in baking parchment and chill for at least 20 minutes.

3 Preheat a baking sheet in the centre of a 200°C/400°F/Gas 6 oven.

4 On a lightly floured surface, roll out the larger pastry ball to a thickness of about 3mm/⅛in.

5 ▼ Roll the pastry around the rolling pin and transfer to a 23cm/9in pie dish. Trim the edge to leave a 1cm/½in overhang.

6 Chill the pastry case (pie shell) while making the filling.

7 In a mixing bowl, combine the rhubarb, cherries, sugar and tapioca, and spoon into the pie shell.

8 ▲ Roll out the remaining pastry and cut out leaf shapes.

9 Transfer the pastry lid to the pie and trim to leave a 2cm/¾in overhang. Fold the top edge under the bottom, and flute. Roll small balls from the scraps. Mark veins in the pastry leaves and place on top with the balls.

10 Glaze the top and bake until golden, 40–50 minutes.

Peach Leaf Pie

SERVES 8

1.2kg/2¹/₂lb ripe peaches
juice of 1 lemon
90g/3¹/₂oz/¹/₂ cup caster (superfine) sugar
45ml/3 tbsp cornflour (cornstarch)
1.5ml/¹/₄ tsp grated nutmeg
2.5ml/¹/₂ tsp ground cinnamon
25g/1oz/2 tbsp butter, diced
FOR THE CRUST
275g/10oz/2¹/₂ cups plain (all-purpose) flour
4ml/³/₄ tsp salt
115g/4oz/¹/₂ cup cold butter, cut into pieces
60g/2¹/₄oz/generous ¹/₃ cup cold white vegetable fat (shortening), cut into pieces
60–75ml/5–6 tbsp iced water
1 egg beaten with 15ml/1 tbsp water, for glazing

1 For the pastry, sift the flour and salt into a bowl. Add the butter and fat and rub in with your fingertips until the mixture resembles coarse breadcrumbs.

2 ▲ With a fork, stir in just enough water to bind the dough. Gather into two balls, one slightly larger than the other. Wrap in clear film (plastic wrap) and chill for 20 minutes.

3 Place a baking sheet in the oven and preheat to 220°C/425°F/Gas 7.

4 ▲ Drop a few peaches at a time into boiling water for 20 seconds, then transfer to a bowl of cold water. When cool, peel off the skins.

5 Slice the peaches and combine with the lemon juice, sugar, cornflour and spices. Set aside.

6 ▲ On a lightly floured surface, roll out the larger dough ball to about 3mm/¹/₈in thick. Transfer to a 23cm/9in pie tin (pan) and trim. Chill.

7 ▲ Roll out the remaining dough 5mm/¹/₄in thick. Cut out leaf shapes 7.5cm/3in long, using a template if needed. Mark veins with a knife. With the scraps, roll a few balls.

8 ▲ Brush the bottom of the pastry case (pie shell) with egg glaze. Add the peaches, piling them higher in the centre. Dot with the butter.

9 ▲ To assemble, start from the outside edge and cover the peaches with a ring of leaves. Place a second ring of leaves above, staggering the positions. Continue with rows of leaves until covered. Place the balls in the centre. Brush with glaze.

10 Bake for 10 minutes. Lower the heat to 180°C/350°F/Gas 4 and bake for 35–40 minutes more.

~ COOK'S TIP ~

Baking the pie on a preheated baking sheet helps to make the bottom crust crisp. The moisture from the filling keeps the bottom crust more humid than the top, but this baking method helps to compensate for the top crust being more exposed to the heat source.

Peach Tart with Almond Cream

SERVES 8–10

4 large ripe peaches
115g/4oz/²/₃ cup blanched almonds
30ml/2 tbsp plain (all-purpose) flour
90g/3¹/₂oz/7 tbsp unsalted (sweet) butter, at room temperature
115g/4oz/¹/₂ cup plus 30ml/2 tbsp caster (superfine) sugar
1 egg
1 egg yolk
2.5ml/¹/₂ tsp vanilla extract, or 10ml/2 tsp rum
FOR THE PASTRY
190g/6¹/₂oz/1²/₃ cups plain (all-purpose) flour
4ml/³/₄ tsp salt
90g/3¹/₂oz/7 tbsp cold unsalted (sweet) butter, cut in pieces
1 egg yolk
40–45ml/2¹/₂–3 tbsp iced water

1 ▲ For the pastry, sift the flour and salt into a bowl.

2 Add the butter and cut in with a pastry blender until the mixture resembles coarse breadcrumbs. Stir in the egg yolk and just enough water to bind the pastry. Gather into a ball, wrap in baking parchment and chill for at least 20 minutes.

3 Preheat a baking sheet in the centre of a 200°C/400°F/Gas 6 oven.

4 ▲ On a floured surface, roll out the pastry to 3mm/¹/₈in thick. Transfer to a 25cm/10in pie dish. Trim the edge, prick the base and chill.

5 ▲ Score the bottoms of the peaches. Drop the peaches, one at a time, into boiling water. Boil for 20 seconds, then dip in cold water. Peel off the skins using a sharp knife.

6 ▲ Grind the almonds finely with the flour in a food processor, blender or grinder. With an electric mixer, cream the butter and 115g/4oz/generous ¹/₂ cup of the sugar until light and fluffy. Gradually beat in the egg and yolk. Stir in the almonds and vanilla or rum. Spread in the pastry case(pie shell).

7 ▲ Halve the peaches and remove the stones (pits). Cut crossways in thin slices and arrange on top of the almond cream like the spokes of a wheel; keep the slices of each peach-half together. Fan out by pressing down gently at a slight angle.

8 ▲ Bake until the pastry begins to brown, 10–15 minutes. Lower the heat to 180°C/350°F/Gas 4 and continue baking until the almond cream sets, about 15 minutes more. Ten minutes before the end of the cooking time, sprinkle with the remaining 30ml/2 tbsp of sugar.

~ VARIATION ~

For a Nectarine and Apricot Tart with Almond Cream, replace the peaches with nectarines, prepared and arranged the same way. Peel and chop three fresh apricots. Fill the spaces between the fanned-out nectarines with 15ml/1 tbsp of chopped apricots. Bake as above.

Apple and Cranberry Lattice Pie

SERVES 8

grated rind of 1 orange
45ml/3 tbsp fresh orange juice
2 large, tart cooking apples
175g/6oz/1¹/₂ cups cranberries
65g/2¹/₂oz/¹/₂ cup raisins
25g/1oz/2 tbsp walnuts, chopped
215g/7¹/₂oz/generous 1 cup caster (superfine) sugar
115g/4oz/¹/₂ cup soft dark brown sugar
30ml/2 tbsp plain (all-purpose) flour
FOR THE CRUST
275g/10oz/2¹/₂ cups plain flour
2.5ml/¹/₂ tsp salt
75g/3oz/6 tbsp cold butter, cut into pieces
75g/3oz/¹/₂ cup cold white vegetable fat (shortening), cut into pieces
60–120ml/2–4fl oz/¹/₄–¹/₂ cup iced water

1 ▼ For the crust, sift the flour and salt into a bowl. Add the butter and fat and rub in with your fingertips until the mixture resembles coarse breadcrumbs. With a fork, stir in just enough water to bind the dough. Gather into two equal balls, wrap in clear film (plastic wrap), and chill for at least 20 minutes.

2 ▲ Put the orange rind and juice into a mixing bowl. Peel and core the apples and grate into the bowl. Stir in the cranberries, raisins, walnuts, all except 15g/¹/₂oz/1 tbsp of the caster sugar, the brown sugar and flour.

3 Place a baking sheet in the oven and preheat to 200°C/400°F/Gas 6.

4 On a lightly floured surface, roll out one ball of dough to about 3mm/¹/₈in thick. Transfer to a 23cm/9in pie plate and trim. Spoon the cranberry and apple mixture into the pastry case (pie shell).

5 ▲ Roll out the remaining dough to a circle about 28cm/11in in diameter. With a serrated pastry wheel, cut the dough into ten strips, 2cm/³/₄in wide. Place five strips horizontally across the top of the tart at 2.5cm/1in intervals. Weave in five vertical strips and trim. Sprinkle the top with the remaining sugar.

6 Bake the pie for 20 minutes. Reduce the heat to 180°C/350°F/Gas 4 and bake for about 15 minutes more, until the crust is golden and the filling is bubbling.

Open Apple Pie

SERVES 8

1.3kg/3lb sweet, tart firm eating or
  cooking apples
50g/2oz/¼ cup caster (superfine) sugar
10ml/2 tsp ground cinnamon
grated rind and juice of 1 lemon
25g/1oz/2 tbsp butter, diced
30–45ml/2–3 tbsp honey
FOR THE CRUST
275g/10oz/2½ cups plain (all-purpose) flour
2.5ml/½ tsp salt
115g/4oz/½ cup cold butter, cut into pieces
60g/2¼oz/generous ⅓ cup cold white
  vegetable fat (shortening), cut into pieces
75–90ml/5–6 tbsp iced water

1 For the crust, sift the flour and salt into a bowl. Add the butter and fat and rub in with your fingertips until the mixture resembles coarse breadcrumbs.

2 ▲ With a fork, stir in just enough water to bind the dough. Gather into a ball, wrap in clear film (plastic wrap), and chill for at least 20 minutes.

3 Place a baking sheet in the centre of the oven and preheat to 200°C/400°F/Gas 6.

4 ▼ Peel, core, and slice the apples. Combine the sugar and cinnamon in a bowl. Add the apples, lemon rind and juice, and stir.

5 On a lightly floured surface, roll out the dough to a circle about 30cm/12in in diameter. Transfer to a 23cm/9in diameter deep pie dish; leave the dough hanging over the edge. Fill with the apple slices.

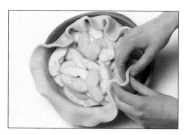

6 ▲ Fold in the edges and crimp loosely for a decorative border. Dot the apples with diced butter.

7 Bake on the hot sheet until the pastry is golden and the apples are tender, about 45 minutes.

8 Melt the honey in a pan and brush over the apples to glaze. Serve warm or at room temperature.

Apple Pie

SERVES 8

900g/2lb tart cooking apples
30ml/2 tbsp plain (all-purpose) flour
115g/4oz/generous ¹/₂ cup caster (superfine) sugar
25ml/1¹/₂ tbsp fresh lemon juice
2.5ml/¹/₂ tsp ground cinnamon
2.5ml/¹/₂ tsp ground allspice
1.5ml/¹/₄ tsp ground ginger
1.5ml/¹/₄ tsp freshly grated nutmeg
1.5ml/¹/₄ tsp salt
50g/2oz/¹/₄ cup butter, diced

FOR THE PASTRY

275g/10oz/2¹/₂ cups plain (all-purpose) flour
5ml/1 tsp salt
75g/3oz/6 tbsp cold butter, cut in pieces
50g/2oz/¹/₃ cup cold white vegetable fat (shortening), cut in pieces
50–120ml/2–4fl oz/¹/₄–¹/₂ cup iced water

1 ▲ For the crust, sift the flour and salt into a bowl.

2 Add the butter and fat and cut in with a pastry blender or rub between your fingertips until the mixture resembles coarse breadcrumbs. With a fork, stir in just enough water to bind the pastry.

3 ▲ Form two balls, wrap in clear film (plastic wrap). Chill for 20 minutes.

4 ▲ On a lightly floured surface, roll out one ball 3mm/¹/₈in thick. Transfer to a 23cm/9in pie dish and trim the edge. Preheat a baking sheet in the centre of a 220°C/425°F/Gas 7 oven.

5 ▲ Peel, core and slice the apples into a bowl. Toss with the flour, sugar, lemon juice, spices and salt. Spoon into the pastry case (pie shell), dot with butter.

6 ▲ Roll out the remaining pastry. Place on top of the pie and trim to leave a 2cm/³/₄in overhang. Fold the overhang under the pastry base and press to seal. Crimp the edge.

7 ▲ Roll out the scraps and cut out leaf shapes and roll balls. Arrange on top of the pie. Cut steam vents.

8 Bake for 10 minutes. Reduce the heat to 180°C/350°F/Gas 4 and bake until golden, 40–45 minutes more. If the pie browns too quickly, protect with foil.

~ COOK'S TIP ~

Instead of using cooking apples, choose crisp eaters such as Granny Smith, which will not soften too much during cooking.

Pear and Apple Crumble Pie

SERVES 8

3 firm pears

4 cooking apples

175g/6oz/scant 1 cup caster (superfine) sugar

30ml/2 tbsp cornflour (cornstarch)

pinch of salt

grated rind of 1 lemon

30ml/2 tbsp fresh lemon juice

75g/3oz/²⁄₃ cup raisins

75g/3oz/²⁄₃ cup plain (all-purpose) flour

5ml/1 tsp ground cinnamon

75g/3oz/6 tbsp cold butter, cut in pieces

FOR THE PASTRY

150g/5oz/1¼ cups plain flour

2.5ml/¹⁄₂ tsp salt

65g/2¹⁄₂oz/scant ¹⁄₂ cup cold white vegetable fat (shortening), cut in pieces

30ml/2 tbsp iced water

1 For the pastry, combine the flour and salt in a bowl. Add the fat and cut in with a pastry blender until the mixture resembles coarse breadcrumbs. Stir in just enough water to bind the pastry. Gather into a ball and transfer to a lightly floured surface. Roll out 3mm/¹⁄₈in thick.

2 ▲ Transfer to a shallow 23cm/9in pie dish and trim to leave a 1cm/¹⁄₂in overhang. Fold the overhang under for double thickness. Flute the edge. Chill.

3 Preheat a baking sheet in the centre of a 230°C/450°F/Gas 8 oven.

4 ▲ Peel and core the pears. Slice them into a bowl. Peel, core and slice the apples. Add to the pears. Stir in one-third of the sugar, the cornflour, salt and lemon rind. Add the lemon juice and raisins, and stir to blend.

5 For the crumble topping, combine the remaining sugar, flour, cinnamon, and butter in a bowl. Blend with your fingertips until the mixture resembles coarse breadcrumbs. Set aside.

6 ▲ Spoon the fruit filling into the prepared pastry case (pie shell). Sprinkle the crumbs lightly and evenly over the top.

7 Bake for 10 minutes, then reduce the heat to 180°C/350°F/Gas 4. Cover the top of the pie loosely with a sheet of foil and continue baking until browned, 35–40 minutes more.

Chocolate Pear Tart

SERVES 8

115g/4oz plain (semisweet)
  chocolate, grated

3 large firm, ripe pears

1 egg

1 egg yolk

120ml/4fl oz/½ cup single (light) cream

2.5ml/½ tsp vanilla extract

45ml/3 tbsp caster (superfine) sugar

FOR THE PASTRY

150g/5oz/1¼ cups plain (all-purpose) flour

pinch of salt

30ml/2 tbsp sugar

115g/4oz/½ cup cold unsalted (sweet)
  butter, cut into pieces

1 egg yolk

15ml/1 tbsp fresh lemon juice

1 For the pastry, sift the flour and salt into a bowl. Add the sugar and butter. Cut in with a pastry blender until the mixture resembles coarse breadcrumbs. Stir in the egg yolk and lemon juice until the mixture forms a ball. Wrap in clear film (plastic wrap) and chill for at least 20 minutes.

2 Preheat a baking sheet in the centre of a 200°C/400°F/Gas 6 oven.

3 On a lightly floured surface, roll out the pastry 3mm/⅛in thick. Transfer to a 25cm/10in tart dish and trim.

4 ▲ Sprinkle the base of the pastry case (pie shell) with the grated chocolate.

5 ▲ Peel, halve and core the pears. Cut in thin slices crossways, then fan them out slightly.

6 Transfer the pear halves to the tart with the help of a metal spatula and arrange on top of the chocolate like the spokes of a wheel.

7 ▼ Whisk together the egg and egg yolk, cream and vanilla. Ladle over the pears, then sprinkle with sugar.

8 Bake for 10 minutes. Reduce the heat to 180°C/350°F/Gas 4 and cook until the custard is set and the pears begin to caramelize, about 20 minutes more. Serve warm.

Caramelized Upside-down Pear Pie

SERVES 8

5–6 firm, ripe pears

175g/6oz/scant 1 cup sugar

115g/4oz/1/2 cup unsalted (sweet) butter

whipped cream, for serving

FOR THE PASTRY

115g/4oz/1 cup plain (all-purpose) flour

1.5ml/1/4 tsp salt

130g/41/2oz/generous 1/2 cup cold butter,
cut into pieces

40g/11/2oz/1/4 cup cold white vegetable fat
(shortening), cut into pieces

60ml/4 tbsp iced water

1 ▲ For the pastry, combine the flour and salt in a bowl. Add the butter and vegetable fat and cut in with a pastry blender until the mixture resembles coarse crumbs. With a fork, stir in enough iced water to bind the dough. Gather into a ball, wrap in clear film (plastic wrap) and chill for at least 20 minutes. Preheat the oven to 200°C/400°F/Gas 6.

~ **VARIATION** ~

For Caramelized Upside-Down Apple Pie, replace the pears with 8–9 firm, tart apples. There may seem to be too many apples, but they shrink slightly as they cook.

2 ▲ Quarter, peel and core the pears. Place in a bowl and toss with a few tablespoons of the sugar.

3 ▲ In a 27cm/101/2in ovenproof frying pan, melt the butter over moderately high heat. Add the remaining sugar. When it starts to colour, arrange the pears evenly around the edge and in the centre.

4 ▲ Continue cooking, uncovered, until caramelized, about 20 minutes.

5 ▲ Leave the fruit to cool. Roll out a circle of dough slightly larger than the diameter of the pan. Place the dough on top of the pears, tucking it around the edges. Transfer the pan to the oven and bake for 15 minutes, then reduce the heat to 180°C/350°F/Gas 4. Bake until golden, about 15 minutes more.

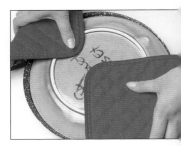

6 ▲ Let the pie cool in the pan for about 3–4 minutes. Run a knife around the edge of the pan to loosen the pie, ensuring that the knife reaches down to the bottom of the pan. Invert a plate on top and, protecting your hands with oven gloves, hold plate and pan firmly, and turn them both over quickly.

7 Lift off the pan. If any pears stick to the pan, remove them gently with a metal spatula and replace them carefully on the pie. Serve warm, with the whipped cream passed round separately.

Lime Tart

SERVES 8

3 large egg yolks

1 × 400g/14oz can sweetened
    condensed milk

15ml/1 tbsp grated lime rind

120ml/4fl oz/¹/₂ cup fresh lime juice

green food colouring (optional)

120ml/4fl oz/¹/₂ cup whipping cream

FOR THE BASE

115g/4oz/2 cups digestive biscuits
    (graham crackers), crushed

65g/2¹/₂oz/5 tbsp butter or
    margarine, melted

1 Preheat the oven to 180°C/350°F/
Gas 4.

2 ▲ For the base, place the crushed
biscuits in a bowl and add the butter
or margarine. Mix to combine.

~ VARIATION ~

Use lemons instead of limes,
with yellow food colouring.

3 Press the mixture evenly over the
base and sides of a 23cm/9in pie dish.
Bake for 8 minutes. Leave to cool.

4 ▲ Beat the yolks until thick. Beat
in the milk, lime rind and juice and
colouring, if using. Pour into the
pastry case (pie shell) and chill until
set, about 4 hours. To serve, whip the
cream. Pipe a lattice pattern on top.

Fruit Tartlets

MAKES 8

175ml/6fl oz/³/₄ cup redcurrant jelly

15ml/1 tbsp fresh lemon juice

175ml/6fl oz/³/₄ cup whipping cream

675g/1¹/₂lb fresh fruit, such as
    strawberries, raspberries, kiwi fruit,
    peaches, grapes or currants, peeled
    and sliced as necessary

FOR THE PASTRY

150g/5oz/10 tbsp cold butter, cut in pieces

65g/2¹/₂oz/generous ¹/₄ cup soft dark
    brown sugar

45ml/3 tbsp unsweetened cocoa powder

200g/7oz/1³/₄ cups plain
    (all-purpose) flour

1 egg white

1 For the pastry, combine the butter,
brown sugar and cocoa over low heat.
When the butter is melted, remove
from the heat and sift over the flour.
Stir, then add just enough egg white
to bind the mixture. Gather into a
ball, wrap in clear film (plastic wrap)
and chill for 30 minutes.

2 ▲ Grease eight 7.5cm/3in tartlet tins
(muffin pans). Roll out pastry between
2 sheets of baking parchment. Cut eight
10cm/4in rounds with a fluted cutter.

3 Line the tartlet tins. Prick the
base. Chill for 15 minutes. Preheat
the oven to 180°C/350°F/Gas 4.

4 Bake until firm, 20–25 minutes.
Cool, then remove from the tins.

5 ▲ Melt the jelly with the lemon
juice. Brush a thin layer in the bottom
of the tartlets. Whip the cream and
spread a thin layer in the tartlet cases.
Arrange the fruit on top. Brush with
the glaze and serve.

Lime Tart (top), Fruit Tartlets

Chocolate Lemon Tart

SERVES 8–10

250g/9oz/1¼ cups caster (superfine) sugar

6 eggs

grated rind of 2 lemons

175ml/6fl oz/¾ cup lemon juice

175ml/6fl oz/¾ cup whipping cream

chocolate curls, for decorating

FOR THE CRUST

190g/6½oz/1⅔ cups plain
     (all-purpose) flour

30ml/2 tbsp unsweetened cocoa powder

25g/1oz/¼ cup icing (confectioners') sugar

2.5ml/½ tsp salt

115g/4oz/½ cup butter or margarine

15ml/1 tbsp water

1 ▲ Grease a 25cm/10in tart tin (pan).

2 For the crust, sift the flour, cocoa powder, icing sugar and salt into a bowl. Set aside.

3 ▲ Melt the butter and water over a low heat. Pour over the flour mixture and stir with a wooden spoon until the dough is smooth and the flour has absorbed all the liquid.

4 Press the dough evenly over the base and side of the prepared tart tin. Chill the pastry case (pie shell) while preparing the filling.

5 Preheat a baking sheet in a 190°C/375°F/Gas 5 oven.

6 ▲ Whisk the sugar and eggs until the sugar is dissolved. Add the lemon rind and juice, and mix well. Add the cream. Taste the mixture and add more lemon juice or sugar if needed. It should taste tart but also sweet.

7 Pour the filling into the tart shell and bake on the hot sheet until the filling is set, 20–25 minutes. Cool on a rack. When cool, decorate with the chocolate curls.

Lemon Almond Tart

SERVES 8

165g/5¹/₂oz/scant 1 cup whole
  blanched almonds

70g/3¹/₂oz/¹/₂ cup sugar

eggs

grated rind and juice of 1¹/₂ lemons

115g/4oz/¹/₂ cup butter, melted

strips of lemon rind, for decorating

FOR THE CRUST

190g/6¹/₂oz/1²/₃ cups plain (all-purpose) flour

15ml/1 tbsp caster (superfine) sugar

2.5ml/¹/₂ tsp salt

2.5ml/¹/₂ tsp baking powder

75g/3oz/6 tbsp cold unsalted (sweet)
  butter, cut into pieces

45–60ml/3–4 tbsp whipping cream

1 For the crust, sift the flour, sugar,
salt and baking powder into a bowl.
Add the butter and rub in with your
fingertips until the mixture resembles
coarse breadcrumbs.

2 ▲ With a fork, stir in just enough
cream to bind the dough.

3 Gather into a ball and transfer to
a lightly floured surface. Roll out the
dough about 3mm/¹/₈in thick and
carefully transfer to a 23cm/9in tart
tin (pan). Trim and prick the base all
over with a fork. Chill for at least
20 minutes.

4 Preheat a baking sheet in a 200°C/
400°F/Gas 6 oven.

5 Line the tart shell with crumpled
baking parchment and fill with dried
beans. Bake for 12 minutes. Remove
the paper and beans and continue
baking until golden, 6–8 minutes
more. Reduce the oven temperature
to 180°C/350°F/Gas 4.

6 ▲ Grind the almonds finely with
15ml/1 tbsp of the sugar in a food
processor, blender, or coffee grinder.

7 ▲ Set a mixing bowl over a pan
of hot water. Add the eggs and the
remaining sugar, and beat with an
electric mixer until the mixture is
thick enough to leave a ribbon trail
when the beaters are lifted.

8 Stir in the lemon rind and juice,
butter and ground almonds.

9 Pour into the pastry case (pie shell).
Bake until the filling is golden and set,
35 minutes. Decorate with lemon rind.

Lemon Meringue Pie

SERVES 8

grated rind and juice of 1 large lemon

250ml/8fl oz/1 cup plus 15ml/1 tbsp cold water

115g/4oz/generous $^1\!/_2$ cup plus 75g/3oz/ 6 tbsp caster (superfine) sugar

25g/1oz/2 tbsp butter

45ml/3 tbsp cornflour (cornstarch)

3 eggs, separated

pinch of salt

pinch of cream of tartar

FOR THE PASTRY

150g/5oz/1$^1\!/_4$ cups plain (all-purpose) flour

2.5ml/$^1\!/_2$ tsp salt

65g/2$^1\!/_2$oz/scant $^1\!/_2$ cup cold white vegetable fat (shortening), cut in pieces

30ml/2 tbsp iced water

1 For the pastry, sift the flour and salt into a bowl. Add the fat and cut in with a pastry blender until the mixture resembles coarse breadcrumbs. With a fork, stir in just enough water to bind the mixture. Gather into a ball.

2 ▲ On a lightly floured surface, roll out the pastry about 3mm/$^1\!/_8$in thick. Transfer to a 23cm/9in pie dish and trim the edge to leave a 2cm/$^1\!/_2$in overhang.

3 ▲ Fold the overhang under and crimp the edge. Chill the pastry case (pie shell) for at least 20 minutes.

4 Preheat oven to 200°C/400°F/Gas 6.

5 ▲ Prick the case all over with a fork. Line with crumpled baking parchment and fill with baking beans. Bake for 12 minutes. Remove the paper and beans and continue baking until golden, 6–8 minutes more.

6 In a pan, combine the lemon rind and juice, 250ml/8fl oz/1 cup of the water, 115g/4oz/generous $^1\!/_2$ cup of the sugar, and butter. Bring the mixture to the boil.

7 Meanwhile, in a mixing bowl, dissolve the cornflour in the remaining water.

> ~ VARIATION ~
>
> For Lime Meringue Pie, substitute the grated rind and juice of two medium-size limes for the lemon.

8 ▲ Add the egg yolks to the lemon mixture and return to the boil, whisking continuously until the mixture thickens, about 5 minutes.

9 Cover the surface with baking parchment and leave to cool.

10 ▲ For the meringue, using an electric mixer beat the egg whites with the salt and cream of tartar until they hold stiff peaks. Add the remaining sugar and beat until glossy.

11 ▲ Spoon the lemon mixture into the pastry case and level. Spoon the meringue on top, smoothing it up to the pastry rim to seal. Bake until golden, 12–15 minutes.

Orange Tart

SERVES 8

200g/7oz/1 cup sugar

250ml/8fl oz/1 cup fresh orange juice, strained

2 large navel oranges

165g/5½oz/scant 1 cup whole blanched almonds

50g/2oz/¼ cup butter

1 egg

15ml/1 tbsp plain (all-purpose) flour

45ml/3 tbsp apricot jam

FOR THE CRUST

215g/7½oz/scant 2 cups plain flour

2.5ml/½ tsp salt

50g/2oz/¼ cup cold butter, cut into pieces

40g/1½oz/3 tbsp cold margarine, cut into pieces

45–60ml/3–4 tbsp iced water

1 For the crust, sift the flour and salt into a bowl. Add the butter and margarine and rub in with your fingertips until the mixture resembles coarse breadcrumbs. Stir in just enough water to bind the dough. Gather into a ball, wrap in clear film (plastic wrap), and chill for at least 20 minutes.

2 On a lightly floured surface, roll out the dough 5mm/¼in thick and transfer to an 20cm/8in tart tin (pan). Trim off the overhang. Chill until needed.

3 In a pan, combine 165g/5½oz/ generous ¾ cup of the sugar and the orange juice and boil until thick and syrupy, about 10 minutes.

4 ▲ Cut the oranges into 5mm/¼in slices. Do not peel. Add to the syrup. Simmer gently for 10 minutes, or until glazed. Transfer to a rack to dry. When cool, cut in half. Reserve the syrup. Place a baking sheet in the oven and heat to 200°C/400°F/Gas 6

5 Grind the almonds finely in a food processor, blender or coffee grinder. With an electric mixer, cream the butter and remaining sugar until light and fluffy. Beat in the egg and 30ml/ 2 tbsp of the orange syrup. Stir in the almonds and flour.

6 Melt the jam over a low heat, then brush over the pastry case (pie shell). Pour in the almond mixture. Bake until set, about 20 minutes. Leave to cool.

7 ▲ Arrange overlapping orange slices on top. Boil the remaining syrup until thick. Brush on top to glaze.

Pumpkin Pie

SERVES 8

450g/1lb cooked or canned pumpkin

250ml/8fl oz/1 cup whipping cream

2 eggs

115g/4oz/¹/₂ cup soft dark brown sugar

60ml/4 tbsp golden (light corn) syrup

7.5ml/1¹/₂ tsp ground cinnamon

5ml/1 tsp ground ginger

1.5ml/¹/₄ tsp ground cloves

2.5ml/¹/₂ tsp salt

FOR THE PASTRY

175g/6oz/1¹/₂ cups plain (all-purpose) flour

2.5ml/¹/₂ tsp salt

75g/3oz/6 tbsp cold butter, cut into pieces

40g/1¹/₂oz/3 tbsp cold white vegetable fat (shortening), cut into pieces

45–60ml/3–4 tbsp iced water

For the pastry, sift the flour and salt into a bowl. Cut in the butter and fat until it resembles coarse crumbs. Bind with iced water. Wrap in clear film (plastic wrap) and chill for 20 minutes.

Roll out the dough and line a 23cm/9in pie tin (pan). Trim off the overhang. Roll out the trimmings and cut out leaf shapes. Wet the rim of the pastry case (pie shell) with a brush dipped in water.

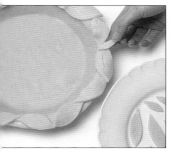

▲ Place the dough leaves around the rim of the pastry case. Chill for about 20 minutes. Preheat the oven to 200°C/400°F/Gas 6.

4 ▲ Line the pastry case with baking parchment. Fill with baking beans and bake for 12 minutes. Remove paper and beans and bake until golden, 6–8 minutes more. Reduce the heat to 190°C/375°F/Gas 5.

5 ▼ Beat together the pumpkin, cream, eggs, sugar, golden syrup, spices and salt. Pour into the pastry case and bake until set, 40 minutes.

Maple Walnut Tart

SERVES 8

3 eggs

pinch of salt

50g/2oz/¹/₄ cup caster (superfine) sugar

50g/2oz/¹/₄ cup butter or margarine, melted

250ml/8fl oz/1 cup pure maple syrup

115g/4oz/1 cup chopped walnuts

whipped cream, for decorating

FOR THE PASTRY

65g/2¹/₂oz/9 tbsp plain (all-purpose) flour

65g/2¹/₂oz/9 tbsp wholemeal (whole-wheat) flour

pinch of salt

50g/2oz/¹/₄ cup cold butter, cut in pieces

40g/1¹/₂oz/3 tbsp cold white vegetable fat (shortening), cut in pieces

1 egg yolk

30–45ml/2–3 tbsp iced water

1 ▼ For the pastry, mix the flours and salt in a bowl. Add the butter and fat and cut in with a pastry blender until the mixture resembles coarse breadcrumbs. With a fork, stir in the egg yolk and just enough water to bind the pastry. Form into a ball.

2 Wrap in baking parchment and chill for 20 minutes.

3 Preheat oven to 220°C/425°F/Gas 7

4 On a lightly floured surface, roll out the pastry about 3mm/¹/₈in thick and transfer to a 23cm/9in pie dish. Trim the edge. To decorate, roll out the trimmings. With a small heart-shaped cutter, stamp out enough hearts to go around the rim of the pie Brush the edge with water, then arrange the pastry hearts all around.

5 ▲ Prick the bottom with a fork. Line with crumpled baking parchmen and fill with baking beans. Bake for 10 minutes. Remove the paper and beans and continue baking until golden brown, 3–6 minutes more.

6 In a bowl, whisk the eggs, salt and sugar together. Stir in the butter and maple syrup.

7 ▲ Set the pastry case (pie shell) on a baking sheet. Pour in the filling, then sprinkle the nuts over the top.

8 Bake until just set, about 35 minutes Cool on a rack. Decorate with whipped cream, if you like.

Pecan Tart

SERVES 8

 eggs

inch of salt

00g/7oz/scant 1 cup soft dark brown sugar

20ml/4fl oz/¹/₂ cup golden
  (light corn) syrup

0ml/2 tbsp fresh lemon juice

5g/3oz/6 tbsp butter, melted

50g/5oz/1¹/₄ cups chopped pecan nuts

0g/2oz/¹/₂ cup pecan halves

OR THE PASTRY

75g/6oz/1¹/₂ cups plain (all-purpose) flour

5ml/1 tbsp caster (superfine) sugar

ml/1 tsp baking powder

.5ml/¹/₂ tsp salt

5g/3oz/6 tbsp cold unsalted (sweet)
  butter, cut in pieces

 egg yolk

5–60ml/3–4 tbsp whipping cream

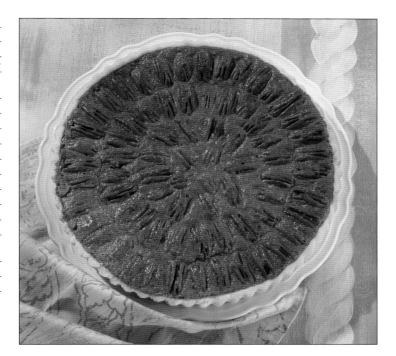

 For the pastry, sift the flour, sugar,
aking powder and salt into a bowl.
Add the butter and cut in with a
astry blender until the mixture
esembles coarse breadcrumbs.

▼ In a bowl, beat together the egg
olk and cream until blended.

6 In a bowl, lightly whisk the eggs
and salt. Add the sugar, syrup, lemon
juice and butter. Mix well and stir in
the chopped nuts.

3 ▲ Pour the cream mixture into the
flour mixture and stir with a fork.

4 Gather the pastry into a ball. On a
lightly floured surface, roll out 3mm/
¹/₈in thick and transfer to a 23cm/9in
pie dish. Trim the overhang and flute
the edge with your fingers. Chill for at
least 20 minutes.

5 Preheat a baking sheet in the
middle of a 200°C/400°F/Gas 6 oven.

7 ▲ Pour into the pastry case (pie
shell) and arrange the pecan halves
in concentric circles on top.

8 Bake for 10 minutes. Reduce
the heat to 170°C/325°F/Gas 3
and continue baking for 25 minutes.

~ COOK'S TIP ~

Serve this tart warm,
accompanied by ice cream or
whipped cream, if you like.

Mince Pies

MAKES 36

175g/6oz/1½ cups finely chopped
   blanched almonds

150g/5oz/generous ½ cup ready-to-eat
   dried apricots, finely chopped

175g/6oz/generous 1 cup raisins

150g/5oz/⅔ cup currants

150g/5oz/⅔ cup glacé (candied)
   cherries, chopped

150g/5oz/¾ cup cut mixed (candied)
   peel, chopped

115g/4oz/1 cup finely chopped beef suet

grated rind and juice of 2 lemons

grated rind and juice of 1 orange

200g/7oz/scant 1 cup soft dark brown sugar

4 cooking apples, peeled, cored and chopped

10ml/2 tsp ground cinnamon

5ml/1 tsp freshly grated nutmeg

2.5ml/½ tsp ground cloves

250ml/8fl oz/1 cup brandy

225g/8oz/1 cup cream cheese

30ml/2 tbsp caster (superfine) sugar

icing (confectioners') sugar, for dusting

FOR THE PASTRY

425g/15oz/3½ cups plain (all-purpose) flour

150g/5oz/1¼ cups icing (confectioners') sugar

350g/12oz/1½ cups cold butter, cut in pieces

grated rind and juice of 1 orange

milk, for glazing

1 Mix the nuts, dried and preserved
fruit, suet, citrus rind and juice,
brown sugar, apples and spices.

2 ▲ Stir in the brandy. Cover and
leave in a cool place for 2 days.

3 For the pastry, sift the flour and
icing sugar into a bowl. Cut in the
butter until the mixture resembles
coarse breadcrumbs.

4 ▲ Add the orange rind. Stir in just
enough orange juice to bind. Gather
into a ball, wrap in baking parchment
and chill for at least 20 minutes.

5 Preheat the oven to 220°C/425°F/
Gas 7. Grease two or three bun trays.
Beat together the cream cheese and sugar.

6 ▲ Roll out the pastry 5mm/¼ in
thick. With a fluted pastry cutter, stamp
out 36 8cm/3in rounds.

~ COOK'S TIP ~

The mincemeat mixture may be
packed into sterilized jars and
sealed. It will keep refrigerated for
several months. Add a few
tablespoonfuls to give apple pies a
lift, or make small mincemeat-
filled parcels using filo pastry.

7 ▲ Transfer the rounds to the bun
tray. Fill halfway with mincemeat.
Top with a teaspoonful of the cream
cheese mixture.

8 ▲ Roll out the remaining pastry
and stamp out 36 5cm/2in rounds
with a fluted cutter. Brush the edges
of the pies with milk, then set the
rounds on top. Cut a small steam
vent in the top of each pie.

9 ▲ Brush lightly with milk.
Bake until golden, 15–20 minutes.
Leave to cool for 10 minutes before
turning out. Dust with icing sugar,
if you like.

Shoofly Pie

SERVES 8

115g/4oz/1 cup plain (all-purpose) flour

115g/4oz/1 cup soft dark brown sugar

1.5ml/^{1}/4 tsp each salt, ground ginger, cinnamon, mace and grated nutmeg

75g/3oz/6 tbsp cold butter, cut into pieces

2 eggs

120ml/4fl oz/^{1}/2 cup molasses

120ml/4fl oz/^{1}/2 cup boiling water

2.5ml/^{1}/2 tsp bicarbonate of soda (baking soda)

FOR THE PASTRY

115g/4oz/^{1}/2 cup cream cheese, at room temperature, cut into pieces

115g/4oz/^{1}/2 cup cold butter, at room temperature, cut into pieces

115g/4oz/1 cup plain flour

1 For the pastry, put the cream cheese and butter in a mixing bowl. Sift over the flour.

2 ▲ Cut in with a pastry blender until the dough just holds together. Wrap in clear film (plastic wrap) and chill for at least 30 minutes.

3 Put a baking sheet in the centre of the oven and preheat the oven to 190°C/375°F/Gas 5.

4 In a bowl, mix the flour, sugar, salt and spices. Rub in the butter with your fingertips until the mixture resembles coarse crumbs. Set aside.

5 On a lightly floured surface, roll out the dough and line a 23cm/9in pie tin (pan). Trim the overhanging pastry and flute the rim.

6 ▲ Spoon a third of the crumbed mixture into the pastry case (pie shell).

7 ▲ To complete the filling, whisk the eggs with the molasses in a large bowl until combined.

8 Pour the boiling water into a small bowl. Stir in the bicarbonate of soda; the mixture will foam. Immediately whisk into the egg mixture. Pour carefully into the pastry case and sprinkle the remaining crumbed mixture evenly over the top.

9 Stand on the hot baking sheet and bake until browned, about 35 minutes. Leave to cool to room temperature, then serve.

Treacle Tart

SERVES 4–6

175ml/6fl oz/³/₄ cup golden
   (light corn) syrup

75g/3oz/1¹/₂ cups fresh white breadcrumbs

grated rind of 1 lemon

30ml/2 tbsp lemon juice

FOR THE PASTRY

175g/6oz/1¹/₂ cups plain (all-purpose) flour

2.5ml/¹/₂ tsp salt

75g/3oz/6 tbsp cold butter, cut in pieces

40g/1¹/₂oz/3 tbsp cold margarine,
   cut in pieces

45–60ml/3–4 tbsp iced water

For the pastry, combine the flour and salt in a bowl. Add the butter and margarine, and cut in with a pastry blender until the mixture resembles coarse breadcrumbs.

▲ With a fork, stir in just enough water to bind the pastry. Gather into a ball, wrap in clear film (plastic wrap) and chill for at least 20 minutes.

On a lightly floured surface, roll out the pastry to a thickness of 3mm/¹/₈in. Transfer to an 20cm/8in pie dish and trim off the overhang. Chill for at least 20 minutes. Reserve the trimmings for the lattice top.

Preheat a baking sheet at the top of 200°C/400°F/Gas 6 oven.

In a pan, warm the syrup until thin and runny.

6 ▲ Remove from the heat and stir in the breadcrumbs and lemon rind. Leave for 10 minutes so that the bread can absorb the syrup. Add more breadcrumbs if the mixture is thin. Stir in the lemon juice and spread evenly in the pastry case (pie shell).

7 Roll out the pastry trimmings and cut into 10–12 thin strips.

8 ▼ Lay half the strips on the filling, then lay the remaining strips at an angle over them to form a lattice.

9 Place on the hot sheet and bake for 10 minutes. Lower the heat to 190°C/375°F/Gas 5. Bake until golden, about 15 minutes more. Serve warm or cold.

Chess Pie

SERVES 8

2 eggs

45ml/3 tbsp whipping cream

115g/4oz/¹/² cup soft dark brown sugar

30ml/2 tbsp granulated sugar

30ml/2 tbsp plain (all-purpose) flour

15ml/1 tbsp whisky

40g/1¹/²oz/3 tbsp butter, melted

50g/2oz/¹/² cup chopped walnuts

75g/3oz/¹/² cup pitted dates, chopped

whipped cream, for serving

FOR THE PASTRY

75g/3oz/6 tbsp cold butter

40g/1¹/²oz/3 tbsp cold vegetable fat

175g/6oz/1¹/² cups plain flour

2.5ml/¹/² tsp salt

45–60ml/3–4 tbsp iced water

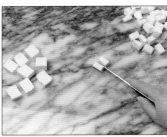

1 ▲ For the pastry, cut the butter and fat into small pieces.

2 Sift the flour and salt into a bowl. With a pastry blender, cut in the butter and fat until the mixture resembles coarse crumbs. Stir in just enough water to bind. Gather into a ball, wrap in baking parchment and chill for at least 20 minutes.

3 Place a baking sheet in the oven and preheat it to 190°C/375°F/Gas 5.

4 Roll out the dough thinly and line a 23cm/9in pie tin (pan). Trim the edge. Roll out the trimmings, cut thin strips and braid them. Brush the edge of the pastry case (pie shell) with water and fit the pastry braids around the rim.

5 ▲ In a mixing bowl, whisk together the eggs and cream.

6 Add both sugars and beat until well combined. Sift over 15ml/1 tbsp of the flour and stir in. Add the whisky, the melted butter and the walnuts. Stir to combine.

7 ▲ Mix the dates with the remaining flour and stir into the walnut mixture.

8 Pour into the pastry case and bake until the pastry is golden and the filling puffed up, about 35 minutes. Serve at room temperature, with whipped cream, if you like.

Coconut Cream Tart

SERVES 8

150g/5oz/scant 1½ cups desiccated
(dry unsweetened) coconut

150g/5oz/¾ cup caster (superfine) sugar

60ml/4 tbsp cornflour (cornstarch)

pinch of salt

600ml/1 pint/2½ cups milk

60ml/2fl oz/¼ cup whipping cream

4 egg yolks

25g/1oz/2 tbsp unsalted (sweet) butter

10ml/2 tsp vanilla extract

FOR THE PASTRY

150g/5oz/1¼ cups plain (all-purpose) flour

1.5ml/¼ tsp salt

40g/1½oz/3 tbsp cold butter, cut in pieces

25g/1oz/2 tbsp cold white vegetable fat
(shortening)

30–45ml/2–3 tbsp iced water

1 For the pastry, sift the flour and salt, then cut in the butter and fat until it resembles coarse breadcrumbs.

2 ▲ With a fork, stir in just enough water to bind the pastry. Gather into a ball, wrap in baking parchment and chill for 20 minutes.

3 Preheat the oven to 220°C/425°F/Gas 7. Roll out the pastry 3mm/⅛in thick. Line a 23cm/9in pie dish. Trim and flute the edges. Prick the base. Line with baking parchment and fill with baking beans. Bake for 10–12 minutes. Remove paper and beans, reduce heat to 180°C/350°F/Gas 4 and bake until brown, 10–15 minutes.

4 ▲ Spread 50g/2oz of the coconut on a baking sheet and toast in the oven until golden, 6–8 minutes, stirring often. Set aside for decorating.

5 Put the sugar, cornflour and salt in a pan. In a bowl, whisk the milk, cream and egg yolks. Add the egg mixture to the pan.

6 ▼ Cook over a low heat, stirring, until the mixture comes to the boil. Boil for 1 minute, then remove from the heat. Add the butter, vanilla and remaining coconut.

7 Pour into the prebaked pastry case (pie shell). When cool, sprinkle toasted coconut in a ring in the centre.

Black Bottom Pie

SERVES 8

10ml/2 tsp gelatine
45ml/3 tbsp cold water
2 eggs, separated
150g/5oz/1¼ cups caster (superfine) sugar
15g/½oz/2 tbsp cornflour (cornstarch)
2.5ml/½ tsp salt
475ml/16fl oz/2 cups milk
50g/2oz plain (semisweet) chocolate, finely chopped
30ml/2 tbsp rum
1.5ml/¼ tsp cream of tartar
chocolate curls, for decorating
FOR THE CRUST
175g/6oz/3 cups gingersnaps, crushed
65g/2½oz/5 tbsp butter, melted

1 Preheat the oven to 180°C/350°F/Gas 4.

2 For the crust, mix the crushed gingersnaps and melted butter.

3 ▲ Press the mixture evenly over the bottom and side of a 23cm/9in pie plate. Bake for 6 minutes.

4 Sprinkle the gelatine over the water and leave to soften.

5 Beat the egg yolks in a large mixing bowl and set aside.

6 In a pan, combine half the sugar, the cornflour and salt. Gradually stir in the milk. Boil for 1 minute, stirring constantly.

7 ▲ Whisk the hot milk mixture into the yolks, then pour all back into the pan and return to the boil, whisking. Cook for 1 minute, still whisking. Remove from the heat.

8 ▲ Measure out 225g/8oz of the hot custard mixture and pour into a bowl. Add the chopped chocolate to the bowl, and stir until melted. Stir in half the rum and pour into the pastry case (pie shell).

9 ▲ Whisk the softened gelatine into the plain custard until it has dissolved, then stir in the remaining rum. Set the pan in cold water until it reaches room temperature.

10 ▲ With an electric mixer, beat the egg whites and cream of tartar until they hold stiff peaks. Add the remaining sugar gradually, beating or whisking thoroughly at each addition.

11 ▲ Fold the custard into the egg whites, then spoon over the chocolate mixture in the pastry case. Chill until set, about 2 hours.

12 Decorate the top with chocolate curls. Keep the pie chilled until ready to serve.

~ COOK'S TIP ~

To make chocolate curls, melt 225g/8oz plain chocolate over hot water, stir in 15ml/1 tbsp white vegetable fat (shortening) and mould in a small foil-lined loaf tin (pan). For large curls, soften the bar between your hands and scrape off curls from the wide side with a vegetable peeler; for small curls, grate from the narrow side using a box grater.

Velvety Mocha Tart

SERVES 8

10ml/2 tsp instant espresso coffee
30ml/2 tbsp hot water
350ml/12fl oz/1¹/₂ cups whipping cream
175g/6oz plain (semisweet) chocolate
25g/1oz dark (bittersweet) cooking chocolate
120ml/4fl oz/¹/₂ cup whipped cream, for decorating
chocolate-covered coffee beans, for decorating
FOR THE BASE
150g/5oz/2¹/₂ cups chocolate wafers, crushed
30ml/2 tbsp caster (superfine) sugar
65g/2¹/₂oz/5 tbsp butter, melted

1 ▲ For the base, mix the crushed chocolate wafers and sugar together, then stir in the melted butter.

2 Press the mixture evenly over the base and sides of a 23cm/9in pie dish. Chill until firm.

3 In a bowl, dissolve the coffee in the water and set aside.

4 Pour the cream into a mixing bowl. Set the bowl in hot water to warm the cream, bringing it closer to the temperature of the chocolate.

5 Melt both the chocolates in the top of a double boiler, or in a heatproof bowl set over a pan of hot water. Remove from the heat when nearly melted and stir to continue melting. Set the base of the pan in cool water to reduce the temperature. Be careful not to splash any water on the chocolate or it will become grainy.

6 ▲ With an electric mixer, whip the cream until it is lightly fluffy. Add the dissolved coffee and whip until the cream just holds its shape.

7 ▲ When the chocolate is at room temperature, fold it gently into the cream with a large metal spoon.

8 Pour into the chilled biscuit base and chill until firm. To serve, pipe a ring of whipped cream rosettes around the edge, then place a chocolate-covered coffee bean in the centre of each rosette.

Brandy Alexander Tart

SERVES 8

120ml/4fl oz/½ cup cold water

15ml/1 tbsp powdered gelatine

115g/4oz/generous ½ cup caster
(superfine) sugar

3 eggs, separated

60ml/4 tbsp brandy

60ml/4 tbsp crème de cacao

pinch of salt

300ml/½ pint/1¼ cups whipping cream

chocolate curls, for decorating

FOR THE BISCUIT CRUST

225g/8oz/4cups digestive biscuits
(graham crackers), crumbed

65g/2½oz/5 tbsp butter, melted

15ml/1 tbsp caster sugar

1 Preheat oven to 190°C/375°F/ Gas 5.

2 For the crust, mix the biscuit crumbs
with the butter and sugar in a bowl.

3 ▲ Press the crumbs evenly on to
the base and sides of a 23cm/9in tart
tin (pan). Bake until just brown,
about 10 minutes. Cool on a rack.

4 Place the water in the top of a
double boiler set over hot water.
Sprinkle over the powdered gelatine
and leave to stand for 5 minutes to
soften. Add half the sugar and the
egg yolks. Whisk constantly over
a very low heat until the gelatine
dissolves and the mixture has
thickened slightly. Do not allow
the mixture to boil.

5 ▲ Remove from the heat and stir
in the brandy and crème de cacao.

6 Set the pan over iced water and
stir occasionally until it cools and
thickens; it should not set firmly.

7 With an electric mixer, beat the
egg whites and salt until they hold
stiff peaks. Beat in the remaining sugar.
Spoon a dollop of whites into the yolk
mixture and fold in to lighten.

8 ▼ Pour the egg yolk mixture over
the remaining whites and fold together.

9 Whip the cream until soft peaks
form, then gently fold into the filling.
Spoon into the baked biscuit case
and chill until set, 3–4 hours.
Decorate the top with chocolate
curls before serving.

Candied Fruit Pie

SERVES 10

15ml/1 tbsp rum

50g/2oz/¼ cup mixed glacé (candied) fruit, chopped

450ml/¾ pint/scant 2 cups milk

20ml/4 tsp gelatine

90g/3½oz/½ cup caster (superfine) sugar

2.5ml/½ tsp salt

3 eggs, separated

250ml/8fl oz/1 cup whipping cream

chocolate curls, for decorating

FOR THE CRUST

175g/6oz/3 cups digestive biscuits (graham crackers), crushed

65g/2½oz/5 tbsp butter, melted

15ml/1 tbsp sugar

1 For the crust, mix the crushed digestive biscuits, butter and sugar. Press evenly and firmly over the base and side of a 23cm/9in pie plate. Chill until firm.

2 ▲ In a bowl, stir together the rum and glacé fruit. Set aside.

3 Pour 120ml/4fl oz/½ cup of the milk into a bowl. Sprinkle over the gelatine. Leave to soften for 5 minutes.

4 ▲ In the top of a double boiler, combine 50g/2oz/¼ cup of the sugar, the remaining milk and salt. Stir in the gelatine mixture. Cook over hot water, stirring, until the gelatine dissolves.

5 Whisk in the egg yolks and cook, stirring, until thick enough to coat a spoon. Do not boil. Pour the custard over the glacé fruit mixture. Set in a bowl of iced water to cool. Whip the cream lightly. Set aside.

6 With an electric mixer, beat the egg whites until they hold soft peaks. Add the remaining sugar and beat just enough to blend. Fold in a large dollop of the egg whites into the cooled gelatine mixture. Pour into the remaining egg whites and carefully fold together. Fold in the cream.

7 ▲ Pour into the biscuit base and chill until firm. Decorate the top with chocolate curls.

Chocolate Chiffon Pie

200g/7oz plain (semisweet) chocolate

250ml/8fl oz/1 cup milk

15ml/1 tbsp gelatine

90g/3¹/₂oz/¹/₂ cup sugar

4 large (US extra-large) eggs, separated

5ml/1 tsp vanilla extract

350ml/12fl oz/1¹/₂ cups whipping cream

pinch of salt

whipped cream and chocolate curls, for decorating

FOR THE CRUST

200g/7oz/3¹/₂ cups digestive biscuits (graham crackers), crushed

75g/3oz/6 tbsp butter, melted

1 Place a baking sheet in the oven and preheat to 180°C/350°F/Gas 4.

2 For the crust, mix the crushed digestive biscuits and butter in a bowl. Press evenly over the base and side of a 23cm/9in pie plate. Bake for 8 minutes. Leave to cool.

3 Chop the chocolate, then grate in a food processor or blender. Set aside.

4 Place the milk in the top of a double boiler. Sprinkle over the gelatine. Leave to stand for 5 minutes to soften.

5 ▲ Set the top of a double boiler over hot water. Add 40g/1¹/₂oz/3 tbsp sugar, the chocolate and the egg yolks. Stir until dissolved. Add the vanilla extract.

6 ▲ Set the top of the double boiler in a bowl of ice and stir until the mixture reaches room temperature. Remove from the ice and set aside.

7 Whip the cream lightly. Set aside. With an electric mixer, beat the egg whites and salt until they hold soft peaks. Add the remaining sugar and beat only enough to blend.

8 Fold a dollop of egg whites into the chocolate mixture, then pour back into the whites and fold in.

9 ▲ Fold in the whipped cream and pour into the biscuit base. Put in the freezer until just set, about 5 minutes. If the centre sinks, fill with any remaining mixture. Chill for 3–4 hours. Decorate with whipped cream and chocolate curls. Serve cold.

Chocolate Cheesecake Tart

SERVES 8

350g/12oz/1½ cups cream cheese
60ml/4 tbsp whipping cream
225g/8oz/generous 1 cup caster (superfine) sugar
50g/2oz/½ cup unsweetened cocoa powder
2.5ml/½ tsp ground cinnamon
3 eggs
whipped cream, for decorating
chocolate curls, for decorating

FOR THE BASE

75g/3oz/1½ cups digestive biscuits (graham crackers), crushed
40g/1½oz/¾ cup crushed amaretti biscuits (if unavailable, use extra crushed digestive biscuits)
75g/3oz/6 tbsp butter, melted

1 Preheat a baking sheet in the centre of a 180°C/350°F/Gas 4 oven.

2 For the base, mix the crushed biscuits and butter in a bowl.

3 ▲ With a spoon, press the mixture over the base and sides of a 23cm/9in pie dish. Bake for 8 minutes. Leave to cool. Keep the oven on.

4 With an electric mixer, beat the cheese and cream together until smooth. Beat in the sugar, cocoa and cinnamon until blended.

5 ▼ Add the eggs, one at a time, beating just enough to blend.

6 Pour into the biscuit base and bake on the hot sheet for 25–30 minutes. The filling will sink down as it cools. Decorate with whipped cream and chocolate curls.

Frozen Strawberry Tart

SERVES 8

225g/8oz/1 cup cream cheese
250ml/8fl oz/1 cup sour cream
500g/1¼lb/5 cups frozen strawberries, thawed and sliced

FOR THE BASE

115g/4oz/2 cups digestive biscuits (graham crackers), crushed
15ml/1 tbsp caster (superfine) sugar
70g/2½oz/5 tbsp butter, melted

~ VARIATION ~

For Frozen Raspberry Tart, use raspberries in place of the strawberries, and prepare the same way, or try other frozen fruit.

1 ▲ For the base, mix together the biscuits, sugar and butter.

2 Press the mixture evenly and firmly over the base and sides of a 23cm/9in pie dish. Freeze until firm.

3 ▼ Blend together the cream cheese and sour cream. Reserve 90ml/6 tbsp of the strawberries. Add the remainder to the cream cheese mixture.

4 Pour the filling into the biscuit base and freeze for 6–8 hours until firm. To serve, spoon some of the reserved berries and juice on top.

Chocolate Cheesecake Pie (top), Frozen Strawberry Tart

Kiwi Ricotta Cheese Tart

SERVES 8

75g/3oz/1/2 cup blanched almonds, ground

90g/31/2oz/1/2 cup caster (superfine) sugar

900g/2lb/4 cups ricotta cheese

250ml/8fl oz/1 cup whipping cream

1 egg and 3 egg yolks

15ml/1 tbsp plain (all-purpose) flour

pinch of salt

30ml/2 tbsp rum

grated rind of 1 lemon

40ml/21/2 tbsp lemon juice

30ml/2 tbsp honey

5 kiwi fruit

FOR THE PASTRY

150g/5oz/11/4 cups plain (all-purpose) flour

15ml/1 tbsp caster (superfine) sugar

2.5ml/1/2 tsp salt

2.5ml/1/2 tsp baking powder

75g/3oz/6 tbsp butter

1 egg yolk

45–60ml/3–4 tbsp whipping cream

1 For the pastry, mix together the flour, sugar, salt and baking powder in a large bowl. Cut the butter into cubes and gradually rub it into the pastry mixture. Mix together the egg yolk and cream. Stir in just enough to bind the pastry.

2 ▲ Transfer to a lightly floured surface, flatten slightly, wrap and chill for 30 minutes. Preheat the oven to 220°C/425°F/Gas 7.

3 ▲ On a lightly floured surface, roll out the dough to 3mm/1/8in thickness. Transfer to a 23cm/9in springform tart tin (pan). Crimp the edge.

4 ▲ Prick the pastry with a fork. Line with baking parchment and fill with dried beans. Bake for 10 minutes. Remove the paper and beans and bake for 6–8 minutes more until golden. Leave to cool. Reduce the temperature to 180°C/350°F/Gas 4.

5 ▲ Mix the almonds with 15ml/1 tbsp of the sugar in a food processor or blender.

6 Beat the ricotta until creamy. Add the cream, egg, yolks, remaining sugar, flour, salt, rum, lemon rind and 30ml/2 tbsp of lemon juice. Combine.

7 ▲ Stir in the ground almonds until well blended.

8 Pour into a pastry case (pie shell) and bake for 1 hour. Chill, loosely covered, for 2–3 hours. Turn out on to a plate.

9 Combine the honey and remaining lemon juice for the glaze.

10 ▲ Peel the kiwi fruits. Halve them lengthways, then slice. Arrange the slices in rows across the top of the tart. Just before serving, brush with the honey glaze.

Apple Strudel

SERVES 10–12

75g/3oz/generous ¹/₂ cup raisins
30ml/2 tbsp brandy
5 eating apples, such as Granny Smith or Cox's
3 large cooking apples
90g/3¹/₂oz/scant ¹/₂ cup soft dark brown sugar
5ml/1 tsp ground cinnamon
grated rind and juice of 1 lemon
25g/1oz/¹/₂ cup dry breadcrumbs
50g/2oz/¹/₂ cup chopped pecan nuts or walnuts
12 sheets frozen filo pastry, thawed if frozen
175g/6oz/³/₄ cup butter, melted
icing (confectioners') sugar, for dusting

1 Soak the raisins in the brandy for at least 15 minutes.

2 ▼ Peel, core and thinly slice the apples. In a bowl, combine the sugar, cinnamon and lemon rind. Stir in the apples and half the breadcrumbs.

3 Add the raisins, nuts and lemon juice, and stir until blended.

4 Preheat the oven to 190°C/375°F/ Gas 5. Grease two baking sheets.

5 ▲ Carefully unfold the filo sheets. Keep the unused sheets covered with baking parchment. Lift off one sheet, place on a clean surface and brush with melted butter. Lay a second sheet on top and brush with butter. Continue until you have a stack of six buttered sheets.

6 Sprinkle a few tablespoons of breadcrumbs over the last sheet and spoon half the apple mixture along the bottom edge of the strip.

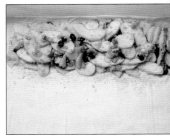

7 ▲ Starting at the apple-filled end roll up the pastry, as for a Swiss roll tin (jelly roll pan). Place on a baking sheet, seam-side down, and carefully fold under the ends to seal. Repeat the procedure to make a second strudel. Brush both with butter.

8 Bake the strudels for 45 minutes. Leave to cool slightly. Using a small sieve (strainer), dust with a fine layer of icing sugar. Serve warm.

Cherry Strudel

SERVES 8

55g/2¹/₂oz/generous 1 cup fresh
   breadcrumbs
175g/6oz/³/₄ cup butter, melted
200g/7oz/1 cup caster (superfine) sugar
15ml/1 tbsp ground cinnamon
5ml/1 tsp grated lemon rind
450g/1lb sour cherries, pitted
8 sheets filo pastry, thawed if frozen
icing (confectioners') sugar, for dusting

1 In a frying pan, lightly fry the
fresh breadcrumbs in 65g/2¹/₂oz of the
melted butter until golden. Set aside
to cool.

2 ▲ In a large mixing bowl, toss
together the sugar, cinnamon and
lemon rind.

3 Stir in the cherries.

4 Preheat the oven to 190°C/375°F/
Gas 5. Grease a baking sheet.

5 Carefully unfold the filo sheets.
Keep the unused sheets covered with
damp kitchen paper. Lift off one
sheet, place on a flat surface lined
with baking parchment. Brush the
pastry with melted butter. Sprinkle
about an eighth of the breadcrumbs
evenly over the surface.

6 ▲ Lay a second sheet of filo on top,
brush with butter and sprinkle with
crumbs. Continue until you have a
stack of eight buttered, crumbed sheets.

7 Spoon the cherry mixture along the
bottom edge of the strip. Starting at the
cherry-filled end, roll up the dough as
for a Swiss roll tin (jelly roll pan). Use
the paper to help flip the strudel on to
the baking sheet, seam-side down.

8 ▼ Carefully fold under the ends
to seal in the fruit. Brush the top with
any remaining butter.

9 Bake the strudel for 45 minutes.
Leave to cool slightly. Using a small
sieve (strainer), dust with a fine layer
of icing sugar.

Mushroom Quiche

SERVES 8

450g/1lb/6 cups mushrooms

30ml/2 tbsp olive oil

15ml/1 tbsp butter

1 clove garlic, finely chopped

15ml/1 tbsp lemon juice

30ml/2 tbsp finely chopped fresh parsley

3 eggs

350ml/12fl oz/1½ cups whipping cream

65g/2½oz/¾ cup freshly grated
    Parmesan cheese

salt and ground black pepper

FOR THE CRUST

190g/6½oz/1⅔ cups plain
    (all-purpose) flour

2.5ml/½ tsp salt

75g/3oz cold butter, cut into pieces

50g/2oz/¼ cup cold margarine, cut into
    pieces

45–60ml/3–4 tbsp iced water

1 For the crust, sift the flour and salt. Rub in the butter and margarine until it resembles coarse breadcrumbs. Stir in enough water to bind.

2 Gather into a ball, wrap in clear film (plastic wrap) and chill for 20 minutes.

3 Preheat a baking sheet in a 190°C/375°F/Gas 5 oven.

4 Roll out the dough 3mm/⅛in thick. Transfer to a 23cm/9in quiche tin (pan) and trim. Prick the base all over with a fork. Line with baking parchment and fill with dried beans. Bake for 12 minutes. Remove the paper and beans and continue baking until golden, about 5 minutes more.

5 ▲ Wipe the mushrooms with damp kitchen paper to remove any dirt. Trim the ends of the stalks, place on a cutting board, and slice thinly.

6 Heat the oil and butter in a frying pan. Stir in the mushrooms, garlic and lemon juice. Season with salt and pepper. Cook until the mushrooms render their liquid, then raise the heat and cook until dry.

7 ▼ Stir in the parsley and add more salt and pepper if necessary.

8 Whisk the eggs and cream together, then stir in the mushrooms. Sprinkle the cheese over the base of the prebaked pastry case (pie shell) and pour the mushroom filling over the top.

9 Bake until puffed and brown, about 30 minutes. Serve the quiche warm.

Bacon and Cheese Quiche

SERVES 8

115g/4oz medium-thick bacon slices

3 eggs

350ml/12fl oz/1½ cups whipping cream

90g/3½oz Gruyère cheese, grated

pinch of freshly grated nutmeg

salt and ground black pepper

FOR THE CRUST

190g/6½oz/1⅔ cups plain (all-purpose) flour

2.5ml/½ tsp salt

75g/3oz/6 tbsp cold butter, cut into pieces

40g/1½oz/3 tbsp cold margarine,
    cut into pieces

45–60ml/3–4 tbsp iced water

1 Make the crust as per steps 1–4 above. Keep the oven at 190°C/375°F/Gas 5.

2 ▲ Fry the bacon until crisp. Drain, then crumble into small pieces. Sprinkle in the pastry case (pie shell).

3 ▲ Beat together the eggs, cream, cheese, nutmeg, salt and pepper. Pour over the bacon and bake until puffed and brown, about 30 minutes. Serve the quiche warm.

Mushroom Quiche (top), Bacon and Cheese Quiche

Cheese and Tomato Quiche

SERVES 6–8

10 medium tomatoes

1 × 50g/2oz can anchovy fillets, drained
and finely chopped

120ml/4fl oz/½ cup whipping cream

200g/7oz/1¾ cups mature Cheddar
cheese, grated

25g/1oz/½ cup wholemeal
(whole-wheat) breadcrumbs

2.5ml/½ tsp dried thyme

salt and ground black pepper

FOR THE CRUST

215g/7½oz/scant 2 cups plain
(all-purpose) flour

115g/4oz/½ cup cold butter,
cut into pieces

1 egg yolk

30–45ml/2–3 tbsp iced water

1 Preheat the oven to 200°C/400°F/
Gas 6.

2 For the crust, sift the flour and ½ tsp
salt into a bowl. Rub in the butter
with your fingertips until the mixture
resembles coarse breadcrumbs.

3 ▲ With a fork, stir in the egg yolk
and enough water to bind the dough.

4 Roll out the dough to about 3mm/
⅛in thick and transfer to a 23cm/9in
quiche tin (pan). Chill the dough
until needed.

5 ▲ Score the bottoms of the
tomatoes. Plunge in boiling water
for 1 minute. Remove and peel off
the skin with a knife. Cut in quarters
and remove the seeds with a spoon.

6 ▲ In a bowl, mix the anchovies
and cream. Stir in the cheese.

7 Sprinkle the breadcrumbs in the
crust. Arrange the tomatoes on top.
Season with thyme, salt and pepper.

8 ▲ Spoon the cheese mixture on
top. Bake until golden, 25–30 minutes.
Serve warm.

Onion and Anchovy Tart

SERVES 8

60ml/4 tbsp olive oil
900g/2lb onions, sliced
5ml/1 tsp dried thyme
2–3 tomatoes, sliced
24 small black olives, pitted
1 × 50g/2oz can anchovy fillets, drained and sliced
6 sun-dried tomatoes, cut into slivers
salt and ground black pepper
FOR THE CRUST
190g/6$\frac{1}{2}$oz/1$\frac{2}{3}$ cups plain (all-purpose) flour
2.5ml/$\frac{1}{2}$ tsp salt
115g/4oz/$\frac{1}{2}$ cup cold butter, cut into pieces
1 egg yolk
30–45ml/2–3 tbsp iced water

1 ▲ For the crust, sift the flour and salt into a bowl. Rub in the butter with your fingertips until the mixture resembles coarse breadcrumbs. Stir in the yolk and enough water to bind.

2 ▲ Roll out the dough to a thickness of about 3mm/$\frac{1}{8}$in. Transfer to a 23cm/9in quiche tin (pan) and trim the edge. Chill in the refrigerator until needed.

3 ▲ Heat the oil in a frying pan. Add the onions, thyme and seasoning. Cook over low heat, covered, for 25 minutes. Uncover and continue cooking until soft. Cool. Preheat the oven to 200°C/400°F/Gas 6.

4 ▼ Spoon the onions into the pastry case (pie shell) and top with the tomato slices. Arrange the olives in rows. Make a lattice pattern, alternating lines of anchovies and sun-dried tomatoes. Bake until golden, 20–25 minutes.

Ricotta and Basil Tart

SERVES 8–10

50g/2oz/2 cups basil leaves
25g/1oz/1 cup flat-leaf parsley
120ml/4fl oz/¹/₂ cup extra-virgin olive oil
2 eggs
1 egg yolk
800g/1³/4lb/3¹/₂ cups ricotta cheese
90g/3¹/₂oz/scant 1 cup black olives, pitted
65g/2¹/₂oz/³/4 cup freshly grated Parmesan cheese
salt and ground black pepper
FOR THE CRUST
190g/6¹/₂oz/1²/₃ cups plain (all-purpose) flour
2.5ml/¹/₂ tsp salt
75g/3oz/6 tbsp cold butter, cut into pieces
40g/1¹/₂oz/3 tbsp cold margarine, cut into pieces
45–60ml/3–4 tbsp iced water

1 ▲ For the crust, combine the flour and salt in a bowl. Add the butter and margarine.

2 Rub in with your fingertips until the mixture resembles coarse breadcrumbs. With a fork, stir in just enough water to bind the dough. Gather into a ball, wrap in clear film (plastic wrap), and chill for 20 minutes.

3 Preheat a baking sheet in a 190°C/375°F/Gas 5 oven.

4 Roll out the dough 3mm/¹/₈in thick and transfer to a 25cm/10in quiche tin (pan). Prick the base with a fork and line with baking parchment. Fill with dried beans and bake for 12 minutes. Remove the paper and beans and bake until golden, 3–5 minutes more. Lower the heat to 180°C/350°F/Gas 4.

5 ▲ In a food processor or blender, combine the basil, parsley and olive oil. Season well with salt and pepper and process until finely chopped.

6 In a bowl, whisk the eggs and yolk to blend. Gently fold in the ricotta.

7 ▲ Fold in the basil mixture and olives until well combined. Stir in the Parmesan and adjust the seasoning.

8 Pour into the prebaked pastry case (pie shell) and bake until set, about 30–35 minutes.

Pennsylvania Dutch Ham and Apple Pie

SERVES 6–8

5 tart cooking apples

60ml/4 tbsp soft light brown sugar

15ml/1 tbsp plain (all-purpose) flour

pinch of ground cloves

pinch of ground black pepper

175g/6oz sliced cooked ham

25g/1oz/2 tbsp butter or margarine

60ml/4 tbsp whipping cream

1 egg yolk

FOR THE PASTRY

225g/8oz/2 cups plain (all-purpose) flour

2.5ml/¹/₂ tsp salt

75g/3oz/6 tbsp cold butter, cut into pieces

60g/2oz/¹/₄ cup cold margarine,
    cut into pieces

60–120ml/4–8 tbsp iced water

1 For the pastry, sift the flour and salt into a large bowl. Rub in the butter and margarine until the mixture resembles coarse crumbs. Stir in enough water to bind together, gather into two balls, and wrap in clear film (plastic wrap). Chill for 20 minutes. Preheat the oven to 220°C/425°F/Gas 7.

2 ▲ Quarter, core, peel and thinly slice the apples. Place in a bowl and toss with the sugar, flour, cloves and pepper to coat evenly. Set aside.

3 Roll out one dough ball thinly and line a 25cm/10in pie tin (pan), letting the excess pastry hang over the edge.

4 Arrange half the ham slices in the bottom of the pastry case. Top with a ring of spiced apple slices, then dot with half the butter or margarine.

5 ▲ Repeat the layers, finishing with apples. Dot with butter or margarine. Pour over 45ml/3 tbsp of the cream.

6 Roll out the remaining pastry to make a lid. Place it on top, fold the top edge under the bottom and press.

7 ▲ Roll out the pastry scraps and cut out decorative shapes. Arrange on top of the pie. Scallop the edge, using your fingers and a fork. Cut steam vents. Mix the egg yolk and remaining cream and brush on top to glaze.

8 Bake for 10 minutes. Reduce the heat to 180°C/350°F/Gas 4 and bake until golden, 30–35 minutes more. Serve hot.

CAKES & GATEAUX

AS DELICIOUS AS THEY ARE
BEAUTIFUL, THESE CAKES AND
GÂTEAUX ARE PERFECT TO SERVE
AT TEATIME OR FOR DESSERT.
DELIGHTFUL PARTY CAKES MAKE
SPECIAL OCCASIONS MEMORABLE.

Angel Cake

130g/4¹/₂oz/generous 1 cup sifted plain (all-purpose) flour

30ml/2 tbsp cornflour (cornstarch)

300g/11oz/generous 1¹/₂ cups caster (superfine) sugar

275–300g/10–11oz egg whites (about 10–11 eggs)

6.5ml/1¹/₄ tsp cream of tartar

1.5ml/¹/₄ tsp salt

5ml/1 tsp vanilla extract

1.5ml/¹/₄ tsp almond extract

icing (confectioners') sugar, for dusting

1 Preheat the oven to 160°C/325°F/ Gas 3.

2 ▼ Sift the flours before measuring, then sift them four times with 90g/ 3¹/₂oz/¹/₂ cup of the sugar.

3 With an electric mixer, beat the egg whites until foamy. Sift over the cream of tartar and salt, and continue to beat until the whites hold soft peaks when the beaters are lifted.

4 ▲ Add the remaining sugar in three batches, beating well after each addition. Stir in the vanilla and almond extracts.

5 ▲ Add the flour mixture, in two batches, and fold in with a large metal spoon after each addition.

6 Transfer to an ungreased 25cm/ 10in tube tin (pan) and bake until just browned on top, about 1 hour.

7 ▲ Turn the tin upside down on to a cake rack and leave to cool for 1 hour. If the cake does not turn out, run a knife around the edge to loosen it. Invert on a serving plate.

8 When cool, lay a star-shaped template on top of the cake, sift over icing sugar and remove template.

Marbled Ring Cake

SERVES 16

115g/4oz plain (semisweet) chocolate

350g/12oz/3 cups plain (all-purpose) flour

5ml/1 tsp baking powder

450g/1lb/2 cups butter, at room temperature

325g/1lb 10oz/3¹/₂ cups caster
  (superfine) sugar

15ml/1 tbsp vanilla extract

10 eggs, at room temperature

icing (confectioners') sugar, for dusting

▲ Preheat the oven to 180°C/350°F/
Gas 4. Line a 25 × 10cm/10 × 4in ring
mould with baking parchment and
grease the paper. Dust with flour.

▲ Melt the chocolate in the top of
a double boiler, or in a heatproof bowl
set over a pan of hot water. Stir
occasionally. Set aside.

3 In a bowl, sift together the flour
and baking powder. In another bowl,
cream the butter, sugar and vanilla
with an electric mixer until light and
fluffy. Add the eggs, two at a time,
then gradually incorporate the flour
mixture on low speed.

4 ▲ Spoon half of the mixture into
the prepared tin (pan).

5 ▲ Stir the chocolate into the
remaining mixture, then spoon into
the tin. With a metal spatula, swirl
the mixtures for a marbled effect.

6 Bake until a skewer inserted into
the centre comes out clean, about
1 hour 45 minutes. Cover with foil
halfway through baking. Leave to
stand for 15 minutes, then turn out
and transfer to a cooling rack. To
serve, dust with icing sugar.

Coffee-iced Ring

SERVES 16

275g/10oz/2¹/₂ cups plain (all-purpose) flour
15ml/1 tbsp baking powder
5ml/1 tsp salt
350g/12oz/1³/₄ cup caster (superfine) sugar
120ml/4fl oz/¹/₂ cup vegetable oil
7 eggs, at room temperature, separated
175ml/6fl oz/³/₄ cup cold water
10ml/2 tsp vanilla extract
10ml/2 tsp grated lemon rind
2.5ml/¹/₂ tsp cream of tartar
FOR THE ICING
165g/5¹/₂oz unsalted (sweet) butter
575g/1lb 4oz/5 cups icing (confectioners') sugar
20ml/4 tsp instant coffee dissolved in 60ml/4 tbsp hot water

1 Preheat the oven to 170°C/325°F/ Gas 3.

2 ▼ Sift the flour, baking powder and salt into a bowl. Stir in 225g/8oz of the sugar. Make a well in the centre and add the oil, egg yolks, water, vanilla and lemon rind. Beat with a whisk or metal spoon until smooth.

3 With an electric mixer, beat the egg whites with the cream of tartar until they hold soft peaks. Add the remaining sugar and beat until the mixture holds stiff peaks.

4 ▲ Pour the flour mixture over the whites in three batches, folding well after each addition.

5 Transfer the mixture to a 25 × 10cm/ 10 × 4in ring mould and bake until the top springs back when touched lightly, about 1 hour.

6 ▲ When baked, remove from the oven and immediately hang the cake upside-down over the neck of a funnel or a narrow bottle. Leave to cool. To remove the cake, run a knife around the inside to loosen, then turn the tin over and tap the sides sharply. Invert the cake on to a serving plate.

7 For the icing, beat together the butter and icing sugar with an electric mixer until smooth. Add the coffee and beat until fluffy. With a metal spatula, spread over the sides and top of the cake.

Spice Cake with Cream Cheese Icing

SERVES 10–12

300ml/1/2 pint/1 1/4 cups milk
30ml/2 tbsp golden (light corn) syrup
10ml/2 tsp vanilla extract
75g/3oz/1/2 cup walnuts, chopped
175g/6oz/3/4 cup butter, at room temperature
300g/11oz/generous 1 1/2 cups caster (superfine) sugar
1 egg, at room temperature
2 egg yolks, at room temperature
275g/10oz/2 1/2 cups plain (all-purpose) flour
15ml/1 tbsp baking powder
5ml/1 tsp freshly grated nutmeg
5ml/1 tsp ground cinnamon
2.5ml/1/2 tsp ground cloves
1.5ml/1/4 tsp ground ginger
1.5ml/1/4 tsp ground allspice
FOR THE ICING
175g/6oz/3/4 cup cream cheese
25g/1oz/2 tbsp unsalted (sweet) butter
200g/7oz/1 3/4 cups icing (confectioners') sugar
30ml/2 tbsp finely chopped stem ginger
30ml/2 tbsp syrup from stem ginger
stem ginger pieces, for decorating

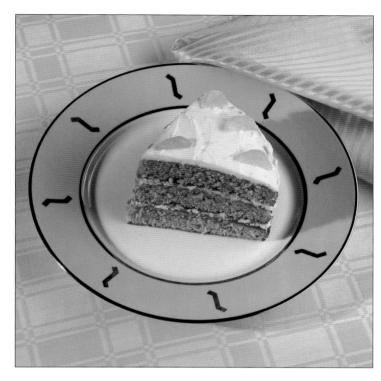

1 Preheat the oven to 180°C/350°F/ Gas 4. Line three 20cm/8in cake tins (pans) with baking parchment and grease. In a bowl, combine the milk, syrup, vanilla and walnuts.

2 ▼ With an electric mixer, cream the butter and sugar until light and fluffy. Beat in the egg and egg yolks. Add the milk mixture and stir well.

3 Sift together the flour, baking powder and spices three times.

4 ▲ Add the flour mixture to the egg mixture in four batches, and fold in carefully after each addition.

5 Divide the cake mixture between the tins. Bake until the cakes spring back when touched lightly, about 25 minutes. Leave to stand for 5 minutes, then turn out and cool on a rack.

6 ▼ For the icing, combine all the ingredients and beat with an electric mixer. Spread the icing between the layers and over the top. Decorate with pieces of stem ginger.

Caramel Layer Cake

SERVES 8–10

275g/10oz/2¹/2 cups plain (all-purpose) flour
7.5ml/1¹/2 tsp baking powder
175g/6oz/³/4 cup butter, at room temperature
165g/5¹/2oz/generous ³/4 cup caster (superfine) sugar
4 eggs, at room temperature, beaten
5ml/1 tsp vanilla extract
120ml/4fl oz/¹/2 cup milk
whipped cream, for decorating
caramel threads, for decorating (optional, see below)
FOR THE ICING
300g/11oz/scant 1¹/3 cups soft dark brown sugar
250ml/8fl oz/1 cup milk
25g/1oz/2 tbsp unsalted (sweet) butter
45–75ml/3–5 tbsp whipping cream

1 Preheat the oven to 180°C/350°F/ Gas 4. Line two 20cm/8in cake tins (pans) with baking parchment; grease lightly.

2 ▲ Sift the flour and baking powder together three times. Set aside.

~ COOK'S TIP ~

To make caramel threads, combine 65g/2¹/2oz/5 tbsp sugar and 50ml/ 2fl oz/¹/4 cup water in a heavy pan. Boil until light brown. Dip the pan in cold water to halt cooking. Trail from a spoon on an oiled baking sheet.

3 With an electric mixer, cream the butter and caster sugar until light and fluffy.

4 ▲ Slowly mix in the beaten eggs. Add the vanilla. Fold in the flour mixture, alternating with the milk.

5 ▲ Divide the batter between the prepared tins and spread evenly, hollowing out the centres slightly.

6 Bake until the cakes pull away from the sides of the tin, about 30 minutes. Leave to stand for 5 minutes, then turn out and cool on a rack.

7 ▲ For the icing, combine the brown sugar and milk in a pan.

8 Bring to the boil, cover and cook for 3 minutes. Remove the lid and continue to boil, without stirring, until the mixture reaches 119°C/238°F (soft ball stage) on a sugar thermometer.

9 ▲ Immediately remove the pan from the heat and add the butter, but do not stir it in. Cool until lukewarm, then beat until the mixture is smooth and creamy.

10 Stir in enough cream to obtain a spreadable consistency. If necessary, chill to thicken more.

11 ▲ Spread a layer of icing on top of one cake. Sandwich with the second cake, then spread the top and sides with the rest of the icing and smooth the surface.

12 To decorate, pipe whipped cream rosettes around the edge. Place a mound of caramel threads, if using, in the centre before serving.

Lady Baltimore Cake

SERVES 8–10

275g/10oz/2¹/₂ cups plain (all-purpose) flour
12.5ml/2¹/₂ tsp baking powder
2.5ml/¹/₂ tsp salt
4 eggs
350g/12oz/1³/₄ cups caster (superfine) sugar
grated rind of 1 large orange
250ml/8fl oz/1 cup fresh orange juice
250ml/8fl oz/1 cup vegetable oil
18 pecan halves, for decorating
FOR THE FROSTING
2 egg whites
350g/12oz/1³/₄ cups caster sugar
75ml/5 tbsp cold water
1.5ml/¹/₄ tsp cream of tartar
5ml/1 tsp vanilla extract
50g/2oz/¹/₃ cup pecan nuts, finely chopped
75g/3oz/²/₃ cup raisins, chopped
3 dried figs, finely chopped

1 Preheat the oven to 180°C/350°F/Gas 4. Grease two 23cm/9in round cake tins (pans) and line with baking parchment. Grease the paper. In a bowl, sift together the flour, baking powder and salt. Set aside.

2 ▲ With an electric mixer, beat the eggs and sugar until thick and lemon-coloured. Beat in the orange rind and juice, then the oil.

3 On low speed, beat in the flour mixture in three batches. Divide the cake mixture between the tins.

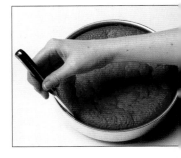

4 ▲ Bake until a skewer inserted into the centre comes out clean, about 30 minutes. Leave to stand for 15 minutes, then run a knife around the inside of the cakes and transfer them to racks to cool completely.

5 ▲ For the icing, combine the egg whites, sugar, water and cream of tartar in the top of a double boiler, or in a heatproof bowl set over boiling water. With an electric mixer, beat until glossy and thick. Off the heat, add the vanilla extract and continue beating until thick. Fold in the pecan nuts, raisins and figs.

6 Spread a layer of icing on top of one cake. Sandwich with the second cake, then spread the top and sides with the rest of the icing. Arrange the pecan halves on top.

Carrot Cake

SERVES 12

450g/1lb carrots, peeled

175g/6oz/1¹/₂ cups plain (all-purpose) flour

10ml/2 tsp baking powder

2.5ml/¹/₂ tsp bicarbonate of soda
(baking soda)

5ml/1 tsp salt

10ml/2 tsp ground cinnamon

4 eggs

10ml/2 tsp vanilla extract

115g/4oz/¹/₂ cup soft dark brown sugar

50g/2oz/¹/₄ cup caster (superfine) sugar

300ml/¹/₂ pint/1¹/₄ cups sunflower oil

115g/4oz/1 cup finely chopped walnuts

75g/3oz/²/₃ cup raisins

walnut halves, for decorating (optional)

FOR THE ICING

75g/3oz/6 tbsp unsalted (sweet) butter

350g/12oz/3 cups icing (confectioners')
sugar

60ml/2fl oz/¹/₄ cup maple syrup

1 Preheat the oven to 180°C/350°F/
Gas 4. Line a 28 × 20cm/11 × 8in tin
(pan) with baking parchment; grease.

2 ▲ Grate the carrots and set aside.

3 Sift the flour, baking powder,
bicarbonate of soda, salt and
cinnamon into a bowl. Set aside.

4 With an electric mixer, beat the
eggs until blended. Add the vanilla,
sugars and oil; beat to incorporate. Add
the dry ingredients, in three batches,
folding in well after each addition.

5 ▲ Add the carrots, walnuts and
raisins, and fold in thoroughly.

6 Pour the mixture into the prepared
tin and bake until the cake springs
back when touched lightly, 40–45
minutes. Leave for 10 minutes, then
turn out and transfer to a rack.

7 ▼ For the icing, cream the butter
with half the icing sugar until soft.
Add the syrup, then beat in the
remaining sugar until blended.

8 Spread the icing over the top of the
cake. Using the tip of a metal spatula,
make decorative ridges in the icing.
Cut into squares. Decorate with
walnut halves, if you like.

Cranberry Upside-down Cake

SERVES 8

350–400g/12–14oz/3–3¹/₂ cups
fresh cranberries

50g/2oz/¹/₄ cup butter

150g/5oz/³/₄ cup caster (superfine) sugar

FOR THE CAKE MIXTURE

65g/2¹/₂oz/9 tbsp plain (all-purpose) flour

5ml/1 tsp baking powder

3 eggs

115g/4oz/generous ¹/₂ cup sugar

grated rind of 1 orange

40g/1¹/₂oz/3 tbsp butter, melted

1 Preheat the oven to 180°C/350°F/ Gas 4. Place a baking sheet on the middle shelf of the oven.

2 Wash the cranberries and pat dry. Thickly smear the butter on the bottom and sides of a 23 × 5cm/ 9 × 2in round cake tin (pan). Add the sugar and swirl the tin to coat evenly.

3 ▲ Add the cranberries and spread in an even layer over the bottom of the tin.

4 For the cake mixture, sift the flour and baking powder twice. Set aside.

5 ▲ Combine the eggs, sugar and orange rind in a heatproof bowl set over a pan of hot but not boiling water. With an electric mixer, beat until the eggs leave a ribbon trail when the beaters are lifted.

6 Add the flour mixture in three batches, folding in well after each addition. Gently fold in the melted butter, then pour over the cranberries.

7 Bake for 40 minutes. Leave to cool for 5 minutes, then run a knife around the inside edge to loosen.

8 ▲ While the cake is still warm, invert a plate on top of the tin. Protecting your hands with oven gloves, hold the plate and tin firmly and turn them both over quickly. Lift off the tin carefully.

Pineapple Upside-down Cake

SERVES 8

115g/4oz/¹/₂ cup butter

200g/7oz/scant 1 cup soft dark brown sugar

450g/1lb canned pineapple slices, drained

4 eggs, separated

grated rind of 1 lemon

pinch of salt

115g/4oz/generous ¹/₂ cup caster (superfine) sugar

75g/3oz/²/₃ cup plain (all-purpose) flour

5ml/1 tsp baking powder

1 Preheat the oven to 180°C/350°F/ Gas 4.

2 Melt the butter in a 25cm/10in ovenproof frying pan. Remove about 15ml/1 tbsp of the melted butter and set aside.

3 ▲ Add the brown sugar to the pan and stir until blended. Place the drained pineapple slices on top in one layer. Set aside.

4 In a bowl, whisk together the egg yolks, reserved butter and lemon rind until well blended. Set aside.

5 ▼ With an electric mixer, beat the egg whites with the salt until stiff. Fold in the caster sugar, 25g/1oz/ 2 tbsp at a time. Fold in the egg yolk mixture.

6 Sift the flour and baking powder together. Carefully fold into the egg mixture in three batches.

7 ▲ Pour the mixture over the pineapple and smooth level.

8 Bake until a skewer inserted into the centre comes out clean, about 30 minutes.

9 While still hot, place a serving plate on top of the pan, bottom-side up. Holding them tightly together with oven gloves, quickly flip over. Serve hot or cold.

~ **VARIATION** ~

For Apricot Upside-down Cake, replace the pineapple slices with 225g/8oz/1 cup ready-to-eat dried apricots. If they need softening, simmer them in about 120ml/4fl oz/¹/₂ cup orange juice until plump and soft. Drain the apricots and discard any remaining cooking liquid.

Lemon Coconut Layer Cake

SERVES 8–10

175g/6oz/1¹/₂ cups plain (all-purpose) flour

pinch of salt

7 eggs

350g/12oz/scant 1³/₄ cups caster (superfine) sugar

15ml/1 tbsp grated orange rind

grated rind of 2 lemons

juice of 1¹/₂ lemon

65g/2¹/₂oz/scant 1 cup desiccated (dry sweetened) coconut

15ml/1 tbsp cornflour (cornstarch)

120ml/4fl oz/¹/₂ cup water

40g/1¹/₂oz/3 tbsp butter

FOR THE ICING

75g/3oz/6 tbsp unsalted (sweet) butter

175g/6oz/1¹/₂ cups icing (confectioners') sugar

grated rind of 1¹/₂ lemons

30ml/2 tbsp lemon juice

200g/7oz/2¹/₂ cups desiccated (dry sweetened) coconut

1 Preheat the oven to 180°C/350°F/ Gas 4. Line three 20cm/8in cake tins (pans) with baking parchment and grease. In a bowl, sift together the flour and salt and set aside.

2 ▲ Place six of the eggs in a large heatproof bowl set over hot water. With an electric mixer, beat until frothy. Gradually beat in 225g/8oz/ generous 1 cup caster sugar until the mixture doubles in volume and leaves a ribbon trail when the beaters are lifted, about 10 minutes.

3 ▲ Remove the bowl from the hot water. Fold in the orange rind, half the grated lemon rind and 15ml/1 tbsp of the lemon juice until blended. Fold in the coconut.

4 Sift over the flour mixture in three batches, gently folding in thoroughly after each addition.

5 ▲ Divide the mixture between the prepared tins.

6 Bake until the cakes pull away from the sides of the tins, 20–25 minutes. Leave to stand for 3–5 minutes, then turn out to cool on a rack.

7 In a bowl, blend the cornflour with a little cold water to dissolve. Whisk in the remaining egg until just blended. Set aside.

8 ▲ In a pan, combine the remaining lemon rind and juice, the water, remaining sugar and butter.

9 Over medium heat, bring the mixture to the boil. Whisk in the eggs and cornflour mixture, and return to the boil. Whisk continuously until thick, about 5 minutes. Remove from the heat and pour into a bowl. Cover with clear film (plastic wrap); set aside.

10 ▲ For the frosting, cream the butter and icing sugar until smooth. Stir in the lemon rind and enough lemon juice to obtain a thick, spreadable consistency.

11 Sandwich the three cake layers with the lemon custard mixture. Spread the frosting over the top and sides. Cover the cake with the coconut, pressing it in gently.

Lemon Yogurt Ring

SERVES 12

225g/8oz/1 cup butter,
  at room temperature

300g/11oz/generous 1¹/₂ cups caster
  (superfine) sugar

4 eggs, at room temperature, separated

10ml/2 tsp grated lemon rind

85ml/3fl oz/generous ¹/₃ cup lemon juice

250ml/8fl oz/1 cup plain (natural) yogurt

275g/10oz/2¹/₂ cups plain
  (all-purpose) flour

10ml/2 tsp baking powder

5ml/1 tsp bicarbonate of soda
  (baking soda)

2.5ml/¹/₂ tsp salt

FOR THE GLAZE

115g/4oz/1 cup icing
  (confectioners') sugar

30ml/2 tbsp lemon juice

45–60ml/3–4 tbsp plain (natural) yogurt

1 Preheat oven to 180°C/350°F/Gas 4. Grease a 3 litre/5¹/₄ pint/13¹/₄ cup bundt or fluted tube tin (pan) and dust with flour.

2 With an electric mixer, cream the butter and caster sugar until light and fluffy. Add the egg yolks, one at a time, beating well after each addition.

3 ▲ Add the lemon rind, juice and yogurt, and stir to blend.

4 Sift together the flour, baking powder and bicarbonate of soda. In another bowl, beat the egg whites and salt until they hold stiff peaks.

5 ▲ Fold the dry ingredients into the butter mixture, then fold in a dollop of egg whites. Fold in the remaining whites until blended.

6 Pour into the tin and bake until a skewer inserted into the centre comes out clean, about 50 minutes. Leave to stand for 15 minutes, then turn out and cool on a rack.

7 For the glaze, sift the icing sugar into a bowl. Stir in the lemon juice and just enough yogurt to make a smooth glaze.

8 ▲ Set the cooled cake on the rack over a sheet of baking parchment or a baking sheet. Pour over the glaze and let it drip down the sides. Allow the glaze to set before serving.

Sour Cream Crumble Cake

SERVES 12–14

115g/4oz/¹/₂ cup butter, at room temperature

130g/4¹/₂oz/scant ³/₄ cup caster
(superfine) sugar

3 eggs, at room temperature

215g/7¹/₂oz/scant 2 cups plain
(all-purpose) flour

5ml/1 tsp bicarbonate of soda (baking soda)

5ml/1 tsp baking powder

250ml/8fl oz/1 cup sour cream

FOR THE TOPPING

225g/8oz/1 cup soft dark brown sugar

10ml/2 tsp ground cinnamon

115g/4oz/²/₃ cup walnuts, finely chopped

60g/2oz/¹/₄ cup cold butter, cut into pieces

1 Preheat the oven to 180°C/350°F/
Gas 4. Line the base of a 23cm/9in
square cake tin (pan) with baking
parchment and grease.

2 ▲ For the topping, place the
brown sugar, cinnamon and walnuts
in a bowl. Mix with your fingertips,
then add the butter and continue
working with your fingertips until
the mixture resembles breadcrumbs.

3 To make the cake, cream the butter
with an electric mixer until soft. Add
the sugar and continue beating until
the mixture is light and fluffy.

4 Add the eggs, one at a time,
beating well after each addition.

5 In another bowl, sift the flour,
bicarbonate of soda and baking
powder together three times.

6 ▲ Fold the dry ingredients into
the butter mixture in three batches,
alternating with the sour cream. Fold
until blended after each addition.

7 ▲ Pour half the batter into the
prepared tin and sprinkle over half
the walnut crumb topping mixture.

8 Pour the remaining batter on top
and sprinkle over the remaining
walnut crumb mixture.

9 Bake until browned, 60–70
minutes. Leave to stand for 5 minutes,
then turn out and cool on a rack.

Plum Crumble Cake

SERVES 8–10

150g/5oz/10 tbsp butter or margarine, at room temperature

150g/5oz/³/4 cup caster (superfine) sugar

4 eggs, at room temperature

7.5ml/1¹/2 tsp vanilla extract

150g/5oz/1¹/4 cups plain flour

5ml/1 tsp baking powder

675g/1¹/2lb red plums, halved and stoned (pitted)

FOR THE TOPPING

115g/4oz/1 cup plain (all-purpose) flour

130g/4¹/2oz/generous ¹/2 cup soft light brown sugar

7.5ml/1¹/2 tsp ground cinnamon

75g/3oz/6 tbsp butter, cut in pieces

1 Preheat the oven to 180°C/350°F/ Gas 4.

2 For the topping, combine the flour, light brown sugar and cinnamon in a bowl. Add the butter and work the mixture with your fingertips until it resembles coarse breadcrumbs. Set aside.

3 ▲ Line a 25 × 5cm/10 × 2in tin (pan) with baking parchment and grease.

4 Cream the butter and sugar until light and fluffy.

5 ▲ Beat in the eggs, one at a time. Stir in the vanilla.

6 In a bowl, sift together the flour and baking powder, then fold into the butter mixture in three batches.

7 ▲ Pour the mixture into the tin. Arrange the plums on top.

8 ▲ Sprinkle the topping over the plums in an even layer.

9 Bake until a skewer inserted into the centre comes out clean, about 45 minutes. Leave to cool in the tin.

10 To serve, run a knife around the inside edge and invert on to a plate. Invert again on to a serving plate so that the topping is right-side up.

~ VARIATION ~

This cake can also be made with the same quantity of apricots, peeled, if preferred, or stoned cherries, or use a mixture of fruit, such as red or yellow plums, greengages and apricots.

Peach Torte

SERVES 8

115g/4oz/1 cup plain (all-purpose) flour

5ml/1 tsp baking powder

pinch of salt

115g/4oz/¹/₂ cup unsalted (sweet) butter, at room temperature

175g/6oz/scant 1 cup caster (superfine) sugar

2 eggs, at room temperature

6–7 peaches

sugar and lemon juice, for sprinkling

whipped cream, for serving (optional)

1 Preheat the oven to 180°C/350°F/ Gas 4. Grease a 25cm/10in springform cake tin (pan).

2 ▲ Sift together the flour, baking powder and salt. Set aside.

3 With an electric mixer, cream the butter and sugar until light and fluffy. Beat in the eggs, then fold in the dry ingredients until blended.

4 ▲ Spoon the mixture into the tin and smooth it to make an even layer over the bottom.

5 ▼ To skin the peaches, drop several at a time into a pan of gently boiling water. Boil for 10 seconds, then remove with a slotted spoon. Peel off the skin with the aid of a sharp knife. Cut the peaches in half and discard the stones (pits).

6 ▲ Arrange the peach halves on top of the mixture. Sprinkle lightly with sugar and lemon juice.

7 Bake until golden brown and set, 50–60 minutes. Serve warm, with whipped cream, if you like.

Apple Ring Cake

SERVES 12

7 eating apples, such as Cox's or Granny Smith
350ml/12fl oz/1¹/₂ cups vegetable oil
450g/1lb/2¹/₄ cups caster (superfine) sugar
3 eggs
425g/15oz/3¹/₂ cups plain (all-purpose) flour
5ml/1 tsp salt
5ml/1 tsp bicarbonate of soda (baking soda)
5ml/1 tsp ground cinnamon
5ml/1 tsp vanilla extract
115g/4oz/1 cup chopped walnuts
175g/6oz/generous 1 cup raisins
icing (confectioners') sugar, for dusting

1 Preheat the oven to 180°C/350°F/ Gas 4. Grease a 23cm/9in ring mould.

2 ▲ Quarter, peel, core and slice the apples into a bowl. Set aside.

3 With an electric mixer, beat the oil and sugar together until blended. Add the eggs and continue beating until the mixture is creamy.

4 Sift together the flour, salt, bicarbonate of soda and cinnamon.

5 ▼ Fold the flour mixture into the egg mixture with the vanilla. Stir in the apples, walnuts and raisins.

6 Pour into the tin (pan) and bake until the cake springs back when touched lightly, about 1¹/₄ hours. Leave to stand for 15 minutes, then turn out and transfer to a cooling rack. Dust with a layer of icing sugar before serving.

Orange Cake

SERVES 6

175g/6oz/1¹/₂ cups plain (all-purpose) flour
pinch of salt
7.5ml/1¹/₂ tsp baking powder
115g/4oz/¹/₂ cup butter or margarine
115g/4oz/generous ¹/₂ cup caster (superfine) sugar
grated rind of 1 large orange
2 eggs, at room temperature
30ml/2 tbsp milk
FOR THE SYRUP AND DECORATION
115g/4oz/generous ¹/₂ cup caster (superfine) sugar
250ml/8fl oz/1 cup fresh orange juice, strained
3 orange slices, for decorating

1 Preheat the oven to 180°C/350°F/ Gas 4. Line a 20cm/8in cake tin (pan) with baking parchment and grease the paper.

2 ▲ Sift the flour, salt and baking powder on to baking parchment.

3 With an electric mixer, cream the butter or margarine until soft. Add the sugar and orange rind, and beat until light and fluffy. Beat in the eggs, one at a time. Fold in the flour in three batches, then add the milk.

4 Spoon into the tin and bake until the cake pulls away from the sides, about 30 minutes. Remove from the oven but leave it in the tin.

5 Meanwhile, for the syrup, dissolve the sugar in the orange juice over a low heat. Add the orange slices and simmer for 10 minutes. Remove and drain. Leave the syrup to cool.

6 ▲ Prick the cake all over with a fine skewer. Pour the syrup over the hot cake. It may seem at first that there is too much syrup for the cake to absorb, but it will soak it all up. Turn out when completely cooled and decorate with small triangles of the orange slices arranged on top.

Apple Ring Cake (top), Orange Cake

Orange and Walnut Roll

SERVES 8

4 eggs, separated

115g/4oz/generous ¹/₂ cup caster (superfine) sugar

115g/4oz/1 cup very finely chopped walnuts

pinch of cream of tartar

pinch of salt

icing (confectioners') sugar, for dusting

FOR THE FILLING

300ml/¹/₂ pint/1¹/₄ cups whipping cream

15ml/1 tbsp caster (superfine) sugar

grated rind of 1 orange

15ml/1 tbsp orange liqueur, such as Grand Marnier

1 Preheat the oven to 180°C/350°F/ Gas 4. Line a 30 × 24cm/12 × 9¹/₂in Swiss roll tin (jelly roll pan) with baking parchment and grease the paper.

2 With an electric mixer, beat the egg yolks and sugar until thick.

3 ▲ Stir in the walnuts.

4 In another bowl, beat the egg whites with the cream of tartar and salt until they hold stiff peaks. Fold gently but thoroughly into the walnut mixture.

5 Pour the mixture into the prepared tin and spread level with a spatula. Bake for 15 minutes.

6 Run a knife along the inside edge to loosen, then invert the cake on to a sheet of baking parchment dusted with icing sugar.

7 ▲ Peel off the baking parchment. Roll up the cake while it is still warm with the help of the sugared paper. Set aside to cool.

8 For the filling, whip the cream until it holds soft peaks. Stir together the caster sugar and orange rind, then fold into the whipped cream. Add the liqueur.

9 ▲ Gently unroll the cake. Spread the inside with a layer of orange whipped cream, then re-roll. Keep chilled until ready to serve. Dust the top with icing sugar just before serving.

Chocolate Roll

SERVES 10

225g/8oz plain (semisweet) chocolate

45ml/3 tbsp water

30ml/2 tbsp rum, brandy or strong coffee

7 eggs, separated

175g/6oz/scant 1 cup caster
(superfine) sugar

pinch of salt

350ml/12fl oz/1½ cups whipping cream

icing (confectioners') sugar, for dusting

1 Preheat the oven to 180°C/350°F/
Gas 4. Line a 38 × 33cm/15 × 13in
Swiss roll tin (jelly roll pan) with
baking parchment and grease the paper.

2 ▲ Combine the chocolate, water
and rum or other flavouring in the top
of a double boiler, or in a heatproof
bowl set over hot water. Heat until
melted. Set aside.

3 With an electric mixer, beat the
egg yolks and sugar until thick.

4 ▲ Stir in the melted chocolate.

5 In another bowl, beat the egg
whites and salt until they hold stiff
peaks. Fold a large dollop of the egg
whites into the yolk mixture to
lighten it, then carefully fold in
the rest of the whites.

6 ▼ Pour the mixture into the pan;
smooth evenly with a metal spatula.

7 Bake for 15 minutes. Remove
from the oven, cover with baking
parchment and a damp dish towel.
Leave to stand for 1–2 hours.

8 With an electric mixer, whip the
cream until stiff. Set aside.

9 Run a knife along the inside edge
to loosen, then invert the cake on to
a sheet of baking parchment that has
been dusted with icing sugar.

10 Peel off the baking parchment.
Spread with an even layer of whipped
cream, then roll up the cake with the
help of the sugared paper.

11 Chill for several hours. Before
serving, dust with an even layer of
icing sugar.

Chocolate Frosted Layer Cake

SERVES 8

225g/8oz/1 cup butter or margarine,
  at room temperature

300g/11oz/generous 1¹/₂ cups caster
  (superfine) sugar

4 eggs, at room temperature, separated

10ml/2 tsp vanilla extract

385g/13¹/₂oz/3¹/₃ cups plain (all-purpose) flour

10ml/2 tsp baking powder

pinch of salt

250ml/8fl oz/1 cup milk

FOR THE ICING

150g/5oz plain (semisweet) chocolate

120ml/4fl oz/¹/₂ cup sour cream

pinch of salt

1 Preheat the oven to 180°C/350°F/
Gas 4. Line two 20cm/8in round cake
tins (pans) with baking parchment and
grease. Dust with flour and shake to
distribute. Tap to dislodge excess flour.

2 With an electric mixer, cream
the butter or margarine until soft.
Gradually add the sugar and continue
beating until light and fluffy.

3 ▲ Lightly beat the egg yolks, then
mix into the creamed butter and sugar
with the vanilla.

4 Sift the flour with the baking
powder three times. Set aside.

5 In another bowl, beat the egg
whites with the salt until they hold
stiff peaks. Set aside.

6 ▲ Gently fold the dry ingredients
into the butter mixture in three
batches, alternating with the milk.

7 Add a large dollop of the whites
and fold in to lighten the mixture.
Carefully fold in the remaining whites
until just blended.

8 Divide the batter between the tins
and bake until the cakes pull away
from the sides of the tins, about 30
minutes. Leave to stand for 5 minutes.
Turn out and cool on a rack.

9 ▲ For the icing, melt the chocolate
in the top of a double boiler or a bowl
set over hot water. When cool, stir in
the sour cream and salt.

10 Sandwich the layers with icing,
then spread on the top and side.

Devil's Food Cake with Orange Icing

SERVES 8–10

50g/2oz/¹/₂ cup unsweetened cocoa powder

175ml/6fl oz/³/₄ cup boiling water

175g/6oz/³/₄ cup butter, at room temperature

350g/12oz/1¹/₂ cups soft dark brown sugar

3 eggs, at room temperature

275g/10oz/2¹/₂ cups plain (all-purpose) flour

7.5ml/1¹/₂ tsp bicarbonate of soda (baking soda)

1.5ml/¹/₄ tsp baking powder

120ml/4fl oz/¹/₂ cup sour cream

orange rind strips, for decoration

FOR THE ICING

300g/11oz/generous 1¹/₂ cups caster (superfine) sugar

2 egg whites

60ml/4 tbsp frozen orange juice concentrate

15ml/1 tbsp lemon juice

grated rind of 1 orange

1 Preheat the oven to 180°C/350°F/ Gas 4. Line two 23cm/9in cake tins (pans) with baking parchment and grease. In a bowl, mix the cocoa and water until smooth. Set aside.

2 With an electric mixer, cream the butter and sugar until light and fluffy. Add the eggs, one at a time, beating well after each addition.

3 ▲ When the cocoa mixture is lukewarm, add to the butter mixture.

4 ▼ Sift together the flour, soda and baking powder twice. Fold into the cocoa mixture in three batches, alternating with the sour cream.

5 Pour into the tins and bake until the cakes pull away from the sides of the tins, 30–35 minutes. Leave for 15 minutes. Turn out on to a rack.

6 Thinly slice the orange rind strips. Blanch in boiling water for 1 minute.

7 ▲ For the icing, place all the ingredients in the top of a double boiler or in a bowl set over hot water. With an electric mixer, beat until the mixture holds soft peaks. Continue beating off the heat until thick enough to spread.

8 Sandwich the cake layers with icing, then spread over the top and side. Arrange the blanched orange rind strips on top of the cake.

Best-ever Chocolate Sandwich

SERVES 12–14

115g/4oz/¹/₂ cup unsalted (sweet) butter
115g/4oz/1 cup plain (all-purpose) flour
50g/2oz/¹/₂ cup unsweetened cocoa powder
5ml/1 tsp baking powder
pinch of salt
6 eggs
225g/8oz/generous 1 cup caster (superfine) sugar
10ml/2 tsp vanilla extract
FOR THE ICING
225g/8oz plain (semisweet) chocolate,
75g/3oz/6 tbsp unsalted butter
3 eggs, separated
250ml/8fl oz/1 cup whipping cream
45ml/3 tbsp caster sugar

1 Preheat the oven to 180°C/350°F/ Gas 4. Line three 20 × 3cm/8 × 1¹/₂in round tins (pans) with baking parchment and grease.

2 ▲ Dust evenly with flour and spread with a brush. Set aside.

~ VARIATION ~

For a simpler icing, combine 250ml/ 8fl oz/1 cup whipping cream with 225g/8oz finely chopped plain chocolate in a pan. Stir over a low heat until the chocolate has melted. Cool and whisk to spreading consistency.

3 ▲ Melt the butter over a low heat. With a spoon, skim off any foam that rises to the surface. Set aside.

4 ▲ Sift the flour, cocoa, baking powder and salt together three times and set aside.

5 Place the eggs and sugar in a large heatproof bowl set over a pan of hot water. With an electric mixer, beat until the mixture doubles in volume and is thick enough to leave a ribbon trail when the beaters are lifted, about 10 minutes. Add the vanilla.

6 ▲ Sift over the dry ingredients in three batches, folding in carefully after each addition. Fold in the butter.

7 Divide the mixture between the tins and bake until the cakes pull away from the sides of the tin, about 25 minutes. Transfer to a rack.

8 For the icing, chop the chocolate and melt in the top of a double boiler, or in a heatproof bowl set over hot water.

9 ▲ Off the heat, stir in the butter and egg yolks. Return to a low heat and stir until thick. Remove from the heat and set aside.

10 Whip the cream until firm; set aside. In another bowl, beat the egg whites until stiff. Add the sugar and beat until glossy.

11 Fold the cream into the chocolate mixture, then carefully fold in the egg whites. Chill for 20 minutes to thicken the icing.

12 ▲ Sandwich the cake layers with icing, stacking them carefully. Spread the remaining icing evenly over the top and sides of the cake.

Rich Chocolate Nut Cake

SERVES 10

225g/8oz/1 cup butter

225g/8oz plain (semisweet) chocolate

115g/4oz/1 cup unsweetened cocoa powder

350g/12oz/1³/₄ cups caster (superfine) sugar

6 eggs

85ml/3fl oz/generous ¹/₃ cup brandy
or cognac

225g/8oz/2 cups finely chopped hazelnuts

FOR THE GLAZE

50g/2oz/¹/₄ cup butter

150g/5oz dark (bittersweet) chocolate

30ml/2 tbsp milk

5ml/1 tsp vanilla essence extract

1 Preheat the oven to 180°C/350°F/
Gas 4. Line a 23 × 5cm/9 × 2in round
tin (pan) with baking parchment; grease.

2 Melt the butter and chocolate
together in the top of a double boiler,
or in a heatproof bowl set over hot
water. Set aside to cool.

3 ▼ Sift the cocoa into a bowl. Add
the sugar and eggs, and stir until just
combined. Pour in the melted
chocolate mixture and brandy.

4 Fold in three-quarters of the nuts,
then pour the mixture into the
prepared tin.

5 ▲ Set the tin inside a roasting pan
containing 2.5cm/1in of hot water.
Bake until the cake is firm to the
touch, about 45 minutes. Leave to
stand for 15 minutes, then turn out
and transfer to a cooling rack.

6 Wrap the cake in baking
parchment and chill for 6 hours.

7 For the glaze, combine the butter,
chocolate, milk and vanilla in the top
of a double boiler or in a heatproof
bowl set over hot water, until melted.

8 Place a piece of baking parchment
under the cake, then drizzle spoonfuls
of glaze along the edge to drip down
and coat the sides. Pour the remaining
glaze on top of the cake.

9 ▲ Cover the sides of the cake with
the remaining nuts, gently pressing
them on with the palm of your hand.

Chocolate Layer Cake

SERVES 8–10

115g/4oz plain (semisweet) chocolate

175g/6oz/³/4 cup butter

450g/1lb/2¹/4 cups caster (superfine) sugar

3 eggs

5ml/1 tsp vanilla extract

175g/6oz/1¹/2 cups plain (all-purpose) flour

5ml/1 tsp baking powder

115g/4oz/1 cup chopped walnuts

FOR THE TOPPING

350ml/12fl oz/1¹/2 cups whipping cream

225g/8oz plain chocolate

15ml/1 tbsp vegetable oil

1 Preheat the oven to 180°C/350°F/
Gas 4. Line two 20cm/8in cake tins
(pans), at least 4.5cm/1¹/2in deep,
with baking parchment and grease.

2 Melt the chocolate and butter
together in the top of a double boiler,
or in a heatproof bowl set over a
pan of hot water.

3 ▲ Transfer to a mixing bowl and
stir in the sugar. Add the eggs and
vanilla, and mix until well blended.

~ VARIATION ~

To make Chocolate Ice Cream
Layer Cake, sandwich the cake
layers with softened vanilla ice cream.
Freeze before serving.

4 ▲ Sift over the flour and baking
powder. Stir in the walnuts.

5 Divide the mixture between the
prepared tins and spread level.

6 Bake until a skewer inserted into
the centre comes out clean, about
30 minutes. Leave for 10 minutes,
then turn out and transfer to a rack.

7 When the cakes are cool, whip the
cream until firm. With a long serrated
knife, carefully slice each cake in half
horizontally.

8 Sandwich the layers with some
of the whipped cream and spread the
remainder over the top and sides of
the cake. Chill until needed.

9 ▼ For the chocolate curls, melt
the chocolate and oil in the top of
a double boiler or a bowl set over
hot water. Transfer to a non-porous
surface. Spread to a 1cm/¹/2in thick
rectangle. Just before the chocolate
sets, hold the blade of a straight knife
at an angle to the chocolate and
scrape across the surface to make
curls. Place on top of the cake.

Sachertorte

SERVES 8–10

115g/4oz plain (semisweet) chocolate
75g/3oz/6 tbsp unsalted (sweet) butter, at room temperature
50g/2oz/¼ cup caster (superfine) sugar
4 eggs, separated
1 extra egg white
1.5ml/¼ tsp salt
65g/2½oz/9 tbsp plain (all-purpose) flour, sifted
FOR THE TOPPING
75ml/5 tbsp apricot jam
250ml/8fl oz/1 cup plus 15ml/1 tbsp water
15g/½oz/1 tbsp unsalted butter
175g/6oz plain chocolate
75g/3oz/scant ½ cup caster sugar
ready-made chocolate decorating icing (optional)

1 Preheat the oven to 160°C/325°F/ Gas 3. Line a 23 × 5cm/9 × 2in cake tin (pan) with greaseproof paper and grease.

2 ▲ Melt the chocolate in the top of a double boiler, or in a heatproof bowl set over hot water. Set aside.

3 With an electric mixer, cream the butter and sugar until light and fluffy. Stir in the chocolate.

4 ▲ Beat in the yolks, one at a time.

5 In another bowl, beat the egg whites with the salt until stiff.

6 ▲ Fold a dollop of whites into the chocolate mixture to lighten it. Fold in the remaining whites in three batches, alternating with the sifted flour.

7 ▲ Pour into the tin and bake until a skewer comes out clean, about 45 minutes. Turn out on to a rack.

8 ▲ Meanwhile, melt the jam with 15ml/1 tbsp of the water over low heat, then strain for a smooth consistency.

9 For the frosting, melt the butter and chocolate in the top of a double boiler or a bowl set over hot water.

10 ▲ In a heavy pan, dissolve the sugar in the remaining water over low heat. Raise the heat and boil until it reaches 107°C/225°F (thread stage) on a sugar thermometer. Immediately plunge the bottom of the pan into cold water for 1 minute. Pour into the chocolate mixture and stir to blend. Leave to cool for a few minutes.

11 To assemble, brush the warm jam over the cake. Starting in the centre, pour over the frosting and work outward in a circular movement. Tilt the rack to spread; use a palette knife to smooth the side of the cake. Leave to set overnight. If you like, decorate with chocolate icing.

Raspberry and Hazelnut Meringue Cake

SERVES 8

150g/5oz/1¼ cups hazelnuts
4 egg whites
pinch of salt
200g/7oz/1 cup caster (superfine) sugar
2.5ml/½ tsp vanilla extract
FOR THE FILLING
300ml/½ pint/1¼ cups whipping cream
675g/1½lb raspberries

1 Preheat the oven to 180°C/350°F/Gas 4. Line the base of two 20cm/8in cake tins (pans) with baking parchment and grease.

2 Spread the hazelnuts on a baking sheet and bake until lightly toasted, about 8 minutes. Cool slightly.

3 ▲ Rub the hazelnuts vigorously in a clean dishtowel to remove most of the skins.

4 Grind the nuts in a food processor, blender, or coffee grinder until they are the consistency of coarse sand.

5 Reduce oven to 150°C/300°F/Gas 2.

6 With an electric mixer, beat the egg whites and salt until they hold stiff peaks. Beat in 25g/1oz/2 tbsp of the sugar, then fold in the remaining sugar, a few tablespoons at a time, with a rubber scraper. Fold in the vanilla and the hazelnuts.

7 ▲ Divide the batter between the prepared tins and spread level.

8 Bake for 1¼ hours. If the meringues brown too quickly, protect with a sheet of foil. Leave to stand for 5 minutes, then carefully run a knife around the inside edge of the tins to loosen. Turn out on to a rack to cool.

9 For the filling, whip the cream until just firm.

10 ▲ Spread half the cream in an even layer on one meringue round and top with half the raspberries.

11 Top with the other meringue round. Spread the remaining cream on top and arrange the remaining raspberries over the cream. Chill for 1 hour for easy cutting.

Forgotten Gâteau

SERVES 6

6 egg whites, at room temperature

2.5ml/¹/₂ tsp cream of tartar

pinch of salt

300g/11oz/generous 1¹/₂ cups caster
  (superfine) sugar

5ml/1 tsp vanilla extract

175ml/6fl oz/³/₄ cup whipping cream

FOR THE SAUCE

350g/12oz/2 cups fresh or thawed
  frozen raspberries

30–45ml/2–3 tbsp icing (confectioners') sugar

1   Preheat the oven to 230°C/450°F/
Gas 8.

2   ▲ Grease a 1.5 litre/2¹/₂ pint/6¹/₄ cup
ring mould. Beat the egg whites, cream
of tartar and salt until they hold soft
peaks. Add the sugar and beat until
glossy and stiff. Fold in the vanilla.

3   ▲ Spoon into the prepared mould
and smooth the top level.

4   Place in the oven, then turn the
oven off. Leave overnight; do not
open the oven door at any time.

5   ▼ To serve, gently loosen the edge
with a sharp knife and turn out on to
a serving plate. Whip the cream until
firm. Spread it over the top and upper
sides of the meringue and decorate
with any meringue crumbs.

6   ▲ For the sauce, purée the fruit,
then strain. Sweeten to taste. Serve
with the gâteau.

~ COOK'S TIP ~

This recipe is not suitable for fan
assisted and solid fuel ovens.

Nut and Apple Gâteau

SERVES 8

115g/4oz/²/₃ cup pecan nuts or walnuts

50g/2oz/¹/₂ cup plain (all-purpose) flour

10ml/2 tsp baking powder

1.5ml/¹/₄ tsp salt

2 large cooking apples

3 eggs

225g/8oz/generous 1 cup caster
  (superfine) sugar

5ml/1 tsp vanilla extract

175ml/6fl oz/³/₄ cup whipping cream

1 Preheat the oven to 160°C/325°F/
Gas 3. Line two 23cm/9in cake tins
(pans) with baking parchment and
grease the paper. Spread the nuts on a
baking sheet and bake for 10 minutes.

2 Finely chop the nuts. Reserve 20g/
³/₄oz/1¹/₂ tbsp and place the rest in a
mixing bowl. Sift over the flour,
baking powder and salt, and stir.

3 ▲ Quarter, core and peel the
apples. Cut into 3mm/¹/₈in dice, then
stir into the nut-flour mixture.

4 ▲ With an electric mixer, beat
the eggs until frothy. Gradually add
the sugar and vanilla, and beat until
a ribbon forms, about 8 minutes.
Gently fold in the flour mixture.

5 Pour into the tins and level the
tops. Bake until a skewer inserted into
the centre comes out clean, about 35
minutes. Leave to stand for 10 minutes.

6 ▲ To loosen, run a knife around
the inside edge of each layer. Cool.

7 ▲ Whip the cream until firm.
Spread half over the cake. Top with
the second cake. Pipe whipped cream
rosettes on top and sprinkle over the
reserved nuts before serving.

Almond Cake

SERVES 4–6

225g/8oz/1¹/₃ cups blanched whole
  almonds, plus more for decorating
25g/1oz/2 tbsp butter
75g/3oz/6 tbsp icing (confectioners') sugar
3 eggs
2.5ml/¹/₂ tsp almond extract
25g/1oz/¹/₄ cup plain (all-purpose) flour
3 egg whites
15ml/1 tbsp caster (superfine) sugar

1 ▲ Preheat the oven to 160°C/325°F/
Gas 3. Line a 23cm/9in round cake tin
(pan) with baking parchment; grease.

2 ▲ Spread the almonds in a baking
tray and toast for 10 minutes. Cool, then
coarsely chop 185g/6¹/₂oz/generous 1 cup.

3 Melt the butter and set aside.
Increase oven temperature to
200°C/400°F/Gas 6.

4 Grind the chopped almonds with
half the icing sugar in a food processor,
blender or grinder. Transfer to a
mixing bowl.

5 ▲ Add the whole eggs and
remaining icing sugar. With an
electric mixer, beat until the mixture
forms a ribbon when the beaters are
lifted. Mix in the butter and almond
essence. Sift over the flour and fold
in gently.

6 With an electric mixer, beat the
egg whites until they hold soft peaks.
Add the caster sugar and beat until
stiff and glossy.

7 ▲ Fold the whites into the almond
mixture in four batches.

8 Spoon the mixture into the
prepared tin and bake in the centre
of the oven until golden brown, about
15–20 minutes. Decorate the top with
the remaining toasted whole almonds.
Serve warm.

Walnut Coffee Gâteau

SERVES 8–10

150g/5oz/1¼ cups walnuts
165g/5½oz/generous ¾ cup caster (superfine) sugar
5 eggs, separated
50g/2oz/1 cup dry breadcrumbs
15ml/1 tbsp unsweetened cocoa powder
15ml/1 tbsp instant coffee
30ml/2 tbsp rum or lemon juice
pinch of salt
90ml/6 tbsp redcurrant jelly
chopped walnuts, for decorating
FOR THE ICING
225g/8oz plain (semisweet) chocolate
750ml/1¼ pints/3 cups whipping cream

1 ▲ For the icing, combine the chocolate and cream in the top of a double boiler, or in a heatproof bowl set over simmering water. Stir until the chocolate melts. Leave to cool, then cover and chill overnight or until the mixture is firm.

2 Preheat the oven to 180°C/350°F/ Gas 4. Line a 23 × 5cm/9 × 2in cake tin (pan) with baking parchment and grease.

3 ▲ Grind the nuts with 40g/1½oz/ 3 tbsp of the sugar in a food processor, blender, or coffee grinder.

4 With an electric mixer, beat the egg yolks and remaining sugar until thick and lemon-coloured.

5 ▲ Fold in the walnuts. Stir in the breadcrumbs, cocoa, coffee and rum or lemon juice.

6 ▲ In another bowl, beat the egg whites with the salt until they hold stiff peaks. Fold carefully into the walnut mixture with a rubber scraper.

7 Pour the meringue batter into the prepared tin and bake until the top of the cake springs back when touched lightly, about 45 minutes. Let the cake stand for 5 minutes, then turn out and cool on a rack.

8 ▲ When cool, slice the cake in half horizontally.

9 With an electric mixer, beat the chocolate icing mixture on low speed until it becomes lighter, about 30 seconds. Do not overbeat or it may become grainy.

10 ▲ Warm the jelly in a pan until melted, then brush over the cut cake layer. Spread with some of the chocolate icing, then sandwich with the remaining cake layer. Brush the top of the cake with jelly, then cover the side and top with the remaining chocolate icing. Make a starburst pattern by pressing gently with a table knife in lines radiating from the centre. Arrange the chopped walnuts around the edge.

Light Fruit Cake

MAKES 2 LOAVES

225g/8oz/1 cup prunes
225g/8oz/1½ cups dates
225g/8oz/1 cup currants
225g/8oz/1⅓ cups sultanas (golden raisins)
250ml/8fl oz/1 cup dry white wine
250ml/8fl oz/1 cup rum
350g/12oz/3 cups plain (all-purpose) flour
10ml/2 tsp baking powder
5ml/1 tsp ground cinnamon
2.5ml/½ tsp freshly grated nutmeg
225g/8oz/1 cup butter, at room temperature
225g/8oz/generous 1 cup caster (superfine) sugar
4 eggs, at room temperature, lightly beaten
5ml/1 tsp vanilla extract

1 Pit the prunes and dates and chop finely. Place in a bowl with the currants and sultanas.

2 ▲ Stir in the wine and rum and leave to stand, covered, for 48 hours. Stir occasionally.

3 Preheat the oven to 150°C/300°F/ Gas 2 with a tray of hot water in the bottom. Line two 23 × 13cm/9 × 5in tins (pans) with baking parchment; grease.

4 Sift together the flour, baking powder, cinnamon, and nutmeg.

5 ▲ With an electric mixer, cream the butter and sugar together until light and fluffy.

6 Gradually add the eggs and vanilla. Fold in the flour mixture in three batches. Fold in the dried fruit mixture and its soaking liquid.

7 ▲ Divide the mixture between the tins and bake until a skewer inserted into the centre comes out clean, about 1½ hours.

8 Leave the cake to stand for 20 minutes, then turn out and transfer to a cooling rack. Wrap in foil and store in an airtight container. If possible, leave for at least 1 week before serving to allow the flavours to mellow.

Rich Fruit Cake

SERVES 12

150g/5oz/²/₃ cup currants

175g/6oz/generous 1 cup raisins

50g/2oz/¹/₃ cup sultanas (golden raisins)

50g/2oz/¹/₄ cup glacé (candied)
  cherries, halved

45ml/3 tbsp sweet sherry

175g/6oz/³/₄ cup butter

200g/7oz/scant 1 cup soft dark
  brown sugar

3 eggs, at room temperature

200g/7oz/1³/₄ cups plain (all-purpose) flour

10ml/2 tsp baking powder

10ml/2 tsp each ground ginger, allspice,
  and cinnamon

15ml/1 tbsp golden (light corn) syrup

15ml/1 tbsp milk

50g/2oz/¹/₃ cup cut mixed (candied) peel

115g/4oz/1 cup chopped walnuts

FOR THE DECORATION

225g/8oz/generous 1 cup caster
  (superfine) sugar

120ml/4fl oz/¹/₂ cup water

1 lemon, thinly sliced

¹/₂ orange, thinly sliced

120ml/4fl oz/¹/₂ cup orange marmalade

glacé cherries

1 One day before preparing, combine
the currants, raisins, sultanas and
cherries in a bowl. Stir in the sherry.
Cover and leave overnight to soak.

2 Preheat the oven to 150°C/300°F/
Gas 2. Line a 23 × 7.5cm/9 × 3in
springform cake tin (pan) with baking
parchment and grease. Place a tray of
hot water on the bottom of the oven.

3 With an electric mixer, cream the
butter and sugar until light and fluffy.
Beat in the eggs, one at a time.

4 ▲ Sift the flour, baking powder
and spices together three times. Fold
into the butter mixture in three
batches. Fold in the syrup, milk, dried
fruit and liquid, mixed peel and nuts.

5 ▲ Spoon into the tin, spreading
out so there is a slight depression in
the centre of the mixture.

6 Bake until a skewer inserted into the
centre comes out clean, 2¹/₂–3 hours.
Cover with foil when the top is
golden to prevent over-browning.
Cool in the tin on a rack.

7 ▲ For the decoration, combine the
sugar and water in a pan and bring to
the boil. Add the lemon and orange
slices and cook until crystallized,
about 20 minutes. Work in batches,
if necessary. Remove the fruit with
a slotted spoon. Pour the remaining
syrup over the cake and cool. Melt
the marmalade over low heat, then
brush over the top of the cake.
Decorate with the crystallized citrus
slices and cherries.

Whiskey Cake

MAKES 1 LOAF

175g/6oz/1^{1}/2 cups chopped walnuts
75g/3oz/^{2}/3 cup raisins, chopped
75g/3oz/^{2}/3 cup currants
115g/4oz/1 cup plain (all-purpose) flour
5ml/1 tsp baking powder
1.5ml/^{1}/4 tsp salt
115g/4oz/^{1}/2 cup butter
225g/8oz/1 cup caster (superfine) sugar
3 eggs, at room temperature, separated
5ml/1 tsp freshly grated nutmeg
2.5ml/^{1}/2 tsp ground cinnamon
85ml/3fl oz/generous ^{1}/3 cup Irish whiskey
icing (confectioners') sugar, for dusting

1 ▼ Preheat the oven to 160°C/325°F/Gas 3. Line a 23 × 13cm/9 × 5in loaf tin (pan) with baking parchment. Grease the paper and sides of the pan.

2 ▲ Place the walnuts, raisins, and currants in a bowl. Sprinkle over 15g/^{1}/2oz/2 tbsp of the flour, mix and set aside. Sift together the remaining flour, baking powder and salt.

3 ▲ Cream the butter and sugar until light and fluffy. Beat in the egg yolks.

4 Mix the nutmeg, cinnamon and whiskey. Fold into the butter mixture, alternating with the flour mixture.

5 ▲ In another bowl, beat the egg whites until stiff. Fold into the whiskey mixture until just blended. Fold in the walnut mixture.

6 Bake until a skewer inserted into the centre comes out clean, about 1 hour. Cool in the pan. Dust with icing sugar over a template.

Gingerbread

SERVES 8–10

15ml/1 tbsp vinegar

175ml/6fl oz/³/4 cup milk

175g/6oz/1¹/2 cups plain (all-purpose) flour

10ml/2 tsp baking powder

1.5ml/¹/4 tsp bicarbonate of soda (baking soda)

2.5ml/¹/2 tsp salt

10ml/2 tsp ground ginger

5ml/1 tsp ground cinnamon

1.5ml/¹/4 tsp ground cloves

115g/4oz/¹/2 cup butter, at room temperature

115g/4oz/generous ¹/2 cup caster
  (superfine) sugar

1 egg, at room temperature

175ml/6fl oz/³/4 cup black treacle (molasses)

whipped cream, for serving

chopped stem ginger, for decorating

1 ▲ Preheat the oven to 180°C/350°F/
Gas 4. Line an 20cm/8in square cake
tin (pan) with baking parchment and
grease the paper and the sides of the pan.

2 ▲ Add the vinegar to the milk and
set aside. It will curdle.

3 In another mixing bowl, sift all the
dry ingredients together three times
and set aside.

4 With an electric mixer, cream the
butter and sugar until light and fluffy.
Beat in the egg until well combined.

5 ▼ Stir in the black treacle.

6 ▲ Fold in the dry ingredients in
four batches, alternating with the
milk. Mix only enough to blend.

7 Pour into the prepared tin and bake
until firm, 45–50 minutes. Cut into
squares and serve warm, with whipped
cream. Decorate with the stem ginger.

Classic Cheesecake

SERVES 8

50g/2oz/1 cup digestive biscuits
(graham crackers), crushed

900g/2lb/4 cups cream cheese,
at room temperature

240g/8³/₄oz/scant 1¹/₄ cups caster
(superfine) sugar

grated rind of 1 lemon

45ml/3 tbsp lemon juice

5ml/1 tsp vanilla extract

4 eggs, at room temperature

1 Preheat oven to 160°C/325°F/Gas 3. Grease a 20cm/8in springform cake tin (pan). Place on a round of foil 10–13cm/4–5in larger than the diameter of the tin. Press it up the sides to seal tightly.

2 Sprinkle the biscuits in the base of the tin. Press to form an even layer.

3 With an electric mixer, beat the cream cheese until smooth. Add the sugar, lemon rind and juice, and vanilla, and beat until blended. Beat in the eggs, one at a time. Beat just enough to blend thoroughly.

4 ▲ Pour into the prepared tin. Set the tin in a roasting pan and pour enough hot water in the roasting pan to come 2.5cm/1in up the side of the cake tin. place in the oven.

5 Bake until the top of the cake is golden brown, about 1¹/₂ hours. Leave to cool in the tin.

6 ▼ Run a knife around the edge to loosen, then remove the rim of the tin. Chill for at least 4 hours before serving.

Chocolate Cheesecake

SERVES 10–12

275g/10oz plain (semisweet) chocolate

1.2kg/2¹/₂lb/5 cups cream cheese,
at room temperature

200g/7oz/1 cup caster (superfine) sugar

10ml/2 tsp vanilla extract

4 eggs, at room temperature

175ml/6fl oz/³/₄ cup sour cream

15ml/1 tbsp unsweetened cocoa powder

FOR THE BASE

200g/7oz/3¹/₂ cups chocolate biscuits
(cookies), crushed

75g/3oz/6 tbsp butter, melted

2.5ml/¹/₂ tsp ground cinnamon

1 Preheat oven to 180°C/350°F/Gas 4. Grease a 23 × 7.5cm/9 × 3in springform cake tin (pan).

2 ▲ For the base, mix the biscuits with the butter and cinnamon. Press on to the base of the tin.

3 Melt the chocolate in the top of a double boiler, or in a heatproof bowl set over hot water. Set aside.

4 Beat the cream cheese until smooth, then beat in the sugar and vanilla. Add the eggs, one at a time.

5 Stir the sour cream into the cocoa powder to form a paste. Add to the cream cheese mixture. Stir in the melted chocolate.

6 ▼ Pour into the crust. Bake for 1 hour. Cool in the tin; remove the rim. Chill before serving.

Classic Cheesecake (top), Chocolate Cheesecake

Lemon Mousse Cheesecake

SERVES 10–12

1.2kg/2¹/₂lb/5 cups cream cheese,
  at room temperature

350g/12oz/1³/₄ cups caster (superfine) sugar

40g/1¹/₂oz/¹/₃ cup plain (all-purpose) flour

4 eggs, at room temperature, separated

120ml/4fl oz/¹/₂ cup fresh lemon juice

grated rind of 2 lemons

115g/4oz/2 cups digestive biscuits
  (graham crackers), crushed

1 Preheat the oven to 160°C/325°F/
Gas 3. Line a 25 × 5cm/10 × 2in
round cake tin (pan) with baking
parchment and grease the paper.

2 With an electric mixer, beat the
cream cheese until smooth. Gradually
add 275g/10oz/1¹/₂ cups of the sugar,
and beat until light. Beat in the flour.

3 ▲ Add the egg yolks, and lemon
juice and rind, and beat until smooth
and well blended.

4 In another bowl, beat the egg
whites until they hold soft peaks.
Add the remaining sugar and beat
until stiff and glossy.

5 ▲ Add the egg whites to the
cheese mixture and gently fold in.

6 Pour the mixture into the prepared
tin, then place the tin in a roasting
pan. Place in the oven and pour hot
water in the pan to come 2.5cm/1in
up the side of the tin.

7 Bake until golden, 60–65 minutes.
Cool in the tin on a rack. Cover and
chill for at least 4 hours.

8 To turn out, run a knife around
the inside edge. Place a flat plate,
bottom-side up, over the tin and
invert on to the plate. Smooth the
top with a metal spatula.

9 ▲ Sprinkle the biscuits over the
top in an even layer, pressing down
slightly to make a top crust.

10 To serve, cut slices with a sharp
knife dipped in hot water.

Marbled Cheesecake

SERVES 10

50g/2oz/¹/₂ cup unsweetened cocoa powder

75ml/5 tbsp hot water

900g/2lb/4 cups cream cheese,
   at room temperature

200g/7oz/1 cup caster (superfine) sugar

4 eggs

5ml/1 tsp vanilla extract

65g/2¹/₂oz/1¹/₄ cups digestive biscuits
   (graham crackers), crushed

1 Preheat the oven to 180°C/350°F/
Gas 4. Line an 20 × 8cm/8 × 3in cake
tin (pan) with baking parchment; grease.

2 Sift the cocoa powder into a bowl.
Pour over the hot water and stir to
dissolve. Set aside.

3 With an electric mixer, beat the
cheese until smooth and creamy. Add
the sugar and beat to incorporate.
Beat in the eggs, one at a time. Do
not overmix.

4 Divide the mixture evenly between
two bowls. Stir the chocolate mixture
into one, then add the vanilla to the
remaining mixture.

5 ▲ Pour a cupful of the plain
mixture into the centre of the tin; it
will spread out into an even layer.
Slowly pour over a cupful of chocolate
mixture in the centre.

6 ▲ Repeat alternating cupfuls of
the batters in a circular pattern until
both are used up.

7 Set the tin in a roasting pan and
pour in hot water to come 4cm/1¹/₂in
up the sides of the cake tin.

8 Bake until the top of the cake is
golden, about 1¹/₂ hours. It will rise
during baking but will sink later.
Leave to cool in the tin on a rack.

9 To turn out, run a knife around the
inside edge. Place a flat plate, bottom-
side up, over the tin and invert on to
the plate.

10 ▼ Sprinkle the crushed biscuits
evenly over the base, gently place
another plate over them, and invert
again. Cover and chill for at least
3 hours, or overnight. To serve, cut
slices with a sharp knife dipped in
hot water.

Heart Cake

MAKES 1 CAKE

225g/8oz/1 cup butter or margarine

225g/8oz/generous 1 cup caster (superfine) sugar

4 eggs, at room temperature

175g/6oz/1¹/₂ cups plain (all-purpose) flour

5ml/1 tsp baking powder

2.5ml/¹/₂ tsp bicarbonate of soda (baking soda)

30ml/2 tbsp milk

5ml/1 tsp vanilla extract

FOR ICING AND DECORATING

3 egg whites

350g/12oz/1³/₄ cups caster sugar

30ml/2 tbsp cold water

30ml/2 tbsp fresh lemon juice

1.5ml/¹/₄ tsp cream of tartar

pink food colouring

75–115g/3–4oz/6–8 tbsp icing (confectioners') sugar

1 Preheat the oven to 180°C/350°F/ Gas 4. Line a 20cm/8in heart-shaped tin (pan) with baking parchment; grease.

2 ▲ With an electric mixer, cream the butter or margarine and sugar until light and fluffy. Add the eggs, one at a time, beating thoroughly after each addition.

3 Sift the flour, baking powder and baking soda together. Fold the dry ingredients into the butter mixture in three batches, alternating with the milk. Stir in the vanilla.

4 ▲ Spoon the mixture into the prepared tin and bake until a skewer inserted into the centre comes out clean, 35–40 minutes. Leave the cake to stand in the tin for 5 minutes, then turn out and transfer to a rack to cool completely.

5 For the icing, combine two of the egg whites, the caster sugar, water, lemon juice and cream of tartar in the top of a double boiler or in a bowl set over simmering water. With an electric mixer, beat until thick and holding soft peaks, about 7 minutes. Remove from the heat and continue beating until the mixture is thick enough to spread. Tint the icing with the pink food colouring.

6 ▲ Put the cake on a board, about 30cm/12in square, covered in foil or in paper suitable for contact with food. Spread the icing evenly on the cake. Smooth the top and sides. Leave to set for 3–4 hours, or overnight.

7 ▲ For the paper piping (pastry) bags, fold a 28 × 20cm/11 × 8in sheet of baking parchment in half diagonally, then cut into two pieces along the fold mark. Roll over the short side, so that it meets the right-angled corner and forms a cone. To form the piping bag, hold the cone in place with one hand, wrap the point of the long side of the triangle around the cone, and tuck inside, folding over twice to secure. Snip a hole in the pointed end and slip in a small metal piping nozzle to extend about 5mm/¹/₄in.

8 For the piped decorations, place 15ml/1 tbsp of the remaining egg white in a bowl and whisk until frothy. Gradually beat in enough icing sugar to make a stiff mixture suitable for piping.

9 ▲ Spoon into a paper piping bag to half-fill. Fold over the top and squeeze to pipe decorations on the top and sides of the cake.

Iced Fancies

MAKES 16

115g/4oz/¹/₂ cup butter, at room temperature
225g/8oz/generous 1 cup caster (superfine) sugar
2 eggs, at room temperature
175g/6oz/1¹/₂ cups plain (all-purpose) flour
1.5ml/¹/₄ tsp salt
7.5ml/1¹/₂ tsp baking powder
120ml/4fl oz/¹/₂ cup plus 15ml/1 tbsp milk
5ml/1 tsp vanilla extract
FOR ICING AND DECORATING
2 large egg whites
400g/14oz/3¹/₂ cups sifted icing (confectioners') sugar
1–2 drops glycerine
juice of 1 lemon
food colourings
hundreds and thousands, for decorating
crystallized lemon and orange slices

1 Preheat oven to 190°C/375°F/Gas 5.

2 ▲ Line 16 bun-tray cups with fluted paper baking cases, or grease.

~ COOK'S TIP ~

Ready-made cake decorating products are widely available, and may be used, if you prefer, instead of the recipes given for icing and decorating. Coloured icing in ready-to-pipe tubes is useful.

3 With an electric mixer, cream the butter and sugar until light and fluffy. Add the eggs, one at a time, beating well after each addition.

4 Sift together the flour, salt and baking powder. Stir into the butter mixture, alternating with the milk. Stir in the vanilla.

5 ▲ Fill the cups half-full and bake until the tops spring back when touched lightly, about 20 minutes. Let the cakes stand in the tray for 5 minutes, then turn out and transfer to a rack to cool completely.

6 For the icing, beat the egg whites until stiff but not dry. Gradually add the sugar, glycerine and lemon juice, and continue beating for 1 minute. The consistency should be spreadable. If necessary, thin with a little water or add more sifted icing sugar to thicken.

7 ▲ Divide the icing between several bowls and tint with food colourings. Spread different coloured icings over the cooled cakes.

8 ▲ Decorate the cakes as you like, with sugar decorations such as hundreds and thousands.

9 ▲ Other decorations include crystallized orange and lemon slices. Cut into small pieces and arrange on top of the cakes. Alternatively, use other suitable sweets (candies).

10 ▲ To make freehand iced decorations, fill paper piping (pastry) bags with different coloured icings. Pipe on faces, or make other designs.

Snake Cake

SERVES 10–12

225g/8oz/1 cup butter or margarine, at room temperature

grated rind and juice of 1 small orange

225g/8oz/generous 1 cup caster (superfine) sugar

4 eggs, at room temperature, separated

175g/6oz/1½ cups plain (all-purpose) flour

5ml/1 tsp baking powder

pinch of salt

FOR THE ICING AND DECORATING

25g/1oz/2 tbsp butter, at room temperature

350g/12oz/3 cups icing (confectioners') sugar

150g/5oz plain (semisweet) chocolate

pinch of salt

120ml/4fl oz/½ cup sour cream

1 egg white

green and blue food colourings

1 Preheat the oven to 190°C/375°F/Gas 5. Grease two 21cm/8½in ring tins (pans) and dust them with flour.

2 Cream the butter or margarine, orange rind and sugar until light. Beat in the egg yolks, one at a time.

3 Sift the flour and baking powder. Fold into the butter mixture, alternating with the orange juice.

4 ▲ In another bowl, beat the egg whites and salt until stiff.

5 Fold a large dollop of the egg whites into the creamed butter mixture to lighten it, then gently fold in the remaining whites.

6 Divide the mixture between the prepared tins and bake until a skewer inserted into the centre comes out clean, about 25 minutes. Leave to stand for 5 minutes, then turn out on to a wire rack to cool.

7 Prepare a board, 60 × 20cm/24 × 8in, covered in paper suitable for contact with food, or in foil.

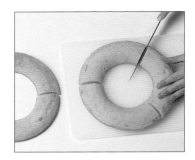

8 ▲ Cut the cakes into three even pieces. Trim to level the flat side, if necessary, and shape the head by cutting off wedges from the front. Shape the tail in the same way.

9 ▲ For the buttercream, mix the butter with 40g/1½oz/scant ½ cup of the icing sugar. Use to join the cake sections and arrange on the board.

10 ▲ For the chocolate icing, melt the chocolate. Stir in the salt and sour cream. When cool, spread over the cake and smooth the surface.

11 ▲ For the decoration, beat the egg white until frothy. Add enough of the remaining icing sugar to obtain a thick mixture. Divide among several bowls and add food colourings.

12 ▲ Fill paper piping (pastry) bags with icing, and pipe decorations along the top of the cake.

Sun Cake

SERVES 10–12

115g/4oz/¹/₂ cup unsalted (sweet) butter	
6 eggs	
225g/8oz/generous 1 cup caster (superfine) sugar	
115g/4oz/1 cup plain (all-purpose) flour	
2.5ml/¹/₂ tsp salt	
5ml/1 tsp vanilla extract	
FOR ICING AND DECORATING	
25g/1oz/2 tbsp unsalted butter, at room temperature	
450g/1lb/4 cups sifted icing (confectioners') sugar	
120ml/4fl oz/¹/₂ cup apricot jam	
30ml/2 tbsp water	
2 large egg whites	
1–2 drops glycerine	
juice of 1 lemon	
yellow and orange food colourings	

1 Preheat the oven to 180°C/350°F/ Gas 4. Line two 20 × 5cm/8 × 2in round cake tins (pans), then grease and flour.

2 In a pan, melt the butter over very low heat. Skim off any foam that rises to the surface, then set aside.

3 ▲ Place a heatproof bowl over a pan of hot water. Add the eggs and sugar. Beat with an electric mixer until the mixture doubles in volume and is thick enough to leave a ribbon trail when the beaters are lifted, 8–10 minutes.

4 Sift the flour and salt together three times. Sift over the egg mixture in three batches, folding in well after each addition. Fold in the melted butter and vanilla.

5 Divide the mixture between the tins. Level the surfaces and bake until the cakes shrink slightly from the sides of the tins, 25–30 minutes. Leave to stand for 5 minutes, then turn out and transfer to a cooling rack.

6 Prepare a board, 40cm/16in square, covered in paper suitable for contact with food, or in foil.

7 ▲ For the sunbeams, cut one of the cakes into eight equal wedges. Cut away a rounded piece from the base of each so that they fit neatly up against the sides of the whole cake.

8 ▲ For the butter icing, mix the butter and 25g/1oz/¹/₄ cup of the icing sugar. Use to attach the sunbeams.

9 ▲ Melt the jam with the water and brush over the cake. Place on the board and straighten, if necessary.

10 ▲ For the icing, beat the egg whites until stiff but not dry. Gradually add 400g/14oz/3¹/₂ cups icing sugar, the glycerine and lemon juice, and continue beating for 1 minute. If necessary, thin with water or add a little more sugar. Tint with yellow food colouring and spread over the cake.

11 ▲ Divide the remaining icing in half and tint with more food colouring to obtain bright yellow and orange. Pipe decorative zigzags on the sunbeams and a face in the middle.

Jack-O'-Lantern Cake

SERVES 8–10

175g/6oz/1¹/₂ cups plain (all-purpose) flour

12.5ml/2¹/₂ tsp baking powder

pinch of salt

115g/4oz/¹/₂ cup butter,
at room temperature

225g/8oz/generous 1 cup caster
(superfine) sugar

3 egg yolks, at room temperature,
well beaten

5ml/1 tsp grated lemon rind

175ml/6fl oz/³/₄ cup milk

FOR THE CAKE COVERING

500–675g/1¹/₄lb–1¹/₂lb/5–6 cups icing
(confectioners') sugar

2 egg whites

30ml/2 tbsp liquid glucose

orange and black food colourings

1 Preheat the oven to 190°C/375°F/
Gas 5. Line a 20cm/8in round cake
tin (pan) with baking parchment
and grease.

2 Sift together the flour, baking
powder and salt. Set aside.

3 With an electric mixer, cream the
butter and sugar until light and fluffy.
Gradually beat in the egg yolks, then
add the lemon rind. Fold in the flour
mixture in three batches, alternating
with the milk.

4 Spoon the mixture into the
prepared tin. Bake until a skewer
inserted into the centre comes out
clean, about 35 minutes. Leave to
stand, then turn out on to a rack.

~ COOK'S TIP ~

If you prefer, use ready-made
roll-out cake covering,
available at cake decorating
suppliers. Knead in food
colouring, if required.

---

5 For the icing, sift 500g/1¹/₄lb/5 cups
of the icing sugar into a bowl. Make a
well in the centre, add 1 egg white,
the glucose and orange food
colouring. Stir until a dough forms.

6 ▲ Transfer to a clean work
surface dusted with icing sugar and
knead briefly.

7 ▲ Carefully roll out the orange
cake covering to a thin sheet.

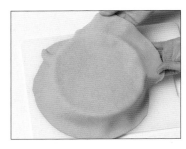

8 ▲ Place the sheet on top of the
cooled cake and smooth the sides.
Trim the excess icing and reserve.

9 ▲ From the trimmings, cut shapes
for the top. Tint the remaining cake
covering trimmings with black food
colouring. Roll out thinly and cut
shapes for the face.

10 ▲ Brush the undersides with
water and arrange the face on top
of the cake.

11 ▲ Place 15ml/1 tbsp of the
remaining egg white in a bowl and
stir in enough icing sugar to make
a thick icing. Tint with black food
colouring, fill a paper piping (pastry)
bag and complete the decoration.

Stars and Stripes Cake

SERVES 20

225g/8oz/1 cup butter or margarine, at room temperature

225g/8oz/1 cup soft dark brown sugar

225g/8oz/generous 1 cup granulated sugar

5 eggs, at room temperature

275g/10oz/2½ cups plain (all-purpose) flour

10ml/2 tsp baking powder

5ml/1 tsp bicarbonate of soda (baking soda)

5ml/1 tsp ground cinnamon

5ml/1 tsp ground ginger

2.5ml/½ tsp ground allspice

1.5ml/¼ tsp ground cloves

1.5ml/¼ tsp salt

350ml/12fl oz/1½ cups buttermilk

75g/3oz/½ cup raisins

FOR THE CAKE COVERING

25g/1oz/2 tbsp butter

1–1.25kg/2¼lb–2lb 10oz/9–10 cups icing (confectioners') sugar

3 egg whites

60ml/4 tbsp liquid glucose

red and blue food colourings

1 Preheat the oven to 180°C/350°F/ Gas 4. Line a 30 × 23cm/12 × 9in baking tin (pan) with baking parchment and lightly grease.

2 With an electric mixer, cream the butter or margarine and sugars until light and fluffy. Gradually beat in the eggs, one at a time, beating well after each addition.

3 Sift together the flour, baking powder, bicarbonate of soda, spices and salt. Fold into the butter mixture in three batches, alternating with the buttermilk. Stir in the raisins.

4 Pour the mixture into the prepared tin and bake until the cake springs back when touched lightly, about 35 minutes. Leave to stand for 10 minutes, then turn out on to a wire rack.

5 Make buttercream for assembling the cake by mixing the butter with 40g/ 1½oz/scant ½ cup of the icing sugar.

6 ▲ When the cake is cool, cut a curved shape from the top.

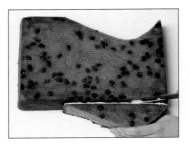

7 ▲ Attach it to the bottom of the cake with the buttercream.

8 Prepare a board, about 40 × 30cm/ 16 × 12in, covered in paper suitable for contact with food, or in foil. Transfer the cake to the board.

9 For the cake covering, sift 1kg/ 2¼lb/9 cups of the icing sugar into a bowl. Add two of the egg whites and the liquid glucose. Stir until the mixture forms a dough.

10 Cover and set aside half of the covering. On a clean work surface lightly dusted with icing sugar, roll out the remaining covering to a sheet. Carefully transfer to the cake. Smooth the sides and trim any excess from the bottom edges.

11 ▲ Tint one-quarter of the remaining covering blue and tint the remainder red. Roll out the blue to a thin sheet and cut out the background for the stars. Place on the cake.

12 ▲ Roll out the red covering, cut out stripes and place on the cake.

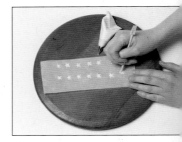

13 ▲ For the stars, mix 15ml/1 tbsp of the egg white with just enough icing sugar to thicken. Pipe small stars on to a sheet of baking parchment and leave to set. When dry, peel them off and place on the blue background.

INDEX